Courtly Art of the
Ancient Maya

Courtly Art of the Ancient Maya

Mary Miller and Simon Martin

Kathleen Berrin, *Curator*

Fine Arts Museums
of San Francisco

Thames & Hudson

Published on the occasion of the exhibition
Courtly Art of the Ancient Maya

National Gallery of Art, Washington
4 April–25 July 2004

Fine Arts Museums of San Francisco
California Palace of the Legion of Honor
4 September 2004–2 January 2005

Courtly Art of the Ancient Maya is organized by the Fine Arts
Museums of San Francisco and the National Gallery of Art.
This exhibition is supported by an indemnity from the Federal
Council on the Arts and Humanities.

The presentation in San Francisco and the publication of the
catalogue are supported, in part, by generous grants from the
National Endowment for the Humanities and the National Endowment
for the Arts, Federal agencies, and Wells Fargo. Additional funding for
the catalogue comes from the Andrew W. Mellon Foundation
Endowment for Publications.

First published in hardcover in the United States of America in 2004
by Thames & Hudson Inc., 500 Fifth Avenue, New York,
New York 10110

thamesandhudsonusa.com

Library of Congress Catalog Card Number 2003111311
ISBN 0-500-05129-1

Designed by Maggi Smith

Printed and bound in Singapore by CS Graphics

Half-title: Worked at small scale and brought to
life with highlights of blue paint, a Maya ruler sits
on a throne covered with a jaguar pelt. The
throne back is carved with a dwarf, providing
him a perpetual attendant; Princeton University.
Gift of Gillett G. Griffin, y1986–87a+b, photo
Bruce M. White (Plate 8).

Frontispiece: A view of Tikal's Great Plaza.
Temple 1 rises up at right; the Central Acropolis,
a great palace, is visible in the foreground;
photo Jorge Pérez de Lara.

Page 8: Yaxchilan, Structure 19. Known today
as the "labyrinth," the building may have been
an elaborate palace in the 8th century; photo
Jorge Pérez de Lara.

Contents

Directors' Foreword

COURTLY ART OF THE ANCIENT MAYA is the result of a collaboration between the Fine Arts Museums of San Francisco; the National Gallery of Art, Washington; and the Instituto Nacional de Antropología e Historia in Mexico. Although specific planning for this exhibition began in 1998, what made such a complex undertaking possible were deep, pre-existing relationships between San Francisco and Mexico, and between Washington and Mexico, that had developed during the last quarter of the 20th century.

For the Fine Arts Museums of San Francisco, relations with Mexico began in the late 1970s and were catalyzed by a large and unexpected bequest of Teotihuacan wall paintings. A series of subsequent collaborative projects focused on all the arts of Teotihuacan and continued for some 25 years. During roughly the same time period, the National Gallery of Art developed several major pre-Columbian exhibitions involving intense collaborations with Mexico: *Art of Aztec Mexico: Treasures of Tenochtitlan* (1983), *Circa 1492: Art in the Age of Exploration* (1991/92), and *Olmec Art of Ancient Mexico* (1996). All of these earlier projects—whether between Mexico and San Francisco, or between Mexico and Washington—required extensive cooperation and perseverance. The result was a foundation of mutual understanding and trust, as well as a desire to create other gratifying collaborative projects in the future.

Until this time, neither the Fine Arts Museums of San Francisco nor the National Gallery of Art had ever originated a major Maya exhibition. When Mary Miller first came to San Francisco with an initial proposal for a related Maya project on the subject of Bonampak, the Fine Arts Museums responded with great enthusiasm, and curator Kathleen Berrin began a long collaboration with Miller as they shaped *Courtly Art of the Ancient Maya*. The exhibition could not have been realized without the combined expertise, talent, and sheer determination of these co-curators. Their years of work, and Mary Miller's and consultant Simon Martin's catalogue text, provide a lasting contribution to this field of study.

Shortly after the planning began, the National Gallery was invited to join as an exhibition partner. Though the Fine Arts Museums have initiated many of the organizing tasks of the exhibition and catalogue, the staff of the National Gallery has played an integral role in shaping the concept and contents.

Every museum exhibition is a product of its own time and draws on the current scholarship and cultural assumptions of its own era. There are over 30 lenders to this project, with the majority of the major loans coming from Mexico. What made this U.S.-based project especially gratifying was the addition of a national Mexican perspective.

The many trips made to Mexico between 1998 and 2003 to carry on discussions about complicated matters pertaining to loans of national cultural patrimony were made pleasant and productive by our gracious Mexican colleagues. Our respective institutions are honored to be able to present these ancient Maya treasures to an international audience and are especially grateful to cultural leaders of the inter-related government agencies of the Consejo Nacional para la Cultura y las Artes and the Instituto Nacional de Antropología e Historia for making so many loans possible. We are indebted to Sari Bermúdez, president of the Consejo Nacional para la Cultura y las Artes, and Sergio Raúl Arroyo, director general of the Instituto Nacional de Antropología e Historia, for the leadership and cooperation that have resulted in this landmark exhibition. This venture could not have been achieved without the expertise of numerous officials at the United States Embassy, and most particularly Bertha Cea Echenique, whose friendship and advice were invaluable. The enormous collaborative efforts of Mexico's greatest cultural leaders and scholars have guided both the exhibition and catalogue.

Harry S. Parker III
Director, Fine Arts Museums of San Francisco

Earl A. Powell III
Director, National Gallery of Art

Foreword by Sari Bermúdez

The presentation of Maya art in the National Gallery of Art in Washington and the Fine Arts Museums of San Francisco is the realization of a desire, shared by various cultural organizations in Mexico and the United States, to broaden the understanding of expressions that have nourished and defined the mosaic that shapes today's world.

While holding the exhibition in such illustrious venues in the United States of America is a source of satisfaction for Mexico, it also fulfills one of the fundamental duties of the Consejo Nacional para la Cultura y las Artes: to coordinate the work of public institutions with regard to research, protection, and diffusion of the historical and cultural heritage of my country.

In this context, we provide continuity in a cultural dialogue that promotes mutual understanding at the same time that it reinforces the bonds of friendship. Within this open and generous spirit of exchange between our nations, *Courtly Art of the Ancient Maya* seeks to introduce to the public in the United States a vision of the cultural legacy of an extraordinary civilization.

This glimpse into the universe of the ancient Maya will bring visitors closer to an essential part of the social structure, organized into differentiated classes, that prevailed there in pre-Hispanic times. The nobility connected their histories to mythical origins and divine acts from the remote past; those who belonged to the upper lineages sought to represent visually their genealogies, memorable dates and feats, and earthly and cosmic events.

Courtly Art of the Ancient Maya is an exhibition composed of objects found throughout the Maya region, and with special emphasis on those found at Palenque. Works found in urban settlements on the banks of the Usumacinta and in other areas of Chiapas, adjoining Mexican states, and from Central America, also provide some of the finest examples. Vestiges of formal conduct as well as of complex rituals, these works strengthened the religious role of the rulers and underscored their power.

The success that we have achieved in this joint effort reaffirms that the sphere of collaboration and cultural exchange has no limits; it notably enriches the artistic offerings available to different publics and renews positive attitudes toward knowledge, and the understanding and respect for cultural diversity. In pursuing this dialogue between our two countries, we have contributed the finest representative works from Maya courts of the Late Classic period to demonstrate our desire, in today's Mexico of change, to promote and create opportunities for understanding between our countries, the nations forming the Americas of our times.

Sari Bermúdez
President
Consejo Nacional para la Cultura y las Artes

Foreword by Sergio Raúl Arroyo

Discovering and delving into the ancient Maya universe has been a key event in world history. The wonder produced by their achievements has been the source of imaginative 19th-century romanticism as well as of scientific notions of history, architecture, and astronomy. For several centuries, that universe also gave rise to the endless creation of stereotypes and fantasies, and to the unprecedented flourishing of different historical disciplines introducing archaeology and anthropology into Mexican academic circles as never before.

One of the challenges posed by Maya civilization over the last two centuries continues to be the subject of heated debate among specialists: how can we explain the complex view of the world underlying the science and arts of a culture, based on clear, indisputable hierarchies and behavior, that inspired the creation of pieces like those assembled in this exhibition? That "lifeworld," as Edmund Husserl referred to it, was gradually lost in the accumulation of events over time, and today it is possible for us to recover it as a luminous and, at the same time, enigmatic fragment of the Mesoamerican past.

Thanks to the dedication of several generations of archaeologists, ethnohistorians, epigraphers, and myriad scholars, little by little we have been uncovering and comprehending the secrets of the Maya, while broadening our vision of their social horizon. It is that exciting work that gives meaning to *Courtly Art of the Ancient Maya*; its content comes from the most recent on-site experiences and conferences of specialists on topics such as the cosmogony that permeated Maya life.

With this exhibition of more than 130 pieces, over half of them from the collections of the Instituto Nacional de Antropología e Historia, Mexico participates in one of the most rigorous thematic exhibitions on the ancient Maya held outside of the country. The aim of the exhibition is to reveal the many faces that defined the structures of that civilization: this is not an easy task because we can barely discern the network of relations that formed their sophisticated political and religious organization. We do not know their rites with complete certainty, nor the rhythm and phonetics of their words. We have only silent vestiges of that civilization that may allow us interpretations, but these interpretations possibly reflect, to a large extent, contemporary issues.

Between approximately AD 550 and 900, Maya ceremonial centers multiplied and expanded. The structures that today we call pyramids were built, and the population grew to levels that indicate complex social and economic organization. Religion with its dense ritual granted a place, a specific role, to each group and individual, as part of an organization in which social mobility must have been regarded as impossible.

As an incarnation of the godhead, the ruler—called Ahaw (lord, king), Ah tepal (king and god), or Halach uinic (true man), whom we perhaps erroneously refer to nowadays as king—was the mediator between the sacred and the profane. He stood at the head of the urban ceremonial center surrounded by smaller settlements distributed in hamlets and agricultural zones. The nobility related by marriage to the ruler aided him in civil and religious matters. The bureaucracy, priests, artisans, and farmers followed them on the social ladder. This social differentiation, and ultimately the strict protocol that it implied, were materially reflected on architectural monuments, commemorative stelae, and numerous works of a religious and ornamental character.

We should recall that stelae at Tikal, Guatemala, narrated rituals of accession of monarchs to the throne at that center. Meanwhile, at Palenque, Chiapas, monuments expressed a combination of historical events with mythical elements, while at Yaxchilan, they displayed the warlike character of their bellicose leaders.

Another theme treated in *Courtly Art of the Ancient Maya* is the fundamental role of Maya women in political stratagems: the matrilineal descent was a decisive factor in succession, and it was precisely the mother who invested the new Ahaw with the emblems of royal power. Women were a primary factor of stability between major centers and secondary cities, for matrimonial alliances forged the networks of political and economic commitments.

However, to understand the role fulfilled by each level, gender, or individual, we must start from the premise that the earthly world was intimately linked with its counterpart in the sacred world: the social hierarchy was a mundane expression of the divine hierarchy. The visitor, therefore, will find interwoven into the dense fabric of the ceremonial realm and political legitimacy another fundamental guiding principle: all human activity for the Maya was aimed at maintaining equilibrium of the cosmos. Man was created by the gods to play a vital role: the remains of this destiny left behind in ceramics, wood, and stone allow us nowadays a hint of their ancient grandeur through the countenances of supernatural forces incarnated in the personal power of Maya rulers.

It is precisely this certainty that perhaps distances us further from the ancient Maya. In that dazzling civilization, human beings were the engine of the universe and they had a function to fulfill. That vital conviction is what confers upon works their powerful beauty; it makes us want to approach their creations with renewed wonder. We modern individuals seek to decipher the mystery of those people and to make their world ours.

Sergio Raúl Arroyo
Director General
Instituto Nacional de Antropología e Historia

Introduction

The Fine Arts Museums of San Francisco have a long-standing interest in the development of art from the ancient Americas. Artworks from ancient Mexico and Central and South America provide unique perspectives on the cultures and civilizations that thrived long before European invaders began their subjection. The names given to great civilizations of the past—Inca, Aztec, Maya, Teotihuacan—are now recognized as counterparts to major cultural developments elsewhere in the world, whether in Egypt, China, Italy, or Greece.

San Francisco's mission to study and disseminate knowledge about ancient artworks from these cultures took a dramatic turn in 1978, when the de Young Museum received a vast, undocumented collection of Teotihuacan murals. The curatorial and conservation departments devoted the next 20 years to studying and restoring these artworks and, in conjunction with the Instituto Nacional de Antropología e Historia of Mexico, to understanding their context and meaning. The project culminated in several exhibitions and ultimately in the voluntary return of over half of the paintings to Mexico (see Berrin 1986). Today the returned murals form an important part of museum displays both at the site of Teotihuacan and the Museo Nacional de Antropología in Mexico City. One cannot study the mural paintings of this powerful culture of the 1st millennium AD and not work with the data, interpretations, and material made possible by the Fine Arts Museums of San Francisco.

In February 1998, the Museums had an opportunity to acquire a remarkable Maya stela (Plate 46). Its legality according to U.S. law was clearly established, for the stela was physically in the United States prior to 1971, but exhaustive research and consultation with scholars did not provide definitive knowledge of its origin. The Fine Arts Museums of San Francisco determined it would be important to talk with the governments of Guatemala as well as Mexico before such an acquisition could be realized, so the staff took an unprecedented step and initiated discussion. Both countries appreciated the Museums' initiative, and after lengthy consultations, neither country objected to the acquisition of the stela. These candid dialogues allowed San Francisco to explore a new relationship with Guatemala, to deepen existing ties with Mexico, and eventually to make the acquisition (see Berrin 1999). The San Francisco stela is one of the most aesthetically compelling works from the ancient Maya to be found in any U.S. collection.

Before and during the acquisition of the stela, many of us at the Fine Arts Museums became fascinated with the prospect of exploring Maya civilization further. How was it that a female could find herself the subject of such a monumental artwork? What was the belief system that gave rise to such a complex artwork? Was the subject matter of the stela religious or political? And what was the significance of the serpent wrapping itself so dramatically around the female dignitary's body?

Over the years I had been in contact with Mary Miller. The groundbreaking exhibition she developed with Linda Schele in 1986, *The Blood of Kings*, had changed the way both scholars and the general public understood Maya art. What had seemed to be arcane and inaccessible narratives of the past came to life, revealing the poignant humanity of the ancient Maya people. Mary, of course, had been working for most of the 1990s on the Maya murals of Bonampak, perhaps the single most vivid depiction of that lost world in action. Together we saw the possibilities of presenting these ideas in an exhibition format and, with the thoughtful input of a wide range of colleagues, we imagined *Courtly Art of the Ancient Maya*. We were excited about taking an in-depth look inside the royal courts where Maya art was made and where such works were commissioned or even demanded in hostile tribute arrangements. We saw that we could tell the story of the life at court—not the entire story of the ancient Maya, by any means, but a concentrated version illuminating a relatively brief period in Maya history. Because of recent interest in the Maya court (Inomata and Houston 2001), and the breakthroughs that have been made in deciphering Maya glyphs and dynastic history by epigraphers such as Simon Martin and Nikolai Grube (2000) in the last decade of the 20th century, we believed that we would gain new insights into this period by intensifying our scrutiny. Simon Martin joined the project in 2001, bringing epigraphic expertise to the collective effort.

While there have been many generalized exhibitions about Maya art, we were determined to focus on a more precise time period. We chose the period often called the Late Classic by some of our authors or simply referred to chronologically by others. The themes played out by Maya kingdoms from AD 600 to 850 seemed to be distinctive and worthy of study. This was a time when the complexity of the court, its arts, and the material wealth inside the royal palace were at their zenith. It was also a time when women played key leadership roles in solidifying power alliances both at home and abroad. This explosion of wealth gave way to experimentation in art forms. Warfare in its various manifestations (real war or reenacted, ritualized war) took place first on the battlefield and then in scripted performance in court. The intense competition and cultural strife between kingdoms vying for power unleashed a social and political dynamism to which the greatest artists had to respond. The social drama, unrest, and turmoil of this period provided a backdrop for the creation of remarkable artistic works, and it was this particular interaction of human circumstances that seems to have been the catalyst for some of the most exciting changes in the visual arts.

Given the complexity of Maya civilization as it has extended during a period of over 2,000 years, there are certainly many other stories of the Maya that could be told, each one deserving its own special focus: the rise of Maya civilization during the 1st millennium BC (often called the

Preclassic or Formative), or the years when the Maya and Teotihuacan civilizations experienced intense interaction (AD 250–550, usually called the Early Classic), or the reconfiguration of Maya society primarily in Yucatan after AD 900 (the Postclassic) and the interaction with groups in Central Mexico. The Spanish conquest of the Maya region (beginning in 1519 with the landing of Hernán Cortés along the Caribbean coast, and ending in 1542 with the founding of Mérida) ushered in the colonial stage of Maya history. Though Spanish rule was to have a devastating effect, Maya history continued to move forward. Today there are several million indigenous Maya peoples who speak over 25 separate languages and are the largest single block of Amerindians north of Peru. Our understanding of all facets of Maya life has deepened considerably, but the story we have chosen to tell here focuses on a unique historic period we call the Late Classic (AD 600–850).

As intermediaries to the gods, Maya lords and ladies lived at the very top of Maya society, in a realm of unbelievable wealth, privilege, and splendor. Between the years AD 600 and 850, these divine kings and queens commissioned great programs of art, inscriptions, and architecture as memorials and to ensure their place in history. They recognized the special value of artists at court, whose work was necessary to convey history as cyclical, as simultaneously past, present, and future. Artists would sometimes depict royal actions as reenactments of cosmic events that had occurred millions of years in the past, reflecting a rich cosmology that knew no beginning or end.

Interpreting the art of the ancient Maya, with its dense iconography and glyphic inscriptions, is never easy. The experience of art in our own time does not in any way begin to prepare us to understand the art of the ancient Maya. Though we may marvel at select works, the visual language of these arts is alien to us—it comes from a different kind of social experience and its messages were aimed at peoples of a different age. The extent to which we can bridge this gap will depend upon our willingness to stand outside our own preconceptions, in an effort to wrap our minds around a radically different belief system and at the same time try to figure out exactly what this system may have meant.

The Miller and Martin texts of this volume—found in the first six chapters and in the catalogue of objects—provide a unified view of a complex subject. Chapter 7, however, is more experimental and suggestive. It is here that we have invited a wide range of distinguished experts to provide brief sketches of some of their latest and most exciting work pertaining to our subject in the fields of art history, archaeology, and epigraphy. As their varied perspectives suggest, burgeoning new data and ideas about the Maya can only enrich our understanding in the future.

If the pinnacles of Maya courtly art commissioned by a narrow stratum of leaders at the top dominate this exhibition, then how did the rest of the Maya population express themselves in art? We may never know for sure—unfortunately most of what all the ancient Maya made, whether rich or poor, urban or rural, was of perishable materials such as wood, feathers, or fiber, and most of these objects have vanished without a trace in the humid tropical environment. We know that religious thought pervaded Maya society, and that art objects must have been made and used at all levels. Sometimes common patterns do emerge, and it may be possible to extrapolate continuities. For example, across Chiapas and Guatemala today, the vibrant textile designs provide living texts that can sharpen our sense of the past as embedded in and revitalized by the present.

It is possible to find occasional views of non-courtly art expression that may surprise us. For example, the Comalcalco bricks (Plate 86), are an unusual form of aesthetic expression; they reveal a preoccupation with the visual arts that we might not expect from working brick-makers. The designs on these bricks were hidden; they were not meant to be seen on courtly buildings. Yet at Comalcalco there were hundreds of these hidden, incised, modeled, or painted bricks, many of them bearing a kind of elegance that goes beyond graffiti. There is often an immediacy or spontaneity in these renderings that reminds us of the flowing line we associate with the artworks prepared by courtly artisans.

As Miller and Martin so vividly describe, Maya aristocratic life seems to have been dedicated to living out cultural ideals, yet it also seems to have been fraught with danger. Archaeology has shown us that precious resources, such as wood, were being used up as the tropical rainforest vanished. The Maya fought over some scarce resources and they squandered others. The ideal script the lords and ladies wrote for their lives increasingly may have been in disharmony with the world around them, and evidently the required price was too high. We are fortunate that it was customary for the courtly world to replicate so many of their beliefs, ideals, and achievements in beautiful, lasting materials. Though precious little remains, it is still possible to reconstruct a glimmer of the ancient splendor.

Kathleen Berrin, Curator in Charge
Arts of Africa, Oceania, and the Americas
Fine Arts Museums of San Francisco

CHAPTER 1 # Life at the Maya Court

Fig. 1   Detail of Monument 168, Tonina, Plate 20. The implacable face of a 6th-century king.

During the 1st millennium BC, the Maya people mastered their harsh tropical environment—the region today covered by southeastern Mexico, Belize, Guatemala, and parts of El Salvador and Honduras—to create one of the most sophisticated civilizations not only of the Americas, but also of the entire ancient world. Skillful management of these shallow soils during annual cycles of deluge and drought produced healthy surpluses and fed a burgeoning population. By 500 BC, one-time villages had grown into the first Maya metropolises, with massive pyramids towering over sweeping plazas and the clustered homes of the rich and powerful.

Maya civilization did not emerge in isolation, but rather as part of a larger cultural flowering in North America. Archaeologists have determined that what is today Mexico, along with much of western Central America, formed a zone of common cultural heritage, and for more than half a century have called it Mesoamerica. The bounty of maize, the indigenous corn first domesticated in Mexico 7,000 to 9,000 years ago, stimulated all the advanced societies of the region. Most of the practices that define the concept of Mesoamerica emerged during the 1st millennium BC, including a sacred divinatory calendar of 260 days and the principles of writing and numerical notation. Others, such as the Mesoamerican ballgame—a sport and ritual played with a rubber ball within two parallel walls—probably developed earlier, among a culture called the Olmec, a people known only archaeologically and who flourished along the Gulf of Mexico Coast, from 1200 BC to 400 BC. One very important feature of this early culture was the emergence of institutionalized leaders, or so modern observers intuit, based on the powerful and dynamic portraiture that survives in stone.

By about AD 250 the Maya had absorbed influences from across Mesoamerica and fashioned their own unique society. The cultural florescence that lasted until AD 900, traditionally known as the "Classic Period," was one that placed special emphasis on dynastic kingship within an expanding landscape of small city-states. Eventually 60 or more fiercely competitive kingdoms dotted the Maya landscape, making for a political history of great complexity.

Each kingdom was ruled by a hereditary lord who entitled himself Ahaw (*ajaw*), "Lord," and "Holy Lord" (*k'uhul ajaw*) (Fig. 2a–c). Succession normally passed from father to son, but the Maya made adjustments when primogeniture could not prevail, so that occasionally one brother succeeded another or the line passed through a female heir. Above the rank of Ahaw lay the higher title of Kaloomte' (*kaloomte'*), of still uncertain meaning, but bearers of the title held a particular association with one of the four cardinal directions; many were known as the "West" Kaloomte', for example (Fig. 2d–f).¹ Titles such as these undoubtedly invoked religious as well as political authority.

Maya royal families may have started out small—although the details through AD 600 are murky at best—but they grew dramatically in the 7th and 8th centuries. Kings took multiple wives,

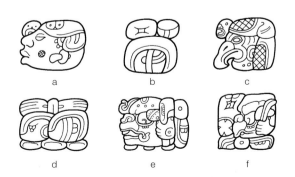

a   b   c

d   e   f

Fig. 2   Titles of kings and lords: a, b, c. Ahaw, "Lord/ruler," in alternative versions; d, e. Kaloomte'; f. West Kaloomte'.

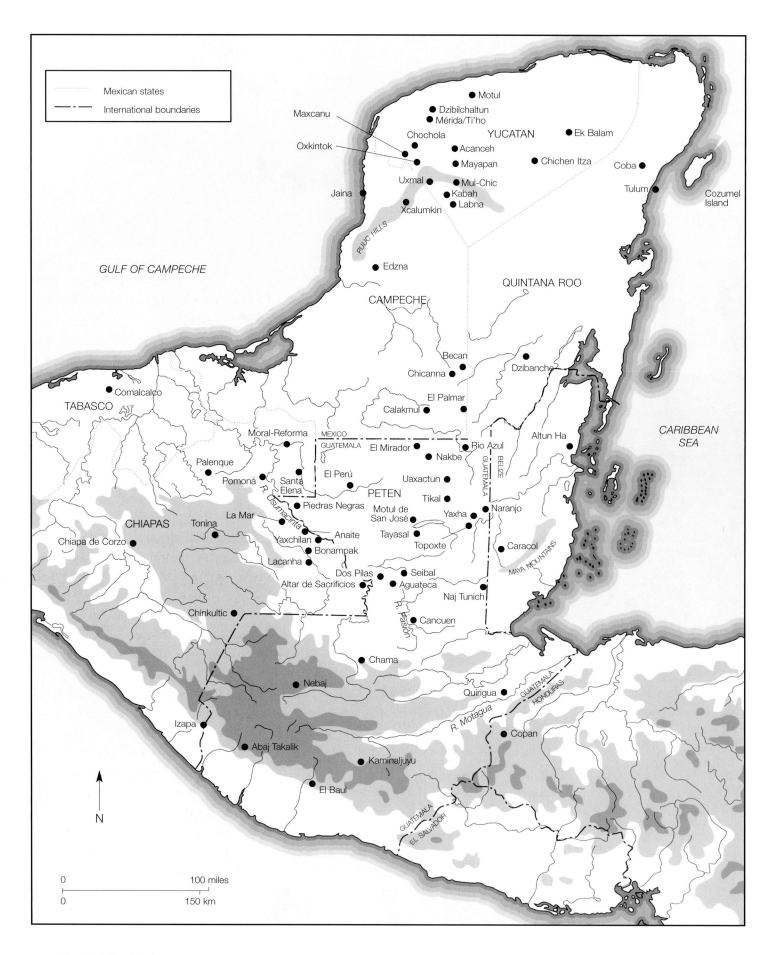

Fig. 4   Graffiti of towering Maya temples, drawing.
From Comalcalco, Chicanna, and Yaxha.

and at least until late in the 8th century, those at the top of the food chain had access to a better life—better diet, better housing, and presumably even better midwifery. Within a few generations the cadet lines expanded, and in some cases, probably contributed to internecine competition, warfare and even treachery. As families grew, they sometimes established new cities or new compounds within existing cities. In other cases, the wealth and power of royal families so enhanced the status of elites at neighboring communities that they, too, became a part of the nobility.

In time, many cities dotted the Maya realm, each the capital of its own city-state. The most famous Maya cities, Tikal, Copan, Palenque, and Yaxchilan (Fig. 3), are known by their towering pyramids or by their fabulous archaeological discoveries. These cities have entered a modern, international consciousness from travel brochures or from movies like *Star Wars*, where Tikal's Temple 2 defined the "rebel planet," or from *National Geographic Magazine*, which has covered Maya discoveries assiduously in recent decades. Major discoveries have created international news, from Palenque, where archaeologists discovered a hidden stairwell inside the Temple of Inscriptions that led to a secret burial chamber in bedrock deep below—a discovery akin to that of Tutankhamun's tomb—to Bonampak, where the finest mural paintings in the New World, with their lively scenes of courtly life, survived over 1,000 years in the rainforest.

Most of all, the Maya are recognized by their iconic pyramids, steep-stepped platforms with stairways leading to lofty temple sanctuaries, the ever-present image of travel brochures and book covers. These great structures may have defined Maya cities to the Maya as well—for they are often the subjects of graffiti, sketched on walls at the great cities and also at lesser centers, perhaps as memories of pilgrimages and journeys to great tombs (Fig. 4). What these discoveries tell us is that Maya pyramids enshrined royal figures, and that ancestor veneration was a central feature of religious practice—as it was for more humble folk, who buried their dead under their houses. One was always living with the ancestors.[2]

But Maya cities were complex living places, not simply mausoleums. At the heart of each lay its royal court, which as home to the ruling king—and occasional queen—served as the supreme seat of authority. The court combined the functions of luxury residence, governmental office, reception center, banqueting hall, school, and courts of justice. It was a place of elegance and entertainment, sumptuously furnished within and splendidly decorated without (Fig. 5). Within what often came to be sprawling complexes, kings commanded their networks of trade and tribute and issued instructions to the hierarchies of lords who administered their realm from small private throne rooms. The royal courts of the Maya should be understood to be both an elite group that dominated the governmental process and the physical constructions that they inhabited and that expressed their power.[3]

During the 7th and 8th centuries AD, elaborate palace culture reached the peak of opulence and refinement. Maya rulers—as kings of the forest—adopted the jaguar as their mascot and metaphor and sat on flayed jaguar skins and pelt cushions (Plates 1, 2, 7, 8, 14). Sitting on wide bench-like

Fig. 3   Map of the Maya region.

thrones, portly lords personified the wealth and power of their divine positions, contemplating their visages in mirrors and smoking thin cigars. Stately women attended their lords and husbands, while a coterie of dwarves and hunchbacks, singers and masked actors, trumpeters and drummers, waiters, dressers and fan bearers—and even the royal flysweep—catered to the lord's every need and desire. Supplicants of lordly favor brought lavish gifts and payments of tribute to his feet: bundles of cloth, chocolate beans, exotic marine shells, and rare feathers—each of which was accounted for by an attendant scribe (Plate 6). The growing court culture bred a range of specializations and ranking offices—each denoted by a specific title—providing ever more refined notions of courtly rights and responsibilities (Plates 5, 9, 14).

One looks in vain for a central religious authority in the Maya world—an equivalent to the Vatican City or Mecca—and just as hopelessly for a central political authority. There was never one Maya. The contrast with contemporary Central Mexico could hardly have been greater. There the great city of Teotihuacan, whose ruins lie just outside modern Mexico City, was the political and religious pivot for a vast region. The largest city of the Western Hemisphere in its day, with a population of 150,000 or more, it pursued an opposing ideal of centrality. The two cultures enjoyed a mutual, if very different, fascination with one another. For the rulers of Teotihuacan, the Maya inhabited an exotic region in which rare and valuable commodities, especially feathers, pelts, and jade, could be found. For the Maya, Teotihuacan represented the home of indomitable war gods and a paragon of military prowess; from them the Maya adopted military ideology, including specific deities, weaponry, and styles of dress. Teotihuacan meddled directly in Maya politics during the 4th century, but there were clearly close cultural exchanges between the two great traditions both before and long after. When Teotihuacan's fortunes waned in the 7th century, the city increasingly took on less tangible but more mythic qualities to the Maya, the kind of sacred place they called "Puh," or "reeds."[4] From the vantage point of the Maya court or courtier, Teotihuacan was always a remote and deeply foreign entity—more the subject of legend than personal experience. Without the counterweight of Teotihuacan during their vibrant peak in the 7th and 8th centuries, the Maya developed largely independently from the rest of Mesoamerica.

Especially through works from the 7th and 8th centuries in the Maya lowlands, we can re-animate the royal courts at the highpoint of Maya civilization. A combination of archaeology, ethnography, art history, and epigraphy—the decipherment of hieroglyphic texts—allows us to see the wealth and texture of this elite world. The now-empty halls of Tikal, Copan, Yaxchilan, Piedras Negras, Tonina, Bonampak, and Palenque, among others, can be re-populated with personalities whose names, life histories, and family relationships are now known to us. We can see how they meted out authority to subsidiary lords and built support among them to secure sometimes tenuous claims to legitimacy. We can similarly chart the fortunes of their kingdoms and their struggles against neighbors and more distant powers. We can even glimpse the supernatural models for Maya kingship and courtly culture that guided and legitimized human action.

While modeling one presentation of courtly kingship at home, Maya kingdoms made bad neighbors to one another, predisposed to mutual animosity and sporadic violence, only occasionally interspersed by alliance and cooperation. Despite the large number of Maya kingdoms, only a few major players dominated the political landscape. The greatest of these, Calakmul, forged alliances and built up hegemonies over great swaths of the region—and fought its rival, Tikal. In equally intense and enduring struggles, Palenque contested the fertile soils of Tabasco with Piedras Negras, and squabbled with Tonina over the mineral-rich highlands of Chiapas. On the great Usumacinta River Piedras Negras and Yaxchilan squared off in a centuries-long contest for pre-eminence. Copan and its one-time vassal Quirigua quarreled, probably over the vast wealth to be exploited in the highland Guatemala jade sources.

In every sense Maya cities of the 7th and 8th centuries competed with one another, and when not engaged on the battlefield they strove to outdo each other in artistic achievement and in the scale of their pomp and circumstance. But they soon faced challenges that dwarfed such petty rivalries. In the early years of the 9th century a lethal combination of factors—of which overpopulation, environmental degradation, and drought are the leading suspects—tipped the Maya world into an abyss. One by one, once proud and populous cities fell first into turmoil and then abandonment and oblivion. The last dated statement from the southern lowlands was posted at Tonina in 909. By then the palaces were deserted of the high and mighty, their place taken by impoverished squatters and refugees.

The Palace Space

The physical space of the court survives as a kind of "self-portrait," a stone and mortar reflection of the cultural activity it once contained. In the same way each Maya city developed its own unique ground plan, so no Maya palace follows a single "typical" template. A palace compound usually began with the construction of a single multi-room stone structure, often with multiple means of access; some rooms were configured for privacy and others for public functions. Over time, additional buildings were added and older ones modified, usually to create a complex of enclosed courtyards, making the spaces within ever more restricted and exclusive.

Archaeologists once doubted that the galleried and multi-chambered buildings they discovered were palaces at all, finding the narrow stone chambers to be dark, cramped, dank, and bat-infested. Yet in their well-maintained heyday, these cool spaces were more than congenial in the tropical heat. Built-in platforms, originally draped with cushions and rugs, formed comfortable family-sized beds. At night, illuminated by flickering torchlight and with curtains drawn across doorways—especially in January when cold *norte* winds rip across the Maya realm—these high-vaulted chambers must have seemed particularly intimate and appealing. At major palaces such at Palenque and elsewhere, architects designed ways to close doors from both the inside and outside (Fig. 6).

Fig. 5   A painted vase in the Pink Glyphs style, rollout photograph. The vessel depicts an enthroned ruler consulting a mirror in its basket while attendants observe.

Though interior spaces could be small, they usually opened out onto wide courtyards. On some buildings, surviving cornice tie-holes show that great awnings and tarpaulins were once stretched out onto the stoop, greatly expanding the available living area. For every square foot of roofed stone palace, there might well have been two of shady space covered in this way, offering protection from the bright sun. These great canvases, furled up and out of use, are frequently shown in representations, as if temporarily pulled back to give the viewer brief access to the intimacies of royal life (Plates 2, 7). Palace galleries, as the wealth of interior tie-holes at Palenque attests, could be subdivided by suspending drapes across doors and hallways, forming room-like spaces that offered at least a modicum of privacy (Fig. 6). Of course there is little privacy to be had on one side of a curtain, whose purpose is visual, much like a Japanese *shoji* screen. Visitors could be housed this way, and their every conversation overheard, using the intricate network of T-shaped windows that penetrate the Palenque walls (Fig. 7).

Whether under canvas or open to the sky, palace courtyards were multi-purpose areas *par excellence*. Here portable furniture—including carved wooden thrones—could be set up and a wide range of different activities engaged in. Certainly the large gatherings assembled for feasts could be accommodated only here—some are known to have been night-time events presumably illuminated by pine torches. Excavations at Tikal and elsewhere have revealed institutional food preparation at the Central Acropolis, a royal palace, with the multiple hearths required to cook for royalty, guests, and retainers. The midden alongside the Palace Reservoir at Tikal reveals that the cooks and attendants hurled broken dishes off the back of the palace.[5]

Inside palace walls, enclosed courtyards make perfect theaters, ideal for private performances, whether sacred ritual or secular entertainment, dances, pageants, and plays. Modern tour guides incessantly clap to demonstrate court and plaza acoustics: without the sound-absorbing grass and foliage found today, the acoustical properties would have been even more pronounced. Open spaces within enclosures would also be practical and cordial surroundings for intellectual life, including education of youths: whether in scribal or arithmetical skills, in the arts of oratory and rhetoric, or in elite crafts such as embroidery and weaving. In more grisly fashion, courtyards were also the venue for parading, humiliating, and torturing of captives—whose anguished images often decorate surrounding walls and stairways.

Specific architectural functions may be revealed in the complex of small rooms along the main plaza at Copan, which include a sweatbath; they may have served as a home for youths in courtly training.[6] We can imagine that they needed space not only for studying mental skills but also for the rigorous workouts and practice combats that would prepare them for warfare. Other structures may well have been allocated to more mundane tasks such as storage. Valuable tribute items needed to be safely secured, while the delicate paraphernalia of ritual display had to be kept dry and protected from pests. The high vaulted ceilings, with their heavy cross-beams, made it possible to hang personal belongings within boxes, baskets, or sacks above normal living space. Other possessions may have been tucked into built-in niches or under benches, out of harm's way. At Piedras Negras, each royal compound featured at least one sweatbath, providing the locus for both ritual purification and healing rituals. The prominence of women at that site makes it possible that some of the baths had gender restrictions, as is known ethnographically elsewhere in Mesoamerica.

Both courtyard and plaza surfaces received frequent coatings of stucco plaster, whose highly polished surfaces of gleaming white would have dazzled the eye. Court buildings themselves were often richly decorated, both inside and out. Especially well-preserved examples, like the one at Palenque, show a riot of exterior color and ornament, with programs of deep red set against the rich polychrome treatments given to stucco-modeled entablatures and piers (Fig. 8). Depictions of

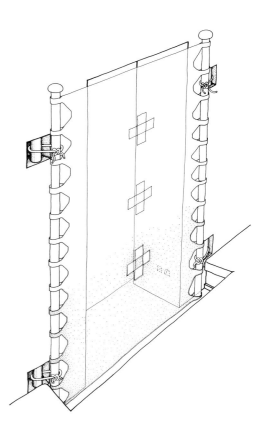

Fig. 6   Cordholders in palaces could have been used to create private spaces. Reconstruction drawing demonstrates possible use at doorway.

Fig. 7   T-shaped windows, Palenque Palace.

cosmic motifs, mythical beasts, deities, and ancestral kings combined to give this elevated "home" the appearance of sacred space. Within the buildings interior decor competed with furnishings such as the great stone thrones. Some thrones were backed by carved limestone relief panels that depict accession to kingship or lengthy hieroglyphic texts.

Such palace inscriptions present a range of topics: dynastic histories, war triumphs, and ritual performances of one sort or another. Of the latter, some of the more important are building dedications: they not only allow us to chart the incremental development of the palace complex but they also name individual structures. For example, House E, the heart of the Palace at Palenque, was originally called the "White Skin House" (*sak nuk naah*): its white-painted exterior spotted with stylized flowers contrasted with the exterior red paint covering most of the palace (Fig. 8). At Piedras Negras one court gallery was called the "Lightning House" (*chahuk naah*), while at Calakmul another structure contained a ceiling capstone inscribed "6 Ahaw House" (*wak ajaw naah*), a reference to a day in the Maya calendar.[7] According to accounts made soon after the Spanish invasion of the Maya region in the 16th century, the nobles who advised the ruler would gather in a "Mat House" (*popol naah*). At more than one ancient city, structures sporting mat-pattern adornments adjoin a throne room (Fig. 9). These texts also tell of the owners of these buildings—stated in the formula "the house of so-and-so"—which were commonly the kings themselves, but sometimes their queens. Despite this wealth of information, we often find ourselves struggling to answer basic questions: How precisely did these buildings function? Did a single king keep multiple palaces? How many nobles might have been in attendance at any one time? When a new building superseded an old one in function, who took over its maintenance? For every question we can answer, there are dozens that remain unanswered.

Life at Court

Works of art open a unique window onto a Maya courtly culture long since vanished. They depict the form, texture, and color of its perishable world—the cushions and pillows, mats and coverings,

Fig. 8   Reconstruction painting by Merle Greene Robertson of Palenque Palace, *c.* AD 670. Copyright Merle Greene Robertson 1986.

Fig. 9   Structure 22A, Copan, a likely "Mat House"
(*popol naah*), a meeting place for nobles.

even the body paint and tattooing of the protagonists—no scrap of which survives today. We are particularly fortunate that so many painted cylindrical vases record vivid scenes of palatial life "behind the curtain." The vessels themselves were designed to hold prestigious beverages—sometimes *balche*, a fermented honey drink, but more often *kakaw*, the bitter, frothy, and chili-laden drink made from chocolate beans (Plates 4, 6, 7, 14, 17). The pots themselves are often shown in the painted scenes, placed in front of, or under, royal thrones, with their contents decanted into gourds or shallow cups. The chocolate drink often accompanies other feast foods commonly represented, particularly tamales dripping with sauce, a Maya favorite.

In monumental scenes of grand royal ceremonies, Maya royals and nobles are weighed down by the panoply of high office: scepters of rulership, tall headdresses, masks, and elaborate apparel (Plates 3, 5, 9, 10, 20, 21). The monuments that depict Maya rulers in this way generally took their place outside, as if permanently representing the ruler on the plaza. But within the palace, as often shown on ceramic vessels, rulers dress for comfort in elegant light cottons. They preside from thrones; empty-handed, they gesture to subordinates. They wear only the most intimate items of jewelry. Carved from jade, shell, or bone, personal possessions such as these regularly carry texts naming their owner, a description of the object itself, and even its individual name.

In addition to thrones themselves, a single furnishing of the palace commonly appears on Maya vessels: the round, framed Maya mirror. When mirrors occur in such scenes, Maya lords stare into their own studied reflections (Plates 4, 7, 14, 17). Among Mesoamerican cultures mirrors were ascribed magical properties, and could be used to "scry," that is, to divine the future, to seek counsel, or to look into otherwise hidden corners of the soul. Lords may have addressed themselves in such devices, since the act of reflection is often by speech, indicated by trailing speech scrolls (Plate 17). The Maya may have understood that these reflections could themselves speak. The mirror may also have protected the speaker from any ills, by reflecting the sound and image, effectively making of him a twin.

The Maya made their mirrors from mosaics of precisely fitted segments, made from either iron pyrite (fool's gold), which gave a glossy, yellowish surface when new, or hematite, another iron ore, which yielded a dark and somewhat misty reflection. A superb mirror recently excavated at Bonampak is composed of 59 such segments attached to a sandstone backing (Plate 15).[8] Its resemblance to a turtle carapace was more than fortuitous, for the Maya viewed the earth itself as a huge cosmic turtle and the metaphorical ground from which the Maize God is annually reborn (Plate 39; Fig. 16). In his reflection, the ruler's own face seems to emerge from the turtle's back, a poignant image of resurrection and renewal. The Maya held the human ideal to be the face and form of the Maize God: as the face in the mirror, the Maize God would always be the "fairest of them all."

A standard pose on cylinder vessels shows a retainer, very often a dwarf, holding the mirror to his lord's gaze. The dwarf mirror-bearer became so standardized an ideal that it was transformed into sculptural form, in which the wooden retainer and his mirror were ever frozen in service (Plate 16). Mirror-backs or frames were often decorated; one made of slate from Topoxte, Guatemala, bears a hieroglyphic text that names its owner and directly describes it as a *nehn,* "mirror."[9] Many mirrors could be worn, like the one with a frame in the shape of a rabbit that appears on the chest of a blue-painted priestly Jaina figurine (Plate 9). The depiction of the mirror on the vessel posed a problem: how to represent the oval or round form when seen from the side? Maya artists developed a conventional solution, depicting half the mirror, to represent a radical foreshortening.

Dwarves served special roles as intimates of the king, in ways that went far beyond holding mirrors. Both dwarves and hunchbacks garnered high status across Mesoamerica (Plates 11, 18). Centuries later, Motecuhzoma, the Aztec ruler, would keep an entourage of dwarves around him, whose political counsel he sought during the Spanish invasion of his empire. Adorned in equally elevated garb but physically unlike the idealized ruler, the dwarf had a relationship with his lord that replicated the mythical one between the Maize God and his dwarf companions—like that between the dominant ear of maize and the stubby, often malformed, ears that also form on the stalk.

The Maya usually represented high nobility with the body and face of the Maize God, eternally young and beautiful, certainly in distinction to the depiction of dwarves and hunchbacks. Firm flesh ("like a tomato," the Aztecs would later say) characterized Maya beauty, along with exaggerated nose, crossed eyes, and tapering forehead. Because most Maya depictions of the human face simplify and idealize, emphasizing these very characteristics, it is often impossible to distinguish one ruler from another by physiognomy alone.

But at Palenque, a true portraiture emerged (Plates 113, 114). Masters of stucco exploited the malleability of their material to take the naturalistic direction of Maya art to its highest achievement. While ceramic figurines, whose faces were often mold-made, usually offer up the standardized ideal, some—particularly representations of captives and servants—go beyond these limitations to demand engagement from the viewer. The old nanny who coaxes the young child may simultaneously represent the old goddess of midwifery, but in her gentle demeanor and grizzled face she also reveals the wisdom of age (Plate 58).

Depictions of powerful women often emphasize their girth, an exaggerated plumpness that indicates their wealth and easy living (Plate 5). Their representation on monumental works of art is most common around AD 700, when women emerge as prominent subjects at certain cities, especially western ones such as Yaxchilan and Piedras Negras (Chapter 3). It would be tempting to read into this some profound transformation of gender relations, but the motivation is probably more prosaic: in a time of enhanced warfare, when larger polities step in to dominate smaller ones, women and the dynastic lines they represent can achieve a new political relevance and thereby a brief foothold on power. Royal wives were often the scions of foreign dynasties sent to forge new alliances and political settlements, and their contacts with their home kingdoms must always have been important. At Yaxchilan, for example, a Calakmul princess bore the great Bird Jaguar, undoubtedly establishing both political and family relationships. Many of these noble women held specific titles of rank, counterparts usually to titles held by men, but not necessarily those of their husbands.

Though few representations of them survive, the palace was also a place for children, and for princesses as well as princes. Young nobles were dubbed a Ch'ok or "Sprout," with the heir to the throne known as Baah Ch'ok (*b'aah ch'ok*) or "Head Sprout" (Fig. 10). They were involved in sacrificial rituals from an early age, with some records indicating accession to the throne by children as young as two years old. There is also reason to think that the offspring of client kings were retained as "guests" at court, there to be kept under the controlling eye of their masters to ensure the good behavior of their kin (Fig. 11).[10]

The most important attendants of the king were his principal nobles (Plate 121). These lords took key roles in the administration of court and kingdom, initially behind the scenes but increasingly publicly during the 8th century. The king's right-hand man was his Baah Ahaw (*b'aah ajaw*) or "Head Lord"—the foremost among a whole stratum of secondary figures. Those entitled Sahal (*sajal*) and Ah K'uhuun (*aj k'uhuun*) seem to perform more specific roles in court officialdom and regional governance, though the terms themselves have thus far resisted decipherment. Such lieutenants to the king passed their authority from one generation to the next—although with the occasional "promotion" to a higher rank not out of the question. Other secondary titles, including Yahaw K'ak' (*yajaw k'ahk'*), "Fire Lord" and Yahaw Te' (*yajaw te'*), "Tree Lord," can be read without

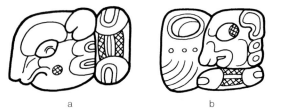

Fig. 10   Titles of young lords: a. Ch'ok, or "Sprout"; b. Baah Ch'ok, "Head Sprout."

Fig. 11   Panel 19, Dos Pilas, drawing. A child at Dos Pilas undergoes a bloodletting rite performed by a kneeling priest or adolescent lord. The event is watched by the Dos Pilas king and his Cancuen queen (at left) and by a lord from Calakmul (second from right) described as the child's "guardian."

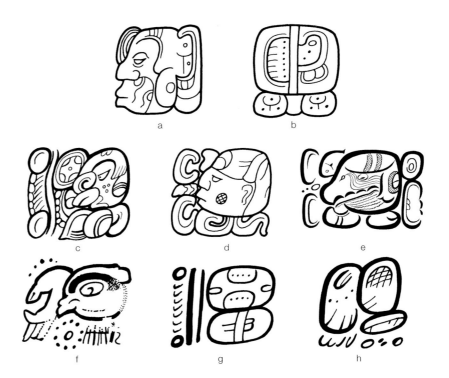

Fig. 12 Titles of secondary lords: a, b. Sahal; c. Ah K'uhuun; d. Yahaw K'ak', "Fire Lord"; e. Yahaw Te', "Tree Lord"; f. [Y]ebet, "[His] Messenger"; g. Ah Baak, "Captive-taker"; h. Baah Pakal, "Head Shield."

comprehending their attendant responsibilities. Those sent on diplomatic missions far from home—probably at some personal risk—were called Ebet or "Messenger." They often wore distinctive white cloaks with shell ornaments and served as the key intermediaries between kings, conducting negotiations, delivering communications, gifts, and tribute from one lord to his rival.

Many nobles had military duties. Their titles boast of the number of prisoners they had taken, or describe themselves as Ah Baak (*aj b'aak*), "Captive-taker" or Baah Pakal (*b'aah pakal*), "Head Shield." Maya warfare often took place away from the city, in the sort of scrub forest depicted in the great battle painting of Bonampak (Fig. 50). Aside from wider strategic considerations the stated goal of Maya combat—like that of Mesoamerican warfare in general—was to capture, not kill, one's enemy. Victorious Maya warriors led their captives back to their home city to be enslaved or sacrificed. Presented to the ruler on palace steps, captives are shown variously pleading for mercy, swearing allegiance to their new masters, or facing with resignation whatever fate awaited them (Plates 2, 93).

Strikingly, a good number of painted ceramic vases show a figure standing behind the throne, a watching bodyguard alert against attempted assassination, or listening out for warnings of approaching attack (Plates 14, 105). The Maya court was a place of pomp and splendor, but it was also one of danger and threat. Those fortunate enough to sit on the jaguar cushion kept themselves there by remaining ever vigilant.

Plate 1

Sculpted throne back

Unknown provenience
AD 700–800
Limestone
44 1/8 x 66 1/2 in. (112.0 x 169.0 cm)
Museo Amparo, Puebla, Mexico
52 22 MA FA 57 PJ1372

This magnificent limestone throne back is the finest of its kind, an innovative piece whose precedents are more to be found in wood carving and stucco modeling than they are in stone. Sculpted thrones feature regularly in courtly scenes, but their rarity in the archaeological record suggests that many were perishable works—probably designed for easy transportation and use in open plazas. By contrast, this monumental piece was a permanent fixture of a palace chamber, probably set into a niche like its closest counterpart, a throne discovered at the city of Piedras Negras. Stylistically we can best place the unknown origin of this work somewhere in the Usumacinta River region.

It was once composed of three figural sections; only two now survive. It shows the god Itzamna (*itzamnaaj*), the supreme sky deity, attended by a wife or other goddess. Between them, gently touched by the back of the woman's hand, is the so-called Pax God, here a bizarre winged character with the glyph for "soot/ink" fixed to his nose. Our interpretation of the scene is greatly aided by the accompanying hieroglyphic text. The opening Calendar Round date (A1–B1) lacks an anchor to

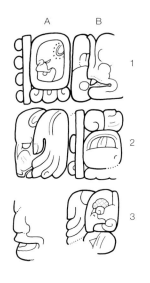

place it in linear time and the following verb (A2) is currently undeciphered. However, the Pax God (A3) is called the *yebet itzamnaaj,* "the messenger of Itzamna" (B3–C1). Maya gods were assisted by various companions and couriers, often birds and winged creatures such as this. All three of our figures are encircled by the masks of animated stone monsters, here bonded into an unbroken chain that defines a "stony" place—probably specifying a cave.

Despite the mythological nature of this piece, we are probably not in the presence of deities so much as their human impersonators, with a masked dwarf playing the diminutive avian. Maya rulers saw their courtly culture as the reflection of divine models, of which the most noble and powerful would be the court of Itzamna. The incomplete text at right (D1–D6) shifts from supernatural affairs to more mundane ones and, when complete, would once have named the earthly king we here see in heavenly guise.

References: Easby and Scott 1970, entry 292; Schmidt et al. 1998, p. 591

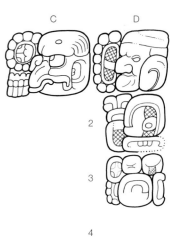

Plate 2
Carved panel with lords and captives

Unknown provenience, Yaxchilan region
AD 783 (9.17.12.13.17 5 Ix *7 Sak)
Limestone, traces of pigments
45⅜ x 35 in. (115.3 x W.88.9 cm)
Kimbell Art Museum, Fort Worth, Texas
AP 1971.07

Framed like a proscenium arch, with swag curtains tied back to reveal the stage, this relief takes us into the court's darker side. In the same way that high nobles present sacks of tribute to their king, so they also bring levies of human beings—prisoners seized in war. Courtyards that more often resounded to family life and entertainments would now host the bloodied victims of battle. Stripped, bound, and humiliated, their ultimate fate—whether servitude, enslavement, torture, or death—is left unstated and suspended in uncertainty.

The orthodox organization of a three-tiered hierarchy—from king, to noble, to captives—is subverted here by the noble placing himself on the prestigious right side of the scene, the preserve of royalty. In this way he makes himself the focus of events, as befitting the location of this carving at his provincial seat. It also serves to illustrate the advances made by the nobility in the 8th century: from one-time anonymity they first share prominence with the king, then ultimately usurp him.

The scene takes place at the court of Yaxchilan king Shield Jaguar III (*itzamnaaj b'ahlam*). His throne carries his hieroglyphic name and titles, here written in reverse to follow the desired reading order from noble to master. The presenting lord is "He of Red Monkey" (*aj chak maax*), who captured the trio of prisoners, each named by caption, on 22 August 783. Three days later he "dressed the captives for his lord"—most probably a reference to the rags pulled through their earlobes in place of fine jewelry. Two of the captives strike pitiful poses, with hands held to their faces in expressions of woe; the third, at right, is more dignified, seemingly resigned to his fate.

The extreme cropping of the leftmost figure is one of the features of late Maya art that most resembles Western representation. Traces of color, on their bodies and elsewhere, reveal the rich, even garish scheme that once enlivened Maya monuments. The sculptor's signature appears in a four-glyph caption close to the throne. It tells us that he was a native of "Sun Water" (*k'ina'*) who also executed other panels that come from this unknown subsidiary of Yaxchilan.

Reference: Schele and Miller 1986, p. 234

Plate 3
Scepter with K'awiil
Unknown provenience
AD 600–900
White stone, probably albite
12⅝ x 4⅞ x ⅞ in. (32.0 x 12.3 x 1.8 cm)
Princeton University Art Museum. Museum purchase,
Fowler McCormick, Class of 1921, Fund
2002–378

The Maya saw K'awiil as a personification of lightning, a divine patron of noble lineages and the essence of fertility, both mental and physical. They conjured him and brought him into existence when they made him emerge in the mist or smoke. They recognized him to be integral to the potency of the Maize God. They also held K'awiil in the hand, as he was commonly rendered on stone monuments.

Almost none of the staffs depicting K'awiil survive; most were probably made of wood, or stucco, making the survival of this white jade K'awiil staff all the more important. What is also remarkable here is that the figure is fully fashioned on every surface, and the rounded shaping of the stone may well indicate the sort of workmanship more characteristic of tropical hardwoods.

K'awiil is one of the most recognizable of Maya gods, with his characteristic serpent foot, snaky face, and a flaming torch in the forehead. He was coincidentally named God K by the early German scholar Paul Schellhas, who assigned letters of the alphabet to Maya deities and their hieroglyphs as he recognized them in the Dresden Codex.

Plate 4

Cylinder vase with lords and mirror

Unknown provenience
AD 600–900
Ceramic
4¹/₂ x 4⁵/₈ in. (11.4 x 11.7 cm)
Dumbarton Oaks Research Library & Collections,
Washington, D.C.
PC.B.569

A Maya lord gazes into a dark mirror in a palace chamber redolent of luxury. Cloth and paper are heaped up behind the throne, and what is probably a bound rubber ball rests within a basket, probably to help retain its shape. A painted pot with the color scheme of codex-style vessels sits directly in front of the ruling lord, who might use his mirror to gaze upon his altered self. Delicate blue and white details were post-fire effects.

Elegant wispy lines attach texts to individuals. This convention indicates first person speech, although the small cursive glyphs here were never meant to be meaningful and simply convey the idea of a spoken dialogue.

Reference: Coe 1975, p. 21

Plate 5

Female figurine

Unknown provenience; probably Campeche, Mexico
AD 600–900
Ceramic
16 3/8 x 9 1/4 x 7 in. (41.6 x 23.5 x 17.8 cm)
Dumbarton Oaks Research Library & Collections,
Washington, D.C.
PC.B.194
Washington, D.C., only

Most Maya figurines are of small scale, rarely
exceeding 10 or 12 in. (25–30 cm), but this seated
woman is almost majestic in her greater size.
The gender of the maker of this and other
figurines from Jaina and the other coastal islands
remains enigmatic, but the large number of female
figures might suggest that women were involved
in their production. Women are more likely to be
the subject of figurines than of stone sculpture
or vase painting.

The sculptor first formed her hollow body
and solid head, probably using a mold for each;
he or she then added solid arms and adornments,
including the flowing cape. Fired within broken
large utilitarian pots, the figures acquired fire
clouds; here the figure's hands, headdress, and
face are dappled with dark smudgy spots. Maya
blue delineates the edge of her dress, both above
her breasts and on the hem at her knees.

Although formed in a mold, the face then
received the maker's attention, and detail is revealed
in visible teeth and raised tattooing. She also has a
nose-piece that extends the nose onto and beyond
the bridge, so as to emphasize this large and
important feature of the face. Blue bands with
flowers anchor the headdress, wrapping long hair
and what would seem to be unspun cotton into
a towering construction—possibly a reference
to Chak Chel and her cult.

Plate 6

Cylinder vase with lords and cloth ("Fenton Vase")

Nebaj, Guatemala
AD 600–800
Ceramic
Diam.: 6³⁄₄ in. (17.2 cm)
Courtesy of the Trustees of The British Museum
1930-F1

Painted vases give insights not only to palatial manners and mythic ideals but also to the more pragmatic economic functions of the court. A recurring theme among palace scenes is the presentation of tribute by a client to his master. Such levies are represented by a formulaic set of items, often shown stacked together: exotic shells and feathers, folded cotton textiles, and bags of cacao beans—the latter often specifying the quantity they contain.

In this fine example excavated from a tomb at Nebaj, Guatemala, in 1904, a basket filled with unidentifiable delicacies—perhaps tamales—sits atop bolts of cloth. A code of gestures, of offering and acceptance, is invariably played out between lord and supplicant. Here the vassal holds one arm in a deferential pose across his body while presenting a valued spondylus shell with the other. Attendants commonly observe such deliveries, but here the courtier sharing the ruler's dais more actively runs his fingers across the open pages of a screenfold book to tally the accounts.

Reference: Schele and Miller 1986, p. 153

Plate 7

Lord of the jaguar pelt vase

Unknown provenience
AD 600–800
Ceramic
8 3/16 x 6 5/16 in. (20.8 x 16.0 cm)
National Gallery of Victoria, Melbourne, Australia
Presented through the NGV Foundation by Mr. John Warner,
Founder Benefactor, 2002
Vernon No. 68966

Enveloped in jewels and quetzal plumes, the Maya ruler sits on a jaguar pelt atop a wide throne, surrounded by the usual coterie of courtiers. Among the standard elements of such scenes— supplicant lords, servants bearing gifts and foodstuffs, fanbearers and flysweeps—there is one very special feature. The ruler's throne is decorated with a red-painted figural scene. At right we see the hand of a two-dimensional dwarf reach out to touch that of his three-dimensional master, in a delightful and unusual interaction between the "real" and "artificial," the interplay of the image-within-an-image.

Plate 8

Seated figurine and throne

Jaina, Mexico

AD 600–900

Ceramic

Figurine: 6⅝ x 4⁹⁄₁₆ in. (16.8 x 11.6 cm); throne: 4³⁄₁₆ x 5 in. (10.6 x 12.6 cm)

Princeton University Art Museum. Gift of Gillett G. Griffin y1986–87a+b

The two parts of this Jaina figure were made as a unit and attest to the artist's skill in working in both two and three dimensions. For the throne, the artist began by rolling out a slab of clay and cutting wedge-shaped legs like those of many full-size Maya thrones (cf. Plates 119 and 120) as supports. The throne back depicts an attendant dwarf, revealed in cut-out and silhouetted low relief, the permanent attendant to the seated lord, even as he screens the dwarf from the observer. The seat is a feline pelt, the flayed cat face revealing a silly smile typical of Maya stone representations but also seen, for example, on the bench from Palenque's Temple 21.

The lord who sits on the jaguar throne has heavy, solid limbs—his oversized hands and feet keep him upright and balanced on the throne; his long, tapering forehead must have once supported a removable headdress, now lost. The lord wears feathered flaps of cloth most commonly worn by warriors—and adapted from a distant Teotihuacan style of armor—but here the ruler takes a relaxed and meditative posture.

Reference: Schele and Miller 1986, p. 78

Plate 9
Standing figurine
Jaina, Mexico
AD 600–900
Ceramic
11½ in. (29.3 cm)
The Metropolitan Museum of Art, The Michael C. Rockefeller
Memorial Collection, Bequest of Nelson A. Rockefeller, 1979
1979.206.953

The full-body feather suit and blue face-paint worn
by this hollow figurine whistle probably indicate
that he is a religious specialist, or priest. His face is
a dramatic one, with features clearly delineated,
especially the raised tattooing on cheek, chin, and
forehead. The large potbelly reveals both age and
high status.

Strikingly, he wears a large pectoral with a
round insert on his chest: this is a rabbit in profile,
presumably a representation of a low-relief, wooden
rabbit with a round mirror forming most of the
body, its large, powerful back feet visible behind
the disk. Such an object would have held powers
of divination, probably channeling the forces of
the moon, understood to take the form of just
such a rabbit in profile. This priest, then, in his
dark blue color, would have controlled nocturnal
forces and been a valued member of the extended
court.

Reference: García Moll 1994, p. 39

Plate 10
Figurine in blue coat
Jaina, Mexico
AD 600–900
Ceramic
10³/₄ x 2⁹/₁₆ in. (27.4 x 11.0 x 6.5 cm)
Museo Nacional de Antropología—INAH, Mexico
10-1215

Travelers—whether hunters, merchants, or messengers—donned broad-brimmed hats for their journeys, as did women who accompanied them. This fellow sports an unusually tall hat, anchored to his head by a headband and smaller disk.

All members of a court might travel, from the king downward, but messengers—perhaps better to be understood in some cases as ambassadors—circulated from one court to another, reporting on tribute, taxes, and perhaps political conditions. Typically such courtiers wear long cloaks—the ones in the Bonampak murals wear mantles that reach the ground—but Aztec sumptuary laws make it clear that specific lengths, especially for merchants, were closely monitored by the ruler's deputies.

Reference: Schmidt et al. 1998, p. 118

Plate 11

Figurine of a seated dwarf

Campeche, Mexico
AD 600–900
Ceramic
8½ x 4½ x 6 in. (21.6 x 11.4 x 15.4 cm)
John G. Bourne Foundation

Maya lords sought the company and advice of
dwarves and hunchbacks, who were thought to
be both entertaining and wise. Certainly their
misshapen bodies kept them from entering any
direct competition with the king, and the court
scenes on Maya vases indicate that they were at
least from time to time the king's closest and most
trusted counselors, a concept probably based in
religious belief, where they are the malformed
companions of the Maize God.

The artist who shaped this large, hollow dwarf
figure understood the conditions of anacephalic
dwarves well, particularly in the representation of
the stumpy but large fingers. The dwarf reaches
one hand to the open mouth, where his teeth are
clearly depicted (they are rarely seen on figurines),
as if speaking or calling; the right hand holds a
small plate of what would seem to be peyote
buttons, a hallucinogen of the Mexican highlands
probably introduced to the Maya by Teotihuacanos.

References: V. Miller 1985; Furst n.d., entry 12

Plate 12
Standing male figure
Jaina, Mexico
AD 600–900
Ceramic
5 3/8 in. (13.7cm)
Los Angeles County Museum of Art, The Phil Berg Collection
M71.73.217

The eloquent face of this standing figure reveals the poignancy of a portrait, as does the attention to an aging male body, indicated by the gentle paunch and the slightness of the arms. He once held a staff and a bag in his hands, probably of perishable materials.

Although limited to a loincloth and hipcloth, the textiles of this figure nevertheless bear a fancy border characteristic of the finest elite cloths. With his small turban, he is probably revealed as a trusted servant, and, like the similarly depicted figure in the Bonampak murals who accompanies the women, possibly a eunuch. In his turned-out stance, he would easily remain at attention in the grave, as well as in life.

Plate 13
Figurine of a singer

Jaina, Mexico
AD 600–900
Ceramic
10½ in. (26.7 cm)
Princeton University Art Museum. Gift of Gillett G. Griffin in
honor of Allen Rosenbaum; with additional support from
Lewis Ranieri in honor of Gillett G. Griffin.
2000–318

Many Jaina figurines represent courtiers. In some
cases, the figurine may represent the interred person
himself or herself, or perhaps in attendance on
greater lords in death. The open mouth, large chest,
and expansive gesture may suggest here the role of
singer, or *k'ayom*, a title that appears for particular
courtiers on Maya vases and in the Bonampak
murals.

The chiseled face with prominent nose,
feathered cape, and slight paunch all attest to the
figure's own high status. The pattern of three dots
on the loincloth textile reflects a tie-dye design
commonly represented in paintings.

Reference: Von Winning 1968, ii

Plate 14
Cylindrical vessel with court scene

Unknown provenience
AD 600–800
Ceramic
9^{7}/$_{16}$ x 6^{11}/$_{16}$ x 6^{11}/$_{16}$ in. (24.0 x 17.0 x 17.0 cm)
National Gallery of Australia, Canberra
82.2292

Court scenes were a favorite topic for Maya vase-painters and inspired some of the more intricate compositions during the 7th and 8th centuries. In this example—one of the most renowned—we see a king of the Motul de San José kingdom reclining against a large cushion, surrounded by his retinue. His rich brown body-paint offsets an ensemble of white jewels, signifying shell or even pearls. He wears a headdress in the form of a wide-eyed rabbit and clutches a flysweep in one hand, while with the other he gesticulates, revealing long, pointed fingernails. A bodyguard peers out from behind the cushion, literally minding his back. Beneath sits a courtier, also equipped with a flysweep, who looks toward a collection of drink containers, including a gourd-shaped pot with its lid set to one side.

The king—named by the caption as Sihyaj K'awiil ("K'awiil is Born")—gazes intently into a mirror held by an impossibly small dwarf. This tiny figure is not a flesh and blood member of the court but rather an effigy, a piece of furniture. Most of the rare wooden figures to survive today once served this purpose (see Plate 16). A real dwarf, sipping from a drinking bowl, a hunchback, and a bouquet-carrying courtier complete a trio of facing characters. Above and behind them, in a dramatic piece of framing, we see a conch-shell trumpet and two wooden horns intrude from the plaza steps outside.

The Motul de San José kingdom, centered around Lake Peten-Itza, specialized in the production of such fine wares, many of which have been excavated well outside its own territory. Indeed, while some may have been made for local consumption, most painted vases seem to have been made as gifts to be bestowed on loyal subjects and visiting dignitaries, often in feasting events.

Plate 15
Mirror
Bonampak, Mexico
AD 600–900
Pyrite, sandstone, and adhesive
Diam.: 13 in. (33.0 cm)
Centro INAH, Tuxtla Gutiérrez, Chiapas, Mexico
10-588889

Nearly a foot in diameter, this remarkable mirror was buried at its owner's feet, perhaps propped up for his eternal gaze. Unlike any other known example, the 59 polygonal tesserae form an idealized turtle carapace, with smaller mosaic pieces worked to form a perfect oval.

When a king looked into this dark, shiny mirror, he would have seen his face clearly, but fractured by the five-, six-, and seven-sided polygons. In this, he would have seen his own rebirth, like that of the Maize God, from the turtle carapace, widely understood to be the surface of the earth. Maya lords—like Palenque's Pakal and apparently this Bonampak lord—sought to die in the guise of the Maize God, to be reborn after death.

Reference: Schmidt et al. 1998, p. 569

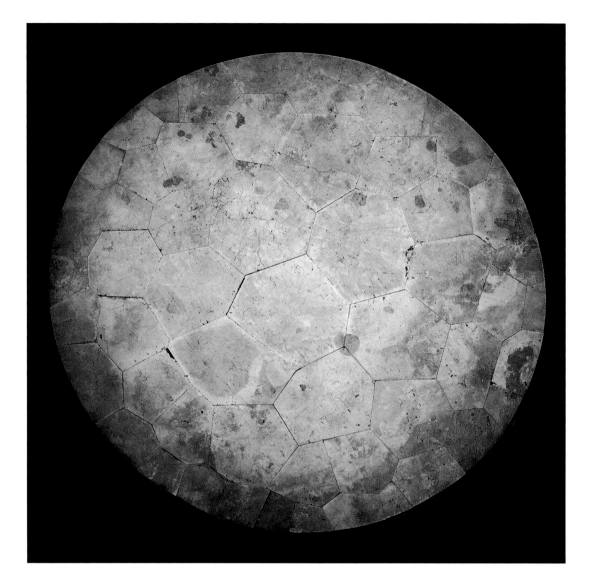

Plate 16

Human effigy mirror-holder

Unknown provenience
AD 600–800
Wood figure and hematite mirror
13 in. (33 cm); mirror diam.: 4¹/₈ in. (10.5 cm)
Princeton University Art Museum. Museum purchase,
Fowler McCormick, Class of 1921, Fund
y1990.71 (figure); y1991–6 (mirror)
Washington, D.C., only

This important figure is among very few wooden
sculptures to have survived the humid conditions
of the Maya forest. It represents a court servant
holding a mirror; here an ancient mosaic (found in a
separate context) made of polished iron ore has been
added to the wooden sculpture. Such objects are
sophisticated plays on the nature of representation,
with the act of mirror-holding frozen in effigy to
produce an uncomplaining perpetual servant. The
carved rim of the mirror carries a now-decayed
hieroglyphic inscription. Enough remains to see that
it follows a formula known from excavated mirrors,
such as the example from Topoxte illustrated below.
It includes the dedication section *yuxulil unehn,*
"the carving of his mirror" (D–F).

Reference: Reents-Budet 1994, p. 92

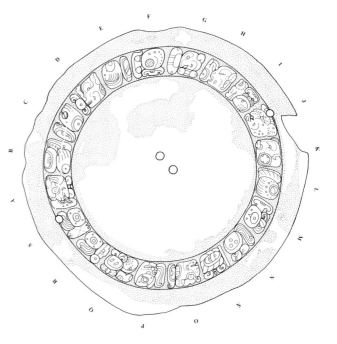

Plate 17

Cylindrical vessel depicting ruler with mirror

Unknown provenience
AD 600
Ceramic
7 x 5 in. (17.8 x 12.7 cm)
Fine Arts Museums of San Francisco. Museum purchase,
Salinger Bequest Fund
78.41

In a palace throne-room, a ruler presides from a
dais while gazing into a mirror that is supported by
a frame of basketry. Subject lords have presumably
presented the cloth heaped up atop baskets in front
of the ruler as tribute payment. Dark curtains
define the architectural space.

The ruler visibly speaks, a trailing speech scroll
emerging from his mouth as if smoke from a
cigarette. Rather remarkably, the mirror also speaks,
as if talking to the ruler or perhaps *for* him. Mirrors
may have functioned as oracles, performing in ways
that protocol or custom did not allow human actors
to communicate. The first of the two seated fellows
in front of the platform also speaks, but the larger
one with fancier jade jewelry and a shell implement
sits behind, and it may be that the first one
translates for his superior.

Here the artist has finished his figures and
painted the text with a strong black line. What
were once green pigments have faded to grey.
Although the head of the principal figure is in
profile and the body is frontal and dramatically
foreshortened, the artist uses the convention of
drawing one shoulder up and one down to
suggest a three-quarters view.

Plate 18

Figurine of a hunchback

Jaina, Mexico
AD 600–900
Ceramic
5¼ in. (13.3 cm)
Fine Arts Museums of San Francisco.
Gift of Mr. and Mrs. Lewis K. Land
76.6.17

On Maya pots and in scenes of impersonation, the Maize God has two steadfast companions, a dwarf and a hunchback, particularly in scenes of dancing. In all likelihood, these companions are his companions in nature, the short, distorted, and misshapen ears that accompany the single ideal ear of maize that grows on the stalk. The hunchback, with his malformed spine, may particularly refer to maize that has been overtaken by corn fungus and takes on its protruding and gnarled features.

The Maya ruler, like the Maize God he emulated, held dwarves and hunchbacks among his esteemed courtiers. The seated Jaina figure of the hunchback wears a turban appropriate to a courtier; his face suggests age and wisdom. The large beads attached to his chest seemingly effeminize him but would have been attached to some sort of cord, perhaps painted onto his body. Two large beads often characterize courtiers.

Plate 19

Figurine of a trumpet player

Jaina, Mexico
AD 600–900
Ceramic
5⅜ x 3 x 5½ in. (13.7 x 7.6 x 14.0 cm)
Sainsbury Centre for Visual Arts. Robert and Lisa Sainsbury
Collection, University of East Anglia
UEA 650

Whether on painted ceramic vessels or in the Bonampak murals, Maya trumpeters bring up the rear of any musical group, the deep sonorous tones juxtaposed with the higher pitch of rattles and flutes. Made of long gourds or wood, trumpets often featured muffles of cloth or feathers to dampen their powerful blasts.

Reference: Miller 1975, p. 3

Plate 20

Stela (Monument 168)

Tonina, Mexico

AD 577 (9.7.4.0.0 4 Ajaw 3 Mak)

Limestone

93 in. (236.0 cm)

Museo de Sitio de Tonina—INAH, Chiapas, Mexico

10-607537

Standing over court and courtier is the Maya king, a supreme ruler and sacred lord. Monument 168 of Tonina reveals a vigorous young king, ready to forge a place for his city in the Maya realm. This sculpture was made after a Maya-wide drought of monument-making, at a time when many new ideas about representation entered sculptural canon.

During the mid-500s, the remote city of Tonina made a decisive break from two-dimensional relief carving and began an entirely new tradition of fully rounded sculpture. As implacable and stony-faced as their forebears, these images nonetheless succeeded in imposing themselves on the viewer in a new way by intruding into the real world and occupying the physical space of the kings they portray. The squat proportions of this monument— one of the earliest of this type—may reflect its sculptor's inexperience, but are as easily explained by the deliberate desire to emphasize the head and its towering, message-laden headdress, stacked with the masks of supernaturals.

The text of 14 glyphs in medallions running down each side of the monument describes the accession of a ruler whose name (B3–B5) is formed from the sequential signs of a jaguar, a bird, and a peccary (the native American boar), on a date best placed in AD 563. The monument itself was dedicated 14 years later in 577.

References: Yadeun 1992, 1993; Mathews 2001; Martin and Grube 2000, pp. 178–179

A   B

1

2

3

4

5

6

7

CHAPTER 2

The Divine Models of Courtly Culture

Fig. 13 Detail of the "Vase of the Seven Gods," Plate 35, rollout photograph. In the Underworld, God L rules his court from a jaguar throne.

Scholars have spilled a great deal of ink in their attempts to discern the "real" from the "supernatural" among the ancient Maya.[1] Scenes that involve dancing animals would seem, on the face of it, to belong to the supernatural realm, while those that depict handsome, simply attired humans would equally seem to belong to a mortal realm. But it is more complex. On the one hand, in the mundane, tangible world the Maya emulated the unearthly palaces in which the gods presided over the sky and netherworlds. On the other hand, some portion of that very unearthly model derived from life on the mortal plain. The royal ideal was a king and court in unison with the cosmos, and to understand courtly culture we must delve into the mythic universe that it sought to replicate on earth—while simultaneously paying attention to what it was on earth that shaped that mythic universe.

Like most pre-modern peoples, the Maya believed the cosmos to have three major planes, the underworld, the sky, and the earth, where mortals reside. The Maya Underworld, dominated largely by aged gods of death and putrefaction, and reached through caves, sinkholes, and sometimes ball courts, bears little resemblance to the fiery Christian hell—nor was it a place of prescribed tortures, like Dante's inferno. The Sun and Itzamna, both aged gods, dominated the Maya sky. The sky at night offered a window on all supernatural doings; like the Greeks and Romans, the Maya configured constellations of gods and places and saw the unfolding of narratives in their seasonal movements, and reckoned there the intersection of all possible worlds. Some gods, especially the strange and multi-faceted K'awiil, could operate on any plane.[2]

Like other Mesoamerican peoples, the Maya assigned colors to each of the cardinal directions—the east is red, for example, and the south green or yellow. They also recognized a fifth direction of center, which, like its other generic counterparts, existed everywhere: just as there is always "east," so too there is always "center." The Maya conceptualized center as a giant ceiba tree that made one level permeable to another. The four- or five-fold quality then applied to many aspects of culture, including the gods, many of whom had individual aspects associated with colors and directions.

Scholars use the terms god and deity to describe the subjects of Maya worship, impersonation, and emulation, but these beings were not discrete, separate entities in the way we think of Greek or Roman gods (Fig. 14a–f). Certain supernatural characters had affinities that caused them to merge with one another in ways that seem fluid and unbounded. Among a bewildering array of different characters some recur with regularity: the sky deity Itzamna (*itzamnaaj*), usually described to be a "paramount" god; Chaak, ostensibly a storm god but of multiple color and form, often with a role in sacrifice (Plate 30); K'inich Ahaw, the sun, and his more dangerous nocturnal aspect, the Jaguar God of the Underworld. The snake-footed K'awiil, especially associated with lightning, commonly forms

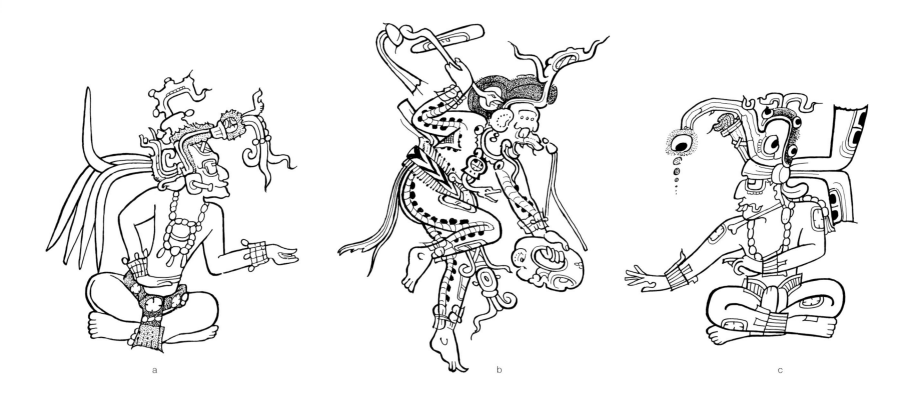

a   b   c

a hand-held scepter of rulership (Plates 3, 31); God L serves as patron of trade, tribute, and commerce, but he is also one of the princes who rules in the darkness of the Underworld (Fig. 13). Good and evil traits are not permanent and immutable characteristics of Maya gods, nor is only good admirable. As we shall see, Maya religious narrative depended on cycles, and what was inappropriate in one season might come to pass in another.

As Karl Taube has demonstrated in recent years, the life-cycle of maize lies at the heart of Maya belief, and is encapsulated in the story of the Maize God (Plate 21). No single figure better exemplifies the intersection of the tangible world and its supernatural counterpart. The Maize God's story is the metaphor of life itself: the cycling of the wet and dry seasons (the seasonality of temperate climes has little meaning in the tropics) and the annual planting, sprouting, ripening, and harvesting of the corn on which all civilization in Mesoamerica depended. Maize required constant human agency: the valuable proteins in maize are released only through the nixtamalization process, in which dried maize kernels are soaked in a quicklime solution, and unlike most plants, it will not self-sow. Yet this was the staff of life, so the Maize God's adventures in the Underworld, particularly his death and resurrection, came to pervade Maya kingship and human endeavor. The tale's dramatis personae, both heroes and villains, appear again and again as subjects for impersonation and re-enactment. Believed to originate in a distant, sacred mountain, maize was understood to emerge time and again from craggy stones. A Maya lord atop a mountain or stone was recognized to fulfill the story of the Maize God (Plate 34).

The Maya bodily ideal is best understood as the perfect form of the young Maize God (Plates 21, 22). The muscular lines of the torso and limbs can be equated with the stout stalk and its verdant leaves. A handsome, high-browed head formed an analog to its crowning cob; thick, lustrous hair akin to its flowing corn silk. The Maya surely knew that individual kernels required individual strands of silk: thick silk—or thick human hair—guaranteed fertility and abundance. In the field, maize is never still. Even without a breeze, it shimmers and waves, making the Maize God a dancer, his body in constant movement (Plate 29). Before it can be eaten or planted, the ear is stripped of its husks. At harvest, the ear of maize is turned downward to complete its drying or snapped off and

Fig. 14 Drawings of Maya gods, as they appear on painted ceramics. Maya names are known for only some of these divinities; some are still known by the alphabetic assignment given early in the 20th century: a. Itzamna; b. Chaak; c. K'inich Ahaw, "Sun Lord"; d. Jaguar God of the Underworld; e. K'awiil; f. God L.

d

e

f

likened to a decapitated head (Plate 28). From the kernels the cycle starts anew. In all this, the story of the Maize God is also the model of courtly life.

Lords and ladies often portrayed themselves as incarnations of the Maize God, whose transformation relied on two precious materials: jade and feathers. As prized in Mesoamerican cultures as gold is in our own, jade represented all that was evergreen and youthful. Impervious to time, it was the distilled essence of fertility and bounty made permanent. The sheer effort required to turn it into works of art—to drill and fashion the super-hard mineral and its greenstone cousins into jewelry, masks, and figurines—gave it incomparable value (Plates 23–27, 38). It was at all times partnered in royal costume by the cascading iridescent-green plumes of the male quetzal bird, whose precious feathers spring and bounce along their flexible "spine," unlike the stiff feathers of most birds. Since the elusive quetzal cannot be raised in captivity and dwells only in the 300–400-ft (*c.* 1000-m) "cloud forest," trained hunters captured, plucked, and released males taking a turn on the nest. Clothed in quetzal feathers and jade, rulers became one with the life-giving corn. For rebirth, like a noble appearing in public, the Maize God needed his jade and feather finery prepared for him (Fig. 15).

As recorded in the Popol Vuh—the great K'iche Maya epic transcribed into the Roman alphabet in highland Guatemala in the mid-16th century—the Maya creator gods made several false starts in setting humanity on the earth. They first gave life to animals: but in their howling and squawking

Fig. 15 Codex-style cup, rollout photograph. On this low cup, we see the Maize God (second from left) receiving the attire and adornments necessary for his rebirth, brought to him by a series of Underworld ladies and his sons the Hero Twins.

they failed to worship their makers, and so they were forever banished to the forest. In their second attempt the gods formed humans from mud, but these succeeded no better; they just crumbled and dissolved away. The next creation saw people carved from wood: but this race quickly forgot their makers, so the angry gods turned all their possessions—even their cooking utensils—against them and brought a black resinous rain down on their heads. In the final, successful attempt, the gods used *masa* or corn dough to create a people of maize. As such, humans not only depended upon maize as the cornerstone of their diet, but they were also *made* of the same stuff.[3]

The Popol Vuh refers to the Maize God story only very sparingly—evidently it was so central to Maya religion that it barely needed repeating. Despite its importance, the Popol Vuh is little more an abridged fragment of a great mythic corpus and, moreover, one separated from the heyday of civilization in the Maya lowlands by some 800 years. It is as if we have a few pages torn from an immense book. Imagine if we had a medieval apocryphal tale related to the story of Jesus of Nazareth, but no complete New Testament as our basis of understanding. To understand the religious narrative of the 1st millennium AD we must combine a range of different sources: the Popol Vuh itself, the significant number of narrative scenes from the 7th and 8th centuries, a bare handful of hieroglyphic texts from roughly those same years, and judicious use of wider Mesoamerican traditions, of which the best known come from Central Mexico. A synopsis of the Hero Twin section of the Popol Vuh can help understand the life of the Maize God, and the roles of other gods.

The Hero Twins and the Maize God in the Popol Vuh

Following the sequential creations and destructions already enumerated, the Popol Vuh, as written down, leaps into the thrilling tale of the Hero Twins, Hunahpu and Xbalanque, twin brothers—blowgun hunters and ballgame players—who defeat the monsters of the earth, particularly the "false sun," or Seven Macaw, and his own two menacing sons (both good and evil in the Popol Vuh emerge in pairs of brothers, usually twins). The story then steps back in time, with the following lines that suggest a transcription from a performance, as well as a story that can be told in different ways.

> And now we shall name the name of the father of Hunahpu and Xbalanque. Let's drink to him, and let's just drink to the telling and accounting of the begetting of Hunahpu and Xbalanque. We shall tell just half of it, just a part of the account of their father...[4]

We learn quickly that Hunahpu and Xbalanque are the children of One Hunahpu, and nephews to his brother Seven Hunahpu, and the story takes us back to the time before the Hero Twins were born. One Hunahpu had married, fathering twins, One Monkey and One Artisan, who became "flautists, singers, and writers; carvers, jewelers, metalworkers as well."[5] The two brothers, One and Seven Hunahpu, played dice and ballgames all day long, usually with the younger boys, eventually disrupting the Underworld gods below.

Called by messenger owls, One and Seven Hunahpu journey to the Underworld, or Xibalba, as it was known, literally "place of fright." They travel down through caves, passing rivers of blood and pus, only to be tricked in many ways by One and Seven Death, chiefs of the Underworld gods, as well as the lesser lights in their retinue, gods with names that suggest corruption and rot ("Pus Master," "Bloody Teeth") rather than the hellfire of the European tradition. As the Popol Vuh author writes, "Xibalba is packed with tests, heaps and piles of tests," all of which the hapless brothers fail.[6] Having silenced the noise that irritated them, the gods do not hesitate to sacrifice the brothers. They bury them "at the Place of Ball Game Sacrifice," but take One Hunahpu's head and stick it in a calabash tree and then forbid all Underworld denizens from visiting it.

A defiant Underworld maiden, Blood Woman, goes to the tree, where the head speaks to her. Marveling, she extends a hand and receives spittle. "Right away, something was generated in her belly, from the saliva alone."[7] Her pregnancy eventually revealed, she survives a perilous flight to the surface of the earth and seeks refuge with her mother-in-law, who, like the lords of the Underworld, administers her own tests—but in this case, the young woman passes.

Still, the half-brothers and grandmother barely accept the twins, Hunahpu and Xbalanque, born to Blood Woman on earth. The older brothers make demands that prompt the younger twins to draw on their greater powers, which, as half mortal and half divine, they discover within themselves as they grow up; eventually they trick the older brothers and turn them into monkeys. These become the supernatural artisans about which we will have more to say in Chapter 4. Presumably the opening scene of this section, the overcoming of the false sun, would take place at about this point, if recorded in a linear sequence.

Like their father and uncle, the Hero Twins excel at the ballgame, creating a ruckus that eventually disturbs Xibalba, and the easily irritated Underworld lords send the messenger owls to fetch them too. In what makes for particularly good storytelling, the trip to Xibalba is both repeated and inverted, for the Hero Twins excel at "heaps and piles of tests." They outwit the dangerous gods at every turn, by stealth, deception, and wit, and never by brawn, numbers, or weaponry. They trick the gods into revealing their names; when placed overnight in one of the six named Underworld "houses," they overcome the tools of sacrifice. They enlist both the animate and inanimate world on their side—from mosquitoes and fireflies and coatimundis (tropical mammals related to raccoons) to flint knives—as if channeling the wrath of the creator gods in earlier creations for their own purposes.

The Twins play ball on a daily basis, playing either to a tie or sometimes losing, but always managing to pay off the wager—until they spend the night in the Bat House. Sleeping inside their blowguns for safety from the vampire bats, the Twins try to decide if dawn has arrived; Hunahpu sticks out his head, only to have it quickly decapitated by a swooping "snatch bat." The Xibalba lords joyfully put the rolling head in play as the ball. Meanwhile Xbalanque desperately negotiates with a possum to keep dawn at bay while he looks for a replacement head for his brother, calling on the animals to present their foodstuffs as candidates. Once Xbalanque selects a round squash for his brother's head, one of the creator gods descends into Xibalba briefly to give it life.

What a ballgame ensues! With Hunahpu's real head rolling around the court, the lords of Xibalba are too overcome with joy to concentrate. Xbalanque kicks the head out of bounds, where a rabbit rolls off and leads the distracted lords on a merry chase; Xbalanque quickly places his brother's head back on his shoulders and introduces the squash as the ball. With one great kick he smashes it, scattering its seeds everywhere and creating mayhem. Surely the audience or reader is supposed to laugh!

Realizing that the Xibalbans can be defeated only by great trickery, the Hero Twins willingly step into a great oven and are killed. Two agents on their side quietly retrieve their bones, and, as if the bones were kernels of maize, they grind them on a metate with a rounded grindstone, making corn *masa*, and throw the stuff into the river. After five days the Hero Twins reappear, reconstituted as it were, first as bottom-feeding catfish, and then as raggedy performers. News of their entertaining performances draws the attention of One Death and Seven Death, who seem to have forgotten about the Hero Twins. The old Underworld gods marvel at a series of sacrifices the Twins perform. First, they sacrifice a dog and then return it to life ("Back and forth he wagged his tail when he came back to life"), then a person, and then Xbalanque sacrifices Hunahpu, who returns again to life. The gods long for this rebirth: "Do it to us! Sacrifice us!" they call out, and the Twins obligingly cut them to bits.[8] Unsurprisingly, there is no resurrection for them and the power of these dark forces is broken for good. In so doing, the Hero Twins offer a route to salvation for all who follow them and assert the cosmic supremacy of the heavens: of the sky, sun, and light. The denouement of the story comes when the Hero Twins resurrect their father and uncle from the ball court where their bodies had been buried—thereby returning maize to the world in an overt metaphor for the first sprouting of the season.

The Maya Maize God and his Milieu

The Popol Vuh has ancient origins in Maya culture—indeed, parts of the epic have been identified in carvings that go back as far as 300 BC or even earlier.[9] Certainly art from the heyday of court society in the 7th and 8th centuries contains many references to these primeval stories. Working with both art and writing it is possible to piece together the myths that had such a formative effect on royal culture.

The father of the Hero Twins, One Hunahpu, is without question the Maize God.[10] As David Stuart has recently proposed, in the lowland regions he was called, at least in part, Huun Ixim or "One Maize."[11] The Hero Twins are readily identifiable, too: Hunahpu can usually be recognized by the spot on his cheek; Xbalanque by a patch of jaguar pelt around his mouth.[12] Their names in the 7th and 8th centuries were close to those in K'iche Maya: Hunahpu translates to the day name Huun Ahaw, while Xbalanque may have been called Yax Balun.[13] The stories from the painted ceramic vessels remind us that the Maize God is father not only to the Hero Twins but also to the Monkey

Fig. 16   Large plate in codex-style. This vessel depicts the Maize God rising from a turtle carapace that symbolizes the earth, with assistance from his sons the Hero Twins: Xbalanque, right, and Hunahpu, left.

Scribes, his progeny by a woman on earth; like his talented offspring, the Maize God is also a scribe, painter, and dancer; the Hero Twins, like their monkey half-brothers, are also dancers.

No single moment may have been more important to the Maya than the rebirth of the Maize God, and no vessel captures the moment of the Maize God's rebirth better than a finely painted large tripod plate (Fig. 16). The Maya often conceptualized the earth as a turtle, the dry cracks in the earth that open during the parched season akin to the crackled lines that define the back of the carapace. On this plate, the Maize God, already dressed in his jade finery, rises from a split in the turtle's back, emerging from a buried skull seed, as can also be seen on other codex-style vessels. The jaguar-patched Xbalanque waters him from a jug containing rainstorm water, while the spotted Hunahpu gently offers a helping hand. On other vessels, Underworld ladies, perhaps including the twins' mother, Blood Woman, dress the god in his jewels and feathers (Fig. 15). Many plates with maize imagery were drilled and then placed upside-down over the face of an interred lord, a channel for rebirth together with a route for the departing soul.[14] In this way, a single ceramic work could convey much of the metaphor embodied in a far more complex work, Stela 11 of Copan, or the entire Palenque Temple of Inscriptions burial chamber (Figs. 17, 18; Plates 65–67; see pp. 206–207).

Copan Stela 11 once belonged to Temple 18, where archaeologists came upon an interior stair-case to a burial chamber, conceptually much like the Palenque tomb, but on a smaller scale. Suitably enough, Stela 11 depicts the city's great king Yax Pasah in the moment of rebirth. Like Palenque's Pakal, he emerges from the "Black Hole," or Xibalba, both as Maize God, whose leafy foliage curls around the back of his head, and as K'awiil, indicated by the smoking tube in the forehead. On Pakal's sarcophagus, not only does the surface depict the king rising from the depths of darkness, but also the sides show the rebirth of his ancestors, each reborn as a fruit-bearing tree. The practice widely documented in Yucatan among humble folk at the time of the Spanish invasion of placing a greenstone bead in the mouth of the deceased symbolically planted the germ of the Maize God, in preparation for rebirth.

Dead kings went to their tombs not with a simple jade bead but with a whole jade costume of the Maize God, with the wealthiest furnished with spectacular jade masks (Plate 24). Some of the

Fig. 17   Detail of Stela 11, Copan, drawing. A Copan king rises from the "jaws of the Underworld."

Fig. 18   Detail of lid of sarcophagus, Temple of Inscriptions, Palenque, drawing. Pakal the Great is depicted at the moment of release from the "jaws of the Underworld."

Fig. 19   Naranjo-style cylinder vessel, section of rollout drawing. The Maize God dances with his dwarf companion.

richest burials unsurprisingly belonged to the most successful Maya kingdoms. Today the buildings at Calakmul, one of the largest of Maya cities of the 1st millennium, reveal little clue to the treasures within—unlike those of Palenque or Copan, little architectural iconography remains in place. But archaeologists there have uncovered elaborate sets of greenstone jewels—all the finery associated with the Maize God's return from the dead (Plates 24–27).

In the prime of life—what we might roughly conceptualize as the time from the milky kernels of green corn, the subject of great festivity among Native Americans in the U.S. Southwest—the Maize God dances. He dances by himself on large plates that may have been used to present tamales or green corn (Plate 29), and such vessels are themselves often depicted in palace scenes. Particularly on vessels from the Naranjo region of Guatemala, the Maize God dances with dwarves and hunch-backs (Fig. 19). These dwarves and hunchbacks, too, probably develop from the natural history of maize. On most maize stalks, a single ear matures; other nubbins may be collected, or they may shrivel, with only a few strands of silk; corn fungus, or *cuitlacoche* as it is known today in Mexico, may take over an ear, deforming it with the bulbous growths.[15] Aztec prayers at the birth of a child invoke the purity of jade beads, suggestive of maize kernels, and decry the "smutty little ear."[16] The Maize God's physical perfection gains by simple comparison.

Lords of the Underworld

If the Maize God embodied everything that was perfect and admirable, the Underworld enemies of the Maize God and the Hero Twins amply manifested the contrasting models of arrogance and greed. Foremost among these was the wealthy god of trade, tribute, and tobacco, whom we know today as God L —the precursor to either the One or Seven Death of the Popol Vuh.[17] As seen on the magnificent "Princeton Vase," he dwells in a luxurious palace, seated on a jaguar pelt throne under swag curtains (Fig. 13; Plates 32, 35). His affluence and lavish palace furnishings were the objects of desire

Fig. 20   Panel flanking internal shrine, Temple of the Cross, Palenque, drawing. God L appears here in a rich jaguar pelt and with a fat cigar in hand.

Fig. 21   Polychrome vessel, rollout drawing. The Hero Twins, seen together at far right, fling God L's finery into the air; another aged god slumps, his open chest bleeding, onto a bone throne. The Moon Goddess and the rabbit watch from above.

for worldly kings, who needed to extend lavish hospitality while keeping the palace economy afloat. Despite disdain for God L's luxury, Maya kings aspired to live as he did, rather than the Maize God.

Like most Underworld gods, God L is depicted to be old and toothless, and with various jaguar attributes. In contrast, representations of humans emphasize firm, youthful skin even in depictions of those who must have been wrinkled and craggy in appearance. God L often smokes a signature cigar (Figs. 13, 20); since tobacco was a common commodity in the Mesoamerican economy, he was his own walking advertisement of the product. For clothes he wears the richest of brocaded capes and an extravagant, feather-trimmed hat in which sits an owl, his messenger and avatar called "13 Sky Owl" (*uxlahuun chan kuy*)—almost certainly one of the "messenger owls" who call on the Hero Twins. Five beautiful young women attend him on the "Princeton Vase," pouring chocolate from one vessel to another to achieve the light, frothy, version of the beverage preferred by Maya lords (Plate 32). God L ties the wristlet of his nearest companion in a lascivious manner, and surely wealth functioned as an aphrodisiac in the past as effectively as it does today. On the "Vase of the Seven Gods" God L lords it over fellow denizens of this realm—half-feline, half-skeletal, often jawless, fiends—who pay him homage and tribute at the dawn of the current universe in 3114 BC (Plate 35). Some clues may link him to world destruction and to the black resinous rain that destroyed the previous race of humans. God L is old, wealthy, and ruthless.

Outside his court God L is equipped with a merchant's pack on his back and a walking staff. As the patron of traders, he peddles the wares that make the Maya elite wealthy and brings them the prestige goods that marked their status. Though God L is the subject of many painted vessels, his monumental representations are largely restricted to the Maya west—a pattern that probably reflects the importance of commerce in a region where the overland trade routes to Central Mexico converge. He was of particular interest at Palenque, where in the company of a fellow Xibalba god he holds up a great war shield on the Tablet of the Sun (Fig. 68a). He is, perhaps, a slave to warfare. Later Aztec traders functioned as the first wave in any military campaign, demanding preferential treatment and provoking conflict, then quietly melting away during battle, returning only to seal unequal deals of trade and punitive taxes.

God L may seem stately and staid enough, but his palace and his world are periodically wracked by turmoil. As in the Popol Vuh, the lords of the Underworld ultimately lose their riches and come to a calamitous fall. The beginning of this undoing is even shown on the "Princeton Vase" (Plate 32).

Fig. 22 Codex-style vessel, section of rollout drawing. The Maize God and his dwarf companion strip God L of hat, clothes, and staff.

Out of sight of the blissfully unaware God L, who is distracted by the beautiful women who attend him, the two disguised Hero Twins are beheading one of his fellow Underworld gods. At God L's feet, a rabbit energetically writes in an open screenfold book, as if recording the ongoing narrative.

The story is advanced on another vase scene (Fig. 21). Here the Hero Twins have shed their masks and have sacrificed the Xibalba lord seated on a bone throne—this time by cutting open his chest, probably to remove the heart. At left a near-naked God L (with one of his names spelled above his head) has been stripped of his fine clothes—his cape, his hat, his staff, and his necklace—which are now contemptuously flung in the air. We know from several pictorial sources that the stripping of God L marks the beginning of his humiliation and defeat, just as it did for vanquished warriors. We know too that the Moon Goddess is a major player in the drama, though mostly by means of her rabbit companion—that same rabbit who serves as scribe on the "Princeton Vase," and is well known as a trickster and companion of the Moon throughout Mesoamerica. In this scene God L appropriately looks up to the Moon, where the Goddess and rabbit conspire with one another. In an

Fig. 23 Naranjo-style polychrome vessel, rollout photograph. God L stands before a triumphant rabbit (left) who holds his clothes and jewels; at right, God L appeals to the Sun God, while the rabbit takes cover behind him.

Fig. 24   Cacaxtla, Tlaxcala, wall paintings in Red Temple. God L plays a prominent role in these Central Mexican wall paintings, where he presides over both cacao and maize. He has balanced his heavy trader's pack against his staff, and he has tied his characteristic hat onto the pack.

otherwise lost episode pictured on a cylinder vase we see the rejuvenated Maize God exacting further revenge on the Underworld lords. Assisted by a dwarf and a hunchback, the Maize God's steadfast companions in many dancing scenes, here he strips and kicks a helpless old God L together with two of his netherworld cronies (Fig. 22).[18]

Surely there were many episodes for these characters, and the send-up of the wealthy has always made for good copy—so we should expect that many pieces of the story remain unknown. Additionally, we note that the Popol Vuh is not told "in order," but rather jumps back and forth in time—undoubtedly the Maya told the accounts as they wanted or needed to, but not necessarily in a linear fashion. For now, the next time we see the defeated God L he is submitting to the authority of the Sun God—the night becoming servant to the day, darkness vassal to the light—to whom he must now pay tribute. The relationship is replicated in Maya political relationships where vassals symbolically deliver their goods in the guise of the feather-headdressed Underworld lord to kings who embody the Sun (Plate 36). But God L's prize possessions, as well as the debt he owes the Sun, end up in the hands of the trickster rabbit on one vessel. God L stands hunched and naked in front of the triumphant rabbit, who holds God L's staff, cape, and headdress as if to taunt him (Fig. 23). In a second scene on the same vessel, God L pleads his case to the Sun God, declaring, in what is a rare example of first-person speech: "Lord, the rabbit took my staff(?), my clothes, my tribute!" The Sun God responds with apparent platitudes, not revealing that he is in cahoots with the rabbit, who mischievously hides behind him. In other scenes, the rabbit has taken the stolen items to his mistress the Moon.[19] God L kneels before them and evidently begs for their return.

God L's fortunes rise and fall, a mirror of the fortunes of the Maize God. Just as the Maize God annually dies at the end of the rainy season, goes dormant, and then re-emerges, so, too, does God L have his season. But his is the dry season, the season of long-distance trade, the same season when Mesoamerican warriors went to war. God L's success as a far-flung trader is most clear at distant Cacaxtla, where strikingly—some 500 miles northwest of Palenque in Central Mexico— God L twice appears in its murals, framing a flight of stairs that depict skeletal captives on treads and town names on risers: submission to God L and his ilk comes with a high price! He rests his trader's pack with its sundry riches, his broad hat propped on its top. There he surveys both a cacao tree and a maize plant—the twin crops of chocolate and corn that underpinned the Maya economy (Fig. 24).

Cacao and Maize

No human dies if unable to obtain chocolate, but cacao held such a special role in ancient Mesoamerica that some members of the nobility might have thought they would! Cacao trees flourish under high rainforest canopy, with plenty of moisture and humidity—where modern-day coffee has often replaced them today. Tiny flowers sprout directly from the trunk or branch; finicky midges pollinate only a small proportion, which ripen into large fruits (Fig. 25). Although the pulp and fresh seeds can be eaten, most "beans" were dried and roasted, to be ground with chili and then blended with water and honey. Maya lords craved the zesty beverage, the caffeine-like substance theobromine providing a rare stimulant in Mesoamerica. Members of the court grew plump drinking the calorie-laden drink. But cacao was more than simply ingested: it functioned as a currency throughout ancient Mesoamerica. A single cacao bean could buy a tomato or a tamale; 100—a standard worker's wage—bought a rabbit or a turkey hen.[20] In Room 1 of the Bonampak paintings the enthroned nobility receive a sack of cacao beans painted with "40,000" to mark the quantity they held. The Spanish complained about forgeries in the marketplace; realistic brown clay effigy beans—possibly intended to deceive—have turned up on the coast of Guatemala; and most recently, archaeologists at Ek Balam, Yucatan, excavated an offering of cacao effigies made of shell, surely intended to provide indestructible cash for eternity (Plate 37).[21]

Unlike maize, which grows almost anywhere—from highland to lowland, from dry to wet— cacao is a delicate crop that flourishes only in the most humid conditions. It prospers best outside the lowland Maya heartland, with many major sources located in Tabasco or points further west in Mexico. Palenque may have been one of the rare Maya sites where the plant flourished wild.

Fig. 25 Chocolate, or cacao (*kakaw*), was a precious foodstuff in ancient Mesoamerica. Europeans incorporated it into elite diet, but the plant will grow only in tropical environments. This botanical drawing, made by Maria Sibylla Merian, a 17th-century natural historian, reveals the tiny white flowers and the large, fruited pods. Reproduced courtesy of Maricel Presilla.

Fig. 26 Polychrome vessel, rollout drawing. In God L's court, K'awiil points to a cacao tree that grows from a prone human body. The kneeling woman in front may be grinding cacao for the court.

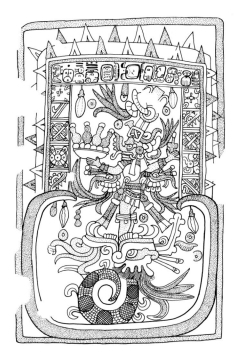

Fig. 27 Capstone, Temple of the Owls, Chichen Itza, drawing. Cacao pods surround K'awiil as he emerges from a sinkhole on this now-lost painting.

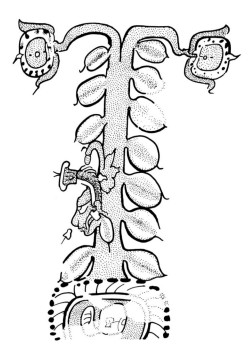

Fig. 28 Polychrome vessel, detail, drawing. Here we see the head of the Maize God sprouting from the trunk of a cacao tree surrounded by ripe pods.

Remarkably, the Maya of parched Yucatan discovered that they could raise cacao in the microclimates of sinkholes—called *cenotes* in Mexico today—along with other valuable fruit trees.[22] The Maya held that animals pursued four roads to cacao and maize, along with other valuable fruit trees—including avocado, nance, zapote—at a mythic place called Sustenance Mountain. The long meandering caves that lead to *cenotes* in Yucatan may have been understood to be the entries to this dangerous place of plenty—as well as entries to the Underworld, or Xibalba. For the Maya living in Yucatan, the ability to grow even a few cacao trees at a *cenote* would have offered both economic power and demonstrated the potency of their sacred channel to another world.[23] The spider monkey was the enemy of both God L and humanity in this endeavor: monkeys covet the just-ripe pods, a subject made fun of on a vessel where the monkey guards his haul (Plate 40).

Yet as different as they are, cacao and maize also share some key characteristics. In both cases, the fruits—the ear of maize, the pod of cacao—grow directly from the main "trunk" of the plant. And both grow individual kernels or beans in rows. Although the pod is thick, sections can be peeled away to reveal the fruit: regular rows of pulpy seeds that look very much like the regular rows of corn.

As the merchant god, God L controlled the traffic in cacao—and he may have had a hand in whatever trade there was in maize. The delivery of both commodities is bound up in the appearance of another character, the mysterious, serpent-footed K'awiil. He is shown in the court of God L, negotiating or receiving instructions, while gesturing toward an anthropomorphic cacao tree in the plaza beyond (Fig. 26). On capstones from Yucatan and Campeche, K'awiil carries sacks of beans, specified in the accompanying texts as containing cacao (Plate 31).[24] On a now-lost lintel from Chichen Itza, K'awiil rises up from a *cenote* bearing the pods (Fig. 24).

Given the sheer commercial importance of chocolate, we might expect to find a god of cacao, something beyond the uncommon anthropomorphic cacao tree. As Michael Coe noted a few years ago, a particularly clear depiction of what would appear to be a god of cacao appears on a stone vessel now part of the Dumbarton Oaks collection (Plate 33), where a lordly figure is covered in sprouting cacao pods. But herein lie more questions than answers. Every one of his other attributes belongs to the Maize God and the explanatory caption calls him the *ixim te'* or "Maize Tree." Other iconographic ties suggest that the Maize God is intimately linked to the cacao tree and this may simply be another stage in his transformation, even a substitute for the calabash tree on which his severed head appears in the Popol Vuh (Fig. 28). Another possibility is that the Maize God, like One Hunahpu and many Maya gods, has a brother. Lords bearing Maize God attributes often appear in pairs, and it is possible that the depiction of Seven Hunahpu—just possibly a patron not of maize but cacao—is so similar as to have escaped detection.[25]

Defeating the Underworld

Generation after generation, the Maya lords recognized that defeat had come to the Underworld by means of the new shoots of maize that appeared with the first rains that initiated the growing season. The hot dry season, then, was the time of the ballgame, the season for combat between young gods and old ones. Although the Maya ballgame originated as a sport—and no doubt the game continued to be played as entertainment and recreation—it was its mythic context, as the site of the netherworld struggle between life and death, that gave it a central place in the rhetoric of Maya kingship. The battle between two teams symbolized conflict in all its guises: the game re-enacted the paradigms for war and sacrifice, where the skillful and blessed triumph and the weak and undeserving are vanquished. The physical presence of earthly ball courts—which take key locations in almost all Maya cities, not least at Palenque, Copan, and Tonina—are testament to their cultural significance. The Underworld and warfare allusions are perhaps clearest at Tonina, where the court is sunk deep into the plaza in an overt reference to descent into the watery abyss; its steep walls are decorated with the projecting torsos of bound captives (Figs. 29, 30). Markers down the alley or sides both pinpoint locations for scoring and denote openings to the Underworld.

The common depiction of paired players may suggest that, like the Hero Twins, ballplayers normally played in teams of two (Plate 45). A pair of Jaina figurines of players calls to the mind the unseen ball (Plates 41, 42). In every respect, the ballplayer personifies the qualities of Maya manhood and a frequent title of kings was simply "ballplayer" (*aj pitzal*). The players wear sturdy padding on at least one arm and leg, as well as the midsection (Plate 44); they struck the heavy rubber ball with upper arms and thighs and, as in modern soccer, did not use their hands. Both accounts from the 16th century and modern survivals of the game in rural Mexico suggest that points were scored in different ways at different times and in different courts.

Fig. 29   Large sunken ball court, Tonina. Laid out in the shape of an H with wide "end zones," this playing arena was commissioned in AD 699.

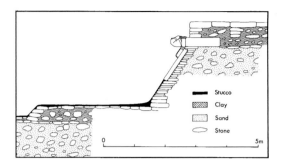

Fig. 30 Large sunken ball court, Tonina, section. The Tonina ball court (Fig. 29) featured six sculptured prisoners, their tenoned bodies projecting out from the walls of the court. Carved feathered shields beneath each one carry inscriptions describing their titles and origins.

Sometimes ball courts illustrate key moments from the drama, as when an alleyway marker shows the incident when the death gods have introduced Hunahpu's head for the ball (Plate 43). But this work raises a troublesome question: why would the king impersonate a death god playing against a Hero Twin? The Maya had a rather more complex relationship with their religious ideology than simple distinctions between good and evil: just as a king might choose to take on God L's attributes to illustrate a particular kind of event or relationship, so too might he seek to harness infernal forces if it increased his grip on earthly power. In short, the king could play as the Maize God or he could embody his nemesis, winning on either side.

The Royal Ideal

In some respects we know more about the supernatural model of the royal ideal than its execution on earth. After all, the highly narrative scenes involving gods and heroes—say, in a work like the "Princeton Vase"—offer a more subtly informative picture of the intrigue at court than most specifically historical scenes, although the Bonampak murals would stand out as a great exception. But the one informs the other: in the opposition between the Maize God and God L we also see the conflict between agricultural wealth and commercial wealth, the familiar contrast of old and new money. We see the pleasure that wealth buys, as well as the peril.

The Maya elite would have understood the tenuousness of their privileged lives and the capricious play of fate—how easily they might end their days trussed and humiliated at the feet of an opposing king. The tales of the stripped and stricken God L might raise a wry smile, but with some acknowledgment that here was a parable of the great lord brought low despite all his one-time grandeur and riches. In all this, the ballgame served as a metaphor of the shifting cycles in movement: the ball was Hunahpu's head, but it was also the sun, and probably also the moon, if not occasionally a carved squash about to shatter on the ground.

Plate 21
Maize God
Temple 22, Copan, Honduras
AD 680–750
Volcanic tuff
35³/₈ x 21³/₈ in. (89.7 x 54.2 cm)
Courtesy of the Trustees of The British Museum
1886-321

Maize Gods adorned the cornice of Copan's Structure 22 until the building collapsed in an ancient earthquake. Excavating the rubble in the 19th century, Alfred Percival Maudslay recognized this nearly lifesize bust as the Maize God and sent him to the British Museum, where later curators mistakenly labeled the work "Singing Girl" for many years.

Hands in motion, his face young, firm, and idealized, with maize foliage falling forward over his head in a jester-like crest, this Maize God—along with others—emerged from carved representations of mountains, embodying the Maya sacred narrative of the annual renewal of the Maize God from the darkness of the Underworld.

References: Taube 1985; Schele and Miller 1986, p. 154

Plate 22
Hacha with human profile
Unknown provenience
AD 650–800
Sandstone
12 in. (30.5 cm)
The Art Institute of Chicago. Ada Turnbull Hertle Fund
1974.23

With its idealized human features and luxurious tresses—a long sloping forehead and thick, brushed-back bangs—this head depicts the young Maize God. More than a simple portrait, this disembodied depiction alludes to his annual "harvest" and decapitation at the end of the growing season. With his skull sown like the lifeless corn kernel, his resurrection comes with the onset of the tropical rains, when the fresh shoots break through the parched ground. In the Popol Vuh this takes place in the ball court where his body had been buried.

Appropriately enough, this carving is an item of ballplaying equipment. Dubbed an *hacha,* it was worn at the waist, attached to a broad belt made of perishable, cushioning materials. In this case, the wear patterns among the cut-out holes in the hair, along the forehead, and at the nape of the neck indicate that the work received substantial use and was tied at these points.

Although essentially "flat" and only a few centimeters thick, the face is fully articulated on both sides, as if completely three-dimensional. If seen face on, however, the sculpture essentially vanishes, reducing itself to a thin blade. Rather remarkably, a recently discovered work featuring two ballplayers at Tonina, Mexico, depicts *hachas* both from the side and straight on (see drawing at left).

Reference: Gallenkamp and Johnson et al. 1985, p. 189

Plate 23
Jester God

Unknown provenience
AD 600–800
Jade with traces of cinnabar
5⁵/₁₆ x 3¹/₂ x 1³/₈ in. (13.5 x 9.0 x 3.5 cm)
On loan from the Permanent Collection, Utah Museum of Fine
Arts, Salt Lake City
1985.020

Among all the supernatural patrons of Maya
kingship, one of the most enigmatic was the Jester
God. So named because of the three jewel-tipped
points that crown his head in most representations,
his image served as a crowning emblem for both
rulers and deities, tied either to an elaborate
headdress or a simple paper or cloth scarf (see below,
detail of Plate 106)—collectively called *huun* by the
Maya. This example, one of the largest known,
shows the drilled holes used to attach it to its
mount in the manner seen in a number of works
in this volume (Plates 29, 101, 106).

The Jester God encompassed a complex range
of ideas and takes a series of forms that are still
incompletely understood. These concerned notions
of centrality and the *axis mundi*, understood by the
Maya to be a great tree that stood at the earth's
center and supported the sky. The tri-pointed crest
is clearly derived from leaves, as if he were a
personified tree. The frequent grouping of Jester
Gods in threes has led Karl Taube to suggest that
another allusion is to the three hearth stones of the
Maya fireplace, traditionally considered the center
of the home, and by extension, the world. Although
they usually have the somewhat reptilian face of
many Maya gods, certain Jester Gods also display
bird or shark traits. On the rare occasions when we
receive personal names for different Jester Gods
they often include *xook,* the word for "shark." An
ancient motif in Mesoamerica, the Jester God can
be recognized on portraits from the Olmec culture.

References: Schele and Miller 1986, p. 79; Fields 1989; Taube 1999

Plate 24

Jade mask with flares

Calakmul, Mexico

AD 600–800

Jade with obsidian and shell

Mask, 5⅞ x 5⅛ in. (15.0 x 13.0 cm); flares, *c.* 4 in. (10.0 cm)

Museo Arqueológico de Campeche "Fuerte de San Miguel"—INAH, Mexico

Mask, 10-290542; flares, 10-290543, 10-290544

Of all the faces created by the ancient Maya, none engages our stare so intently as this vividly naturalistic mask from Calakmul. Here the ideal of male beauty, as represented in the person of the young Maize God, is realized in jade—the material that epitomized fertility and preciousness throughout Mesoamerica. A work of profound quality, this closely fitted mosaic gives the impression of a fractured whole rather than the sum of many parts. At first sight, the intense green color distances us from human flesh; yet closer inspection reveals the very skin-like surface transparency of jadeite, whose sheen glows like a human face in the tropics.

Usually placed over the face of the deceased, these "death masks"—which lack the eye-holes of their functional counterparts—reveal royal aspirations to become one with the Maize God. Jade mosaic masks are rare: finds have been concentrated at powerful and wealthy cities like Palenque, Tikal, and most especially Calakmul, where six full size versions have been excavated thus far. Such objects represent immense value, since to the cost of the material we must add the weeks, or more likely months, of labor to cut, carve, fit, and polish the tesserae. This one—the pieces so closely matched in texture and hue that much of the jadeite itself must have been extracted from the same boulder—was discovered in a well-built crypt at the summit of the lofty pyramid Calakmul Structure 7. It dates to the late 7th or more likely 8th century, but sadly no inscriptions were left to identify its undoubtedly royal occupant.

References: Carrasco 2000, pp. 16–17; Schmidt et al. 1998, p. 555

Plate 25

Necklace with *ik'* motif on pendant

Calakmul, Mexico

AD 600–800

Jade

2⁷⁄₈ x 4⁹⁄₁₆ in. (7.2 x 11.6 cm)

Museo Arqueológico de Campeche "Fuerte de San Miguel"—
INAH, Mexico

10-290657 0/45

Jade jewelry was always something more for the Maya than an advertisement of their wealth and elevated status. On a deeper level it emulated the finery of the Maize God, whose splendid jewels were metaphors for the verdant green foliage of the sprouting cornstalk. Maya royalty went to their graves believing that they would follow his footsteps into the Underworld, defeat the lords of death and experience the same rebirth and elevation into the sky. They therefore prepared for this resurrection by dressing their corpses in the same jewelry worn in life: jade necklaces, ear ornaments, wristlets, and belts—sometimes even mosaic masks (Plate 24).

Technically speaking, true Mesoamerican jade is jadeite, a silicate of sodium and aluminum colored with various trace elements. It comes from highland Guatemala, where important sources worked in ancient times have recently been rediscovered. It is harder, though slightly more brittle than its cousin in China, nephrite. In fact, jadeite is notably harder than steel, something that makes the skill and technical know-how with which it was fashioned, without any metal tools, so very impressive. Jadeite was actually only one of several greenstones worked by the Maya (others include albite, diopside, serpentine, and chrysoprase) which are often grouped under the rubric "jade," and which probably made up the majority of their output.

The items in this collection were found in a variety of tombs at Calakmul. The centerpiece is a sizable "wind jewel" pectoral, representing the hieroglyph *ik',* meaning "breath," "wind," and "vital essence," and which can sometimes be seen as the pectoral of the god K'awiil on Plate 3. It comes from under Structure 2D, part of a massive pyramid in the heart of the city.

Reference: Schmidt et al. 1998, p. 555

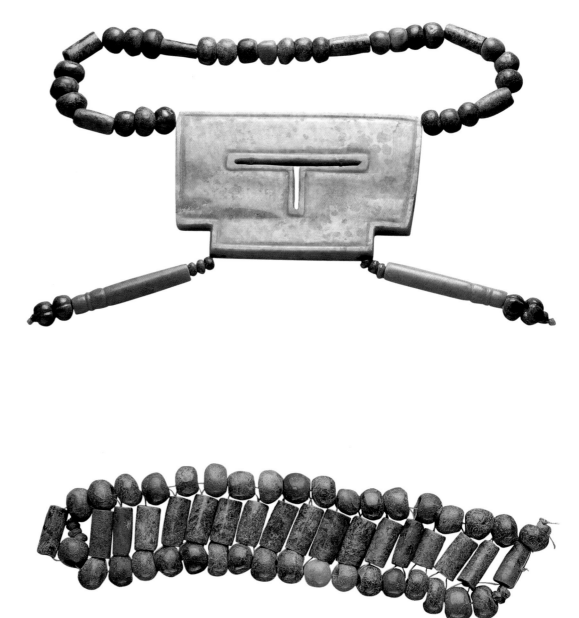

Plate 26

Bracelet

Calakmul, Mexico

AD 600–800

Jade

6¹⁄₂ x 1³⁄₈ in. (16.5 x 3.5 cm)

Museo Arqueológico de Campeche "Fuerte de San Miguel"—
INAH, Mexico

10-568481 0/30

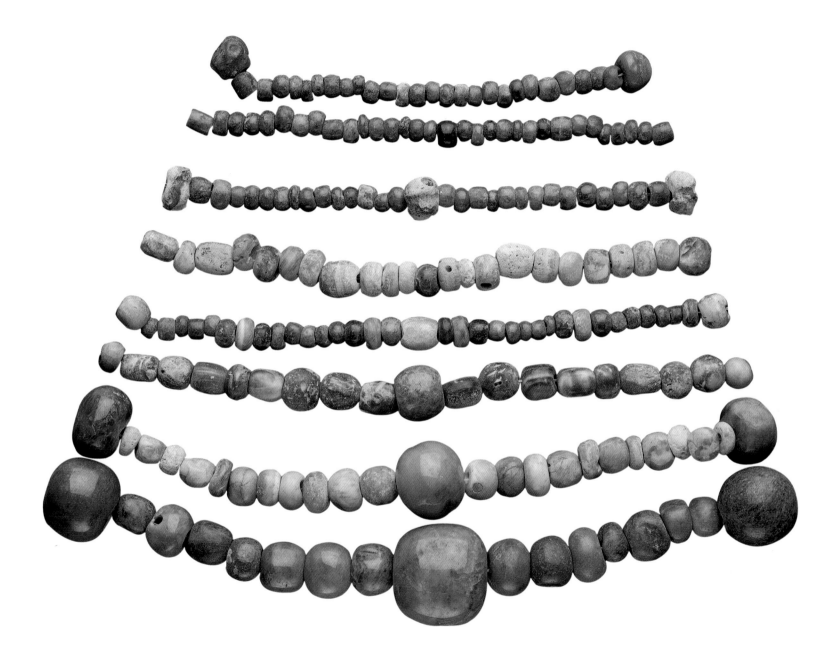

Plate 27
Collar of eight strands of beads
Calakmul, Mexico
AD 600–800
Jade and spondylus shell
c. 8 x 8 in. (*c.* 20.3 x 20.3 cm), mounted
Museo Arqueológico de Campeche "Fuerte de San Miguel"—
INAH, Mexico
10-566761 0/211

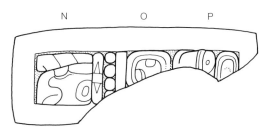

Plate 28
Jade head in a limestone box
Unknown provenience
Box: *c.* AD 750; Head: AD 600–800
Jade and limestone
Box: 9⅝ x 7 x 2½ in. (24.5 x 17.8 x 6.4 cm)
Head: 8⅝ x 6¹/₁₆ x 3¹⁵/₁₆ in. (22.0 x 15.5 x 10.0 cm)
National Gallery of Australia, Canberra
78.1297

This pairing of a jade head and the stone tray in which it snuggly sits is distinctly unusual. Polished greenstone maskettes such as this one were made to be belt ornaments, usually in a set of three. Many seem to represent the idealized face of the young Maize God, although some are fused with, or substituted for, ancestral portraits. The tray is evidently an upturned box lid, as suggested by the inverted inscription on all four sides. The configuration may be a reference to the decapitated Maize God, whose head is sometimes shown in plates or trays much like this one (see below).

The text on the box is equally peculiar, especially with its truncated sequence of 260-day calendar positions (A, K, O). We can read that it was made for the Tonina king "Stone Centipede-God" (*k'inich tuun chapaat*) (I–J), and dedicated to his personal goddess (F–G). Although we lack firm dates for his reign it occurred sometime in the mid-8th century and during an unexplained 50-year silence in Tonina's monumental record.

References: Coe 1973, pp. 32–33; Martin and Grube 2000, p. 187

Plate 29
Plate with Maize God
Unknown provenience
AD 600–800
Ceramic
Diam.: 16³/4 in. (42.6 cm)
New Orleans Museum of Art: Museum purchase through
the Ella West Freeman Foundation Matching Fund
69.2

The Maya buried their noble and royal dead
with large plates bearing images of the Maize
God. Some may have held tamales, food for the
Underworld journey; others specifically carried
the message of renewal and rebirth.

Having never been ritually drilled or "killed,"
this large plate probably held foodstuffs. The Maize
God's jade adornments—attached to his tiny
diadem, woven into his hair, or worn as swinging
necklace and jeweled loincloth—give evidence of
the young god at the seasonal height of his powers,
between the "green corn" of milky kernels and
the fulfillment of harvest, his annual death. The
surrounding text is dominated by a repeating
phrase, which, if it has any true meaning, is a
simple statement of ownership.

Reference: Coe 1973, p. 35

Plate 30

Chaak with bird headdress

Copan, Honduras

AD 600–700

Carved volcanic stone

30 x 36 in. (76.2 x 91.4 cm)

Instituto Hondureño de Antropología e Historia: Museo Regional de Copan, Honduras

Carved from a single block of stone, this sculpture depicts the storm god Chaak in a particularly snake-like form, with upturned snout and sharp tooth. With a great bird rearing back, fish in mouth, to form the headdress, this figure can be identified as a particular version or aspect of Chaak dubbed GI (one), of the Palenque Triad Gods. This god was especially important at the city of Palenque, where he was impersonated by kings on a number of monuments (see Plate 118; Fig. 93).

Archaeologists found this example at Copan, Honduras, along with other, broken examples, deep within Structure 26. They believe that these figures once adorned a building laid waste by the mid-8th-century construction of the mammoth Hieroglyphic Stairway that now elaborates the front of Structure 26. The volcanic tuff used in Copan construction was ideal for such three-dimensional architectural sculpture: soft when first quarried, the stone later hardened to a surface that defied wind and rain.

Plate 31
Capstone with K'awiil
Campeche, Mexico
AD 600–800
Paint on limestone
26¹/₂ x 14³/₈ in. (67.5 x 36.5 cm)
Museo Amparo, Puebla, Mexico
52 22 MA FA 57PJ 1465

This lively rendering of the serpent-footed deity K'awiil comes from the northern Maya area, probably the state of Campeche. Painted on the underside of a capstone—one of a row of slabs that closed the vault of a corbel chamber—it shows him running or dancing while carrying a bursting sack of beans. The hieroglyph on this bag reads literally "nine eight-thousands"—although "nine" in Mayan languages is frequently used simply to mean "many." The glyphic spelling of *kakaw*, "cacao," appears here in the lower text band identifying its contents as raw chocolate, while another in the scene itself reads *ox wi'il* or "an abundance of food."

K'awiil is closely associated with corn, no doubt because he embodies lightning, the sacred force that many Mesoamerican accounts credit with striking and splitting open a sacred mountain to release maize hidden in a cave. Indeed, among all his other attributes, he often displays the Maize God's extended forehead and fringe of hair, allusions to the ripe cob. But cacao was another of the valuable foodstuffs to emerge from the split mountain, and the Maya seem to have credited K'awiil with its recovery too. On one painted vessel K'awiil is seen at the court of God L—the Underworld god of trade, tribute, and wealth—and gestures toward a cacao tree (Fig. 26). Another painted capstone, this time from Chichen Itza, Yucatan, shows him rising from a cacao-studded sinkhole, an allegorical entrance to the Underworld, bearing the gift of chocolate (Fig. 27).

References: Arellano 2002; Uriarte ed. 1998, p. 67

Plate 32

Cylinder vase with underworld scene ("Princeton Vase")

Unknown provenience
AD 600–800
Ceramic
8½ x 6½ in. (21.5 x 16.6 cm)
Princeton University Art Museum. Museum purchase, gift of A. Widenmann, Class of 1918, and Dorothy Widenmann Foundation
y1975-17

On perhaps the most famous of all painted Maya ceramic scenes—a true masterpiece of codex-style painting—we enter the Underworld court of God L at a crucial moment. Gleeful, almost chortling, the old toothless god ties the wristlet of one of five beautiful young women arranged around him. Often interpreted as concubines, they might equally well be his daughters. One of the girls pours chocolate from one vessel to another from waist height, creating the frothy beverage enjoyed throughout Mesoamerica. A rabbit scribe sits below the dais and writes in an open jaguar-skin-covered book with a brush or a quill pen. Although seemingly a functionary of the Underworld court, the rabbit comes to play a bigger role in the saga. This idyll is disturbed by something going on around the other side of the vessel; one girl, already alerted, taps another on the ankle to attract her attention.

The other side of the vessel reveals a horrific scene. Here we see two standing lords, each wearing a mask and armed with an axe. The first stoops to behead a bound and nearly naked figure. An umbilicus-like snake emerges from the victim's belly, and seems to strike at the second executioner. The identities of both the masked characters and the sacrificial victim have long been a topic of debate. Fortunately, another vessel now casts some useful light on the story (Fig. 21).

Outwardly rather different, this vase offers a closely related scene that pushes the story forward a little in time. To the left we see the standing figure of God L, his name (here *13 Muy? Chan*) written in a caption above his head. Now virtually naked, to the right we see his clothes—his long cape, his hat (now rather effaced), and his staff—all flung into the air. This stripping of God L appears on other vessels, where it marks the beginning of his defeat and humiliation. On Fig. 21 we see another Underworld lord—identified by the disembodied eyes and skeletal "centipede" headdress—sitting on a throne made from femurs. He has recently been sacrificed and blood spills forth from an open wound to his chest. The same umbilicus-like snake seen on the "Princeton Vase" rises from his body and identifies him as the same victim seen on the "Princeton Vase." To the right we see the executioners, the triumphant Hero Twins, having now shed their disguises. One contemptuously tosses God L's necklace into the air. These events closely parallel those described in the Popol Vuh, where the disguised Hero Twins put the co-rulers of the Underworld to death. The appearance of a second Underworld lord distinct from God L suggests that this deity shared the dualism of the Hero Twins or Monkey Scribes—as one lone carving already hinted (Fig. 68a).

References: Coe 1973, pp. 90–93; Schele and Miller 1986, pp. 286–287; Reents-Budet 1994, p. 356

Plate 33

Bowl with images of the "Chocolate God"

Mexico or Guatemala
AD 400–600
Stone
3³⁄₈ x 6¹⁄₄ in. (8.6 x 15.9 cm)
Dumbarton Oaks Research Library & Collections,
Washington, D.C.
PC.B.208

This small, delicately worked stone bowl provides information of considerable interest to Maya mythology. The exterior features three figural medallions with hieroglyphic captions, interspersed with columns of additional glyphs. Each medallion features the same character, one whom we can identify, from the cacao pods that sprout from his body, and the "wood" motifs he is marked with, to be a personified cacao tree: in other words, a god of chocolate. In one scene he points to a ceramic vessel, presumably one containing a chocolate drink, while on another he lies on a throne and contemplates a book (the third scene is largely destroyed).

But this "Chocolate God" has something special about him. His sloping forehead and crowning jewels are characteristic features of the young Maize God. The glyphic captions confirm this by naming him *ixim te'* or literally "maize tree." The significance of the word *ixim* in early Mayan languages is complex and probably not restricted to the physical material of maize so much as to underlying mythical concepts. Interestingly, the inscribed contents of chocolate vessels are frequently said to be *iximte'el kakaw* or "maize-tree-like cacao"—underscoring that the cacao plant was indeed known by this name.

The Maya recognized an intimate relationship between maize and cacao in their belief system, reflecting the special place of these two foodstuffs in Maya culture: one the ultimate dietary staple, the other the ultimate symbol of wealth and privilege. Although the Popol Vuh tells us that the head of the decapitated Maize God came to life from a calabash tree, earlier depictions show a cacao plant in this same role and it seems that his embodiment or rebirth from a cacao tree was a key stage in his revival (Fig. 28). Rare depictions reveal that the Maize God, like One Hunahpu in the Popol Vuh, had a brother. It is worth exploring the idea that it was this hitherto unidentified character who had a special affinity with cacao.

References: Coe 1975, pp. 11–12; Taube 1985; Stuart 1989

Plate 34

Limestone panel with seated lord

Lacanha, Mexico
AD 746 (9.15.15.0.0 9 Ajaw 18 Xul)
Limestone
27¹/₂ x 66 in. (69.9 x 167.6 cm)
Dumbarton Oaks Research Library & Collections,
Washington, D.C.
PC.B.145
Washington, D.C., only

One of the most elegant low-relief sculptures dedicated to any Maya noble, this panel is a fine example of the growing naturalism of the 8th century. On it, a seated lord extends his hands to hold a long bar scepter from which heads of the deity K'awiil emerge at either end. As the small nearby caption explains, the lord is performing a piece of religious theater; he is conjuring, and thus giving birth to, a version of K'awiil especially associated with fecundity and the release of maize from its hiding place in a sacred mountain. This birth takes place deep in the "Black Hole"—a primary name of the Underworld, called Xibalba in the Popol Vuh.

The surrounding text identifies the lord as

He of White Lizard (*aj sak teleech*), who acceded to the rank of Sahal (*sajal*) in 743. He evidently ruled the city of Lacanha where this stone was found, although only under the overlordship of Knot-Eye Jaguar, king of the unified Bonampak-Lacanha kingdom. He of White Lizard was the son of a Sahal himself but he may have later achieved kingship either through promotion or usurpation. Texts from nearby Bonampak later accord him full royal titles, and he was father to Lord of the Sky Hawk (*yajaw chan muwaan*), who ruled Bonampak-Lacanha from 776 and commissioned the famous Bonampak murals. There is some hint that internal strife accompanied these developments: in a lintel text associated with the Bonampak murals, He of

White Lizard is shown capturing another one of Knot-Eye Jaguar's vassals in 748, just two years after this panel was commissioned.

Wearing beads braided into his hair, a nosebead, and minimal clothing, this lord personifies courtly refinement and elegance. He sits atop a living stone, a place of rebirth for the Maize God. The slight mustache and beard are characteristic of the Bonampak region, whence comes the sculpture. The sculptor convincingly foreshortens legs and arms, creating a sense of depth for the figure. The panel would have been set into the rear wall of a small structure.

References: Coe and Benson 1966; Mathews 1980

Plate 35

Cylinder vessel with underworld scene ("Vase of the Seven Gods")

Naranjo region, Guatemala or Belize
AD 755–784
Ceramic
9¹/₂ x 6 in. (24.1 x 15.2 cm)
Anonymous loan, courtesy of The Art Institute of Chicago
42.1992

Known as the "Vase of the Seven Gods," this painted vase shows a scene from the first day of "creation" in 3114 BC. It is set in the court of God L, who is shown here as the presiding ruler of the Underworld. Seated on a jaguar-pelt-covered throne, he can be recognized from his feather-trimmed hat complete with his owl messenger nested in its crown. God L was the wealthy god of trade and tribute; the thin cigar he smokes is an allusion to another area of his interests, tobacco. Elsewhere he is associated with rain as well, possibly night rain and the black resin of world destruction that ended the era previous to our own.

Before him sit six fearsome deities: the first among them at top is the Jaguar God of the Underworld, another key deity of the "Black Hole," as the ancient Maya called Xibalba. The hieroglyphic text between God L and his minions gives the date of the creation of the current era before going on to talk about an "ordering" of the pictured gods; it then lists each by name.

The vase was evidently made at the city of Naranjo in the latter half of the 8th century. A second version of this event on an unusual rectangular vase shows not 7 but 11 deities, but is otherwise so similar in its details that both may have been copied from a single original, possibly one painted in a long-lost book.

The artist of this vessel mastered distinctive styles of painting and here demonstrates his skill with the "black background" technique, in which the background is painted first, reserving the areas for figures with a strong contour line.

References: Coe 1973, pp. 106–109; Freidel et al. 1993; Reents-Budet 1994, p. 319

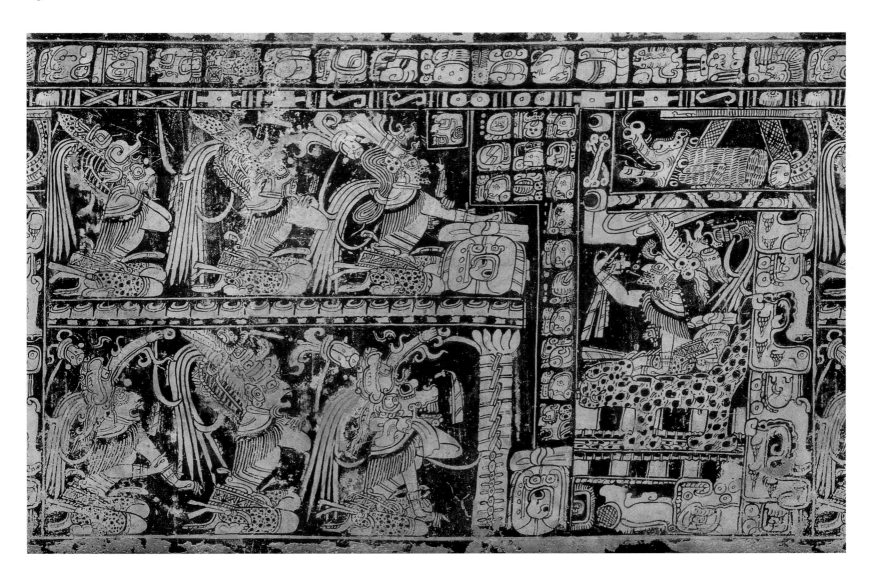

Plate 36

Carved panel with kneeling God L impersonator

Palenque region, Mexico

c. AD 700

Limestone

39 1/8 x 26 1/2 x 1 3/4 in. (99.4 x 67.3 x 4.4 cm)

The Museum of Fine Arts, Houston; Museum purchase

62.42

This fragmentary carving is the lower left corner of a much larger panel that once formed the centerpiece of a temple sanctuary or palace chamber. It shows a lord dressed as the Underworld deity God L, identified by his headdress of black-tipped feathers with a nested owl at its core. Among other things, God L was the god of tribute; here his impersonator plays the supplicant making an offering. In his plate there is a mask and headdress in the style of the distant metropolis Teotihuacan. The small arching proboscis identifies the costume to be one of the strange warrior butterflies of Central Mexico.

In the original composition—which can be partly reconstructed from fragments in several locations—our kneeling figure is one of two that flanked an unidentified central character in full Teotihuacano dress. Since the 19th century, the right-hand figure has been in the Museo Nacional de Antropología in Mexico City, and it depicts the Palenque king Kan Bahlam II in the guise of K'uk'ulkan, the Maya version of the Mexican deity Quetzalcoatl. Sections of surviving text (not shown here) suggest that this panel might come from a provincial satellite of Palenque, though in many ways it remains a unsolved puzzle.

References: Schaffer 1987; Hales, n.d; Taube 1992; personal communication, Gunter to Martin 2000

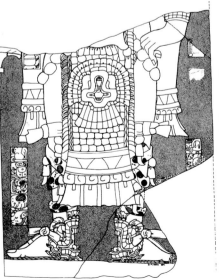

Plate 38
Headdress ornament
Unknown provenience
AD 600–900
Jade
2¹/₂ x 1¹/₂ x 1⁵/₈ in. (6.4 x 3.8 x 4.1 cm)
Fine Arts Museums of San Francisco.
Museum purchase, Fine Arts Museums Acquisition Fund
in memory of James Medley Jr.
1988.4

The Maya held rare apple-green to be the most valuable color for the precious jadeite found in highland Guatemala. The brilliant apple color occurs in thin veins, often deep within boulders of more banal grey-green. Here the artist has located the valued color at the front of the head, with the lighter tones falling to the back, where it is perforated by holds for suspension or attachment.

Maya kings wore small jade adornments at the centers of their headdresses, most frequently Jester Gods (Plate 23) worked as thin, if not openwork, representations of the head of the deity. Yet here the deity depicted is the patron of arts and writing, the personified head of Number 13, a highly auspicious and favored number among the Maya. Characteristic of this god is the knotted tie atop a waterlily pad, visible here on the headdress. The wearer of this adornment was probably known for his artistry.

Reference: Robertson 1990

Plate 37
Shell cacao beans in bowl
Ek Balam, Mexico
AD 600–900
Shell and ceramic
Bowl, c. 4 in. (10.0 cm)—reproduced larger than actual size
Museo Regional de Yucatan "Palacio Cantón"—INAH, Mexico
10-626558 0/136, 10-596932 (bowl)

Ek Balam was a thriving city in the northern Maya realm before the rise of its neighbor Chichen Itza. Investigators Leticia Vargas de la Peña and Victor Castillo Borges have recently uncovered the magnificent tomb of a great Ek Balam ruler. Among the burial offerings were these pieces of shell, finely worked to take the form of snow-white cacao beans. Not only would they have functioned as incorruptible cash for the afterlife, but they also hint at one source of Ek Balam's wealth, since local sinkholes would have provided the ideal micro-climate for the cultivation of their real cousins.

Plate 39

Lidded turtle shell vessel

Unknown provenience
AD 350–500
Ceramic
8¹/₂ x 16 in. (21.6 x 40.6 cm)
Promised gift to the Fine Arts Museums of San Francisco
L03.59

The Maya likened the hard, articulated shell of the turtle to the dry, cracked earth from which maize would emerge with annual rains. In this way, they understood the turtle to *be* the earth in miniature, both earth and stone. Like the landmass of the earth, the turtle is rounded, lumbers slowly, if at all, and is surrounded by water. The ancient Maya believed that the Maize God would be reborn time and again from its surface.

Ceramic vessels of this sort are known as basal-flange bowls because of the lower flange that makes them easy to carry and support. Most examples come from 4th- and 5th-century tombs and held foodstuffs for the interred. In a tomb, such a work offered the promise of eternal renewal.

Plate 40

Lid of vessel with monkey and cacao pods

Tonina, Mexico
AD 600–900
Ceramic
7³/₁₆ x 13 in. (18.3 x 33.0 cm)
Museo de Sitio de Tonina—INAH, Chiapas, Mexico
10-569388

The greatest threat to the cacao harvest was the clever spider monkey, whose desire for chocolate is the subject of many painted ceramic vessels—most of which were made for serving the valuable beverage. Although only the lid of this vessel survives, it brings the story into three dimensions: here the spider monkey's body becomes the chocolate vessel, and his carefully rendered (and very human) hands seemingly control the valuable liquid. The monkey's characteristic face is rendered to emphasize thick eyebrows, squat nose, and lolling tongue, all of which are antithetical to Maya canons of beauty. He wears pods of fresh cacao around his neck. Postfire pigments bring the work to life.

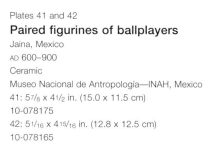

Plates 41 and 42

Paired figurines of ballplayers

Jaina, Mexico

AD 600–900

Ceramic

Museo Nacional de Antropología—INAH, Mexico

41: 5⁷⁄₈ x 4¹⁄₂ in. (15.0 x 11.5 cm)

10-078175

42: 5¹⁄₁₆ x 4¹⁵⁄₁₆ in. (12.8 x 12.5 cm)

10-078165

Found together during Mexican excavations on Jaina Island in the early 1960s, these ballplayer figurines work together as a pair. Each goes down on his left knee and cocks the left arm, and they can easily be arranged to be in eternal play, the ball suspended in the observer's mind for all time.

The maker of these figurines took care to detail the costumes. Protective wraps shield only one arm, from wrist to elbow, along with a single knee pad. Thick cotton quilting, perhaps attached to wicker or wood, is then held in place with great ropes or bands. The simple caps on their heads suggest that the figurines may once have sported elaborate headgear, now lost; ballplayers often wear vulture or deer headdresses (Plate 45).

Reference: Piña Chán 1968

Plate 43

Ballcourt marker

La Esperanza, Mexico
AD 591 (9.7.17.12.14 11 Ix 7 Sotz')
Limestone
Diam.: 22 in. (56.0 cm)
Museo Nacional de Antropología—INAH, Mexico
10-225798

Circular stones were often set face-up in the central alley of ball courts where, as one of three, they demarked playing zones or scoring devices in the game. This example from La Esperanza, a small site near the larger one of Chinkultic, Chiapas, Mexico, carries an especially well preserved scene.

The ballplayer wears a long kilt of animal hide, along with a heavy waist belt, knee and forearm protectors, as he kneels to strike a ball. The ball itself displays the finely incised portrait of Hunahpu, one of the Hero Twins and a son of the Maize God. According to the Popol Vuh, the Underworld foes outwit Hunahpu, decapitate him, and introduce his head as a ball in the game. The scalloped cut-shell design of his headdress identifies the ballplayer himself to be an important Underworld deity. The captions to the scene, however, make clear that this is an impersonation ritual, and that the player is actually a lord of Chinkultic, a kingdom anciently known as Sky (*chan*). The rim inscription describes the dedication of the stone, and probably the ball court it once graced, on 19 May 591.

References: Miller and Houston 1987; Kowalski 1989; Freidel et al. 1993

Plate 44

Figurine of ballplayer

Jaina, Mexico
AD 600–900
Ceramic
13$\frac{1}{2}$ x 7 in. (34.2 x 17.8 cm)
Princeton University Art Museum. Museum purchase, Fowler
McCormick, Class of 1921, Fund, in honor of Gillett G. Griffin
on his seventieth birthday
1998–36

His brow furrowed, this ballplayer captures the concentration, the poise, and the courtly elegance brought to the game. Slightly protected on his right wrist and ankle, he wears a thick ring of padding above the waist, protecting most internal organs from the dangerous, heavy, rubber ball. For a headdress he wears a great vulture, painted a brilliant Maya blue, set in a crown of feathers. Vulture and deer headdresses frequently distinguish teams of players from one another.

Both textiles and jewelry are rendered with unusually fine detail; the cut-out cross motif of the cloth suggests a fine openwork tapestry, in a technique similar to that depicted at Yaxchilan (Plate 50).

Reference: Whittington 2001, p. 233

Plate 45
Cylinder vessel with ballgame scene
Unknown provenience
AD 700–850
Ceramic
6¼ x 4¹/₁₆ in. (15.9 x 10.3 cm)
Dallas Museum of Art, gift of Patsy R. and Raymond D. Nasher
1983.148

The Maya ballgame held a crucial place in royal life and is celebrated in a range of different media. It could symbolize the struggle for life over death performed in the Underworld, and the related metaphors for warfare and the hunt. Like the teams in the Popol Vuh, players worked in pairs, with one player taking the lead position to strike or receive the ball. The heavy rubber ball could cause significant injury and the game required protective clothing: a ubiquitous wide waist belt, as well as arm and knee guards. Decorative costumes were elaborate and the prominence of animals and birds in headdresses—in this case the common deer and vulture motifs—suggests allusions to the hunt.

The rim text tells us that the ruler of Cat Hill (*hix witz*)—a kingdom centered near Zapote Bobal and El Pajaral, Guatemala—once owned the vessel. The vertical column, however, names a king of Motul de San José, an adjacent kingdom to the west that encompassed Lake Peten-Itza. The relationship between the two domains is unclear, but it is possible that this scene alludes to an inter-kingdom contest, rather than the more familiar rituals of post-battle sacrifice or mythic re-enactment of the great Underworld game.

Reference: Schele and Miller 1986, p. 255

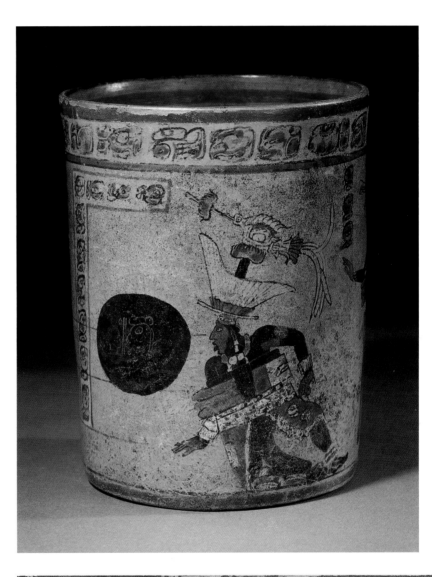

Women at Court

CHAPTER 3

Fig. 31   Detail of Stela, Plate 46. A powerful 8th-century woman conjures a snake from the oversized bone in her arms.

To a degree unprecedented in the ancient New World, Maya women played a prominent role at court. Although few achieved the ultimate status of rulership, women nevertheless held positions of substance and power. From the earliest times, we know that females were accorded elite burial, and a significant number of well-furnished Maya tombs have been found to contain the bones of women.[1] Their appearances in the 5th and 6th centuries—mostly in texts, but with a few depictions on monuments—emphasize their genealogical importance as the mothers of kings. But beginning in the 7th century and continuing well into the 8th century we see a decisive shift, as women rise to a new public role, commanding wealth and prestige in ways previously unseen and never to be repeated. They even came to be represented in ways usually restricted to men, as solo actors on freestanding stone monuments wielding major symbols of supernatural and temporal power (Fig. 31; Plate 46).

Forty years ago, the glyph for "lady" or "woman" (Fig. 32) was one of the first non-calendrical Maya hieroglyphs to be deciphered, appropriately enough by Tatiana Proskouriakoff, the first great female Mayanist. Not only were women's names and life histories suddenly revealed, but certain carved depictions—long misconstrued as male priests in long vestments—could be recognized for what they were, women wearing the traditional *huipil* dress. This introduced a new range of issues to iconographic studies of the Maya and gave notions of dress, gesture, and gender new relevance to the project.[2]

In an era of rising modern expectations for the change of women's roles in society during the later 20th century—initiated by Simone de Beavoir's *The Second Sex* in France and continuing through the failure of the Equal Rights Amendment in the United States—it would be easy to look back on the Maya of the 7th and 8th centuries and read into their art a new assertiveness, a veritable transformation of gender relations and power structures. But this phenomenon of prominent women emerged at a very particular time in the Maya lowlands, one in which broader social forces were at work. Newly crowded with petty states that had absorbed virtually all the remaining productive land, the Maya world experienced a new intensity of complex power plays among royal houses. To be successful, each petty state needed to pursue ever more involved strategies of warfare, diplomacy, and marriage alliance. Just as the records of conflict pick up, so too do the representations of

Fig. 32   Titles of noble women: a. Ixik', "Lady"; b. Ix Kanal Ahaw, "Lady Ahaw of Calakmul"; c. Ix Kaloomte', "Lady Kaloomte'"; d. Ix Sahal, "Lady Sahal."

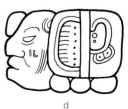

a   b   c   d

women, and it is likely that marriage, always an alternative strategy to war in court society, acquired new value in inter-dynastic relations. If the brief appearance of women in the spotlight reflects the special social circumstances of the 7th and 8th centuries, then their disappearance just as surely indicates that a new epoch had been ushered in. With few exceptions, depictions of women disappear in the 9th century to be replaced by images of armed men (Plate 107).

Through these images and their accompanying texts, along with evidence from archaeology and ethnology, we can gain some access into the lives of women in this period. We see the active part they took in public and private ceremonies, engaging in a full range of religious rituals, including auto-sacrifice, god-conjuring, and impersonation. "Women's work" accrued value in palace culture, making women an indispensable part of the state economy.

The Lives of Courtly Women

The lives of high-ranking women reflect the dual nature of the court, as both an exceptional place of secular authority and an ordinary household writ large—a space of intimate domesticity as well as one with the greatest political and economic import. On one level, elite women replicated the traditional roles of mother, nurse, weaver, and cook, both in practical and symbolic form. While noble ladies clearly lived better than women further down the social scale, we should not imagine that this meant a life of leisure. On another level, the women of the court made a difference in the political agenda, and accordingly, women held titles of note: Lady Ahaw, Lady Kaloomte', and Lady Sahal, among others (Fig. 32a–d). Kings name their mothers as frequently as they name their fathers.

A key responsibility for the woman of an ordinary Maya household was the weaving of cotton cloth, where her labors met the basic clothing needs of the family. Women wove on a backstrap loom, a machine of simple design which has remained essentially unchanged from ancient to modern times. In the form of Jaina figurines, we see Maya noblewomen at work, the loom extending from their waists to a tree, where a companion bird perches on top (Plate 53). The material evidence for weaving activity, spindle-whorls and bone picks, is concentrated in high-status residences—implying, at the very least, that it was performed under elite supervision in ancient times.[3] This connection between weaving and high status is reiterated on the fine bones from more than one kingdom inscribed with *upuutz' b'aak,* "the weaving bone of," followed by the name of a royal wife.[4] We know from elsewhere in Mesoamerica that noblewomen worked with correspondingly elevated materials—expensive dyes, including cochineal, feathers, and pearl beads—and contributed toward the economy of the court as the producers of high-quality gift, trade, and tribute items.[5]

Although precious little Maya cloth has survived the intense humidity of the region, with only a few scraps found in tombs or dredged from the mud of sacrificial sinkholes, representations in carvings and paintings on pots and murals are evidence enough that it was among the world's great textile-making traditions. Spectacular creations not just of woven cloth, but also of batik and tie-dyeing, openwork, tapestry, brocade, and embroidery, show immense variety and inventiveness (see pp. 242–243). Like modern Maya textiles, the designs undoubtedly encoded deep religious and cosmological significance. Some plectogenic designs—that is, patterns constrained by the technology of weaving—may have lent themselves equally to woven fabric and to woven baskets (Plate 52).

Finely woven cloth held great value throughout the pre-industrial world. Among the Incas, for example, it was the principal means of accumulating and storing wealth.[6] Regional lords sent young "chosen women" to the Inca capital to "weave for the sun," and their efforts are today considered the finest surviving artworks of prehispanic Peru. Among the Aztecs, cloth, like cacao, offered a standardized means of exchange. A single blanket-sized *manta* was worth 60 to 100 cacao beans; a slave cost 10 to 40 *mantas.* Although all sorts of fancy textiles are given illustration in the Codex

Magliabecchiano, for example, the single most unusual one merits a page unto itself.[7] Tribute scenes on Maya vases regularly show stacked heaps of cloth, some edged with fine decorative borders, indicating that it was a major commodity here, too. Although part of the ancient economy now largely invisible to us in the Maya case, control of textile production could have meant great wealth.

Not all weaving was of fancy textiles: Maya women also produced elaborate basketry (Plate 49) and other products, such as sleeping mats, made from the fibrous core of palm trees. Many Maya headdresses seem to feature a woven matrix that supports the elaborate towers of feathers, and the Panama-style hats worn among the Maya today have direct antecedents on painted vessels made more than 1,000 years earlier, particularly in the "hunter's hat," a broad-brimmed *sombrero*.[8]

The making of fine ceramics was also a province supervised by the court. Although men generally painted their decoration, contemporary studies emphasize the role of women in forming the vessel itself—achieving a tall thin-walled vessel through the coiling method—and this may well be true of ancient times as well. The Maya enjoyed the play among forms and textures, painting smooth vessels as if they were covered with jaguar pelts or delicately painting the specific weave of a basket onto a vessel's exterior, a sophisticated interplay among the media.

Maya women took responsibility for the preparation of family and court food. Although little is known of ancient Maya cuisine, maize and beans formed the basis of the staple diet then, as now, with the kernels of maize soaked in limewater to release their nutrition. Years of kneeling to grind the softened kernels at the metate leave their mark on Maya bones: women have gnarled knees, calcified toe bones, and powerful arms.[9] Unsurprisingly, few if any elite women display these telltale signs, suggesting that while noblewomen may have cooked and run their own kitchens, the most arduous labor was probably performed by household servants, whose physical remains would be interred elsewhere. One figurine of a noblewoman shows her preparing corn cakes (Plate 57). Clay griddles have not been found in this period, but thick tortillas may have been cooked directly on the hot rocks of the hearth. For the privileged, foodstuffs were considerably more exotic and varied than this. Painted vessels show Maya lords throwing great feasts in their palaces, serving sumptuous platters of tamales, meat stews, and spicy sauces.[10] Indeed, the same figurine shows a fat dog—next in line, perhaps—sitting by her side while the head of another dog stews in her pot.

Supernatural Models of Female Power

The supernatural universe shaped and defined expectations of royal women, just as it did for their male counterparts. In the lives of gods we see a reflection—albeit a dim and distorted one—of the ideals of court society, a mirror held to the aspirations and behavioral norms of a culture. In the lives of women we also see the way the living and the ideal toggle back and forth to a religious paradigm. Among a number of female protagonists in Maya myth, two especially stand out.

The first is Chak Chel, meaning "Red" or "Great" "Rainbow"—later known as Ixchel, "Lady Rainbow"—the supernatural patron of women's work, from weaving to childbirth, from curing to divining. Devotion to her remained keen into the early colonial period: Hernán Cortés, the conqueror of Mexico, commented on the number of pilgrims who visited her shrine on Cozumel Island to seek healthy pregnancies. Like many powerful Maya gods, Chak Chel is shown wrinkled, toothless, and hunched over from old age (Plate 60). She wears a braided headscarf that is simultaneously a skein of cotton and the coils of a serpent—a form still worn by many Maya women in highland Guatemala today. Although rainbows in Western thought bring luck and good tidings, for the ancient Maya they were dangerous emanations from the Underworld, the harbingers of disease.[11] It is little surprise, then, that Chak Chel also bears sinister connections to the Underworld, signaled by her feline ears and claws, and her skirt sometimes marked by disembodied eyes and crossed bones

(Fig. 33a). She is closely involved in scenes of world destruction, specifically with a deluge she pours from a water vessel. She is also a warrior, but here the reference may be as much to her role as midwife as that of a destroyer: Mesoamerican peoples understood birth as an event fraught with danger and conflict, a battle in which an infant could kill its mother. A sympathetic rendering of Chak Chel comes where she holds a young child, probably the young Maize God, highlighting her role as nurse and protector (Plate 58).

The second major female deity, patron of women's progenitive powers and the ruler of her own supernatural court, is the Moon Goddess. She can be recognized by the crescent moon motif that she sits within or by the rabbit she often cradles in her arms (Fig. 33b). Whereas Westerners see a face in the moon, Mesoamericans see a rabbit. According to the Maya, the Moon Goddess gives birth to the rabbit, aided by none other than Chak Chel (Fig. 34). The Moon Goddess—whose original name remains unclear—is often shown in the company of the aged supreme sky deity Itzamna, and she may be his eligible young daughter (Plate 61).

Beautiful and voluptuous, the Moon Goddess is sexually alluring, a lovely temptress. Modern-day Maya stories relate how the Sun took the form of a deer in order to retrieve his young wife from an adulterous assignation with the planet Venus; others say that it took the imprint of a deer hoof to give her a vagina. A hollow figurine from Jaina—a mold-made whistle finished with elaborate detail added by hand—shows the young goddess chucking the chin of the old god with deer headdress (Plate 59). This deer headdress may indicate the Sun God, in an aged phase, or it may also suggest the deer who provides womankind genitalia. The old god lifts her skirt; she smiles demurely but pulls his emaciated body tight to hers. The Maya clearly relished these human foibles played out among the gods.

The Moon Goddess was also closely involved with the mythology of maize. Modern ethnographies describe how sowing of corn kernels is determined by the lunar calendar, while in some communities maize and the moon are together called "Our Mother."[12] We find the same synergy in ancient times, especially where the two deities seem fused together, the gender variously male and female (Fig. 33b). The prime identifier for maize deities is a net overskirt, thought to be composed of linked jade beads.[13] It is worn together with the belt ornament mask of a piscine monster—probably based on a shark—from whose open mouth emerges a large bivalve shell. Both sexes wear this costume, although kings often wear the net as a short hip-length kilt, whereas queens wear it either as a two-piece collar and skirt (Plate 47), or a full-length *huipil* dress (Plate 46). The costume has a regional presence, and it is commonly worn in the Palenque region (Plate 48) by both men and women; whereas at Yaxchilan, for example, neither men nor women adopt this garb. Much has been made of the occasions when men wear the longer version: is cross-dressing going on here? Have men appropriated some fundamental aspect of femininity?[14]

Some element of female fertility is surely suggested in the open half spondylus shell, which is worn over the groin in this costume. The inside of a spiny oyster bivalve yields a rich pink and red surface when its thin, white nacre is scraped off, as is the case with many such shells recovered archaeologically. In body placement, color and shape (the shell is of course concave), the reference is seemingly to female genitalia. Excavated offerings of single jade beads within whole spondylus shells, sometimes with a large dollop of brilliant red cinnabar, recall the Aztec invocation of the newborn infant as a "precious jade bead" and the Maya custom of offering a single jade bead in the mouth of a dead noble (Plate 62). The offering may encapsulate potential life in the womb; its inchoate potential may have made the jade-cinnabar-spondylus the ideal cache offering.

It is the very principle of regeneration and birth-giving that seems to be represented by the Maize God, who was the embodiment of new life. Ever dying, ever being reborn, the Maize God transcends gender rather than appropriates it. The Maya themselves seemed to have had little problem with this sexual blurring, and, indeed the ambiguity may well have been fully intentional.

Fig. 34 Polychrome vessel, rollout photograph. In two scenes, the Moon Goddess (at far right) gives birth to a rabbit while she observes in a mirror; a large red scroll, presumably symbolizing the blood lost at birth, flows from her body. In the next scene, Chak Chel (at left), the midwife, presents the creature to suckle.

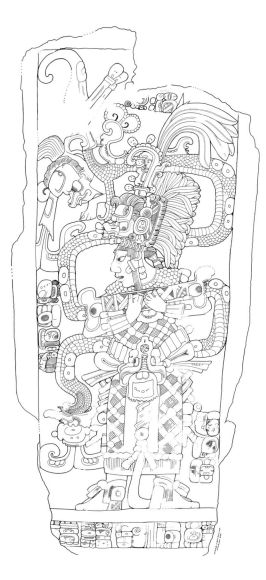

Fig. 35 San Francisco Stela (Plate 46), drawing. A queen called Ix Mutal Ahaw wears the jade costume of maize deities as she conjures a writhing vision serpent. At the center of the body she wears an open shark mouth, with half a spiny oyster shell (spondylus) suspended directly over the groin.

Royal Women in History

Women who reached the heights of fame in the 7th and 8th centuries appear in the guise of these and other deities. Like men, women interacted with the supernatural world to enhance their temporal power. The magnificent San Francisco stela is a case in point (Plate 46; Fig. 35). Wearing the Maize God's net skirt and shark-and-shell belt motif, this otherwise unknown queen Ix Mutal Ahaw grasps an oversized conjuring bone, through which she channels a huge "vision serpent."[15] The snake's mouth gapes open to reveal K'awiil, a deity closely associated with maize—perhaps as the lightning god who first reveals the source of maize inside Sustenance Mountain. The snake bears a motif that links it to lightning, and indeed we can read its whole writhing form as a single bolt of lightning. Vision serpents were instruments of supernatural birth and rebirth, a channel between different realms. Their control by women clearly alludes to their procreative powers.

Another powerful woman pictured in the net skirt was Lady Six Sky of Naranjo (Fig. 37). A scion of the Dos Pilas dynasty, Lady Six Sky arrived at Naranjo in 682.[16] She entered at the time of a political vacuum in Naranjo, in the wake of a conquest of the site that seems to have removed its ruling line, and almost certainly at the behest of Dos Pilas's patrons at Calakmul. She succeeded in initiating a new dynasty, but the name of her husband is notable by its absence. No female in Maya history has a better claim to be a warrior queen, a role she seems to have reveled in. Though acting

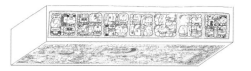

Fig. 36   Structure 23, Yaxchilan, demonstrating lintel position. Lintels 24, 25, and 26 once spanned doorways of Structure 23, as they are oriented in this drawing. The front edge text of Lintel 24 does not survive; here the front text of Lintel 25 has been repeated on 24.

always in the name of her infant son—just five years old at his accession—she presided over a string of captures and conquests. On one monument she tramples a hapless captive underfoot, a device so rare for women that it appears otherwise only at the home of her sponsors at Calakmul.[17]

Lady Xok of Yaxchilan

If Lady Six Sky of Naranjo exemplifies the power of the intrusive, foreign bride, then Lady Xok [pronounced "shoke"] (*ix k'ab'al xook*) from Yaxchilan personifies the power of the local bride and her family. During her era at Yaxchilan, many of the preceding themes come together and find expression in some sublime works of art. Yaxchilan's key position on a promontory at a great sweeping horseshoe bend on the Usumacinta River offered no protection against a troubled history, with lengthy silences in its record pointing to conquests, internal disarray, or subjections to foreign powers. Yet Yaxchilan's fortunes improved markedly during the long reign of Shield Jaguar the Great (*itzamnaaj b'ahlam*), who came to the throne in 681. After a slow start, he initiated a major revival of the city, commissioning numerous monuments to celebrate his military successes over neighboring kingdoms. But it is clear that this renewal was intimately bound up with the role of Lady Xok as his principal wife and queen. Indeed, some of the earliest surviving records from this period are to be found in Temple 23, which—in a rare event—was dedicated to her in 726. This edifice is remarkable not so much for its architecture as for the quality and exceptional character of its monuments (Plates 49–51).

The building contains a total of four carved door lintels: three feature figural scenes and faced out onto the wide central plaza of the city; a fourth, entirely glyphic, remains in place today above a side entrance (Fig. 36). From early in its history the sculptors of Yaxchilan had specialized in the carving of stone lintels, an idiosyncratic format seldom used elsewhere. Set within the narrow doorways of major buildings, they were accessible to very few, and even then, required an uncomfortable craning of the neck to see. The earliest lintels at Yaxchilan are all textual (Plate 70) and worked in a variety of styles, from delicate incision to a rich cameo relief. No previous works, however, prepare the observer for the dramatic human representations on Lintels 24, 25, and 26. The sculptures are simply among the finest Maya accomplishments in relief carving. As if to lay claim to the merit, these artists signed their works—revealing in at least one case that it was the work of an outsider, a specialist drawn from afar to work on an important new commission. These masterpieces mark an entirely new direction in figural carving at the city, and from Lady Xok's time forward there was an identifiable Yaxchilan school of sculpture, characterized by both style of carving and a vivid iconography.

Each lintel shows Lady Xok to be a featured protagonist, performing rituals and ceremonies in the company of her husband.[18] Thus, Lady Xok was both the subject and owner of the building. That in itself would be extraordinary, but the sculptures of this building are unusual in both subject and execution, suggesting her direct involvement in its entire conception. The three lintels suggest a single narrative, reading from left to right: a bloodletting (Lintel 24), precedes a vision (Lintel 25), and ends with a war ceremony (Lintel 26). In fact, the events depicted were widely spaced in time and not even sequential—they have been reconfigured on these monuments to form a narrative with its own motivation and intent, and therefore an attempt to tell two stories at the same time.

Fig. 37   Stela 24, Naranjo, drawing. Lady Six Sky stands atop an unfortunate captive. Dressed in the beaded costume of the Maize God, she may re-enact his victories (see also Fig. 22).

The sequence as given to us begins on Lintel 24 with a sacrificial ritual from the year 709 (Plate 49). On the panel, Lady Xok kneels and pulls a rope studded with thorns through her tongue; blood streams from her mouth to her cheeks and drips to spot the paper in the basket in front of her. Shield Jaguar holds a great torch over her head—described in the text as a "burning spear"—illuminating what was probably a night-time ritual, or one set in the dark recesses of a private chamber. Both king and queen are richly attired. They each wear a Sun God pectoral around the neck, while the human head worn by Shield Jaguar over his brow may be a shrunken trophy of battle. Cloth piles luxuriantly at Lady Xok's knees, and a narrow strip of doublecloth woven in a pattern representing the sky and finished with feathers and what are probably pearls, has been sewn to the border. Shield Jaguar's hipcloth is of a cut-out and embroidered fabric that Lady Xok wears on Lintel 25, casual internal references to the common vocabulary of their dress. Shield Jaguar has donned a fringed short cape, an unusual costume element that seems to allude to the Underworld's God L. The herringbone pattern of his loincloth is also rare.

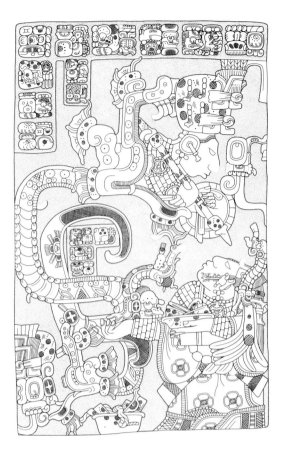

Fig. 38 Lintel 25, Yaxchilan, drawing. Lady Xok, right, sees a warrior within the open maw of a Vision Serpent.

Such detail gives the lintel the richness of an elaborate textile in its own right. Sensuous details urge the eye to linger, re-examine, and even play in the rich patterns. The knots attaching wristlets and other adornments receive lavish attention. The frame of the lintel truncates feathers and smoke curls, an indication of the self-consciousness that this is a rendering rather than life itself.

Lintel 25 effectively shows the result of Lintel 24: Lady Xok sits back on her heels from the kneeling position and receives a vision (Plate 50; Fig. 38). From the bowl where her rope and blood-spattered paper lie rises up a monstrous beast, part-snake, part-centipede. From the monster's mouth emerges a warrior in full regalia, in all likelihood Shield Jaguar himself. The monument indicates that she offered blood, but blood loss alone does not produce this state: she probably also danced, fasted, deprived herself of sleep, and even consumed hallucinogens to achieve her vision. The force of the apparition is emphasized by its representation: it presses against everything it touches—text, frame, even Lady Xok herself—giving the scene great dynamism. When Lady Xok enters a trance, she re-enters moments from the past, and, according to the dates inscribed, this event is the earliest of the three, coinciding with Shield Jaguar's inauguration in office in 681. This is the only known depiction of the rites of this day, and it is highly significant that Lady Xok should be placed so pivotally here. The iconography of rebirth, already examined on the San Francisco stela, seems directed toward fundamental aspects of the city's resurrection, with Lady Xok placed as its instigator and agent.

On Lintel 26, Lady Xok helps Shield Jaguar complete his battle dress, handing him his helmet and shield—an event that took place in 724 (Plate 51). Just as Lady Xok held out her hand to accept the vision, Shield Jaguar now holds out his to accept the helmet, a jaguar head, probably a stuffed skin. Because he bears a hafted knife rather than a spear, he may be preparing for some war-related ceremony or sacrifice rather than battle itself. Yet he is fully prepared for combat: to protect his torso, the king wears the cotton and feather body armor over woven mat seen on his other monuments and those of his son. Lady Xok has donned a *huipil* with stylized frog designs similar to those woven today by the Maya of highland Chiapas (Plate 84). Here, as throughout the program, the faces of Lady Xok and Shield Jaguar are idealized, calm, and of Maize God-like perfection, with their thick, even hair and long, sloping foreheads. Although Shield Jaguar's body turns frontally to assert his greater importance, and he stands a shade taller, in every other respect the two noble figures are visual partners, their arms and hands interlocking at the center of the representation.

The fourth and final lintel (Lintel 23) provides some significant information about the family of Lady Xok, who gives every indication of descent from the local lineage—perhaps even a collateral royal line. Two other women, at least one of which may have been her sister, attend the dedication of this doorway in 724, but no male is recorded as present. In later years at least two burials were laid inside the floor of Temple 23. These graves were found to contain valuable carved bones identified glyphically as the possessions of Lady Xok, heirlooms or personal gifts she made to the deceased (see pp. 268ff, Plates 55, 56). She and her powerful husband may have both been buried in the structure. For the rest of the 8th century, the buildings erected on this strip of the Yaxchilan plaza all engaged in one way or another with Structure 23 and the legacy of Lady Xok. A later set of lintels patterned themselves on her; the building programs also addressed her structure through emulation.

What difference could a woman's ownership have made to this program of sculpture? Would she have supervised the workmanship, instructed the sculptors in the rendering of her own portrait, and insisted on a detailed portrayal of textiles that superseded all precedents and successors? Does the fact that a woman owned the building make it a women's building? We need not assume that the construction costs were drawn from central funds, or were a gift of the king; her local power base would presumably represent a degree of family wealth—giving her the potential to directly commission the whole enterprise.

Of course we cannot know the answers to many of these questions, nor can we know the precise source of any such personal riches. Cacao beans and exotics such as jade, feathers, and marine shells—these were seemingly the domain of men among the ancient Maya, and indeed, control of commerce on the river may have been a general source of income for Yaxchilan as it was for lords at many other pivotal locations. But perhaps there is a clue in the striking depictions of cloth in these carvings. With high-quality weaving under the control of the noble class, we might wonder if this ephemeral medium might have fallen more specifically within the economic orbit of high-ranking females.

Maya weaving generally took place out of doors, and the long open plaza in front of Temple 23, Lady Xok's building, would have been a suitable location for the fabrication of elegant textiles. As previously described, the Maya draped awnings from the cornices of many buildings, making pleasant shady spaces—a sort of portable architecture—of adjacent steps and plaza. The inscriptions on an annex added to Temple 23, called Temple 24, are also concerned with female protagonists (they include a description of Lady Xok's death in 742). It may be that these structures and their plaza space were specifically the province of Yaxchilan's 8th-century *grand dames.*

The rhetoric of Maya kingship obscures many important features of ancient Maya life, and the rare insights we get into the lives of royal women are accordingly precious. There are many things we do not see: we don't find the names of women scribes and artists, for example, yet we find the names of female owners, as if to suggest a noble female literacy. We don't find female soldiers, yet we find women who take the titles generally held by men in political administration. Particularly within the world of the court, a woman's worth could be measured in political and economic terms, giving her some purchase beyond hearth and home.

Plate 46
Stela with supernatural scene
Mexico or Guatemala
AD 761 (9.16.10.0.0 1 Ajaw 3 Sip)
Limestone
92 x 42 x 3 in. (233.7 x 106.7 x 7.6 cm)
Fine Arts Museums of San Francisco. Museum purchase,
Gift of Mrs. Paul Wattis
1999.42a–k

Maya queens were active participants in the supernatural rites that lay at the conceptual heart of royal power. In this superb carving we see a queen in the coils of a grotesque and fearsome serpent, in a demonstration of her ability to harness universal forces of nature. Few sculptures devoted to a woman match the vibrant treatment of this work, created when Maya relief carving had reached the highpoint of its extravagant curves. The similarities it displays in subject matter with painted ceramics suggest a close interaction among artists working in different media, and indeed in different regions and kingdoms.

This woman wears the net overskirt and shark-and-shell belt ornament associated with maize deities. Clasped to her bosom is an oversized femur, and passing through its hollow core is the body of the serpent that she has conjured as a vision. From its open maw emerges an image of the lightning god K'awiil, his signature flaming torch protruding from his forehead. The snake's head is crowned by two spotted curls which represent a form of fire called *tok* associated with lightning—perhaps to be read here as flashes or sparks (see drawing below). In fact, the serpent itself is a zoomorphic bolt of lightning, the same one that elsewhere forms the leg and foot of K'awiil. Some texts actually describe the serpent as K'awiil's *way* or "companion spirit." The Maya believed that a lightning bolt split open the mountain where maize was found. The queen here, dressed as a maize deity, manipulates the regeneration of the maize plant, the food upon which all Mesoamericans ultimately depended.

The monument dates to the year AD 761, but very little is known of its origins or of the woman it celebrates. Her name is Ix Mutal Ahaw—which suggests descent from the royal line of Tikal or Dos Pilas. The inscription begins with the calendrical notation, before describing the erection of the stone itself, specifically said to be *ulakamtuun*, "her stela." Despite her elevated status, the whole event is said to be supervised by a male, presumably her husband. A companion monument may once have clarified his identity. The lower text band features the expression *utz'akaw te'*, literally "he stacked wood," referring to some unknown character. This seems to be a metaphor of some kind; elsewhere it is associated with tribute-giving and/or captive-taking.

References: Berjonneau and Sonnery 1985; Schele and Miller 1986, pp. 176–189; Berrin 1999

CHRONOLOGY			
(9.16.10.0.0)	1 Ajaw 3 Sip	(AD 761)	Her stela is erected
(9.16.9.7.5)	7 Chikchan 13 Yax	(AD 760)	"? stacked wood"
+ 10.15			
(9.16.10.0.0)	1 Ajaw 3 Sip	(AD 761)	(End of the 10th Katun)

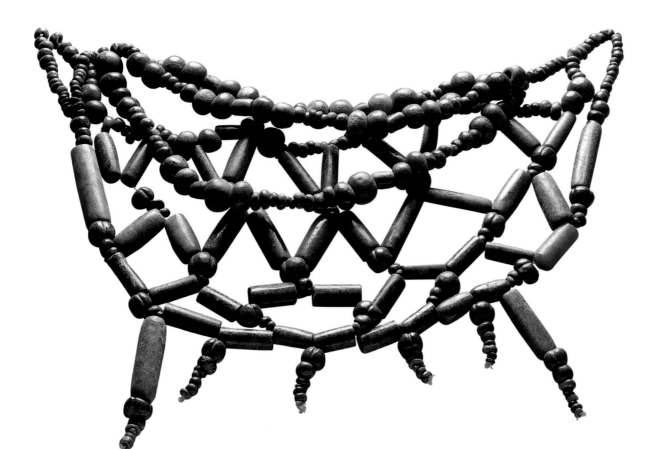

Plate 47
Netted jade collar
Calakmul, Mexico
AD 600–900
Jade
13 x 9½ in. (33.0 x 24.0 cm)
Museo Arqueológico de Campeche "Fuerte de San Miguel"—
INAH, Mexico
10-342994 0/377

A key feature of apparel for maize deities—whether
personified in male or female form—was
a net over-garment made from linked jade beads
(Plates 46, 48). Although common in carved
portraits, few of these items have been recovered
archaeologically. Like certain other items of royal
regalia, these beaded capes or skirts were probably
passed down from one generation to the next. Such
expensive items may have been imitated in other
materials at times, especially by poorer kingdoms.

Reference: Schmidt et al. 1998, p. 555

Plate 48

Panel of woman in jade costume

Xupa, Chiapas, Mexico
AD 600–800
Limestone
44 x 17 x 3 in. (111.8 x 43.2 x 7.6 cm)
Fine Arts Museums of San Francisco. Museum purchase,
Anonymous donor, Art Trust Fund, AOA Art Trust Fund,
J. Alec Merriam Fund
1998.142

Lightly incised, this Palenque-style carving from
the nearby center of Xupa has little of the polish
of the finest Palenque works, but nevertheless
retains its calligraphic flair. The panel once flanked
a temple doorway, according to Austrian explorer
Teobert Maler, who saw the work *in situ* at the
end of the 19th century, only to lament its removal
from the site a short time later.

Here, a woman carries a small platform or
throne. Elsewhere just this kind of throne is used
to present effigies and masks in ceremonies. She
wears the net collar and overskirt of the Maize God,
who can be manifested by both males and females.

Although the woman here is unnamed, a
fragment of related carving, without provenience,
names the birth date of Pakal, suggesting that she
is either his mother or wife.

Reference: Maler 1901

Plate 49
Ruler holding flaming torch (Lintel 24)
Yaxchilan, Mexico
c. AD 725
Limestone
43¼ x 30½ in. (109.7 x 77.3 cm)
Courtesy of the Trustees of The British Museum
1886-317

Lady Xok, the most prominent wife of Shield Jaguar during his lifetime, commissioned three extraordinary sculptures for the front doorways of Structure 23: Lintels 24, 25, and 26. Made during a time of unprecedented wealth and expansion for Yaxchilan, these works mark the emergence of the city from a long and obscure era of troubles into an artistic and political renaissance.

Each lintel was set so that the figural portion faced downward and the glyphic text that runs along one side faced out to form part of the building's facade (lamentably, the German explorer Rockstroh cut off and lost Lintel 24's text in the 19th century) (Fig. 36). All three show the royal couple interacting with one another, with the queen always placed on the privileged right side. They are arranged in such a way that any visitor would have first passed under the depiction of Lady Xok and faced Shield Jaguar before entering the dark chambers. Today, we see them oriented in the manner of wall panels, but they were never viewed this way in antiquity.

Seen in order, Lintels 24-25-26 seem to follow a visual sequence. On Lintel 24, Lady Xok kneels in front of Shield Jaguar, who holds a torch. She runs a thorn-studded rope through her tongue, the principal form of blood sacrifice performed by royal women. On Lintel 25, we see the apparent sequel: Lady Xok now burns blood-spattered paper, creating clouds of smoke in which she witnesses an armed warrior emerging from the mouth of a Vision Serpent. Finally, on Lintel 26, as if acting on the results of divine communication, she prepares Shield Jaguar for war, extending to him both his shield (on the eroded lower half of the sculpture) and his jaguar helmet.

The dates attributed to these events in the accompanying texts, interestingly enough, posit no such sequence: 24 places the bloodletting in AD 709, 25 sets the vision in 681, and 26 calls for arms in 724. The effect is to expand the story and encompass the repetition of these rites over time.

The texts originally set on the edges—together with Lintel 23, set over a side door—establish Structure 23 as an *otoot* or "house" belonging to

Lady Xok and describe the dedications of its carvings in 723. Lintel 26 was finished later and carries a record of its own completion date in 724. The project was completed in 726, marked with an *och k'ahk'* or "fire-entering" ceremony.

What makes these works so exceptional is not only the drama of their subject matter—although that is clearly one key to their attraction—but also the quality of their execution. The relief is unusually high, making it possible for the sculptors to work at a variety of depths and to introduce a modeled, almost three-dimensional approach. The surface detail, from the pearls sewn to the feathers that trim the border of Lady Xok's dress on Lintel 24 to the flower-jeweled headband of Shield Jaguar on Lintel 26, are acutely observed; no other Maya sculptures capture the luxuriant quality of the textiles seen here. The glyphic captions suggest architectural frames, transporting the observer from one interior setting to another.

For generations thereafter, sculptors at Yaxchilan engaged in a dialogue with the works of Structure 23, emulating them with new carved lintels and at least one stela. This gives us some sense that it is not simply a modern eye that puts them on a pedestal. Maya sculptors also signed these works, and Lintel 26 carries the name of a foreign sculptor, raising the possibility that that this eminent school began with outside help

These lintels are the first at Yaxchilan to carry figural scenes; earlier examples were restricted to glyphic text (Plate 70). What we see here is a development in the idea of narrative: from a sequence in which individual doorways effectively act as pages in a book, to one in which events unfold in illustrated form, like murals or vase paintings. Shield Jaguar's successors would repeat the formula many times—but never match the essential quality of the originals.

The British explorer Alfred Percival Maudslay brought Lintels 24 and 25 to the British Museum in 1882 and 1883. Teobert Maler, an Austrian explorer who worked for Harvard's Peabody Museum, explored the rubble in the right-hand doorway of the structure in 1897 and found Lintel 26, which was taken to the Museo Nacional de Antropología e Historia in 1964. Although they have appeared individually in a number of exhibitions, the three lintels have not been seen together since Structure 23 collapsed in the rainforest.

Reference: Schmidt et al. 1998, p. 592

Plate 50

Woman conjuring a giant snake (Lintel 25)

Yaxchilan, Mexico
c. AD 725
Limestone
46½ x 29⅛ in. (118.0 x 74.0 cm)
Courtesy of the Trustees of The British Museum
1886.316

Plate 51 (opposite)

Ruler, his spouse, and a jaguar headdress (Lintel 26)

Yaxchilan, Mexico
c. AD 725
Limestone
84⅝ x 33½ x 10⅝ in. (215.0 x 85.0 x 25.0 cm)
Museo Nacional de Antropología—INAH, Mexico
10-9790

Plate 53

Figurine of a woman at her loom

Jaina, Mexico
AD 600–800
Ceramic
6 11/16 x 3 15/16 x 6 5/16 in. (17.0 x 10.0 x 16.0 cm)
Museo Nacional de Antropología—INAH, Mexico
10-78164

Several examples are known of the woman weaver at her loom, but this particular one, excavated on Jaina Island in the early 1960s, is the finest. Not only is the woman herself rendered with an intent gaze and handsome face, but the attention to the backstrap loom itself is also meticulous. In her right hand she holds a batten, for tightening threads; at the edge of the cloth, the heddles, which hold the threads apart and allow for easier work, are indicated, as are the sticks at the end of the loom and their attachment to the tree stump.

Maya women, like this one, often sit cross-legged rather than kneel, unlike most women of ancient Mesoamerica. A hole in her right shoulder turns her into a whistle that would have made a player hold the object sideways.

Reference: Schele 1997, pp. 40–41

Plate 52

Cylinder vessel with basket-work decoration

Mexico or Guatemala
AD 600–800
Ceramic
5 x 4 3/4 (base), 5 1/4 (rim) in. (12.7 x 12.1 x 13.3 cm)
Duke University Museum of Art. Gift of Mr. Ray Biagiotti
1978.37.3

Maya artists relished imitation of one material with another, particularly in painted renderings that we read as *trompe l'oeil*, in which the eye is "tricked." Here the artist has painted the surface in clay slip in such a way as to make the observer see woven basketry.

None of these perishable works has survived from the 1st millennium AD, and so carved or painted basketwork is our only record of the forms and decoration. Today, among traditional Maya communities, most weaving, whether of cloth or baskets, is considered "women's work," although prehispanic practice is not known.

Reference: Reents-Budet 1994, p. 331

Plate 54

Carved cylinder vessel with depiction of body painting

Yucatan, Mexico
AD 600–800
Ceramic
4 3/16 x 5 7/8 in. (10.6 x 15.3 cm)
American Museum of Natural History
30.3/2484

One of the most important but least understood facets of ancient Maya symbolism were the designs painted on the human body. Lords and ladies, gods and goddesses, all wore painted adornment ranging from simple blocks of color to intricate abstract or figural motifs. Some of these patterns may be reflected in the raised sculptural designs on human bodies, although it is difficult to distinguish body-paint from tattooing or scarification.

On this carved pot in the Chochola style, one of the Hero Twins, Hunahpu, identified by prominent spots on body and cheek, paints spiral designs on a young woman, probably a goddess. She holds out a shell paint pot (Plate 67) for the painter to refill his brush. The text includes the hieroglyph for *cheeb*, or "quill" (below)—though this may be an earlier word for "brush" altered by contact with the 16th-century Spanish and their writing technology.

Reference: Coe and Kerr 1998, p. 149

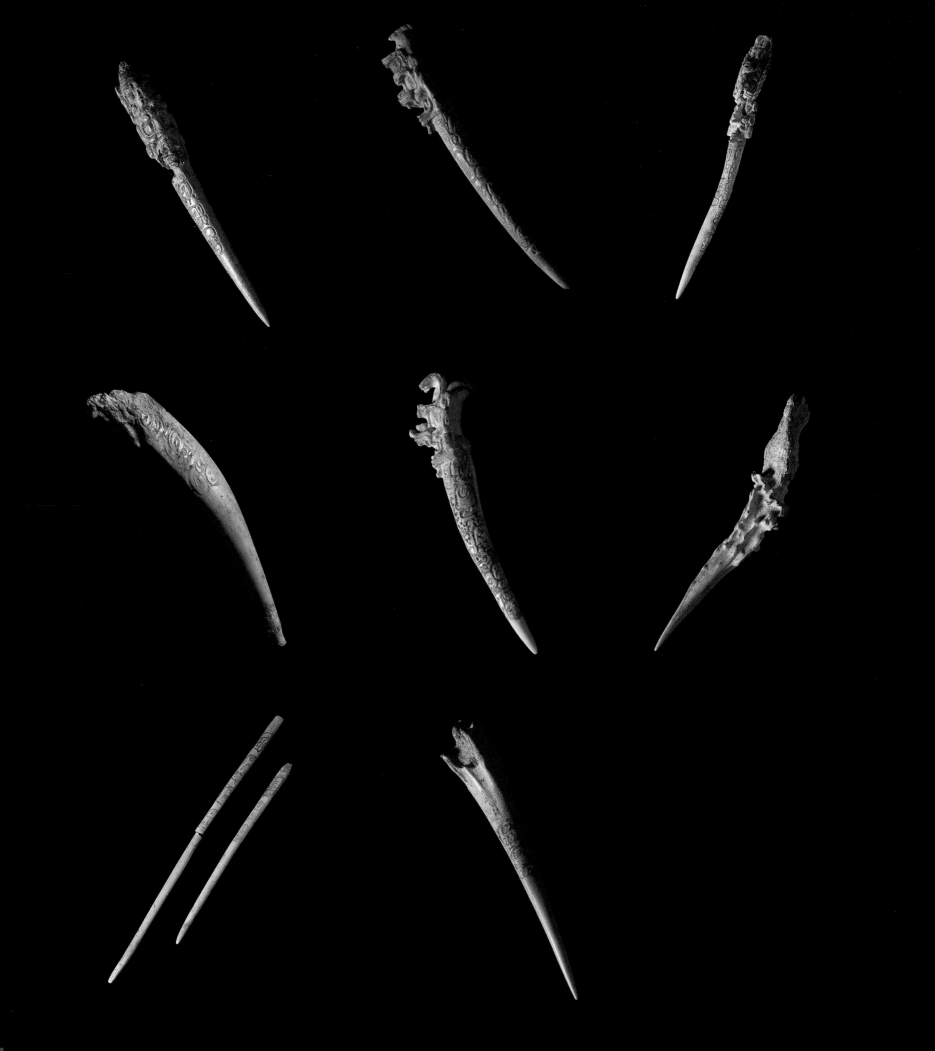

Plate 55

Nine carved bones

Tomb 2, Structure 23, Yaxchilan, Mexico
AD 700–760
Bone
Lengths: 2½–4¾ in. (6.3–12.0 cm)
Dirección de Estudios Arqueológicos—INAH, Mexico
10–342459 0/2, 10–342465, 10–342524, 10–342604,
10–342605, 10–342606, 10–629685, 10–342554

Archaeologist Roberto García Moll discovered carved bones, carved deer antlers, and inscribed stingray spines in Tomb 2 and Tomb 3 within Structure 23 of Yaxchilan. Most came from a small bundle that had been placed at the feet of the interred male of Tomb 2 (pp. 268–270). The short texts inscribed on these objects name Lady Xok or her husband Shield Jaguar, providing important data linking these burials to this king and queen.

Plate 56

Two vases

Yaxchilan, Mexico
AD 700–760
Alabaster
6 11/16 x 5 11/16 in. (17.0 x 14.5 cm)
11 3/8 x 6 5/8 in. (29.0 x 16.8 cm)
Dirección de Estudios Arqueológicos—INAH, Mexico
10–342477, 10–342478

Ancient artisans worked alabaster, a translucent gypsum often quarried in caves, into the forms of objects and vessels. Partly finished works from other parts of Mexico indicate that stone drills were used to create vessels of this sort. The Maya valued translucency in their materials; although alabaster occurs in many colors in Mexico (one thinks of the so-called "onyx" chess sets made today), Maya examples are almost always a snowy white. Most date to the 8th century, and few have been found in Guatemala or Yucatan.

These two examples come from Tomb 2, where archaeologist Roberto García Moll found them outside the mortuary bundle that held the remains of the great king Shield Jaguar (d. 742), where they were in association with other artifacts, including an obsidian axe (Plate 102) and 19 jaguar claws.

Plate 57

Figurine of woman preparing food

Jaina, Mexico
AD 600–900
Ceramic
7 1/2 in. (19.1 cm)
Yale University Art Gallery
Stephen Carlton Clark, B.A. 1903, Fund
1973.88.4

With one hand extending a flat corn cake, or tortilla, this seated noblewoman provides a rare depiction of the preparation of food among the ancient Maya. A fattened dog sits at her left and another head of a dog, presumably now ready to be served up as a meal, rests in the low bowl. The large vessel in front of her would seem to hold yet more of the repast she seems to offer.

Because griddles, or *comales*, traditionally used to make tortillas, are unknown among the Maya until AD 900, scholars have generally assumed that the Maya consumed their maize as tamales, rather than tortillas, until that time. Yet thick tortillas could easily have been cooked on hot stones at the edge of the hearth, as this work would seem to attest.

References: Kubler ed. 1986, p. 135; Schele 1997, p. 42; S. Coe 1994

Plate 58
Figurine of old woman with young child
Jaina, Mexico
AD 600–800
Ceramic
4 7/16 in. (11.3 cm)
Princeton University Art Museum. Gift of Gillett G. Griffin
2003-26

The Maya goddess of weaving, childbirth, and the end of the world, known as Chak Chel, "Great Rainbow," serves as midwife at the birth of at least some Maya gods, as portrayed explicitly on a vessel where she assists a pregnant young woman, possibly the Moon Goddess. Here, the twisted cotton cords in her hair and her wrinkled, sagging body suggest the supernatural midwife, although she is depicted with the empathy felt for a human grandmother. The handsome, idealized face and tapering head of the child she restrains suggest the young Maize God, to whom she now serves as nursemaid.

References: Schele 1997, p. 48; Taube 1994

Plate 59
Figurine pair of couple embracing
Jaina, Mexico
AD 600–900
Ceramic
10 1/8 x 5 1/4 x 3 3/8 in. (25.7 x 13.3 x 8.6 cm)
Dumbarton Oaks Research Library & Collections,
Washington, D.C.
PC.B.195

Erotic imagery is rare in Maya art, but sexual
tension reveals itself in this pair of lovers, an old
man and a young woman. He gently tugs the
woman's skirt and rests his hand above her knee
while they intently gaze into one another's eyes
and wrap their arms around one another's waist.
His toothless face sags and his body is slight and
shrunken, but the lovers study one another
knowingly.

The voluptuous young woman, with quilted
cotton strips forming a crown-like adornment,
probably represents the young Moon Goddess,
while the old man in deer headdress may well
represent her spouse, the aged Sun God, who
disguised himself as a deer in an attempt to catch
her in an act of infidelity.

A craftsman fashioned the body of this work
with a mold: it is hollow, and the back of the object
features a whistle that is played with the figurine
upside-down. The heads are solid and were made
by hand; the faces are exquisite in their detail and
the mastery of sober expression. Blue, white, and
yellow paint were added after firing.

Plate 60

Figurine of Chak Chel

Jaina, Mexico
AD 600–800
Ceramic
10 1/4 in. (26.0 cm)
Princeton University Art Museum. Gift of J. Lionberger Davis,
Class of 1900
y1965.197

The goddess Chak Chel embodied the power of
aged, post-menopausal women. She served as
midwife to young women, and, on painted ceramic
vessels, she attends the birth of both the Maize
God and the rabbit, offspring of the Moon
Goddess. She is also the warrior who unleashes
floods at the end of a previous creation of the earth,
and it is in this particular role that she appears on
this figurine.

Armed with a shield (the weapon in her hand
is modern), Chak Chel appears here as a fearsome
warrior. Her wrinkled, craggy face takes on aspects
of the jaguar, underscored by the snarling mouth
and feline ears she wears in her headdress.

Reference: Schele 1997, p. 165

Plate 61

Cylinder vessel with Itzamna, Moon Goddess, and scribe

Mexico or Guatemala

AD 700–800

Ceramic

9 5/16 x 5 9/16 in. (23.7 x 14.2 cm)

Virginia Museum of Fine Arts, Richmond. The Adolph D. and Wilkins C. Williams Fund

77.98

Itzamna was the paramount sky god of the ancient Maya. Always old and wise, he invented writing and the calendar, according to ethnohistoric sources; and indeed, on this vessel, Itzamna wears the spangled turban and pectoral ornament characteristic of some scribes, while hieroglyphs painted on a wall in the scene also make some mention of scribal activity.

Although information on the familial relationships among the Maya gods is sketchy, Itzamna is often shown with the extended forehead and fringe of hair associated with ripe corn: he may well have been father to the Maize God, who often presents himself at Itzamna's court. Indeed, the visitor facing Itzamna on this red-background vase may be the Maize God in the guise of a hummingbird—indicated solely by a long beak and its pierced flower. Behind Itzamna sits the Moon Goddess, explicitly identified by the sweeping crescent moon behind her. Their relationship is unclear. They share a throne, usually to be taken as a sign of marriage, although here she might be an eligible young daughter. The throne itself is marked with cosmic symbols, identifying their location in the heavens.

Reference: Coe 1978, pp. 73–74

Plate 62

Three spondylus shells with three jade beads

Tonina, Mexico

AD 600–800

Shell, jade

Diams.: shells, 2 15/16–3 3/4 in. (7.5–9.5 cm); beads, 6/16 in. (1 cm)

Museo de Sitio de Toniná, Chiapas—INAH, Mexico

Shells, 10-569368 1/3, 10-569367 1/2, 10-569350 1/2; beads, 1-601697 5/10

Both the spondylus shell and the jade bead are characteristic of Maize God regalia, especially when worn by women. The spondylus usually appears over the groin; even at the time of the Spanish invasion, Bishop Landa would comment on the wearing of a shell below the waist by maidens.

These examples from Tonina, however, like others at the site, formed building dedicatory caches. Part way up the structure, the Maya nestled "sets"—a spondylus with jade bead inside—between ashlars, just at the juncture of building corners. At some other sites cinnabar (the ore of mercury) may have been added inside the mollusk.

CHAPTER 4

Word and Image in the Maya Court

Fig. 39 Detail of Yaxchilan Lintel 48, Plate 70. These six full-figure hieroglyphs open the text, collectively establishing a day in AD 526 as the date.

The Maya court styled itself, among all its other ideals and paragons, as a house of artists and scribes. That the perfect palace should be seen as something of a workshop may surprise modern observers, but this must be read within a mythic context in which the gods played the role of skilled craftspeople and, at the highest level, the "makers" of all things on earth. Accordingly, the Maya elite regarded artistic ability favorably and gave key roles in the intellectual and administrative functioning of the court to those with such gifts. Indeed, deeply engaged with arcane and recondite knowledge, artists and scholars, scribes and administrators, were often one and the same person. The nobility rubbed shoulders with, and to some degree idealized themselves as, a professional class of artisans. Maya art was not only created in the service of a courtly culture, but within and by it.

Even centuries later, at the time of the Spanish invasion, threads of this courtly culture survived. Certainly the very different Maya polities of 16th-century Yucatan had governing courts that performed many of the same functions. Bishop Diego de Landa, second bishop of Yucatan and a man burning to extirpate idolatry, described a priestly elite who were responsible for apportioning priests and books to smaller towns. He went on to say:

> "[The elite] taught the sons of the other priests and second sons of the lords who brought them for this purpose from their infancy, if they saw that they had an inclination for this profession. The sciences which they taught were the computation of the years, months, and days…and their antiquities and how to read and write with the letters and characters, with which they wrote, and drawings which illustrate the meaning of the writings."[1]

Like their 16th-century descendants, the Maya of the 1st millennium used one term, Ah Tz'ib (*aj tz'ib*), or "painter," to describe all those who worked with a brush, whether they created images or texts (Fig. 40a).[2] In a phenomenon almost unknown in the ancient world outside Classical Greece, a few Maya artisans signed their works, so we know something of their names and status in society (Plate 85). A separate title, perhaps to be read Ah Uxul (*aj uxul*), "carver," identified those who practiced sculpture or incision using tools of bone, tusk, or the volcanic glass called obsidian (Fig. 40b), and the term Baah Uxul (*b'aah uxul*), or "head carver," is even known (Fig. 40). Carvers often worked together on monuments—up to seven signatures could appear on the same stone—while there is good reason to believe that both scene and text on almost all Maya vases are in a single hand. Signatures tend to have a regional bias, those on sculpture appearing predominantly in the west of the Maya realm, and those on pots in the central zone of the Peten. The artisans' names and elevated titles often place them within the elite class and doubtless quite a number were of noble birth. In

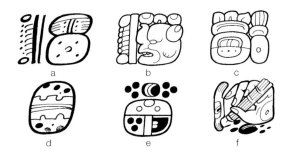

Fig. 40 Titles and glyphs associated with artists: a. Ah Tz'ib, "painter"; b. Ah Uxul? "carver"; c. Itz'aat, "wise one"; d. Huun, "book"; e. Abak? "soot/ink"; f. Utz'ib? "his painting" (note the ink sign beneath).

fact, all young nobles may have received some scribal training—the graffiti in Maya palaces is often literate and demonstrates skill in sketching both architectural scenes and humans caught in motion. Worth noting here is the complete absence of women's names from the ranks of scribes, although there is no particular reason to think of women as illiterate: had paper not survived from 1st-millennium Japan, we would not know of women authors in that ancient society, and the same might pertain to the ancient Maya.

At Aguateca, in Guatemala, Takeshi Inomata has excavated the house of a noble artist, which was set in the midst of a courtly complex within shouting distance of the king's own residence. Here he found tools, including tiny mortars for grinding pigments and diminutive axes, amid dozens of half-worked pieces of jade abandoned during the fire that destroyed the city shortly after AD 800. One recovered shell fragment names its lord as an *itz'aat*, a scribal title meaning "wise one," emphasizing the relationship between scribes and significant offices: bureaucrats, accountants, and notaries. And what of this official's status within the city? He owned at least one finely painted Maya vase that archaeologists found tucked under a bench in his house; under what must have been siege conditions, he mustered dozens of plain vessels to store food and drink in hope of survival. Yet the royal family themselves fled the city ahead of the fire, leaving lesser courtiers, like this artist, to the conflagration.[3]

At the same time that the Maya admired the special talents of artists, they retained ambivalence toward them. Their supernatural patrons were monkey gods: not quite human in their imitation of mortals, yet gifted at mimesis (see p. 239 ff, and Plates 63–66). Monkeys were failed humans from a previous creation—creatures to be both pitied and mocked. Later, the Aztecs would comment that even simple potters can "fabricate," suggesting the transformation of the raw lump of clay into some other form.[4] Art-making was a peculiar and dangerous power, and it was important for the lordly elite to keep these savants in their places, no matter how much they admired their craft.

In all this, there is no specific word in the ancient New World for "art." Works had value because of their material (such as jade or feathers, or the expensive pigments used in paints), because of the skill and labor they took to make, or because they were associated through setting or ownership with the most exalted class of person. Yet at the same time, some works clearly transcended these notions and became exemplars that influenced everything that followed them. For example, the Yaxchilan Lintels 24, 25, and 26—so keenly appreciated by modern observers—must also have been admired by the ancient Maya at Yaxchilan. They remained in place over the doorways of Structure 23 (Fig. 36) on the main plaza, and they transformed the nature of sculpture at the site, where subsequent generations of carvers saw them and emulated them.

But we cannot begin to imagine all the contexts in which fine—and less fine—things were made. Clemency Coggins proposed some years ago that the guests at the funeral of a Tikal king in the 8th century may have painted clay vessels using identical pigments and a series of prepared "blank" pots, resulting in both inept and fine depictions, all of which were placed in the tomb together.[5] Fine painting limns the occasional clumsy and misshapen vessel, as if an adept parent painted the child's trial pot (Fig. 41). All such works help us see the family shop, where some artisans made pots and others painted, where some works must have responded to the commission, and where others sat on the shelf, in hope of a sale.

Fig. 41 Cylinder vessel, codex-style. Despite its eroded condition, this awkwardly formed vessel still reveals the confident hand of an experienced painter.

Script

Writing was one of the foremost achievements of Maya civilization, and one with far-reaching consequences for both its intellectual culture and art. Maya hieroglyphs represent a complete writing system that faithfully reflects the grammar and vocabulary of Mayan languages. In other words, lit-

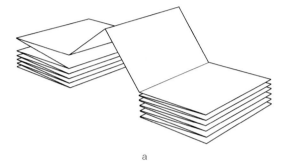

a

b

Fig. 42   a. The Maya made their books of a paper made from beaten bark, joined in sections to form a concertina-like screenfold; b. A supernatural scribe writes in such a book, here covered in jaguar pelt; detail from a painted vase.

erate members of society could have spoken aloud any text put in front of them. Invented during the 1st millennium BC but reaching its greatest sophistication during the 1st millennium AD, Maya writing is what grammatologists call a "mixed system," one that combines signs for whole words with others for syllables and vowels. At any one time the Maya recognized about 500 signs in common use. Startling progress over the past two decades has seen our ability to read the inscriptions transformed, and every year fresh decipherments offer deeper insights into past ideas and practice.

Most of what survives today are formal historical texts on stone monuments, written as terse third-person narratives. Their content dwells on the lives of kings: on ritual performances, genealogies, and political events, all embedded within lengthy calendrical notations. But those texts found in more informal contexts, such as on vases or other personal possessions, often feature very different subjects, from myths to tribute deliveries, sometimes with spoken captions or more flowery descriptions (Plate 69). They give us some glimpse into the content of innumerable lost books that once lay at the core of scholarly and administrative life at court. Many painted scenes depict scribes, both supernatural and mortal, who write and paint in jaguar-skin-bound tomes (Fig. 42a and b). Only a bare handful of late barkpaper almanacs survive today, but colonial-era accounts emphasize the range of topics they covered and the extraordinary value the Maya placed on them. Landa wrote, "We found a large number of books in these characters, and, as they contained nothing in which there were not to be seen superstition and lies of the devil, we burned them all, which they regretted to an amazing degree, and which caused them much affliction."[6] The Spanish collected from their Aztec subjects of the 16th-century tribute lists, histories, mythologies, and divinatory books: surely the Maya wrote such texts and others as well. The story of the Popol Vuh—the great Maya supernatural and historical epic set down in the Roman alphabet in the 16th century, which can be compared with the Hebrew Genesis or the Greek Odyssey—could have been set down in a hieroglyphic book.[7]

At the junction between art and writing lies calligraphy, and the Maya infused their script with the same sureness of line and richness of imagination that characterizes their image-making. The hieroglyphs range from the overtly pictorial—the heads of humans, animals and gods, body parts and depictions of everyday objects—to those that appear wholly abstract (Plates 72, 73). Signs crowd close to one another—some genuinely fused together—challenging the eye to unravel their constituent parts. The resulting blocks of text resemble more the carpet page of a medieval manuscript than the linear registers of Old World writing.

The fluid character of Maya script developed at the point of a brush and found its natural home on the pages of books and in ceramic and mural painting. However, in the 8th century we see a few instances where painting briefly escapes into stone carving, exemplified by the hand of the master scribe or scribes who painted the templates for the "Creation [Throne] Panel" and the "Tablet of the 96 Glyphs" at Palenque (Plates 119–121, 122; Figs. 43, 71). Here, in work comparable to the best of Islamic and Chinese calligraphy, the brush seems to dance across its stony page. Using a fine chisel, probably of obsidian but perhaps of flint, the painted line has been cut into the stone, retaining both whiplash lines and flourishes that waver from thick to thin, as ink might pulse through a brush or pen.

Such was the value placed on writing both as an art form and a mark of social distinction that many vessels carry "pseudo-glyphs"—designs that merely imitate writing. This practice supports the idea that literacy in Maya society was very largely restricted to the highest echelons. Lower classes aspired to the real thing but lacked the wherewithal, or perhaps the permitted rank, to commission a literate work. Pseudo-glyphs also became common among non-Maya speakers in Honduras, where all that mattered was that it looked like writing.

"Full-figure" hieroglyphs represent the deepest expression of the interplay between Maya art and writing. Here signs expand into whole creatures—or perhaps conversely whole creatures reduce themselves to signs—in animated poses that force legibility to its very limits and verge on elaborate, highly decorative, puzzles (Plates 70, 71, 75). This baroque form of writing reached its highest achievement in the eastern cities of Copan and Quirigua during the 8th century, but the earliest dated example comes from Yaxchilan, dedicated around AD 550.

Fig. 43   The Tablet of 96 Glyphs, Palenque, drawing. This small panel, probably a throne seat, exhibits calligraphic flair in which the chisel replicates the line of the brush.

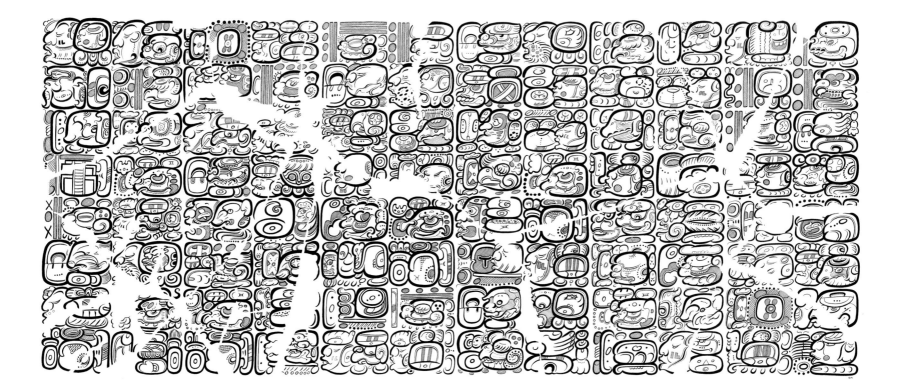

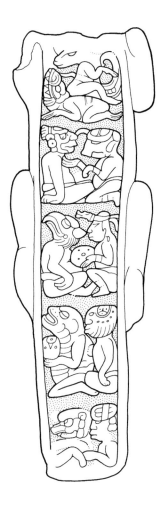

Fig. 44 Carved from a bone, this crocodile features tiny full-figure hieroglyphs on its belly (Plate 71).

The conventions of writing and art-making intersected continually for the Maya. Sculptors shaped quarried limestone blocks into freestanding shafts of stone, called stelae (sing. stela), that modeled themselves on the rough proportions of height to width common for manuscripts. In turn, these pages generally conform, more or less, to the proportions of the human body. In this, we see the Maya human form not only as the obvious basis for human representation, but also as an underpinning of more subtle aspects of Maya design. Screenfold books may have run horizontally as well as vertically (the orientation of the surviving Maya manuscripts), like the surviving books of Oaxaca. Is it the book that influences the overall configuration of Maya art, or is it the human body itself? We may never know, but we can see in these relationships a fundamental humanism unique in ancient Mesoamerica to the Maya.

Numbers, Mathematics, and Calculation

The modern world has long known of the ancient Maya mastery of numbers. Like all Mesoamerican peoples, they based their counting system in 20, rather than 10, although indigenous peoples in other parts of the western hemisphere, including the Iroquois and the Incas, favored the decimal. The Maya also developed the most sophisticated calendars of the New World, chronicling several observable cycles of time—solar, lunar, venutian, martian, all with unequalled accuracy—along with several documentable but invisible cycles—9 days, 819 (the sacred numbers 7 x 9 x 13 = 819) days, and most importantly, 260 days. All these cyclical calendars operated alongside a Long Count calendar, a continuous reckoning of all days elapsed since a supernatural zero date in 3114 BC. The Long Count, which was established in the 1st millenium BC, was calculated by periods of days (*k'in*), 20 days (*winal*), 360 days (*tun*), 20 x 360 days (*katun*), and 400 x 360 days (*baktun*). Like our calendar, the Maya calendar put emphasis on years that closed out "round" numbers, like the turn of our centuries or decades. That "zero" date back in 3114 BC was the completion of a period of 13 *baktuns*, and so the forthcoming completion of 13 *baktuns* on 23 December 2012 should simply turn over from one cycle to another, as do our millennia. Although scholars have quarreled about the correlation between the Maya Long Count records and our own calendar, we use here the revised Goodman-Martinez-Thompson standard (and the Julian calendar). The correlation, which is based in 16th-century records, agrees with radiocarbon dates of the 1st millennium AD.

We know from a handful of monuments—for it was far from common—that the Maya also reckoned numbers of enormous magnitude. Knowing that the *baktun* was 20 *katuns* squared, one can see how quickly the order of magnitude of the periods of the calendar progressed in the Maya mind. In addition to such depth of time, the Maya also had a precision of time, and a facility in calculating numbers of days that our own records do not offer—for example, the number of days between any given first Monday in September and Christmas is something that a school registrar knows by heart but anyone else would have to sit down and count out, day by day. Although not a single transaction—no record of tax, trade, or census—survives, the Maya probably kept good account of such matters, and would have recorded such items using a pure vigesimal system, that is, without the 360-day feature of the calendar that makes a rough accommodation to solar time.[8]

Early in the 20th century, the recognition of the sophistication of their calculations catapulted Maya civilization onto a unique plane, and they came to be known as peaceful timekeepers. Although such a vision of the Maya has been thoroughly discredited, we would emphasize that the Maya did have a notion of time and counting in the ancient New World that exceeded the achievements of all others. Their own interest in the very "art" of this effort can be seen in the emphasis on calligraphy in the reckoning of time, the subject most likely to be inscribed in the full-figure glyphs.

Painting and Ceramics

The greatest ceramic painting workshops developed in the central heartland of Maya civilization, where artists learned to paint with thin suspensions of unwieldy clay slip: like the Greeks, the Maya knew neither glass nor glaze. Artisans in small ateliers worked collectively to make Maya ceramics, first acquiring the clay—usually from locally known sites along riverbanks—and then shaping coils into the tall cylinder shapes characteristic of the best workshops. Women may have made the vessels, but the signatures tell us only of painters who were men. Pigments of minerals—particularly iron ores for the reds and oranges, along with other minerals for blue and green that have since dulled to grey—were ground into the slip and then painted onto unfired vessels using brushes or possibly even pens.[9]

At the same time that particular styles characterize particular regions, individual artists sometimes mastered multiple styles. A handful of pots in "black background" (Plate 35)—or what would be called red-figure in the Greek vase painting tradition—were completed by artists who also worked in more conventional formats. A single workshop produced extraordinary work at the site of Naranjo, with vessels in the conventional red and orange on cream of the region, black on cream, and the "black background" style all at once. One of its painters, a master who signed himself Ah Maxam (*aj maxam*), created one of these pots for a son of the Naranjo king around AD 780 (Plate 85).

Little remains today of the painted architecture revealed on vases, but the jaguar pelt motifs, *k'in*, or "sun," signs, and quatrefoil "opening" signs common on painted vessels probably characterized the ancient buildings themselves. Such motifs would have sanctified the highly restricted spaces of courtly activity. Of the themes treated in Maya vase painting, few are as common as palace interiors where rich description shows us the actors, furnishings, and costuming that lie beyond any archaeological recovery. Books and scribes often appear in these palace scenes, so that one can see the relationship between the artists' milieu and the subject matter of their works.[10] They are *of* the court, and they also *are* the court.

Artists decorated elite structures in both abstract and figural painting in rare cases—most notably in the incomparable program at Bonampak, Mexico. At first sight these unnamed muralists would appear to have transplanted work from ceramics to the stuccoed walls. However, recent study of the paintings of the north walls of Rooms 1 and 2 has revealed an animated contour line akin to the work of monumental sculptors—particularly those at Yaxchilan—based on the way artists worked body details, especially hands, feet, and ears. As far as modern archaeology can tell, the ceramic tradition itself did not flourish in the Maya west to the degree that it did in its center, in the Peten of modern-day Guatemala and southern Campeche; rather, sculpture and monumental painting reigned. We can see that artistic practice was not uniform across the Maya region, and that different expertise thrived in different regions.

We can see some of the more unusual talents of artists on ceramic vessels that depict the *way* (pronounced "why") or "spirit companions" of the lordly elite (Plate 88). This bewildering variety of supernatural creatures—some based in human forms, some in animal—bear texts that identify them as belonging to particular kings or their kingdoms, and, as if to confound modern understanding of them, to gods as well. These *way* seem analogous to mystical alter-egos—or what is usually called the *nagual* elsewhere in Mexico. They often reveal creatures of horror and outright evil, visible nightmares of danger and putrefaction—even representing "animated diseases," as David Stuart has recently suggested.[11] The ability of the elite Maya artist to conjure such imagery and put it to paint must have signaled his status and even his own priestly powers. That the subject matter was not appropriate for stone may also tell us something about the privacy and inner workings of the court: these are aspects that the lords might not have sought to broadcast.

Like other art forms, vase painting also engaged the aesthetic based in the Maya book. Painted with a black clay slip against a cream background and rimmed with red—"the red and the black" as the later Aztecs metaphorically called all writing—the surfaces of "codex-style" vessels are pages wrapped into a cylindrical form (Plates 32, 85). By the 8th century, when the majority of cylinders were painted, the vessels had taken on a life of their own, and we cannot know how engaged they were with the painting of books. Just as dramatically as the cylinder form had arrived, it vanished by 800 or so and a new, jar-shaped pot became prevalent, decorated with a pressed, mass-produced imagery. Screenfold books, by contrast, continued to be made well after the Maya abandoned their greatest cities.

Other local carving and sculpting traditions in clay developed, particularly in the Maya west. The practice of carving vessels when the drying clay reached a fragile leather-hard stage reached its highest development in western Yucatan, where the modern town of Chochola has given its name to the style (Plates 54, 76). Artists in the region also commonly used resist paints—utilizing beeswax, a product of the region—to render what often look like batik designs on these wares. Other vessels were formed in molds, sometimes to be retouched and finished by hand. In areas such as Comalcalco, in the far west of the Maya area where local limestone is absent, clay was baked into tile-like bricks for building temples and palaces. These often carry improvised sketches, graffiti that were hidden once the bricks were laid atop one another, and thus with no thought to future sight (Plate 86). The versatility of clay naturally made it a favorite for modeling figurines. Although they are found across the Maya realm, figurines from the island of Jaina are the most famous (e.g. Plates 41, 42, 44, 94–97). Larger works in clay, such as the incense-burner stands from Palenque, had important roles in ritual (Plates 123–125, 128).

Another plastic material widely employed both for architectural decoration and small works of sculpture was stucco. To make stucco, the Maya burned limestone or seashells until they had a fine powder, which they could then refine and mix with water to make a thick, quick-drying paste. At Palenque, Tonina, and Ek Balam, artists built up layers of the stucco paste on armatures of small stones. Flint hard, stuccoes made for superb architectural sculptures (Plates 91, 113, 114), from larger-than-lifesize figures to delicate renderings of hieroglyphs (Plates 73, 89, 92, 115, 116).

The Maya incised smooth passages of conch shell or bone—usually the femurs of jaguars, tapirs, deer, or humans—with a flowing line (Plate 69). These materials were of continuing significance to their owners, and the inscriptions they carry very often state "this is the jaguar bone of so-and-so." In the case of shell, its natural shape or surface patterning was exploited wherever possible (Plates 67–69, 83, 84).

Another side to the Maya's manipulation of natural materials was their exploration of the replication of perishable objects in stone and clay. The Maya must have used gourds for most common vessels, but in one example they shaped a ceramic vessel into a squash—and then named the vessel as one for their precious chocolate drink, and the prized possession of the king of Acanceh, in northern Yucatan (Plate 74). In another instance a skilled draftsman painted a pot to make it resemble a basket, replicating not only the design that forms the woven basketry but also recognizing the thick-and-thin broken lines the pattern requires (Plate 52). These works strike us as clever today, and the Maya much admired cleverness: in the Popol Vuh it is neither their power nor their humility that makes us admire the Hero Twins but rather their quick wittedness and ingenuity.

Carving in Stone: Lithics and Jade

Along with interest in artifice and transformation, Maya artists also had a fascination for materials in the raw, especially where mastery could be achieved over the most obdurate of them. Specialists knapped flint and obsidian from quarried blanks brought to them as large ovals—whose outline forms define the limits of many "eccentrics" as they are known today (Plates 78–82). Among the most common motifs were human profiles, reduced in flint to their simplest outlines in the lithic equivalent of rapid brushstrokes—though in fact the product of laborious and masterful chipping. They preferred a very dark flint for these eccentrics, and although flint itself is a common material, the source for this particular blackish-brown flint material has never been found.

The Maya prized jade over all other stones, seeing in its range of blues and greens the color not only of the growing maize but also of the sky, oceans, and forest—the color of life itself. The earlier Olmec civilization had mastered jade carving by the 1st millennium BC, and the Maya adopted many of their techniques for string-sawing, drilling, and grinding. Like the Olmecs, the Maya manufactured jewelry and figurines (Plates 24–27, 47, 118), but their innovation was to carve large, flat panels of jade with figural representations engraved on them—often a Maize God or ruler joined by a dwarf—a technical tour-de-force in Mesoamerica's hardest stone (Plate 77).[12]

For all the skill and imagination of portable artworks, the ancient Maya are best known for their monumental work in stone. The entire Maya lowlands lie on a huge limestone shelf and the material for stone-carving was never far from hand. Yet the quality of the natural rock varies markedly across the region. At the great city of Calakmul, for example, the limestone is so weak and powdery that most of its monuments have been eaten away by centuries of exposure to the elements. The limestone around Palenque, by contrast, is of exceptional quality. Dense and fine-grained, it can be split readily into thin plaques ideal for wall panels, with smooth faces immediately available for outline sketching (the traces of which survive in a few cases). Easy to carve when newly exposed, this stone hardens into a resilient, buttery surface perfectly suited to detailed work (Plate 129). In upland regions sandstone was another option, best seen at Tonina, Mexico, and Quirigua, Guatemala. Relatively easy to work when first quarried, the volcanic tuff used for the magnificent three-dimensional work of Copan, Honduras, hardened to adamant after exposure to air (Plate 30). The Maya Mountains of modern-day Belize were an important source of slate, which was employed for large-scale work at nearby centers such as Caracol and transported elsewhere for fashioning into smaller items.[13]

Lost Arts: The Body, Textiles, Wood
Unlike these durable works, much of what constitutes art in its own time is ephemeral. Perhaps the best example is a medium used worldwide, the human body. The Maya painted their faces and torsos in colored blocks and designs, encoding both intelligible iconography (Plate 97) and patterns

Fig. 45 Graffiti from the Central Acropolis, Tikal, drawing. Observers of huge perishable litters sketched these images onto palace walls.

whose meanings elude us (Plate 34). Lost masterpieces of weaving and embroidery are richly represented in Maya art, forcefully demonstrating the intricate design and technical sophistication of ancient textiles (e.g. Plate 49). Equally short-lived are the efforts of feather-workers. Using a range of exotic plumes, including the rare and precious quetzal tailfeathers, they made luxuriant headdresses and high-status garments. Tropical hardwoods, many redolent with fragrance, were hewn into sculptures, musical instruments, utensils, and furniture of all kinds. Precious few of these once ubiquitous works survive; when they do their pitted and decayed surfaces make it hard to imagine their original luster (Plate 16). Papier-mâché—easily formed with manioc or cornstarch—may well have been used to create some of the immense effigies that were trooped around Maya cities like floats in a carnival, as attested in sculpted scenes and in graffiti. Of such perishable works only these secondary representations survive—a half-life in which art reflects other art (Fig. 45).

The Role of the Artist in Maya Art-Making

A carved panel from somewhere near Palenque opens a window onto the role that a noble lord could play in art production (Fig. 46). On it, a high-ranking lord and artist takes a boar's tooth and carves a stone; the text notes that the event takes place seven days after the death of the Palenque king Kan Bahlam.[14] What the noble artist works on is a great head of stone, almost identical to any one of the several such sculptures which personify the animate qualities of rock (Fig. 47). Self-descriptive, the stone object itself spells hieroglyphically *k'antuun,* "yellow/precious stone," the Maya word for limestone. We might presume, based on similar precedents, that the work served as some kind of memorial to the Palenque king. But is it the very passing of Kan Bahlam that liberates the satellite from some prohibition on representation? Does his death result not only in the memorial but also in the freedom to make the memorial? To which object does the act of carving refer? The work depicted or the very panel itself? Would the answer be clear to a contemporary viewer or is the ambiguity intentional?

Nothing like these self-conscious Maya works was being made anywhere else in ancient Mesoamerica at the time, although the allies, enemies, and trading partners of the Maya must have

Fig. 46   Emiliano Zapata Panel, drawing. A seated lord uses a tool tipped with boar tusks to fashion a personified rock.

Fig. 47   Two views of a carved leg, Piedras Negras Altar 4, drawing. The supports of Piedras Negras Altar 4 take the form of personified rocks very much like the one depicted on the Emiliano Zapata Panel (Fig. 46).

been well aware of them. As Esther Pasztory has insisted, the emphasis on different subject matter and the rejection of Maya script must have been active choices for the lords of the great city of Teotihuacan.[15] Teotihuacanos knew of the Maya system and chose not to adopt it, perhaps because the writing system in particular did not lend itself to their multiethnic, multilingual world, or because its specificity and historicity seemed antithetical to their culture.

Certainly Maya art underwent its own transformation, moving from monuments depicting single individuals to dynamic depictions of groups within architectural settings. What makes art change in this way? Most early depictions feature static Maya lords, without a strong temporal or locative inflection. Yet at the same time that such representations were made, by means of their script and the calendar, the Maya narrated the life stories of individual kings, tying their lives to those of their gods, in shifting pasts, presents, and futures that could span millions of years.

In comparison to such writing, the representation of the human figure in time and space lagged behind the inscriptions through the 6th century. Then, during the 7th and 8th centuries, the Maya artist sought to render human and divine actors in just that time and space that the text already had mastered. Because a Maya artist was also a scribe, he would have understood the full range of capability of Maya writing and arithmetic and their ability to represent time, place, and development through time. Of course, all representations always underrepresent the complexity of human actions, but the Maya scribe may well have sought greater visual representation, one with greater specificity of place and one with narration and time embedded, driven by the achievements already in place in writing and calculation.

In their greatest works of the 7th and 8th centuries, Maya artists conflated several aspects of representation, and they may have done this with a careful eye to the ways that visual and verbal representation differed, particularly with regard to pictorial space and its human occupants. Whereas Maya texts carefully record sequential moments, distinguishing events to the day and protagonists precisely, often with the naming of a location that may indicate a city or building within a city, a visual representation collapses and reduces time, while offering specificity of location—the furniture, the awnings—that is not spoken of in texts.

In the case of a work like Piedras Negras Panel 3—a depiction of the court in action created around AD 795, but picturing events from 40 years earlier—we can appreciate one of the last great engagements between Maya text and image (Fig. 48). Here we see a throne-room scene encased in a textual frame that doubles as enclosing architecture. In a composition much influenced by the asymmetry found in ceramic and mural painting, a group of naturalistic, if now rather damaged, characters sit in front of and stand alongside an enthroned ruler. Although painted scenes had included spoken captions for most of the 8th century, the first-person monologue engraved on the "back wall" of this chamber is unique in Maya monumental art. Image and script supply complementary but divergent parts of the overall message, since the climax of the text lies not in the depicted gathering—which we are told is a feast—but in the re-entry and burning of the same king's tomb 40 years in the future.

A work like Piedras Negras Panel 3 shows that the Maya artist had learned to trust what the eye sees over what the brain knows—that is, that the thigh of a sitting figure seen face-on will essentially vanish from view, for example. Maya artists can show that space is infinite, captured only in part by any frame. They cut body parts in remarkable ways by means of frames, commonly cutting a figure off, acknowledging that a part can stand for the whole. This concept of synecdoche—the part standing for the whole—was an essential notion of classical Greek and Roman poetics; in the visual arts its introduction in Europe is often heralded as a step toward modernism. For the Maya, the sense of infinite space is paired with an interest in illusionistic space: indeed the Maya saw these as two differ-

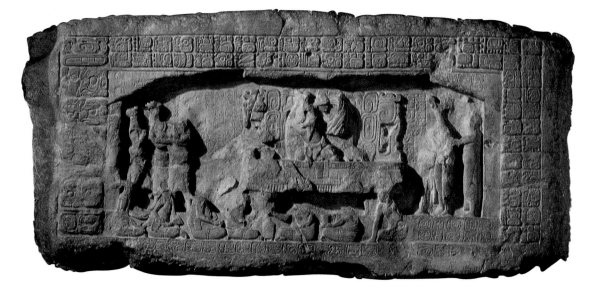

Fig. 48 Piedras Negras Panel 3. Made during the last years of the Piedras Negras court, this small but very fine carving retrospectively depicts a ruler and his courtly retinue of the mid-8th century.

ent problems, although they were for the European artist usually a single problem. The Maya established the principle that figures set higher up in architectural settings were more distant, while figures along the ground line were understood to be close, and indeed sometimes adjacent to, the viewer.

Especially in the 8th century and using all these tools, Maya artists began to assemble far more complex compositions, works that sometimes capture an event as if seen from slightly different points of view, or as if over a brief period of time, say, the time of a long exhalation or the turning of the head. Panel 3 from Piedras Negras or the Kimbell Panel (Plate 2) both feature this "ripple in time," in which the eye moves from one protagonist to another, detecting movement and progression, hierarchies, spatial relationships, and ultimately, the passage of time. The furled awnings add to the sense of transience, whether it is of the viewer's ephemeral opportunity to see (will the moment vanish?) or the event altogether. These Maya artists so mastered the word and image of the court that even now, over 1,000 years later, we catch our breath at the sense of the moment revealed, and at the mastery of the makers.

Plate 63

Sculpture of a scribe
Copan, Honduras
AD 650–800
Stone
22 7/16 x 14 9/16 in. (57.0 x 37.0 cm)
Instituto Hondureño de Antropología e Historia
CPN-P-3446

Ranking lords at Copan severed the head from the body of this sculpture, burned the head and then deposited the two parts separately into the rubble foundation of a late-8th-century structure owned and used by a lineage of scribes, according to the building's inscriptions. This sculpture presumably belonged to this same lineage that constructed the new building, but who nevertheless felt the need to "terminate" the old work.

Probably from the early 8th century, this seated scribe is about half life size and may once have been set inside a niche. He hunches forward, and although his hands rest on his knees, he's poised with brush to inscribe the next line of text, drawing pigment from the sliced shell paint pot in his left hand.

Like many other scribes, this profoundly human figure displays aspects of his simian supernatural patrons, the twin Monkey Scribes. His eyes are small and close together, his teeth visible, his forehead broad, and his nose broad and flat, all in direct counter to the reigning canons of beauty. Yet of course it is the scribe and artist who give form to what is beautiful, so in this self-abnegation, one sees a carefully cultivated representation of humility and effacement.

References: Webster ed. 1989; Schele and Miller 1986, p. 151

Plate 64
Cylinder vessel with Monkey Scribes
Mexico or Guatemala
AD 700–800
Ceramic
4 5/8 x 4 7/8 in. (11.2 x 12.4 cm)
New Orleans Museum of Art: Museum purchase, Women's
Volunteer Committee Fund and Anonymous Funds
73.13

This small vessel depicts the Monkey Scribes, twin half-brothers of the Hero Twins. Although of human body, the Monkey Scribes have monkey faces, characterized by hideous jaws and teeth, and a snake-like tongue.

The artist has worked quickly in an extremely fluid and confident line that conveys the intensity of the scribes themselves. They hold jaguar-covered books in their extended left hands; their right hands may be tied, perhaps an indication of the binding of the writing pen to the hand.

Reference: Schele and Miller 1986, p. 151

Plate 65
Human artisan
Unknown provenience
AD 250–600
Ceramic
22 7/16 in. (57.0 cm)
The Cleveland Museum of Art. John L. Severance Fund
1994.12.1

Maya artisans created these ceramic figures as a pair
to represent their divine counterparts, the patrons
of art and writing in Maya culture (see p. 239).
They appear in the Popol Vuh epic as the elder
half-brothers of the Hero Twins; they are sons of
the Maize God but of a different mother. They
mastered the arts, and they were singers and
musicians as well as carvers and painters. But
despite their talents they were also jealous bullies
who persecuted their younger siblings. The Hero
Twins eventually avenged themselves by tricking
their tormentors into climbing a tree; having
trapped them there, the Hero Twins transformed
their half-brothers into monkeys. The defeated
brothers are common subjects in ancient Maya
art where they are represented in both human
and simian form, and often, as here, as one of each.

   Both of these finely detailed figures bear their
original paint schemes and would originally have
held perishable tools, a stylus and brush, in their
hands. The simian artisan models a small mask in
his hand; a rearing serpent forms his menacing tail.
His human brother, by contrast, paints on a piece
of bark—a symbolic book since beaten bark was
the paper of the New World. The serpent heads
under his arms are simplified forms of the "number
tree"—a characteristic snake-and-tree outgrowth
marked with Maya bar and dot numbers. The pair
probably date to the 5th century; their domed bases
may have been the lids of incense burners.

Reference: Berjonneau and Sonnery eds. 1985, pp. 236–237

Plate 66
Monkey artisan
Unknown provenience
AD 250–600
Ceramic
23¼ in. (59.0 cm)
The Cleveland Museum of Art.
John L. Severance Fund
1994.12.2

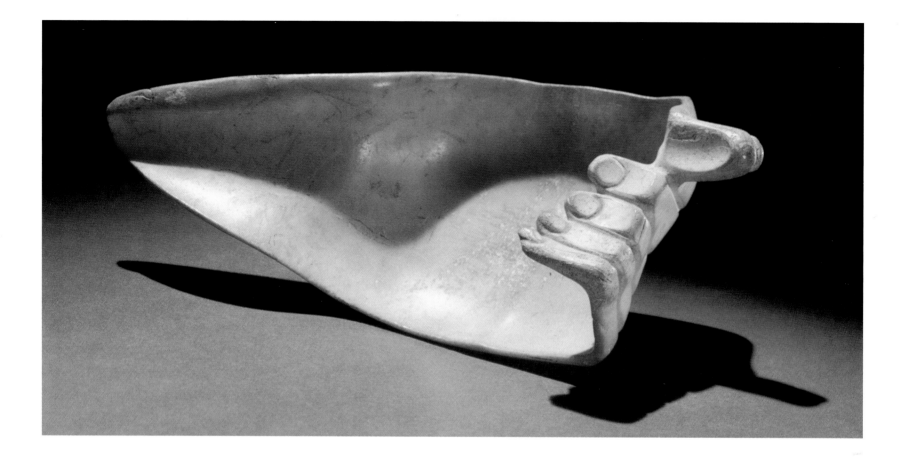

Plate 67
Paint container in form of human hand
Unknown provenience
AD 600–900
Shell
Length, 8 1/16 in. (20.5 cm)
Private Collection, on loan to The Denver Art Museum
277.1997

A Maya artist took a split conch shell and saw in it the potential to shape a sensuous representation of a cupped left hand. The back of the hand follows the curve of the shell, narrowing to an elegant wrist. The concentric and interior whorl of shell forms four fingers and the thumb. It replicates a gesture often depicted in courtly scenes.

An extraordinary personal possession, this object probably belonged to a high-ranking scribe. Scribes used split conch shells as paint pots, as represented in Plate 63. With this vessel the living left hand would have cradled the shell left hand, in what must have been a satisfying interplay between life and art.

Reference: Easby and Scott 1980, entry 199

Plate 68
Flower-shaped earflares
Unknown provenience
AD 600–800
Shell
1 3/8 x 1 13/16 in. (3.4 x 4.6 cm)
Princeton University Art Museum. Gift of Gillett G. Griffin
2003–25 a&b

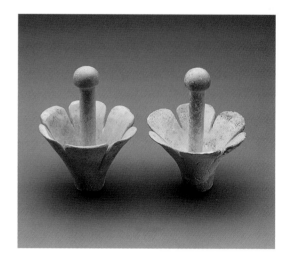

Ear ornaments had a symbolic significance for the Maya that far outstripped simple adornment or beautification. Like the eyes, the mouth, or the nostrils, they believed the ears to be conduits of vital essences—pathways to the mind, the soul, and other spiritual dimensions. Breath, scent, voice, and hearing were all related expressions of *ik'*, literally "wind," but an altogether deeper and more ethereal emanation for the Maya. The examples here take the form of six-petal flowers pierced by long pistils. Floral motifs of this kind allude to the fragrance of lordly *ik'*, a vital essence of the greatest refinement and beauty. Many such earflares are fashioned in precious greenstones, but these are cleverly worked in shell, their maker exploiting the material's natural curvature to create the bell-like blossom.

References: Stuart 1992; Houston and Taube 2000

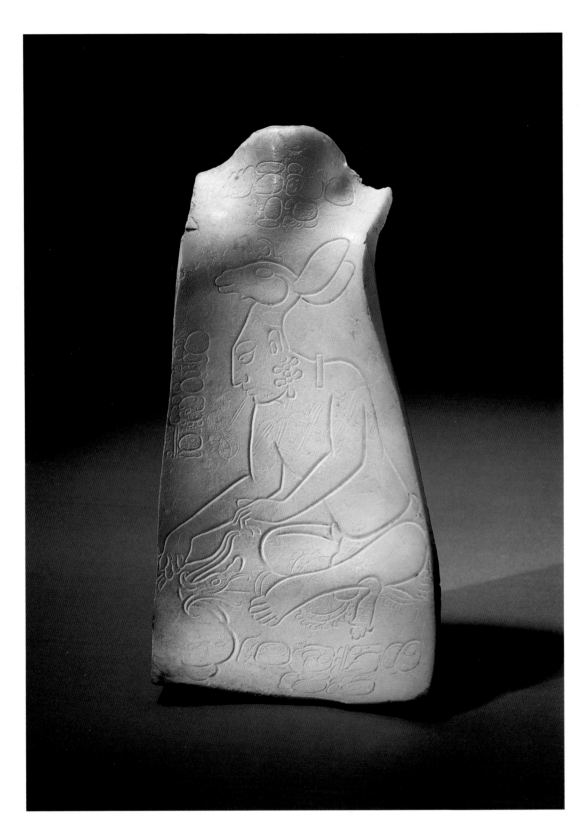

Plate 69
Shell plaque
Unknown provenience
AD 600–800
Shell
6½ in. (16.6 cm)
The Cleveland Museum of Art, The Norweb Collection
1965.550

Some of our best insights into the lifestyle and privileges of the Maya nobility come from their personal possessions: the texts and depictions they left on ceramic vessels, utensils, or items of jewelry. This plaque of marine conch shell is the vehicle for an exquisite piece of incision, a near-calligraphic illustration of a noble in deer-headdress who puffs on a cigar while gesturing daintily toward a snake coiled inside a conch shell. The flower-like medallions across his chest are either bodypaint or designs on a gauze-like textile.

The text is unusually complex for an object of this kind. As part of a spoken caption at top it refers to "great tribute" (*chak patan*); lower down "his incised-thing" (*ujuuch*) introduces the name of the owner, a lord of the Ah K'uhuun status. Some hint that it may be from the Usumacinta region comes from the glyph "Sun Water" (*k'ina'*), an unidentified location also mentioned on Plates 2 and 107, and in various texts from Palenque, Piedras Negras, and the region around Yaxchilan.

Reference: Schele and Miller 1986, p. 155

Plate 70
Lintel with full-figure hieroglyphs (Lintel 48)

Yaxchilan, Mexico
AD 526 (9.4.11.8.16 2 Kib 19 Pax)
Limestone
69 1/4 x 32 5/8 x 9 1/4 in. (176.0 x 83.0 x 23.5 cm)
Museo Nacional de Antropología—INAH, Mexico
10-80370

The most exuberant, complex, and challenging of
Maya inscriptions are those rendered in "full-figure"
form. When written this way, artists expand every
sign into the body image of which the sign was
normally part, in a sort of reverse synecdoche, or
into a new beast altogether; at other times artists
transformed conventional signs into humans,
animals, or birds. The effect was to give every sign
its own life. Twisting and turning, full-figure glyphs
entwine with one another like knotted monograms,
seeming to rage and struggle against their
confinement in the grid of the text. These glyphs
say a great deal not only about the artistry and
invention of their designers, but also about the
Maya understanding of writing as an animate force:
the Maya believed the gods themselves were actively
engaged in rendering an intelligible universe and
the sacred word. From a Maya perspective, it may
be better to see full-figure glyphs not so much as an
elaborated form as the complete one from which
"normal" hieroglyphs were simplified derivatives.

A master of the form created Lintel 48, one of
the earliest examples known. Originally a lintel
spanning a doorway in Yaxchilan Structure 12, it
was commissioned by the 10th king of the city, a
ruler we know as K'inich Tatb'u Skull II. As the
introduction to a longer text running across several
such lintels, it carries an extended date called the
Long Count. The normal numerals and units of the
count are here replaced by full-figure portraits of
their patron deities, decipherable to 9.4.11.8.16
2 Kib 19 Pax (see right) and corresponding to 11
February 526, the day of the king's accession.

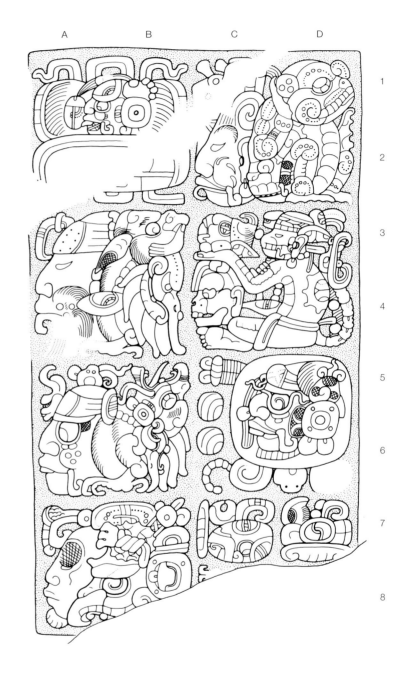

Plate 71
Bone with full-figure hieroglyphs
Unknown provenience
AD 600–800
Bone
5 5/16 x 1 3/4 in. (13.5 x 4.5 cm)—reproduced larger than actual size
Museo Nacional de Antropología—INAH, Mexico
10-1238

Full-figure glyphs of all kinds are rare, but those executed at a miniature scale presented a special challenge to their carvers. Worked from a single bone, the inscription here runs down the belly of a thick-tailed quadruped, most likely a crocodile. Due to breaks at both top and bottom, the text is incomplete. Although most of the signs can be recognized individually, it is difficult to get a clear sense of the message as a whole. The bulk of it seems to consist of a lord's name, including the title Katun Ahaw, which specifies an age of less than 20 years.

Reference: Schmidt et al. 1998, p. 628

Plate 72
Hieroglyphic column

Unknown provenience, Bonampak region
AD 715 (9.14.3.8.4 2 K'an 17 Sotz')
Limestone
22 7/16 x 9 1/16 x 8 3/8 in. (57.0 x 23.0 x 21.3 cm)
The Saint Louis Art Museum. Gift of Morton D. May
384:1978

Carved Maya columns are unusual. Though
some may have been freestanding monuments—
pedestals or altars—they more often played an
architectural role. Maya writing had intimate
relations with the built environment, whether in
identifying buildings and their particular functions
or acting as billboards for broader political messages.

The first part of this text provides the Maya date
9.14.3.8.4 2 K'an 17 Sotz', 28 April 715 (A1–C1). This
was the 13th anniversary of rule for a Bonampak
ruler nicknamed Etz'nab Jawbone (D2–C3). The
final three glyphs provide information, describing
this king's subordination to Baaknal Chaak, ruler
of the highland kingdom of Tonina (D3–D4). Their
relationship presumably began on, or close to, the
implied accession date of 5 July 702 (9.13.10.8.4
2 K'an 2 Mol), which followed on the heels of
Baaknal Chaak's successful military campaigns in
the region c. 699. Baaknal Chaak had died by 708,
and so the effect of this monument was to stress the
bonds between vassal and lord even after death.

References: Liman and Durbin 1975; Martin and Grube
2000, p. 184

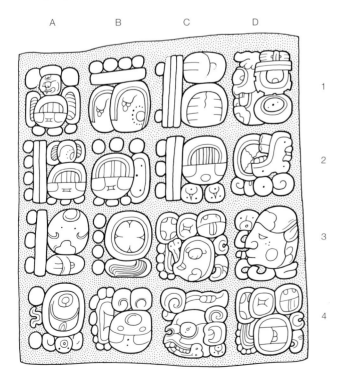

Plate 73
Stucco glyphs

Tonina, Mexico
AD 700–900
Stucco
Each, c. 2½ in. sq. (c. 6.4 cm sq.)
Museo de Sitio de Tonina, Chiapas—INAH, Mexico
10–607730–32, 10–607734–42, 10–607744–45

This group of stucco hieroglyphs—survivors from
what was once a much longer text—originally
formed part of some architectural frieze or figural
tableau. Crisply delineated, these unusually small
signs are fashioned not only by wet modeling and
impression, but also by a significant degree of dry
carving. Like random words cut from a page they
form no narrative in themselves, but do provide
a few clues to the topics originally described. In
particular, the presence of the term *yotoot,* "the
house of," points to dedication ceremonies for
the building that housed this text. Although other
signs mention dates and a ruler's name, these are
not sufficient to place these wonderful minatures
in time. Stylistically, they are best placed in the
8th century, when writing began to look back to
its origins in calligraphy and received a more fluid
and dynamic treatment.

Plate 74

Squash effigy vessel

Acanceh, Mexico
AD 600–800
Ceramic
5 9/16 x 6 7/8 in. (14.1 x 17.5 cm)
Museo Regional de Yucatán "Palacio Cantón"—INAH, Mexico
10-426169

The Maya had a strong interest in mimesis of material in their crafts, especially the reproduction of perishable items in more durable form. Here the bulbous form of a squash is reproduced as a ceramic vessel. Though the humble squash is an outwardly prosaic vegetable, like many other aspects of Maya daily life it was also imbued with mythic significance. In the ballgame described in the Popol Vuh in which the Hero Twins take on the lords of the Underworld in a life-or-death struggle, Xbalanque partially restores his decapitated brother Hunahpu by substituting a squash for the missing head.

This particular vessel was found at Acanceh, Yucatan, Mexico—a town in which ancient pyramids intermingle with a modern street-plan. The vessel carries a six-glyph text incised in an elegant hand. It begins by describing itself as a carved vessel (Glyphs 1–2) before telling us that it was intended for a particular type of cacao drink called *bukutz kakaw* (Glyph 3). The other side features the name of its owner (Glyphs 4–5). The last sign is the king's royal title or "emblem glyph" (Glyph 6). As recently demonstrated by Nikolai Grube, the glyph can be read as a combination of *akan*, the name of a Death God associated with drunkenness, and *keh*, the Yukatek word for deer. It is clear that Akankeh, the ancient name for the town, has survived unchanged for over 1300 years.

References: Grube and Nahm 1994, p. 709; Schmidt et al. 1998, p. 130

Plate 75

Full-figure hieroglyph

Tonina, Mexico
AD 600–800
Sandstone
12 5/8 x 12 5/8 in. (32.0 x 32.0 cm)
Museo del Sitio de Tonina, Chiapas—INAH, Mexico
10–601017

With a wizened face arching skyward, this sculpture represents one of the finest instances of a god's name spelled in full-figure form. The entity is a strange, human-headed bird, ostensibly an amalgam of three different subjects. First there is Itzamna (*itzamnaaj*), the supreme sky deity, identified by his flowery headband marked with the sign for darkness, *ak'ab* (see also Glyph 2). At the same time, he fuses with the aged earth deity, the toothless God N (see also Glyph 1). Finally there is the supernatural bird in the mix, with its stylized serpent mask wings and gnarled talons. Itzamna often takes an avian form such as this, which here perches on the hieroglyph *ti*. This phonetic sign is the expected suffix to the term *muut,* "bird," indicating the presence of this word in the overall reading.

An important challenge remaining in Maya studies is to achieve a fuller understanding of these fused, multi-faceted supernatural characters. Like many Egyptian deities, Maya gods can merge one into another, resisting the easy categorization often imposed upon them.

Plate 76

Cylinder vessel carved in Chochola style

Unknown provenience, Dzibilchaltun region, Yucatan, Mexico
AD 600–800
Ceramic
5½ x 5⅞ in. (14.0 x 14.9 cm)
Dumbarton Oaks Research Library & Collections, Washington, D.C.
PC.B.530

Artists of western Yucatan developed a carved style of ceramics that matches the painted codex-style vessels for calligraphic flair. Originating in western Yucatan, and linking the ancient cities of Oxkintok, Edzna, and Dzibilchaltun (and the modern towns of Chochola and Maxcanu), the Chochola technique involves taking a leather-hard clay cylinder and carving it into expressive forms that have much the feel and appearance of woodcarving. This magnificent example shows a deity who holds a personified axe; he is surrounded by fiery volutes. His shell ear ornament and mouth barbel identify him as one of the watery gods associated with Chaak. Original red pigment still adheres to much of the surface.

A short accompanying inscription names the vessel as the property of a lord from Ti'ho (*ti'jo*) (Glyph 6). When the Spanish seized the Yucatan peninsula in 1542, they founded the modern capital of Mérida on the razed remains of a city bearing this name. But the name Ti'ho is of even greater antiquity; in the years 600–800, the name appears on the monuments of Dzibilchaltun, a city in ruins just north of Mérida, one of whose lords probably commissioned this work in the 8th century.

References: Grube 1990; Schele, Grube, and Boot n.d.; Ardren 1996; Maldonado, Voss, and Góngora 2002; Tate 1985

1

2

3

4

5

6

Plate 77

Carved plaque with ruler and dwarf

Nebaj, Guatemala
AD 600–800
Jade
4³/₁₆ x 5³/₄ in. (10.6 x 14.6 cm)
Museo Nacional de Arqueología y Etnología de Guatemala
MNAE 4733

The largest known complete carved jade Maya plaques have been found not at great Maya cities but at Nebaj, in the Guatemala highlands, close to abundant sources of jade. Divers and dredges have retrieved many broken examples from the Sacred Cenote at Chichen Itza; other examples have been collected at distant Teotihuacan and Xochicalco.

Archaeologists excavated tombs and caches in the late 1940s just to the southwest of the modern Ixil Maya town of Nebaj and found remarkable wealth in offerings that spanned more than 1,000 years. The ancient inhabitants used fine Maya ceramics, acquired more pyrite mirrors than have been found anywhere else, and, after the year 1000 or so, had access to copper bells, all of which found their way into offerings. A large ceramic urn (16½ in. or 42 cm) buried under a stairway held the richest cache at the site and included several jade plaques, among them this one. Five large, round beads may have formed a quincunx, a Maya symbol for the five directions.

This jade plaque features a Maize God, or his human impersonator, surrounded by abundant foliage, sitting on a throne and leaning against a feathered cushion. He is attended by his faithful dwarf. At the sides of the plaque, heads yield maize plants, with young Maize God heads emergent.

Reference: Smith and Kidder 1951

Plate 78

Flint with human faces

El Palmar, Quintana Roo, Mexico

c. AD 711

Flint

12³/₁₆ x 9 ¹⁴/₁₆ in. (31.0 x 25.0 cm)

Museo Nacional de Antropología—INAH, Mexico

10-9648

When Carnegie Institution of Washington archaeologists moved Stela 10 at El Palmar, Quintana Roo, Mexico, in 1936, they found a cache of obsidian cores, flints, and eccentric flints at its base. Among the pieces was this extraordinary black flint, gently knapped to create human and god faces at the four corners. When Stela 10 was set in place to dedicate the Maya date 9.14.0.0.0, or AD 711, this flint was the jewel among many plainer pieces.

Although flints have been recovered throughout the Maya area, the most unusual ones have turned up to the south and east. The raw material, a fine-granular limestone quartz, was widespread in the Maya lowlands, but the best sources appear to have been in modern-day Belize. For ceremonial objects the Maya preferred black and dark brown flints whose stark silhouettes stood out against the sky. A ceremonial flint, like any other flint, yields sparks when struck.

Although the suggestion has been made that the El Palmar flint may have once been attached to a ceremonial staff, the object seems to defy a single orientation. The juxtaposed human and god heads as seen in this photograph create a cleft, possibly the place for emergence of maize and humanity.

Reference: Thompson 1936

Plate 79
Three eccentric flints
Centro Regional, Copan, Honduras
c. AD 755
Flint
12¹/₈ x 4¹⁵/₁₆ in. (30.9 x 12.5 cm), 10⁵/₈ x 5⁵/₈ in.
(27.0 x 14.4 cm), 13¹/₄ x 5⁵/₁₆ (33.5 x 13.5 cm)
Instituto Hondureño de Antropología e Historia
CPN-P-1, 2, 3

The Maya created dedicatory caches inside buildings and under stelae, time capsule assemblages but ones whose message in large part escapes modern scholars. The Maya considered eccentric flints critical to such offerings; unlike the jades that often accompany them in such offerings, flints do not occur in burials or tombs. The material itself may have been relevant: the Maya believed that flint came into being where lightning struck. These offered flints became the tangible evidence of lightning strikes.

Craftsmen at Copan excelled at carving flints, and in recent years archaeologists tunneling deep into the site have recovered many of them. The raw material may have been shipped to Copan in large oval blades—each one retains the original frame, now willfully opened by the vision of the artist. Using subtle pressure with a deer antler, the artist learned to release tiny chips to form the principal figure, achieving both the pouty lips and subtle indentations that suggest eyes and ornament. Any process of reduction like this requires no false moves or the work will be ruined. In their uniformity, these three flints probably came from a single hand.

Each flint represents a single anthropomorphic figure with K'awiil features, given the perforated forehead that characterizes the god. But each appendage or protrusion—forehead, arms, headdress, even penis—takes on its own animated quality, turning into another head. A Maya king may have borne such a flint as a scepter of authority, like the K'awiil scepters often held in the hand. Yet none of these shows evidence of any sort of haft, and the razor-sharp blade could not have been easily handled.

Reference: Schmidt et al. 1998, p. 607

Plate 80
Eccentric flint head of K'awiil
Unknown provenience
AD 600–800
Flint
3¹⁄₂ x 2³⁄₄ in. (8.9 x 7.0 cm)
Dumbarton Oaks Research Library & Collections,
Washington, D.C.
PC.B.587

Plate 81
Eccentric flint
Unknown provenience
AD 600–800
Flint
9¹⁄₈ x 5³⁄₈ in. (23.2 x 13.7 cm)
Dumbarton Oaks Research Library & Collections,
Washington, D.C.
PC.B.588

Plate 82
Eccentric flint
Unknown provenience
AD 600–800
Flint
9¹⁄₂ x 5¹⁄₈ in. (24.1 x 13.0 cm)
Dumbarton Oaks Research Library & Collections,
Washington, D.C.
PC.B.589

At accession, many Maya kings take K'awiil scepters (Plate 3), and some may have been eccentric flints like these. Whether representations of humans or deities, eccentrics usually emphasize the god K'awiil, the serpent-footed god, characterized by a smoking tube or axe pierced through the forehead. Here, the human heads have transformed into K'awiil.

Among natural forces, K'awiil represents lightning. Because the Maya believed that flint was formed where lightning struck, the material itself is K'awiil's essence, perhaps accounting for the consistency of K'awiil representations among eccentric flints in general.

The Maya deposited such flints inside building or stelae caches, often in multiples, as the Copan examples suggest. The same artist fashioned at least the two large examples at Dumbarton Oaks, and perhaps the K'awiil head as well, suggesting that this group, as well, may have formed a single offering.

Plate 83

Profile of a Death God

Topoxte, Peten, Guatemala
AD 750–800
Shell (Mother-of-Pearl)
5 7/8 x 4 1/8 in. (15.0 x 10.5 cm)
Museo Nacional de Arqueología y Etnología de Guatemala
17.7.21.210B

Plate 84

Frog

Topoxte, Peten, Guatemala
AD 750–800
Shell
2 3/4 x 2 1/2 in. (7.0 x 6.4 cm)—reproduced larger than actual size
Museo Nacional de Arqueología y Etnología de Guatemala
17.7.21.210C

During the 8th century, lords at Topoxte, an island site in Lake Yaxha, Peten, rebuilt what is known today as Structure A. Some of the motivation for this reconstruction was the interment of an important lord at mid-century, in what is known as Burial 49, although there was little other elite activity at the site at the time. The island may have come to be the refuge of an exiled ruler.

This lord took remarkable worldly possessions with him into death—elaborate jade jewelry, including rare examples of Jester God headdress ornaments, a valuable inscribed bone that names an otherwise unknown personage linked to the Naranjo dynasty, at least one mirror, possibly two, and musical instruments. These two shell objects were among the most unusual works in the tomb.

Archaeologists found these intact objects among the remnants of what seems to have been a large mosaic that was once attached to a perishable armature—possibly a headdress assemblage. Plate 83 is a Death God, skeletal of limb and distended with rot; Plate 84 is a shell frog with quartz eyes. The craftsman has captured the movement of the swimming frog, with one leg extended in water. The surface of the frog suggests a textile pattern; many patterns in use today in Guatemala include the frog as a feature.

References: Wurster ed. 2000, p. 130; Centro Cultural de la Villa de Madrid 2002, pp. 220–221

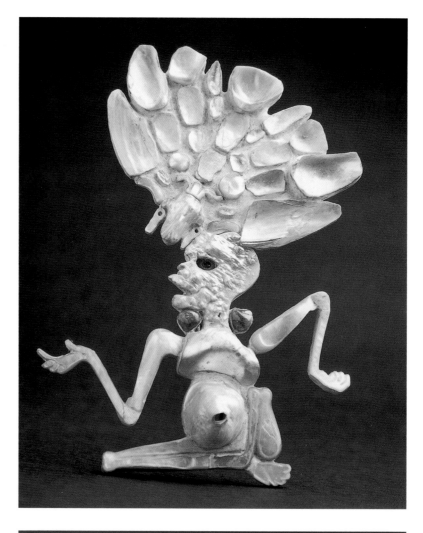

Plate 85

Cylinder vessel with flower motifs ("Fleur-de-lis Vase")

Unknown provenience

c. AD 780

Ceramic

9⁷/₁₆ x 6⁵/₁₆ in. (24.0 x 16.0 cm)

The Art Institute of Chicago, Ethel Scarborough Fund

1986.10.80

Without surviving books from the 1st millennium AD, one turns to the calligraphy of ceramic vessels for some impression of a vast but now lost corpus of painted manuscripts. The kingdom of Naranjo produced thin-walled cylinders with elaborate decoration, particularly in black background, red-on-cream, and black-on-cream schemes. Dubbed the "Fleur-de-lis Vase," this vessel features a striking black-on-white repeat design of a stylized flower.

A long text begins on the upper band, where we receive formulaic descriptions of the function as a chocolate vessel, before the text names its owner as a lord of "Rabbit," probably a satellite center near Naranjo. The lower band names the lord as the son of Naranjo's ruling king and queen. His father (*k'ahk' ukalaw chan chaak*) ruled between 755 and 784, and this vessel presumably dates to his reign. The artist is named here as "He of Maxam," one of several place-names associated with the Naranjo kingdom.

References: Coe 1973, pp. 102–103; Stuart 1989; Reents-Budet 1994, p. 319

Plate 86

Nine bricks with incisions or modeling

Comalcalco, Tabasco, Mexico
AD 600–800
Ceramic
Largest, 14 1/8 in. (36 cm); smallest, 8 3/8 in. (21.3 cm)
Museo de Sitio de Comalcalco—INAH, Mexico
10–508174, 10–508194, 10–508209, 10–575769, 10–575893,
10–575775, 10–575756, 10–575776, 10–575768

Most Mesoamerican builders used stone to construct works in urban settings. Some domestic structures were fashioned of sun-dried adobe bricks. True fired bricks are rare. But at Comalcalco, in the Tabascan flood plain, the most western of all Maya cities, stone was the rare material. Accordingly, the Maya at the site learned to make fired bricks, and they made them by the thousands.

Archaeologists discovered that the makers of hundreds of these bricks had taken time to mark them, occasionally with intelligible script—often a day sign—or more typically a sketch, and more rarely, with relief sculpture or paint. Yet when workers laid these bricks into walls, not a single mark remained in view. Some larger bricks took a position as part of a door lintel, but stucco coatings capped any imagery on the bricks themselves.

The articulated bricks reveal a range of skills. One talented draftsman took a tool and quickly drew a member of the court, a dwarf in a bird costume, a confident work informed by subtle, elite knowledge. Another, somewhat less trained artist sketched a scene from a plaza procession, revealing a lord in a litter, his bearers, and a parasol.

Who incised or painted or sculpted these works? Were they foremen, trained in courtly arts? Slaves from another city, assigned to menial tasks? Whoever they were, they surely knew that their efforts would not be seen. The bricks provide quiet testimony to the Maya call of art-making, a call that insisted on response, even when futile.

Reference: Álvarez Aguilar et al. 1990

Plate 87

Two tenoned heads

Comalcalco, Tabasco, Mexico
AD 600–900
Ceramic
6⁵⁄₁₆ x 5¹⁄₂ in. (16.0 x 14.0 cm)
6¹⁄₄ x 4¹⁄₄ in. (15.9 x 10.9 cm)
Museo de Sitio de Comalcalco—INAH, Mexico
10-575760, 10–576814

With little available local stone, Comalcalco
builders turned to brick for most construction,
using little more than mud as mortar in most
cases. In place of the customary stucco exterior
decoration, they also turned to clay, firing pieces
independently before assembling the exteriors.
Among the most handsome examples of terracotta
tenoned heads are these two, from the North Plaza
of the site, and from adjoining Structures 3 and 3a.

Facial scarification extends out from the mouth
on both heads, along with a prominent feature on
the forehead. Both sorts of scarification are also
common among Jaina figurines. Their mouths are
partly open, revealing perfect teeth, but also making
the heads particularly lifelike, as if they were
breathing.

Plate 88
Cylinder vessel with companion spirits
Unknown provenience
AD 600–800
Ceramic
11 x 5¾ in. (20.4 x 16.3 cm)
Princeton University Art Museum. Museum purchase,
Fowler McCormick, Class of 1921, Fund
y1993-17

Among the supernatural realms of the Maya, one
of the strangest was that inhabited by the alter-egos
of various kingly offices. Called *way* (pronounced
"why") by the Maya, these fantastical fusions of
gods, humans, and beasts represent companion
spirits that roam the dream world of sleep. Similar
entities have a presence in modern Maya lore,
where they are said to leave the body at night to
make mischief. Depicted in numerous painted
vases in the 7th and 8th centuries, they are by
turn frightening and loathsome and may personify
diseases and other forms of misfortune.

This vessel, one of a number executed by the
same artist, features nine such spirits. Individual
captions identify them to be the *way* of kings from
various locations, including the major kingdoms
of Caracol and Seibal. Their forms incorporate
those of jaguars, dogs, birds, and various death
gods. This vessel was originally created for the
king of Motul de San José, Guatemala, probably
in the mid-8th century.

References: Houston and Stuart 1989; Grube and Nahm 1994;
Calvin 1997

Plate 89
Stucco hieroglyph

Tonina, Mexico
AD 600–800
Stucco
Diam.: 6 in. (15.2 cm)
Museo de Sitio de Tonina, Chiapas—INAH, Mexico
10–604265

This rounded stucco hieroglyph once filled a medallion decorating the leg of a monumental throne at Tonina. It represents the kingly title called an "emblem glyph," a reference to a "holy lord" of a particular kingdom. The large central element that dominates the emblem is called the "main sign" by scholars and represents the kingdom name. Maya scribes enjoyed fusing glyphs and in this case have inserted the sign for a star (*ek'*) set into the eye of a jaguar (*b'ahlam*). The whole compound combines to read *k'uhul ek' b'ahlam ajaw,* or "Holy Lord of Star Jaguar."

Coincidentally, in both modern and ancient times, the name Ek Balam has belonged to a distant site north of Chichen Itza. It is unclear what it referred to at Tonina, especially if it occupied so prominent a position on a throne. One possibility is that it constitutes a kingdom in the Chiapas highlands that formed part of Tonina's regional hegemony; another is that it is an obscure title used by the Tonina king.

References: Yadeun 1992, p. 133; Lacadena, personal communication to Simon Martin, 2001

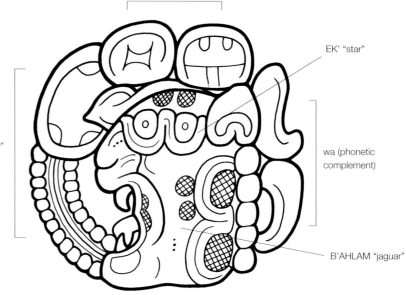

AJAW "lord/ruler"

EK' "star"

K'UHUL "holy"

wa (phonetic complement)

B'AHLAM "jaguar"

B

1
2
3
4
5
6
7

Plate 90
Two celts
Tonina, Mexico
c. AD 598
Stone
13 1/8 x 1 in. (33.5 x 2.5 cm), 11 5/16 x 1 7/8 in. (28.7 x 4.7 cm)
Museo de Sitio de Tonina, Chiapas—INAH, Mexico
10-607683; 10-607684

Axe blades hewn from jade and other hard stones were some of the most ancient and prized artifacts in Mesoamerica, with origins among the Olmec culture (1200–400 BC). Although inspired by humble tools, these polished "celts" had higher functions: as the embodiments of elemental forces and, as a result, as the accoutrements of gods and rulers.

For the Maya, the axe was the instrument of the storm god Chaak and symbolized his lightning bolt: a combination of stony core, fire, and serpent qualities that finds its fullest personification in the snake-footed character of K'awiil. Chaak strikes the earth to sacrifice the parched months of the dry season and supply the rains that bring forth the green shoots of a new season. It is perhaps for this reason that celts have links to maize and fertility more generally and are usually worked in greenstone: jadeite or one of its cousins.

The two blades here, discovered at Tonina, are hewn from an almost black stone with lighter green veins. One celt carries an incised text on both its faces. The first side commemorates the end of a calendrical cycle that took place in AD 598. This serves as the anchor date for the event on the second side (shown here), the dedication of the stone itself a year later. The celt is given its own name, which is evidently linked to the aforementioned embodiment of K'awiil since it includes his name.

Reference: Yadeun 1993, p. 131

CHRONOLOGY		
(9.8.5.0.0) 11 Ajaw 18 Yaxk'in (AD 598)	Period Ending
(9.8.5.12.19) 10 Kawak 12 Wo (AD 599)	Dedication of the celt

Plate 91
Head of old man

Tonina, Mexico
AD 600–800
Stucco
13¹/₈ x 7¹/₄ x 9 in. (33.5 x 18.5 x 23.0 cm)
Museo de Sitio de Tonina, Chiapas—INAH, Mexico
10-569198

Archaeologist Juan Yadeun has uncovered dozens of remarkable stucco heads from the rubble of collapsed buildings. Some depict gods, especially Chaak, and others represent idealized human faces. This life-size head is distinctive in its attention to the qualities of an old man's face—the craggy nose, the toothless mouth, the eyes sunk deep in their sockets, and the heavy wrinkles gained over time.

A stucco head like this one would have had a body, usually formed in lower relief and assembled in stucco on top of a stone armature. At Tonina, artists created huge friezes against the natural setbacks of the site, some with dozens of individual figures.

Plate 92

Stucco hieroglyph

Tonina, Mexico
AD 600–800
Stucco
5¹/₂ x 5¹/₂ in. (14 x 14 cm)
Museo de Sitio de Toniná, Chiapas—INAH, Mexico
10–607721

One of the strongest regional art traditions of the western Maya realm was the working of stucco— richly revealed at Palenque, Comalcalco, and Tonina among other places—and this hieroglyph, a recent find from Tonina, is another fine example. Although worked by both hand and tool, only the piece's characteristically powdery surface and deep undercutting immediately distinguish it from carved stone.

For all its beauty, its meaning is prosaic. It describes a time period of eight Maya years, or 2,880 days. The numeral *waxak*, "eight," appears in its "head variant" form: the portrait of a youthful Maize God, with a leaf forming his trailing hair. The unit *haab'*, "year," appears in its skeletal deity version, marked by a stylized jaguar ear. This glyph once appeared in the midst of a much longer sequence, detailing the amount of time that had elapsed between two significant dates.

CHAPTER 5   # The Court at War

Fig. 49 Detail of carved panel, Plate 107. This rendering of a noble warrior comes from an unknown site in the Lacandon forest, south of the Usumacinta River. A late work dated to AD 864, the active body pose and stylized costume characterize the troubled, strife-filled final years of the Maya stela tradition.

For most of its days, the Maya court was an unhurried place of mundane business. Scribes sat cross-legged, copying old records, entering sums in ledgers, and grinding pigments as they needed; kneeling women chatted among themselves as they wove the finest of cotton fabrics or embroidered the edges with pearls and feathers. When kings received visiting lords and their retinues, the feasts and festivities introduced new life into the daily rhythm, particular highlights for those on the cusp of adulthood. Yet just a little farther away, while their attendants repaired equipment and armor, young men and experienced soldiers sparred with one another, staying constantly in shape and always at the ready, preparing for the inevitable return of warfare.

When war struck this world, it did so suddenly, shocking these quiet routines with noise and terror, initiating disruptions that might last days or weeks, and in repercussions, years. Invading warriors might arrive at night, or at dusk or dawn, bearing torches both to light the way and to lay waste the thatch roofs of home and hearth. They might come in silence, quietly taking a valued hostage or two before suddenly sounding the trumpets and charging into battle. Battle might begin at a pre-arranged time and place, but chaos would soon reign. Active battle could also devolve into something far more arduous: late 1980s excavations at Dos Pilas yielded evidence of a grueling existence; desperate residents of the city dismantled expensive buildings to throw up walls for palisades, only to be burned to the ground eventually. At nearby Aguateca the royal family walled up treasure within a single palace chamber and presumably fled. Less fortunate residents, including many courtiers, stayed behind as trouble brewed. Attackers set the city on fire, and artisans and nobles died alongside slaves and servants when the firestorm swept the city. Some fleeing inhabitants were driven over a precipice and into a deep ravine at Aguateca.[1] Although most cities recovered, sought revenge, or built new alliances, others were never the same again. The powerful punctuation of war—even when rare—could dominate life at court.

Accordingly the themes of war and sacrifice became common in the artistic output of almost every Maya city, particularly during the fractious 8th century, when these disturbing intervals and their cultural convulsions came more and more frequently. Whether fixed in the sculptural and architectural programs of the royal court itself or depicted in the many painted scenes of courtly life, such images expose a view of court spaces sharply different from those we have examined thus far. Alongside all its intimate, household functions, its quotidian successes, the court emerges as an arena of state, where the business of inter-kingdom rivalry was conducted and where military and economic prowess took center stage.

By their very nature, representations and textual descriptions can only allude to the real world in a stylized and idealized fashion. But they always reflect the special concerns and priorities of their makers: in this way their rhetoric reveals both ancient mentalities and the relationships between commissioners of art and their intended audiences. Significantly, what we see in the art of war is rarely a distant clash of arms—the king and his captains on campaign—but homecomings: the display of prisoners in the heart of the victorious city, the ultimate humiliation of reversal in a public forum. In a pattern familiar across ancient Mesoamerica, the victorious performed warfare as if it were a two-act play: the first act on the battlefield then completed by a second, its reenactment and denouement at home (Plate 108). The first is distant, unruly, chaotic, and set in places of tangible risk and subject to high emotion by all concerned. At the return to the city, a scripted picture of order and control emerges, with emotion manifest only in the forms of tormented prisoners who become a special focus of war representation. A king whose henchmen might keep him closely encircled and protected in combat could now emerge with an enhanced role back at court.

Spanish accounts of their 16th-century battles against the Maya describe furious charges from warriors bedecked in elaborate costumes, their bodies painted red or black, carrying banners and sacred images, all to the accompanying din of horns, drums, and war cries.[2] The few representations of combat provided by the Maya show this same kind of ferocious melee: a tangle of fighters dressed in tall headdresses topped with feathers and animal effigies, encouraged by musicians and standard-bearers. The Bonampak battle includes a tussle over a box; this may be the sort of coffered chest in which the first Spanish invaders quickly learned that the Maya kept their most valuable possessions,

Fig. 50   Bonampak, Room 2. Reconstruction of east, south, and west walls by Heather Hurst with Leonard Ashby. A battle rages across three walls, in a vivid depiction of the confusion of hand-to-hand combat. The Bonampak king, Yahaw Chan Muwan, "Lord of the Sky Hawk," can be seen taking a captive toward the right side of the central (south) wall.

including feather-work and books.[3] The battle panorama that covers three walls of Bonampak Room 2 is by far the most comprehensive of these rare survivals (Fig. 50). Maya war is portrayed as chaotic, wild, uninhibited—in keeping with its wilderness setting of hill and dale. Whatever formations may have existed at the outset, or tactics employed, it is clear that the struggle quickly descended into one-on-one combat with friend and foe hopelessly intermingled, only to eventually clarify into groups of two or three who gang up on a single captive, who is then disarmed, disrobed, and bound. The symmetries and centralities that characterize all the courtly scenes are shattered here, and the main focus of the fight in Room 2—including the image of the king himself—is set off to one side.

In the Maya ideal of heroic combat, warriors fought toe-to-toe, thrusting with heavy lances or wielding clubs, axes, flints, and even obsidian-edged swords (Plates 103, 106). The spearthrower, or *atlatl* to the later Aztecs, represented long-range weaponry to the Maya. With this wooden sling, warriors unleashed a hail of javelin-like darts with deadly accuracy. Maya warriors defended themselves with shields of two kinds. One was small and circular, rimmed with feathers and embellished with the heads of deities or hieroglyphs (Plate 110). Worn with the imagery upside-down on the arm, it turned right side up when the arm protected the face, making the warrior the god depicted or named on the shield, usually the Jaguar God of the Underworld, a powerful war deity. Although this design predominates in ceremonial contexts, another is more typical of battle scenes: a larger and mat-like shield, woven from a flexible, fibrous material, usually cotton or palm, and sometimes covered and always edged with feathers (Plates 111, 112). Decorative helmets and masks may have offered limited protection for the head and face; a mask of a skull would have made a warrior into a terrifying ghoul (Plate 110). An armor of woven cotton, strips of palm, or close-fitting hide jerkins protected the body (Plate 51). Much of the finery that may seem to be merely cumbersome was in fact also practical, particularly the protective pelts and hides that provided insignia of what may have been fighting orders.

Warriors shared the predatory status of big cats, raptorial birds, and venomous snakes at the top of the food chain. Among the ancient Maya, as throughout Mesoamerica, these powerful animals defined both warrior orders and warrior garb, including fearsome effigy headdresses and masks, as well as actual jaguar pelts, eagle and owl feathers, and stuffed snake skins. Clothed in animals' fur and feathers, embodying their vital spirits, combatants mirror the primeval battle of nature, a struggle for survival played out in the wild and frightening forest. The Maya would call on these same animals as spirit companions (Plate 88).

There was another way in which warfare was rendered foreign and in the thrall of outside forces. Maya war iconography relentlessly explored the art and ideas of a distant Goliath, the Mexican metropolis of Teotihuacan.[4] A contemporary of the Maya until its fall somewhere close to AD 650, this single city of perhaps 150,000 people or more represented the military might and orthodoxy of a Rome or Jerusalem to the scattered Maya city-states. Although many of the specifics of Teotihuacan's history remain largely unknown to us, there were close contacts between the two civilizations. Teotihuacan may have taken up arms against the Maya in 378 in some kind of intervention, although it probably did not last beyond a generation.[5] But the decisive factor in this context was the superior military reputation of Teotihuacan, whose aura long outlived its actual existence as a major power.[6] The Maya manipulated Teotihuacan imagery, especially the plated and mosaic-made image of the Mexican War Serpent, a deity the Maya enigmatically called "18 heads/images of the snake" (*waxaklajuun ub'aah kaan*); with little writing from Teotihuacan itself, we learn about the mysterious city from the Maya interpretation (Plate 109). Warriors wore the War Serpent as headdress and armor; they wielded a fearsome miniature as a weapon (Fig. 52). They also took the imagery of Tlaloc—the Central Mexican patron of storms and war—stripped him of any agricultural benevolence, and wore his fanged face with goggle eyes as a cut-away mask or headdress. Frequently the Maya added a stuffed-deerskin "balloon" headdress to Tlaloc's image (Plate 50). Maya artists represented these "foreign" images in the angular, geometric style of Teotihuacan, a self-conscious contrast with the organic, flowing forms characteristic of Maya art. The Maya sought to evoke the aid of these foreign deities, but they also recognized that when they made war, especially on other Maya, they sought to step outside the norms of behavior; they became foreigners, if only for as long as they wore their alien costumes.

In the art of Teotihuacan the images of warriors reflect an aesthetic of conformity, resembling so many automatons. Not so for the Maya who here, as elsewhere, prized individuality. Each combatant is distinguished not only by body paint, personal weaponry, and costume—particularly oversized, almost heraldic headdresses—but, as at Bonampak, even by individual hieroglyphic captions. This emphasis on individuality is no less true of the captives seized in battle: they bear either captions or headdress designs that provide a hieroglyphic spelling of their names (Plate 104). One can well imagine the honor and fame that accrued from the seizure of a high-born or powerful opponent. But we might also consider the economic dimension of the prize, that a prisoner of note represented a much wider set of obligations and resources—be it a ransom that could be extorted or tribute that could be demanded: lands and labor, slaves, brides and concubines.

Indeed, this focus of Maya combat on the capture of live opponents—a characteristic they share with the rest of Mesoamerica—is demonstrated not only in art but in the inscriptions, where *chuhkaj*, "he is seized/roped," is the most common of all verbs referring to warfare. The name of the victim invariably follows. What is astonishing is that even in the midst of the Bonampak battle, the emphasis is on individual capture, so that the principal battle text names prisoners taken by Yahaw Chan Muwan (*yajaw chan muwaan*), rather than making any larger political statement in the text (Fig. 50). Such achievements were commemorated in titles the victor often carried throughout his lifetime: the master of "so-and-so." Sheer quantity was meritorious and reflected the title "he of 'so many' captives" prevalent in some western regions. The fixation on personal capture was reflected even in military ranks or offices such as "captive-taker" (Fig. 12g).

No single work encapsulates these themes better than the north wall of Room 2 at Bonampak (Plate 93). This sets out a vision of the court in its role as the center of politics, as the lair of a predatory force, and as the setting for the state-sanctioned violence that undergirds early complex societies wherever we may find them in the world. Ostensibly, the mural offers a single field of view: a vista of arraigned lords, warriors, and captives, set among courtly architecture. But it also works in the manner of a diagram, in which the stairs serve as both a visual hierarchy and narrative device, in which time itself unfolds and life gives way to death. Seen today, out of its architectural context, the central figure of the ruler dominates. The artists of the paintings portray attendant lieutenants; close family members, among them wives and mothers; functionaries and servants, lower-ranking warriors, and prisoners not only in a code of elevation but also with intentional placements to the right or left, all of which would have been readily intelligible to an elite Maya observer. Similar scenes occur on painted cylinder vases, where the same ranking of participants is explored time and again (Plate 105). Nevertheless, the beautifully rendered naked captives at center dominate the picture plane.

Other surviving sculptures suggest that the captives of the Bonampak North Wall fulfill an existing script: sculptural fragments of captives from Tonina, for example, some of which are in this exhibition, conform to the same postures, as if once part of a sculptural tableau made up of many individual slabs.[7] Some prisoners express something more than their own dejection and were clearly part of some mythic re-enactment as sacred victims for sacrifices. Some victims are dressed-up in the accoutrements of deities, such as the Jaguar God of the Underworld (Fig. 54a; Plates 95, 100). On one painted vessel we see this warlike patron of fire meet his end when he is bound and immolated by a heroic young god (Fig. 54b). Presumably the same fate now awaits his human impersonators. In

Fig. 51 Drawing of Plate 107. This late Maya lord wears the typical battle garb of short-sleeved hide jerkin; he is armed with a heavy thrusting lance.

this way we can see that warfare and sacrifice, like the other practices of the court, follow a program ordained by the gods.

Perhaps one of the most striking features of the Bonampak captives—and of the Tonina carvings, for that matter—is the sympathetic and emotional rendering of the captives, particularly when juxtaposed in the case of Bonampak with the detached depiction of the ruler. The rendering of the dead captive, poised diagonally just above the doorway on the North Wall of Bonampak Room 2, calls on the observer to study the sensuous if not erotic body, the dripping blood, the limp hand; the pleading captive on the riser above seemingly gasps for assistance; his pate seems to hang loose on his head—yet the king he addresses makes no eye contact. Because of the sharp slope inward of the wall, an observer seated on the bench built into this room easily sees the captives, who cluster around the doorway and at eye height, but not their captors, whose depictions press to the margins.

The enduring image of Maya war is therefore less the strutting warrior king with his captains and warriors—though we certainly have those—but instead that of the miserable prisoner. Depictions of victors read to us as impassive and cold, even as lords take physical control of both their prisoners and themselves. The vanquished, by contrast, express their distress; they bend into bodily contortions, their faces grimace in pain, and they cast their eyes down in sorrow, shame, or simple exhaustion.[8] When not bound tightly to them by ropes, the arms and hands of captives perform a range of plaintive gestures. Captives beseech with hands outstretched, they accede with one hand to the forehead, and they acquiesce, with one hand at the mouth.[9] The defeated are physically imperfect, even ugly and misshapen—although some of this results from batterings already meted out to them. Their flesh, sometimes even genitalia, is exposed—a great indignity for a people with strict ideas of public modesty even in the heat and humidity of the rainforest.

Inscriptions, however, prefer to talk about their *nahwaj,* seemingly referring to "presentation or adorning" (Fig. 53d). In many cases long strips of rag or paper have been drawn through prisoners' earlobes—tokens that mock the fine greenstone jewels they have replaced (e.g. Plates 2, 97, 98, 100, 101, 104, 105) and underscore the transfer of the wealth to the victors. These bear zigzag tears or partially cut-out holes that produce hanging flaps.[10] Female prisoners, though exceedingly rare in Maya art, can have their *huipil* dresses cut up in the same manner (Plate 96).[11] Under normal circumstances, the Maya never cut or tore cloth; the ripping of cloth may well have been analogous to the tearing of flesh. These materials then are defiled and useless—matching the wretched status of their wearers.

Many stelae—including some featuring women (Fig. 37)—emphasize a ruling lord standing atop an abject captive. The act of "trampling" for the Maya had the kind of resonance that "smiting" did for the ancient Egyptians, where it served as shorthand for the king's absolute victory, with monolithic scenes showing him literally crushing and mangling his enemies underfoot. We see much the same idea in a pair of sandals from the pharoah Tutankhamun's tomb, whose innersoles bear depictions of bound Nubian and Asiatic prisoners—forever downtrodden. The Maya convey similar power by carving the images of captives on the treads of stairs. These steps—or sometimes stone carvings flanking steps—take on a central role in city architecture in the 8th century, often right within palace confines (Plate 104).

Stairs may have been the single most common architectural feature that the Maya designed to celebrate victory and to bring the battle back to the court. The North Wall of Room 2 at Bonampak suggests the staging of the stairs, but many steps themselves were inscribed with texts and images that celebrated warfare. These carved risers offer an ongoing performance rather than a static memory of the past. In this way they make past warfare tangible in some later present, particularly in a visual sense, so that memory is refreshed and vivid. A carved staircase made the war of a past generation a living and tangible feature of a subsequent king.

Fig. 52 Panel from Temple 17, Palenque. The ruler Kan Bahlam reigns over his bound and kneeling captive. The victorious king wears the headdress of the distinctly foreign War Serpent, a character whose origins lie in Central Mexico.

Who carved the depictions of captives? Many representations of captives suggest that artists pressed to service from the defeated city made some of the carvings. On Tonina's Fifth Terrace, the discourse between the victors and the defeated may have been played out not only in carving style but also in the interplay between two and three dimensions: Tonina's traditional three-dimensional carving characterized victorious lords; regional two-dimensional carving styles of lowland Chiapas characterized the captives. Some individual figures (Plate 100) seem to have been developed from a single prototype, nearly identical to sculptural examples known from the Yaxchilan region, as well as the Bonampak paintings, and probably common to now-lost Maya books. Of varying size and format, the Tonina captive panels could have been assembled over time and rearranged as new panels were added (Plates 98, 99). Over the course of more than 50 years, dozens of lords had their humiliated representations committed to stone.

Most striking among these carvings is Monument 122, which records the ignominious fate of Palenque's king K'an Hoy Chitam II (*k'inich k'an joy chitam*), captured by with Tonina in 711 (Plate 101). Although worked of local sandstone, the figure belongs to the Palenque canon, especially in the rendering of hair, hands, and posture. Here, as elsewhere, we can see that victory in battle resulted in tribute labor—on Monument 122, artists made their home city's defeat manifest for all time, with a work that inserts Palenque's elegant, languid line into the artistic program of Tonina.

Although there is little specific evidence for it today, the Fifth Terrace panels probably formed a staircase, flanked by vertical panels, creating a tableau of assembled captives. Monument 27 is a stair riser depicting a lord from Palenque or one of its allies; his subordinate status is indicated by the rings on his headdress (Plate 104). Carved so that his nose, shoulder, and knee protrude just above the step line, the captive's body would engage a living protagonist, whose feet must touch the stone. The sculptor renders the figure without the idealization reserved for victorious lords; the captive's humble face and contorted body are confined to the stone block and yet protruding from it.

Two additional monuments form a pair in scale, stone, and costume (Plate 98; Fig. 55); they may once have flanked a course of risers. Each captive reveals one hand bound behind him, long, flowing hair, and flapped ear cloths; they are so similar as to be brothers, if not twins. One captive can be assigned securely to Calakmul, a trophy from the period 708–723, when Calakmul's fortunes began to wane.

What was the ultimate fate of these unfortunates? Would they endure hours—if not days—of tests of strength before yielding to death, as seems to have been the case of the noble captive whose story survives in the 16th-century Maya epic, the Rabinal Achí?[12] There is ample visual evidence for the torture of prisoners in the 1st millennium: the slicing of fingers and tearing out of fingernails, the burning with torches or tied stacks of tinder. One mural at the northern site of Mul-Chic shows prisoners hanged in trees, an immediate dispatching at the scene of the battle. Roped and marched back home (Plate 108), others underwent sacrifice before a home audience: garroted, their chests or stomachs cut open, or beheaded. In more elaborate rituals victims took part in ballgames, not as players but as the ball—with legs and arms bound tightly behind them they were thrown down stairways.[13] The human remains of such rituals could become grisly trophies. The glyph for "shield" is the image of a flayed human face stretched across the warrior's round shield (Fig. 53e); lords frequently wear what seem to be shrunken heads as part of their battle dress, and occasionally entire shrunken bodies.[14]

Some well-documented victims miraculously turn up in history again as the kings of their original realms—as if, having suffered their defeat and humiliation, having submitted to the authority of a new master, they were free to resume their lives—though now shackled by new obligations of servitude.[15] Many lords may have been ransomed: the debilitating price-tag may have cast the home city into submission as much by penury as overt control. A good number of captives are free of restraining ropes and

a   b   c   d

e   f   g   h

Fig. 53 Glyphs associated with warfare: a. Chuhkaj, "(he) is seized"; b. Ucha'an? "the master/guardian of"; c. Ah Wuk Baak, "he of seven captives"; d. Nahwaj, "(he) is dressed"; e. Pakal, "shield"; f. Utook' Pakal, "his flint (and) shield"; g. "Star War at Seibal"; h. Ch'ahkaj, "(it) is axed."

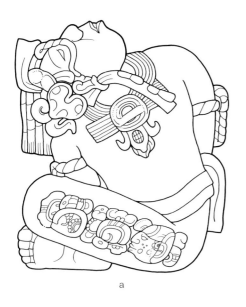

Fig. 54   a. Drawing of Plate 100, this captive lord is dressed in the jaguar ear, nose "cruller" and pectoral collar of the Jaguar God of the Underworld, a patron of fire and war. The victim may well be destined for the same fiery sacrifice experienced by that deity; b. Drawing from codex-style pot, where a young god ignites the bound Jaguar God with a burning torch.

strike poses of submission instead, with arms held across the chest or kneeling with an inverted fan or broken parasol in hand. These may be newly enlisted vassals rather than captives or slaves.

Meaning and Rhetoric

Were Maya armies large or restricted to a professional elite? Sadly, the inscriptions describe neither the organization nor quantity of combatants. But when the Spanish fought in the region they encountered groups of military specialists drawn from the nobility who, as required, mobilized larger forces of peasant-soldiers drawn from their labors in the field. Evidence that the Maya preferred to do battle when the harvest was in, and therefore when there were the greatest number of men available to fight, may be relevant here. We have long understood that the Aztec dry season at harvest's end brought in not only the "season of hunting" but the season of "hunting of men" as well.[16] Some encounters were doubtless small raids and ambushes. Equally, the storming of foreign capitals described in the texts implies invading armies and sizable forces to defend their homes, king, and kingdom. Although the Bonampak battle takes place on a background of scrub jungle and occasional leafy fronds, the murals at Chichen Itza show the storming of walled cities and the burning of thatched dwellings. Many conflicts must have taken place in the open farmland that surrounded Maya cities. As in all complex societies, conflict doubtless took many guises, occurred in varied environments, and at many different scales—all depending on circumstance. Anyone who searches for some single "model" of Maya conflict is sure to be disappointed.

We might expect that the titles of Maya kings would abound with military epithets. In fact, martial titles more typically belong to their lesser lieutenants, some of whom may have been specialists lacking high noble rank. The inscriptions are richer sources when it comes to the type of clash involved. The most important of these was the "star war," a still undeciphered verb that describes the most decisive encounters, including conquests and the defeats of dynasties. To see the name of a Maya capital set beneath the hieroglyph of a star and its cascade of falling droplets is to anticipate the worst of fates for it (Fig. 53g)—and the Bonampak North Wall tableau, with rendered droplets of blood under the setting of stars, may be analogous to a full-figure hieroglyph of the "star war" itself. Though we can well imagine that court astrologers and seers fervently sought auspicious moments for military action, the idea that the Maya ritualistically timed their battles to a rigid cycle—such as that of the planet Venus—is certainly overstated. Only a few battles took place on genuinely significant dates; we might expect innumerable other auguries to have played their part. The rhetoric of deadly cosmic influence should be balanced by the more practical issue of timing that has governed warfare throughout human history.

Archaeological evidence for Maya warfare is generally scant. Flint blades for both lances and darts are relatively plentiful in excavated sites, but every other item of warrior panoply has succumbed to the humid tropical climate. These conditions, plus the highly acidic soils of the region, mean that skeletal remains survive poorly outside formal tombs, which were largely restricted to the upper classes, if not the royal family. Few battle casualties have been positively identified, although one king at Copan—almost certainly the dynastic founder Yax K'uk' Mo'—had suffered numerous injuries during his lifetime, including those typical of parry wounds to the forearm.[17] Dozens of royal tombs lack specific bones, and the occasional royal interment with the front of the skull cut off suggests a body defaced and humiliated by an opposing lord, yet perhaps returned home for final burial.

The bones of a sacrificed captive may well have had great power. In the Bonampak and Cacaxtla mural programs, both warriors and dancers bear human femurs, sometimes with a hafted blade.[18] While some warriors held real femurs, others—particularly for ceremonial occasions—carried obsidian or flint axes knapped to look like hafted bone weapons (Plates 102, 103, 106). Among the Aztecs, the femurs of women who had died in childbirth enhanced the potency of warriors; grieving families had to fight off attempts to steal these women's body parts. Such women were also understood to be warriors, and it may well be that any warrior's bone could enhance battle efficacy.

In terms of defenses, the Maya built impressive fortifications in the form of ditches at some sites. Many others exploited local topography: Palenque was built on an escarpment with steep mountains at its back. River cities offered limited access to invaders, as well as a quick means of escape. Some settlements built wooden palisades of the kind Hernán Cortés describes during his epic trek through the Maya region in 1524–1525.[19] When under attack during the Spanish invasion, the Maya often fled under cover of night, taking all food with them. This may well have been the practice earlier in the past as well. City dwellers would have returned to a sacked palace to begin the process of rebuilding.

Warfare and Political History

Our understanding of the representation of Maya warfare does little or nothing to explicate the social and political motivations that lay behind it. What did aggressive dynasties hope to achieve by conflict and what were its consequences? Mayanists have differed over the years about the purposes of warfare and the relative importance of symbolic overtones within more prosaic materialism. The Maya would be unprecedented indeed if economic gain of one sort or another was not a primary goal. We know that they had elaborate trade and tribute relationships and there is good reason to suspect that these were the glue that held together the landscape of petty kingdoms developed by the Maya. Warfare played its part in creating new economic obligations.

At first sight there appears to be little shape or pattern to Maya warfare, but neither would there be with a random sample of European conflicts over 600 years of history. By and large, the Maya world saw a struggle between various "overkings," rulers who grasped more than the usual amount of military and economic muscle to cow their peers. Calakmul, Tikal, Palenque, Tonina, Piedras Negras, and Dos Pilas, among others, extended webs of political influence that reduced fellow kingdoms to compliant vassals and clients. The most successful examples, Tikal in the 5th century, Calakmul in the 6th and 7th, seem to be states striving for the role of hegemon. Behind even minor clashes may have lain machinations of a greater order, the pernicious influence of distant power plays, the endless permutations for alliance, betrayal, and warfare anew.[20]

Fig. 55   Captive Panel, Tonina. One of a pair of captive figures at Tonina (see Plate 98), this stone effectively portrays an individual physiognomy, with particular attention to his mustache, nose, and nosepiece. The loincloth text tells us that he is a victim of Tonina Ruler 4, suggesting a date between 708 and 723 for this work.

We must neither sensationalize nor sanitize the ancient Maya. Over the years perspectives have shifted between polar extremes, from seeing a pacifistic society where warfare was almost unknown, to one of unrelenting brutality and bloodlust. Both are caricatures that do an injustice by failing to see the ancient Maya as a sophisticated but competitive culture neither more nor less willing to use armed force than ancient or medieval societies of the Old World. What cannot be denied is that warfare and its consequences provided the inspiration for new and imaginative works of art, often produced under circumstances that would lead to yet more rounds of conflict.

Plate 93
North wall, Room 2, Bonampak
AD 790–800
Reconstruction painted by Heather Hurst with Leonard Ashby
for the Bonampak Documentation Project
Reconstruction: watercolor on paper
Original: paint on stucco

During the final decade of the 8th century, remarkable artists worked at the small site of Bonampak and covered three rooms of a small building with the most sophisticated and complete paintings to survive from the ancient New World. About 16 miles (26 km) from Yaxchilan, Bonampak and its larger neighbor shared intertwined histories for most of the millennium: the last ruler, Yahaw Chan Muwan, married a Yaxchilan princess, and references to Yaxchilan appear throughout the program of paintings.

Rendered at about two-thirds life size, the paintings feature an unprecedented number of individuals, from the trumpet players and cigarette smokers of Room 1 to the messengers in white cloaks who attend powerful lords in Rooms 1 and 3. All three rooms conform to a larger program, giving the paintings a sense of coherence and order despite the very different subject matter of each room.

The second room of Bonampak surrounds the viewer with one of the greatest battles ever captured in paint (Fig. 50). From west to south to east, the warriors of Bonampak parade, attack their enemy, and bring the opposition to heel, one individual at a time. Yahaw Chan Muwan dominates the south wall, attended by his jaguar-pelted lieutenants.

The built-in bench surrounds three sides of the room, inviting the observer to sit and turn to the door, thus observing the north wall. This north wall has long been the most admired section of the painting, and with good reason: perhaps no single image captures so effectively the complexity of Maya warfare at court, especially the relationship between the victor and the victim.

The king stands just to the right of center, receiving his lieutenant's presentation of captives. To the right of the king stand two Yaxchilan henchmen, and beyond them, the king's wife, Lady Rabbit of Yaxchilan, followed by his mother and a conch-playing servant to the women.

For the observer seated on the bench, and given the sharp inward pitch of the vault, what is most legible, however, is not the victorious nobility but rather the captives a step or two below. Dominating the scene is the dead captive who sprawls below the king, his eye aligning with the king's spear. His naked frontal form insists on being read, and the observer lingers on the cut marks across his body, the limpness of the fingers that seem to have just dropped a rope scourge, and the blood that flows from the corpse.

To the dead captive's right, other captives remain erect, as if to contest their status. At far left, where beams once pierced the wall (leaving visible brown circles) a warrior pulls fingernails or trims the ends of phalanges; other captives slump and stare abjectly at their bleeding hands. In front of the king, one seemingly pleads, but to no avail; blood spurts; his pate hangs down.

The viewer absorbs these images of captives at each sitting. At the door frame, painted warriors stand ready to pounce, as if this painting defined a site for captive presentation. Up above, constellations, including the Turtle (the three bright stars on its back are the same ones read as the belt of Orion) and the Peccaries (probably the Pleiades) frame the scene.

Plate 94
Figurine of warrior
Jaina, Mexico
AD 600–900
Ceramic
11 x 4³/₄ x 3 in. (28.0 x 12.0 x 10.0 cm)
Courtesy of the National Museum of the American Indian,
Smithsonian Institution
226348

This Jaina warrior stands on guard and ready to strike, with both lance and knife in hand. He wears a short cape that noble warriors in the Bonampak murals also don, as well as the short, smooth cap of many lieutenants who serve greater lords. Atop the cap are three tied "bowties," often a sign of bloodletting and warfare.

Reference: Schele 1997, p. 99

Plate 95
Figurine of captive
Jaina, Mexico
AD 700–900
Ceramic
7 5/8 in. (19.3 cm)
Princeton University Art Museum. Gift of Gillett G. Griffin
2003-148

With his stately posture and steady countenance, this figurine of a captive epitomizes the dignity and toughness that a defeated noble might bring to torture and death. His paunch suggests a man who has lived well and consumed many cups of *kakaw*. The figurine may have been intentionally mutilated.

What is also compelling about this figure is the representation of the face, with what seems to be a false beard, scalloped eyebrows, and even fish barbels—all characteristics of a supernatural figure who is sometimes subject to a sacrificial burning, as if the captive has become this character. Despite these features, the depiction evokes a particular individual and may be a portrait.

Reference: Schele and Miller 1986, p. 228

Plate 96

Figurine of standing nude girl

Jaina, Mexico
AD 600–900
Ceramic
9 x 3¹/₄ x 2¹³/₁₆ in. (22.8 x 8.3 x 7.1 cm)
Yale University Art Gallery. Gift of the Olsen Foundation
1958.15.9

Female captives are rare in Maya art, as is any sort of nudity. The two known monumental sculptural examples of female captives feature young women, whose fate may have been to enter a rival royal household, either as servant or concubine, rather than to face sacrifice. Indeed, female capture may have been one way to enforce dynastic marriage or to acquire valuable hostages.

This Jaina figure of a naked woman features no bonds to restrain her, but her exposed genitalia and loose, flowing hair both suggest that she has been deprived forcibly of clothing and headdress. Her hands, poised at her waist, may once have been tied by perishable material, or the artist may have emphasized her nakedness by suggesting that she tries to cover her pudendum. Who would have chosen such a companion in a tomb?

Despite her youthful and idealized face— probably crafted in a mold, hand-finished with facial details and hair and attached to a hand-modeled body—this woman is specifically represented with the abdominal rolls and stretchmarks that come from childbirth. Her broad shoulders and heavy thighs suggest a woman of substance, and perhaps she embodies a powerful matriarch, now brought low.

References: Kubler 1986, p. 136; Schele 1997, p. 32

Plate 97
Figurine of captive
Jaina, Mexico
AD 600–900
Ceramic
9³/₄ x 4 in. (24.8 x 10.2 cm)
Promised gift to the Yale University Art Gallery. Anonymous loan
ILE1988.12.3

Traces of the rope that once bound him still survive around the neck of this Jaina figurine. His ample body, particularly the gently protruding belly, suggests an individual who has lived well, even as a captive taken into the tomb, and he retains his dignity.

The date 8 Ahaw has been inscribed on his forehead, in a raised technique that may be tattooing. The strips of torn cloth that hang from his ears—rendered in clay with a simple zigzag pattern—are overt signs of his captive status.

Plate 98
Relief carving of captive
Tonina, Mexico
AD 708–723
Stone
28 x 20½ in. (71.0 x 52.0 cm)
Museo de Sitio de Tonina, Chiapas—INAH, Mexico
10–607609

This figure, one of a pair (see Fig. 55), typifies the recurring theme of capture and imprisonment at Tonina. The heaped humiliations—the kneeling posture, the arms immobilized at his back by prominent rope bindings and long flap-cut paper strips inserted through the earlobes—here reduce a human being to the status of captured game. The two prisoner panels together must have originally flanked some central feature: an entryway, staircase, or a now missing figure.

The inscription on the loincloth of this example provides the victim's name: identified simply as *aj chihk nahb'* or "He of Calakmul." Since he lacks any other title, it seems to have been his famous origin that secures him this sculptural record rather than his individual status. One is left to wonder if Calakmul—so distant from Tonina—was a direct opponent or whether it had instead sent fighters to the aid of one of its nearer allies. The last glyph names the captor, the Tonina king we know only as Ruler 4. Given his accession in AD 708 at the age of just two years, control of the state and its forces must have long lain with the powerful nobles mentioned on several of his monuments.

References: Yadeun 1992, pp. 73–74;
Martin and Grube 2002, p. 184

Plate 99

Relief carving of captive

Tonina, Mexico
AD 600–800
Sandstone
22 1/2 x 19 1/2 in. (57.0 x 49.5 cm)
Museo de Sitio de Tonina, Chiapas—INAH, Mexico
10–569506

The faces and postures of prisoner sculptures at Tonina vary between the dignified and the dejected; between proud princely portraits and representations of ridicule and scorn. Even when his now-broken nose was intact, the wide mustachioed upper lip of this victim gave him the simian features that evoked a "pre-human" state for the Maya. Unlike many other captives, he still wears items of personal clothing and adornment: a cloth headdress and collar, and an ear ornament pierced by what seems to be a longbone with a peccary tusk pendant hanging below.

His name, "4 Jaguar," is carved into his calf. The number four carries a phonetic value in such cases: "four" is *kan* or *chan* depending on the relevant Mayan language and region. Although it is tempting to tie this name to that of the Palenque king, Kan Bahlam, a connection is improbable given the southern location of Tonina, where *chan* is the typical form for "four" (we might similarly note the lack of a high title, or of the name *aj pitzal,* "ballplayer," with which Tonina always refers to this king). The best reading for this character therefore emerges as *chan b'ahlam.* The glyph fragment at top right is enough to know that there was once a caption naming his royal captor.

Plate 100

Relief carving of captive

Tonina, Mexico
c. AD 700
Limestone
22 3/8 x 18 1/8 x 4 in. (56.8 x 46.1 x 10.2 cm)
Museo de Sitio de Tonina, Chiapas—INAH, Mexico
10–588895

Captives are very often shown twisted and contorted, struggling with their bonds and giving bodily expression to their suffering and humiliation. This particular hunched figure was designed to fit within a small niche—a literal place of confinement—which explains his body's square outline. As adornment he wears a twisted cord around his eyes, a jaguar ear issuing flames, and a particular design of pectoral collar, all attributes of the Jaguar God of the Underworld. From various other scenes we know that this deity met a sacrificial end, either immolated by a fiery torch or crushed under a large stone. It seems clear that the victim here has been dressed in emulation of this myth and presumably faces an unpalatable end (Fig. 54).

The name of the prisoner is inscribed along his thigh: "Green Turtle, Lord of Anaayte'" (*yax ahk anaayte' ajaw*). As noted by Peter Mathews, this spelling of Anaayte' almost certainly links him to modern Anaite, the name of a lake, river, and sizable ruin close to the Usumacinta River, not too far from Yaxchilan. Such a strong association over a whole range of different features suggests long continuity; this place-name seems to be one among several that have survived from ancient times to the present day. A stone from the ball court at Tonina tells us that "Green Turtle" was a vassal of the Palenque king Kan Bahlam II. Tonina's war against Anaite seems part of the wider conflict between these two regional rivals.

References: Yadeun 1992, 1993; Ayala 1995;
Martin and Grube 2000, p. 182

Plate 101
Relief sculpture of Palenque king (Monument 122)

Tonina, Mexico

AD 711

Limestone

23¼ x 32⅝ x 5⁵⁄₁₆ in. (59.0 x 83.0 x 13.5 cm)

Museo Regional de Chiapas, Mexico

10–409956

Among Tonina's great litany of prisoner sculptures one stands apart, both in its manner of representation and historical significance. The victim is all but naked and the pose suitably abject. Yet, by the same token, he is accorded refined and idealized features, even a certain elegance—very unlike the ugly and injured prisoner portraits one often sees elsewhere. He also retains much of his jade jewelry, and, most significantly, his royal Jester God diadem. The victim is, in fact, the Palenque king K'an Hoy Chitam II (*k'inich k'an joy chitam*), second son of the illustrious Pakal. His identity is spelled out on his thigh, although with the normal honorific parts of his name and title—the references to being the "Great Sun" and a "Holy" lord—stripped away. Despite his youthful appearance, the king was no less than 66 at the time of the carving.

The top right caption text begins with a date falling in AD 711 and recounts a "star war" defeat of Palenque. This type of action describes the most calamitous of reverses, and suggests that Palenque itself fell to an invading force. Originally thought to be the doing of the Tonina king Baaknal Chaak, this attack can now be recognized to have taken place during the reign of his successor, the child Ruler 4, not yet five years of age, and under the control of his guardians and leading nobles. The final fate of K'an Hoy Chitam remains unclear. The latest evidence suggests that he returned to Palenque and ruled once more, perhaps ransomed or under continued Tonina oversight, until at least 720.

References: Baudez and Mathews 1978; Becquelin, Baudez, and Arnauld 1982–1984; Martin and Grube 2002, pp. 183–184

Plate 103
Carved stone weapon
Unknown provenience
AD 600–900
Flint or chert
16³/₄ x 4¹/₈ in. (42.5 x 10.5 cm)
American Museum of Natural History, New York
30.0/2210

Maya artisans prized flint for their weaponry. Technically a silicified or agatized dolomitic quartz chert, flint was easily knapped and flaked into dangerous weapons that could nevertheless shatter if dropped onto stone.

This example suggests a zoomorph, perhaps a snake in its long, sinuous shape. A Tonina warrior on a recently excavated panel (Plate 106) holds a similarly curved blade. Like other "eccentrics" this piece was designed for ceremonial rather than practical purposes.

Plate 102
Ceremonial axe
Yaxchilan, Mexico
AD 200–900
Obsidian
12³/₄ x 6³/₈ in. (32.3 x 16.1 cm)
Dirección de Estudios Arqueológicos—INAH, Mexico
10-342454

This chipped ceremonial axe—displaying the unmistakable luster of obsidian—was found with other offerings just outside what archaeologists believe to be the mortuary bundle of the ruler Shield Jaguar (*itzamnaaj b'ahlam*) in Tomb 2, Structure 23, at Yaxchilan. This particular blade may be the one the great king wielded in his lifetime.

The Maya associated axes with lightning bolts; the storm god Chaak wielded such a weapon. A hieroglyph that spells the core part of the high title Kaloomte' features an axe-bearing Chaak (Fig. 2e). Shield Jaguar styled himself a "West Kaloomte'," a form that often seems to allude to the authority of Central Mexico and the great city of Teotihuacan (Fig. 2f). As archaeologists Roberto García Moll and Carlos Brokmann have shown, this axe is nearly identical to an example excavated in Belize early in the 20th century. Both were made from Cerro de las Navajas obsidian from Central Mexico, where they were most likely manufactured. With such a source, these axes would have been seen as tangible connections to distant but powerful western lands.

References: Brokmann 2000; Schele and Miller 1986, p. 227; García Moll, this volume, pp. 268–270

Plate 104
Relief step of captive (Monument 27)
Tonina, Mexico
AD 650–800
Stone
8⅝ x 38 x 2⅛ in. (22.0. x 96.5 x 5.5 cm)
Museo Nacional de Antropología—INAH, Mexico
10-1258

Prisoner portraits were preferred subjects for rendering as monumental steps, sometimes as treads, and other times as risers. These steps provided limitless potential to humiliate one's enemies. When arranged in sequence to form a whole stairway, as was often the case, they produce a struggling stack of human misery. This particular victim looks up to meet the feet of his tormentors, accentuating the pathos of his situation.

The unfortunate on this riser from Tonina is called K'awiil Mo', a name that combines that of the well-known lightning deity with the Maya word for "macaw." In a second depiction, on a panel recently excavated at Tonina by Juan Yadeun, we see this name spelled out in his headdress (at right). A third spelling (far right) appears in a stucco glyph, also recovered in recent archaeological work, that once came from an architectural context. These repeated references point to the great importance of K'awiil Mo' as an individual and of the political circumstances of his seizure. As the new panel makes clear, he was taken on 4 October 692 (9.13.0.10.3 3 Ak'bal 11 Keh)—the same day Baaknal Chaak inflicted a significant defeat on his Palenque opponent Kan Bahlam II, Pakal's first son. K'awiil Mo' was presumably one of the Palenque king's confederates or vassals.

References: Martin and Grube 2000; Mathews 2001; Schmidt et al. 1998, p. 538

Plate 105

Cylinder vessel with warriors and captives

Unknown provenience
AD 600–800
Ceramic
11 1/8 in. (28.3 cm)
Princeton University Art Museum. Gift of Mary O'Boyle English
in honor of Woodruff J. English and the Class of 1931
y1986–91

Few painted vessels provide such a clearly defined diorama of militarism and the Maya royal court as does this example, with the position of each actor carefully defined and stratified for the viewer. At the apex of this hierarchy, the Ahaw or "Lord" presides over all. Richly attired in a feather cape and necklace of peccary tusks, he rests upon a dais and a voluminous cushion, from behind which a bodyguard peers out anxiously.

In front of the king kneels a submissive visitor; the inverted severed head on his belt suggests that he is a military captain. The direct correspondence between his headdress and the crest of the covered litter shown at the base of the steps makes clear that he has arrived in grand fashion and is of high status himself. Alongside the litter stands a group of warriors who guard two prisoners, whose earlobes are already marked by the white rags of the defeated and humbled. Close by are set two white bags, likely containing cacao beans in such a context— literally sacks of cash. An accompanying bearer— wearing the same forward-sweeping headdress worn by other household officials in the scene—holds stacks of shell and textiles, evidently additional spoils of war.

Outside the palace proper and at the highest level on the vessel sits a single figure. He gestures and seems to be directing traffic. This may be a rare glimpse of the head courtier at work, the secretary who controlled access to the king and who organized courtly business.

This vessel presents the denouement of battle, the presentation of captives and booty by some regional noble or general to his overlord (compare with Plate 2). Whereas art of earlier times emphasized the personal bravery of the "warrior king," by the 7th and 8th centuries rulers often liked to portray themselves as refined, courtly monarchs distanced from the muddy, bloody realities of war.

In what is a rare occurrence for such a complicated scene, this vessel (above right) has a near-twin painted by a separate artist (below right).

It ostensibly shares the same composition, although with a couple more characters included. Both must be the output of a single workshop in which several painters worked together, and we have good reason to think that this was a common arrangement, perhaps with a single master assisted by a team of apprentices.

Reference: Reents-Budet 1994

Plate 106
Relief of noble with weapon
Tonina, Mexico
AD 613 (9.9.0.0.0 3 Ajaw 3 Sotz')
Stone
44 1/8 x 22 1/8 x 5 15/16 in. (112.0 x 56.0 x 15.0 cm)
Museo de Sitio de Tonina, Chiapas—INAH, Mexico
10–461094

The city of Tonina is unusual in the degree to which the nobility share prominence with the king—even, as in this example, having independent monuments as early as the beginning of the 7th century. A number of Tonina rulers acceded at a tender age, and in doing so ceded very real power to secondary figures acting as regents and guardians.

The lord on this panel wears a Jester God headband of exalted rank, and, in addition to his scimitar-like flint blade, carries an incense bag. His name does not survive, but he describes his accession to the rank of Ah K'uhuun (*aj k'uhuun*) in 612, an era of some turmoil in the region when no ruler of Tonina is currently known. The next king at the city, "Jaguar Centipede" (*hix/b'ahlam chapaat*), would come to power three years later in 615, when he was just eight years old.

CHRONOLOGY		
(9.8.19.8.7)	(2 Kaban 5 Mak)	Accession as Ah K'uhuun
+ 9.3		
9.9.0.0.0	3 Ajaw 3 Sotz'	9th K'atun-ending

Plate 107

Carved stela with warrior

Mexico
AD 864 (10.1.15.0.0 10 Ajaw 8 Mak)
Limestone
40 x 18 in. (101.6 x 45.7 cm)
Private Collection

This small, almost miniature, stela is both rare and anomalous. It is the last known monument for the Usumacinta River and Lacandon rainforest region by more than half a century, and it is clearly the work of a minor center at that. The sculpture represents the only historical record we have for this area at a time when lowland society was in meltdown and when many nearby capitals had already fallen silent or collapsed completely.

The central image is patently late in style, demonstrating weakening traditional canons. The striding figure bears a spear and holds under his arm a basket or folded book. His jaguar-patterned jerkin is typical military gear, but the oliva shells that trim his belt are usually associated with dance events. The zig-zag border and freewheeling strips of cloth and feathers are found on other very late monuments.

Of yet greater interest on this stone is the surrounding 69-glyph inscription—the longest known from the troubled 9th century. It opens with a date in March 864, when an "entering with fire" takes place—a dedicatory ritual normally associated with memorial rites and temple inaugurations. The subject of the ceremony is a carved stone belonging to the central character of the text who, it quickly becomes clear, had died the year before. He is given a full parentage statement and described to have been the "17th" Sahal to rule in that office. There is brief mention of the lord who dedicated the monument, very probably his son since he is called ch'ok, "young noble," and he names only his mother, a lady of "Sun Water" (*k'ina'*). Finally we learn that the deceased was a vassal of the ruler of "White Dog" (*sak tz'i'*), a kingdom of still uncertain location but within the Lacandon forest or adjoining areas.

Reference: Mayer 1980, pp. 50–51

CHRONOLOGY		
10.1.14.9.17	3 Kaban 5 Sek	Fire-entering ceremony
+ 17.13		
(10.1.13.10.4)	1 K'an 17 Sek	819-day count
(10.1.14.0.14)	2 Ix *7 K'ank'in	Death of the lord
+ 17.6		
(10.1.15.0.0)	10 Ajaw 8 Mak	Period ending

Plate 108

Cylinder vase with war party

Unknown provenience
AD 600–800
Ceramic
Diam.: 6⁵/₁₆ in (16.0 cm)
Kimbell Art Museum, Fort Worth, Texas
APx 1976.16

On this vessel we join a war party on its way back to the victor's home city for the inevitable display of wretched prisoners. Four warriors escort a naked captive stripped of all his finery, hands bound behind his back and paper strips inserted through his earlobes. His guards clasp spear and shield and are fitted out in pelts, feathers, and fancy woven textiles. In their headdresses several wear the shell roundels associated with the militarism of highland Mexico and, in two cases, long-handled paintbrushes are thrust into them like giant hatpins. This seemingly incongruous detail serves to emphasize the noble status of these warriors: these are not armed peasants, or even professional soldiers, but literate men, administrators and governors, who might otherwise be painting books in their own palace compounds. It is possible that they are the portraits of individuals known to the vase's original owner, although they could easily represent archetypes—the warrior ideal of courtly culture.

Reference: Schele and Miller 1986, p. 224

Plate 109

Panel with king and warriors (Panel 2)

Piedras Negras, Guatemala

c. AD 660

Limestone

25³/₄ x 53¹/₂ x 7¹/₈ in. (65.5 x 136.0 x 18.0 cm), mounted

Peabody Museum of Archaeology and Ethnology,

Harvard University

00–36–20/C2740

Piedras Negras Ruler 2 dedicated Panel 2 in 667. Although the work features commemoration and mourning of the late Ruler 1, its principal subject is an event over 150 years earlier, in 510, when Piedras Negras staked its claim to rule over the Usumacinta region. In the late 8th century, Ruler 7 then moved the work to a new and central location at O-13, a massive pyramid dedicated to ancestors and their memory. Despite its small size, the panel was an extremely important one, a work that could both invoke the past and reassure Piedras Negras lords of the late 8th century. At the end of the 19th century Teobert Maler found Panel 2 in the debris near the central doorway at the top of O-13 (pp. 277–279). It was first thought to have been a lintel but more likely functioned as an exterior wall panel, thus explaining some confusion in its traditional nomenclature.

On the panel, six armed warriors from Yaxchilan, Lacanha, and Bonampak kneel before the Piedras Negras ruler, who is accompanied in turn by an heir. Both the ruler and the entourage wear war costumes that explicitly evoke Teotihuacan in both iconography and cut of cloth. The kneeling figures wear Teotihuacan "year signs," trapeze-and-ray adornments on their plated helmets and Teotihuacan Tlaloc motifs in their textiles. The king bears a shield with a frontal owl; his heir and the kneeling figures all wear typical Teotihuacan armour.

The Maya adopted foreign attire in warfare, to appropriate the power of the foreigner when making war on other Maya. Here the representation of foreign costume is so complete as to suggest "period" costume of that earlier 6th-century date, although the re-use of this monument throughout Piedras Negras history also suggests that the 510 event was one to be re-enacted.

References: Schele and Miller 1986, p. 84;
Martin and Grube 2000, p. 144

Plate 110

Figurine of warrior with mask

Jaina, Mexico
AD 600–900
Ceramic
10⁵/₁₆ x 5¹/₄ x 2¹/₂ in. (26.2 x 13.3 x 6.4 cm)
Seattle Art Museum, Gift of John H. Hauberg
81.108

With his human skull mask in place, this warrior becomes a terrifying image of death, and the tiny holes at the edge of the mask indicate that it was meant to be worn in such a way. Warriors may also wear human skulls in their headdresses; other warriors appear on stone monuments in "x-ray" or cutaway masks. The ancient Maya collected trophies of human skulls, which can in turn serve as images for renewal and rebirth.

This warrior wears a headdress with great plumes attached to a headband with two distinctive rings. These two rings characterize a particular rank of noble below the king, and may appear on either captor or captive. He also wears a short cape and sleeveless jacket typical of the Yaxchilan kings, among others. At the time of the Spanish invasion, the Maya carried round shields of this sort into battle. An unusual feature is the protective cloth wrapped around a single wrist, usually a marker of a ballplayer: our warrior may be preparing to enter the sacrificial ritual of the ballgame, usually a postlude to war.

Reference: Schele and Miller 1986, p. 224

Plate 111

Figurine of warrior

Jaina, Mexico
AD 700–900
Ceramic
8 5/8 in. (22.0 cm)
Princeton University Art Museum. Gift of Gillett G. Griffin
y1991–69

The face of this soldier is pensive and visibly wrinkled: this is the older warrior, the survivor of battles. Like others, his face is painted or tattooed, and he has had his nose enlarged—possibly through a prosthesis, possibly by means of tattooing.

This warrior's costume is specific to the 8th and 9th centuries, especially the *xicolli*, as the open, sleeveless jacket is known in Central Mexico, whence the style came. Not only is the jacket Central Mexican in origin, but in this case it also bears the stylized motifs of Tlaloc, the Central Mexican god of rain and storm. The close-fitting cap with feathered or scalloped edges belongs to war captains, rather than kings (cf. Plate 2). The flexible feather-trimmed shield served its bearer well, as both protection in battle and also lightweight bedding on the road.

Reference: Schele and Miller 1986, p. 224

Plate 112
Figurine of warrior
Campeche, Mexico
AD 700–900
Ceramic
8¹/₂ x 4 x 3¹/₄ in. (21.6 x 10.2 x 8.3 cm)
The Denver Art Museum. Gift of May D & F Co.
in honor of David Touff
1969.308

Noble in his demeanor, this figure stands at the ready for the call of battle. His right hand once grasped a spear; his left holds a rectangular shield of the sort that is often depicted to be flexible in scenes of active combat.

The low turban characterizes some of the mid-ranking warriors in the Bonampak murals, but the small frontal deity head attached at the center may be that of the Jester God. The artist has worked a raised pattern onto his face, as if to reproduce tattooing or face paint. At the scale of the figurine, this is exacting detail to render, and the imagery is highly specific: the left cheek bears the Jester God, the right woven mat. Both are insignia of rulership.

Reference: Schele and Miller 1986, p. 224

CHAPTER 6 # Palenque: An Exemplary Maya Court

Fig. 56 A bird's-eye view of Palenque, as seen from the northeast. The ball court in the foreground leads to the Palace; the Temple of Inscriptions is built into the hill behind.

Shrouded by the dense foliage of a rich tropical rainforest and frequently bathed in mist and fog, the ruins of Palenque have long captured the imagination of visitors. The first great ancient Maya city to be rediscovered in the high canopy jungle during the 18th century, Palenque drew not only explorers but also artists, whose romantic lithographs portrayed the fallen temples and palaces as an exotic idyll (Fig. 57). The 1952 discovery of an extraordinary tomb at the site sealed a reputation for mystery that has endured to the present day. One suspects that Palenque was legendary even in its own time, with its abundance of water and waterfalls, steep valleys, relative remoteness, and, most important for our discussion here, an exceptional palace to house its royal court.

Fig. 57 Jean-Frédéric Waldeck posed neoclassical figures into romantic landscapes at Palenque, which he visited from 1832 to 1834.

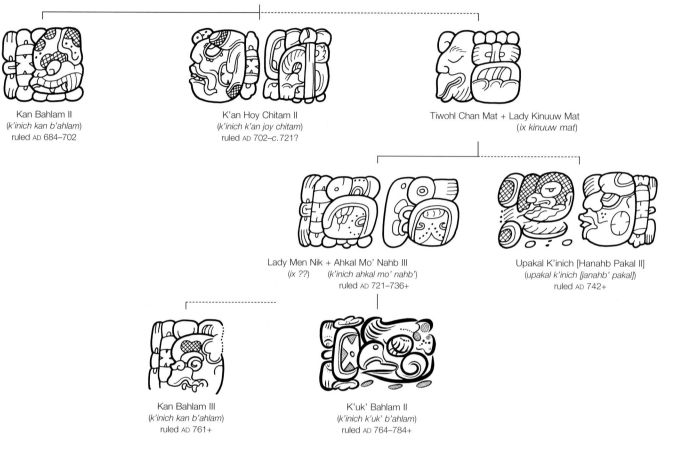

Pakal I (the Great) + Lady Tz'akbu Ahaw
(*k'inich janahb' pakal*)   (*ix tz'akb'u ajaw*)
ruled AD 615–683

Kan Bahlam II
(*k'inich kan b'ahlam*)
ruled AD 684–702

K'an Hoy Chitam II
(*k'inich k'an joy chitam*)
ruled AD 702–*c.*721?

Tiwohl Chan Mat + Lady Kinuuw Mat
(*ix kinuuw mat*)

Lady Men Nik + Ahkal Mo' Nahb III
(*ix ??*)   (*k'inich ahkal mo' nahb'*)
ruled AD 721–736+

Upakal K'inich [Hanahb Pakal II]
(*upakal k'inich [janahb' pakal]*)
ruled AD 742+

Kan Bahlam III
(*k'inich kan b'ahlam*)
ruled AD 761+

K'uk' Bahlam II
(*k'inich k'uk' b'ahlam*)
ruled AD 764–784+

Perhaps more than at any other Maya city, the physical spaces and social arrangements at Palenque demonstrate the ideals of courtly life. Even as the Palenque lords alternately triumphed and then fell prey to the ravages of warfare, they renewed the spaces that had long been the center of court culture. Both in the divine and worldly sphere, women played roles central to the success of the royal and noble families; at one point a queen even took the reins of rulership itself. Palenque kings and queens polished the legends that surrounded their history and promoted the ideals of sacred acts of four millennia before, seeing in them the template for actions in the 7th and 8th centuries; they recorded this charter in works of art that took key locations across the ceremonial heart of the city: in the Palace, the Temple of Inscriptions, the Cross Group, and in Temples 19 and 21.

On the one hand, the familiarity with works at Palenque in the 19th century led modern viewers to think that these works were characteristic of the Maya; on the other hand, the dramatic discovery of new works at the site during the past half-century disrupts any stable understanding of what really is characteristic even of Palenque. As Palenque's complex and often difficult inscriptions have yielded to decipherment, these texts have revealed that many of the works we associate with this sophisticated civilization came into being in the wake of warfare and dynastic struggle. Generation

Fig. 58   The dynasty of Pakal: a family tree of Palenque rulers from AD 615 until *c.* 784.

after generation, Palenque artists invented new compositions and dramatic assemblages while they built on a substantial past and coped with a ruptured present.

Palenque artists matched an exacting eye for form with a profound understanding of their materials. The locally available dense, fine-grained limestone—probably the finest of ancient Mesoamerica—led them to create bas-reliefs abounding in crisply cut edges and buttery smooth surfaces. Their expertise in the making and manipulation of stucco plaster—slow-drying and flint-hard when set—gave them full expression in three dimensions as well. Traces of murals also suggest a once rich corpus of painting, including a bold calligraphic tradition that survives mostly in a late flowering of brush-influenced glyph carving. At the same time, they showed little interest in three-dimensional sculpture in stone, and the painting of cylinder vases, typically such a characteristic of Maya art, did not flourish at Palenque.

What made it possible for Palenque artists to excel in so many media—and yet seemingly exclude others? How was it that innovation could take place in every generation, probably exceeding any other Maya city in this regard? Did they respond to the works produced at other courts—say, Copan or Tonina—or were theirs the works that others responded to? Furthermore, what role did the political environment exert upon the artistic one? To answer these and other questions, we can now go behind the surface of Palenque's stunning artistic production to look at the court society that commissioned the art and the architecture, along with the larger social and political milieu in which artistic traditions developed. Despite the seemingly placid tone and calm demeanor of figures on works at Palenque, the texts on these sculptures reveal tension and dissonance, making it possible to read the works as political artifacts. The rulers of Palenque were deeply concerned with the supernatural origins of their kingdom, and, accordingly, they promulgated the family of gods who defined the city's identity. The story of these gods began in a distant 3309 BC with the account of a divine progenitor and three offspring who would be venerated as its patrons and tutelary gods. Archaeologically, little is known of Palenque's history before the mid-7th century AD; we only have retrospective accounts to fill in the blanks before that time. Anciently known as Lakamha', "Big Water," the site we call Palenque today probably became the seat of the dynasty only in the 6th century. From the beginning the larger Palenque kingdom was known as Baakal, or "Bone"— perhaps some allusion to its westerly place in the Maya world, the land where the sun dies each day.

A succession of rulers for whom we know little more than their names follows until the early 7th century.[1] What seems to have been a modestly successful dynasty came to an end in 611, when enemies from Calakmul attacked the city. Destruction and chaos reigned; enigmatic texts later lament that key rituals were *not* performed and lords and ladies were *lost*.[2]

The Palenque of Pakal

In the wake of all these traumas a 12-year-old boy took the throne. Today the most famous of all Maya kings, Pakal the Great (*k'inich janahb' pakal*)—*pakal* means "shield" in Mayan—had only a tenuous grasp on legitimacy at the outset of his reign. Although no one could have predicted it at the time, his accession was the first step toward stability after years of disruption. Pakal was not the son of a king—there may have been no male heirs—instead, he traced his royal pedigree through his mother, Lady Sak K'uk', "Resplendent Quetzal," and she enjoyed a prominent place during his reign. Pakal clearly had the troubles of the years before his accession to thank for his opportunity: were it not for the defeat of 611 and the extinction of the existing royal line by 612 we might never have heard of him. By the time Pakal died in 683, Palenque had become a key Maya city, not as large as Tikal or Calakmul, and not so old as Copan or Piedras Negras, but a place to be reckoned with nevertheless.

Pakal's early reign is poorly known. Of course he was just a boy at its onset, so presumably his honored parents played key roles in his administration. We know that he married, probably in 626, sired sons in 634 and 644, and a third in 648. But in 654 Calakmul attacked the city once again and it may have been at this point that monuments carrying Pakal's name were destroyed, leaving fragments that later generations would use as building blocks. Whatever the setbacks, Pakal overcame them.[3]

When Pakal hit his stride as a builder in the second half of the 7th century, he focused his attention first on the royal Palace (Fig. 59). He buried the existing complex within a higher platform, turning some chambers into dark and cool subterranean passageways that could be reached only by private stairways that opened into courtyards at the southern end of the Palace. On the new higher level he constructed a multi-chamber throne room, House E, completed in 654; it sheltered one of these stairways to the basement, making for hidden comings and goings from the throne room.

The form of House E acts as a conspicuous display of the king's relationship to his people. In what is a very rare element of architectural ornament, this building features an overhanging cornice of slates cut to imitate Maya thatch. The result is a stone building that emulates humble domestic architecture, and in so doing elevates peasant construction to state architecture. Stone architectural forms created by the Maya bear a relation with their wattle-and-daub antecedents, including the often-criticized corbel vault. Why, people often ask, did the Maya content themselves with this "false" arch when they could have invented something more stable? The answer is that the corbel vault is intended to replicate the perishable hip roof in stone. Pakal's architects took the mimesis of the domestic forms one step further with the stone thatched overhang, as if to state the relationship more explicitly.

Despite House E's exterior appearance, it offered enhanced interior space. Drawing upon the engineering knowledge that may have first been developed at Palenque, House E features two parallel corbel vaults. Although the single Maya vault is inherently unstable, with weight of roof and roofcomb pressing the outer walls out, the vault becomes much stronger in this configuration, in which the outward energy from the two vaults converges in a central, load-bearing wall. This greater stability is attested by the fact that many Palace buildings have stood nearly intact for almost 1,400 years. Pakal's successors would build higher and more dramatic vaults, but the pattern always depended on the parallel vaults that Pakal's program had put into perpetual view.

Pakal named House E the "White Skin House." Years later, when every building at Palenque would be painted red, it remained white, embellished only with painted flowers and symbols of preciousness that were repainted many times across the facade, recalling the many bouquets of flowers brought to court and the symbolic fragrance of its occupants. House E's exterior program made the building seem dressed in the kind of white robe worn by courtiers, their flowers in hand. Amidst all the red buildings, it remained startlingly different, even when later structures pressed in on it and captured the generous patios that had once framed both back and front (Fig. 8).

Pakal set up his principal throne room in House E, whose three large entryways open out onto a western court.[4] The central one frames a throne backed with an unusual rounded relief, known as the Oval Palace Tablet. Mimicking the jaguar skin cushion that supported the king's back, the panel was carved with a scene of Pakal receiving a crown from his mother, Lady Sak K'uk'—freezing the moment of his inauguration and, when viewed through the open doorway, forever setting it upon the king's throne (Fig. 60). Although small in comparison to later Palenque sculptures, the Oval Palace Tablet was a revolutionary work, and like many striking achievements at the city, it seems to have been a homegrown invention. Here, for the first time anywhere in Maya art, was an intimate, indoor scene of accession, dependent in part on dramatic foreshortening for its effect, and carved on

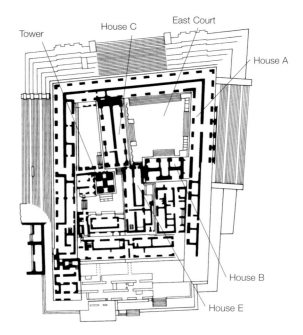

Fig. 59   Plan, Palenque Palace, *c.* AD 800. House E, at center, was among the first buildings to go up; Houses B and C formed spokes that were ultimately surrounded by enclosing colonnades. The tower was one of the last additions.

Fig. 60   Oval Palace Tablet and throne, House E, Palenque Palace. Pakal's mother Lady Sak K'uk' presents her son with a royal headdress. Copyright Merle Greene Robertson.

an unusually shaped interior panel that itself replicated a piece of furniture, the stuffed oval jaguar cushion. Neither figure on the Oval Palace Tablet occupies the center of the picture plane, another innovation. In pushing the figures to the sides, the sculpture places emphasis on the unwritten verb (for the text simply names the protagonists, Pakal and his mother) that is stated visually: the transferring of power is the act, even the subject, of this fresh and adventurous work. Little wonder that subsequent Palenque kings would revere it, adding layers of stucco ornament around it and citing it visually in their own sculptures.

In later years Pakal expanded his complex further, adding House C in 661 and House B at about the same time, the first structures to define a new East Court (Fig. 61a). They radiated from the north end of House E like spokes of a wheel (Fig. 8). From the back doorways of the House E, one could have slipped directly into House B, a building that originally featured a single, vast chamber, but was later subdivided as the Palace grew. Just as House E signals its relation to domestic Maya architecture, House B notes its affiliations by means of the now badly eroded woven mat design on its sloping roof. This motif appears to mark it as a Popol Naah, or "council house," a space reserved for ranking members of local lineages, and whose advice might be sought by the king (or who might impose their will on him).[5]

House C was a reception hall of the kind so often shown in the Palace scenes painted on cylinder vases, including its large frontal stucco heads of gods on both the mansard roof and within the long, open chamber. The front steps form a reviewing stand, a hierarchical space of the kind employed in painted scenes to distinguish differing roles and statuses among courtiers and visitors. The steps themselves carry an inscription, a complex but rather laconic text that runs from tread to riser to tread. The narrative recasts Palenque's perilous conflict with Calakmul into a more favorable light and must be read in conjunction with the sculptures of submissive lords that flank the stairway (Fig. 61a). Carved in a wraparound style characteristic of Tabasco, the figures have their identities drummed home three times: in the stairway text, in their own personal captions, and in the glyphic headdresses they wear. Evidently, they are all captives from sites on the Tabasco plain, where Palenque and Calakmul vied for political dominance and access to the region's deep and fertile soils. Despite this self-acclamation, Pakal's influence in Tabasco seems to have been in decline. In this light, the House C program seems like an elaborate gloss on the true situation.[6]

The House C steps lead down to a sunken patio of the East Court, the key Palace arena for royal receptions. Across this patio (Fig. 61b), House C faces a row of vastly oversized and humiliated

Fig. 61 The East Court of the Palenque Palace: a. View of Houses B and C; b. Some of the oversized captives that flank the steps of House A opposite House C.

a

b

Fig. 62 The Palenque Palace, as seen from the Temple of Inscriptions. The fertile plain of Tabasco can be seen in the distance.

carved figures who strike poses of submission at the base of House A. Probably reset from elsewhere at the site, the sculptures are worked of a variety of rough-grained limestone, varying from white to yellow to gray; the stone may even be imported, shipped to Palenque as part of some tribute arrangement or the booty of war. The figures kneel, press one arm across the chest, or nervously clutch a leg, unlike the submissive figures of House C, who maintain some dignity. One has his genitalia exposed in a mark of abject humiliation. No doubt designed to impress and intimidate visiting dignitaries, these elegant patios were likely—as at Bonampak (Plate 93)—to have been used for the presentation, torture, and execution of prisoners.

In the years to follow, this core group of Palace chambers would be surrounded and cut off from public view by a frame of colonnaded galleries (Fig. 62). Commanding stairways on north, west, and east facades provide attractive and seemingly open approaches to Palace chambers—but the effect is illusory. Long internal walls beyond the colonnade serve to enclose and protect the inner chambers, channeling human movement to a few easily guarded portals. The eastern gallery of House A provides an impressive gateway to the East Court: House A's soaring corbels are cut at right angles by a fabulous fluted Moorish (and corbel) arch, creating a cathedral-like interior space. No other Maya engineers ever approached these architectural feats.

Over time, not only did the Palenque Palace grow, but so also did the profile of the courtiers who attended it. Although they may well have shared communal space within the royal complex, such as House B, they had their own grand residences, many to the east of the Palace across the Otolum River. The new map of Palenque shows how such residences dominate most of the city's prime real estate—stretching downstream where the river by turns cascades and then forms deep iridescent pools.[7] Some featured places of ritual cleansing, such as sweatbaths, as well as sleeping chambers, ancestral shrines, and courtyards for community gatherings. What may seem to be small and cramped spaces today would have been extended with awnings and large parasols. One multi-room palace set in the shadow of the Cross Group was dedicated either to a particular office or to a lineage that monopolized that office. Close to the royal Palace, but not too close, this residence's many private chambers would have served effectively as temporary quarters for visitors or for an expanding and possibly competitive lineage.

Although smaller and less elaborate than the king's abode, these minor palaces still contained artworks and inscriptions commissioned by their owners.[8] Such works offer an especially revealing window on the wider court community and attest to the wealth of the inhabitants who lived just in the shadow of Pakal's own royal residence. Particularly characteristic are elaborate stands once used to support clay pots for the burning of incense, often called censer stands or *incensarios*. Whether of stucco, stone, or terracotta, these censer stands bear the portraits of deceased nobles and were presumably objects of ancestral veneration in household or lineage-based shrines. Carved from stone or shaped in stucco (Plate 122), their texts offer information on the offices held by this stratum of society and describe the rituals and historical celebrations within these lesser courts. An exceptionally handsome figure with a pensive face, detailed mustache, and striking blue paint once held a miniature burner within the headdress (Plate 128). Some works may well be portraits.

Personal portraiture that explored the nature of physiognomy—and possibly attendant issues of the mind behind the face—blossomed under Pakal, with modeled stucco becoming a favorite medium. Across the rest of the Maya world, kings projected impersonal images of youth and vigor, a formal idealism stripped of individuality. Portraits of Pakal, although still stylized, offer a profound move toward naturalism, projecting an innovative vision of Maya kingship, one defined as much by a personality as the institution itself. In many ways this shift can be seen as the logical conclusion of the centuries-long obsession with royal identity. Pakal's most famous likeness, a masterful head in stucco (Plate 113), was torn from some architectural context—part of a bust or full-sized figure on a building facade—and later wedged beneath his sarcophagus as an offering. Stucco frames that may once have surrounded such heads survive along an interior wall of House A in the Palace. A damaged

Fig. 63 Stucco head of Kan Bahlam, *c.* AD 700. Kan Bahlam's protruding lower lip makes him one of the most recognizable of Maya kings.

Fig. 64 Censer stand, Structure 15, Palenque. Although most censer stands that feature human faces cannot be identified, this example depicts a youthful Kan Bahlam.

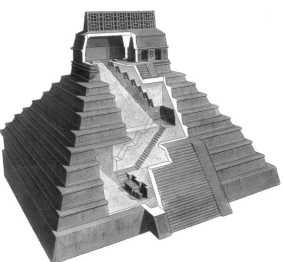

head of Pakal's eldest son Kan Bahlam—one of several retrieved from the rubble of Temple 14—reveals the later king with candor, featuring the protruding lower lip that seemingly violates a typical Maya canon for beauty (Fig. 63). Equally fine examples depict unidentified successors or leading nobles (Plate 114). These stucco heads never smile; the artist captures them in a deeply sober mood. Their eyes meet the viewer's, and one has the sense of intense human thought within these heads.

Pakal directed his greatest efforts at immortality toward his mammoth memorial pyramid, the Temple of Inscriptions, adjacent to the Palace (Fig. 65). Workers first carved a crypt into bedrock and set an immense sarcophagus in place before the pyramid began to rise; engineers designed an 80-ft. (25-m)-long internal stairway that would connect the funerary chamber to a vaulted shrine on the summit. At his death in 683, Pakal's funeral procession carried his body up the front steps of the temple and then down the internal stairs to his waiting sarcophagus, where they laid him into a womb-shaped cavity. When Mexican archaeologist Alberto Ruz Lhuillier[9] opened the tomb in 1952 (Fig. 66), he found the skeleton of a tall man (about 5 ft. 8 in, a veritable giant among the Maya) adorned with several pounds of carved jade: most stunning among these jade offerings is a mosaic mask of jade, shell, and obsidian. Mexican scholars have recently reassembled the jade mask Pakal wore for death's odyssey: fresh and green, it transformed the old man into the youthful and perfect Maize God, while still capturing the essence of his appearance. Perhaps to preserve the body, his funerary attendants anointed his body with cinnabar, and they left a ball of it by his head. Assistants then slid the great sarcophagus lid into place, sealing Pakal's tomb for 1,269 years.

One funerary attendant then placed Pakal's ceremonial belt with jade celts atop the sarcophagus (Plate 133) while a mason connected a hole in the sarcophagus to what archaeologists have called the psychoduct, or spirit tube, a hollow stone channel that runs along the interior stairs, finally issuing into air at top, through a stucco pier, conducting Pakal's spirit or soul to air and fresh air to the sarcophagus. The trapezoidal slab used to close the chamber was then set in place and sealed up with

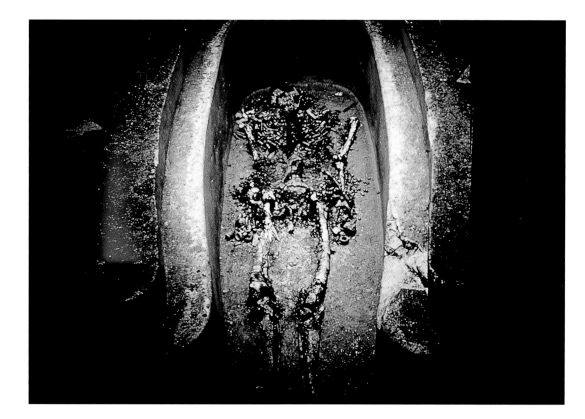

Fig. 66 Sarcophagus, Temple of Inscriptions, Palenque. When the great stone slab (Fig. 67) had been moved aside, archaeologists could see the remains of a single, tall human within.

Fig. 67 Sarcophagus lid, Temple of Inscriptions, Palenque. The surface of Pakal's sarcophagus depicts the king in a state of rapture and rebirth, as he emerges from the jaws of death in a form that combines features of the Maize God, the Sun God, and K'awiil. Copyright Merle Greene Robertson 1967.

plaster, and the entire space was finally sanctified with the blood offering of five sacrificial victims just outside the door. Laborers with tumplines hauled load after load of rubble up the front steps of the temple and slowly sealed the staircase for what was to be eternity. It took Ruz four years to remove the rubble once again.

Within what is an assemblage of mystery and drama, the most extraordinary single work of art in the Temple of Inscriptions is the sarcophagus lid itself (Fig. 67), now a symbol that has transcended Palenque to become an image of modern Mexico, woven into rugs and printed on curtains. Exquisitely drawn and mapped onto the stone, the carving of the lid, sides, and base is nevertheless hasty and unfinished, with tool marks and outline painting readily visible. Perhaps Pakal died unexpectedly, although given his age, that seems unlikely, or perhaps the final carving was held off until his death in 683. On the surface of the sarcophagus, Pakal appears both as the Maize God and as K'awiil, in the moment of rebirth from the Underworld. In his posture of rapturous recline, Pakal also issues forth a great tree from his body, as if to show that by this act the world once again is centered. It also shows Palenque to be the center of that world. On the sides of the sarcophagus, Pakal's ancestors emerge from cracks in the earth, reborn with Pakal. They, too, become trees, and each is an edible fruit: cacao, guava, avocado, and nance among them.

The Next Generation

Pakal's eldest son, Kan Bahlam II, "Snake Jaguar" (*k'inich kan bahlam*), inherited the kingdom at the age of 48. He was already an old man in 7th-century terms, and we do not know how he spent his youth or his manhood up until this time. With his arched nose, protruding lower jaw and lip, and six-toed feet, his is the most recognizable likeness at Palenque, as easily identified in three-dimensions in stucco or ceramic as in stone bas-relief (Figs. 63, 64). Perhaps galvanized by a desire to escape the long shadow of Pakal, Kan Bahlam achieved significant political and military success. Although the father may have been the master of kingly rhetoric, the son established the regional dominance that befitted such posturing.[10] Yet Kan Bahlam also established a new program at Palenque, one that quickly distinguished son from father.

In 692, less than a decade after his accession, Kan Bahlam dedicated his major architectural complex, three major temples known today as the Cross Group. Each Cross building features aspects of a standard program, including a "shrine within a shrine," inset into the rear chamber of the building (Fig. 68). Each interior shrine houses a large carved panel: events in supernatural time on the left of the panel link to historical events on the right, with moments in Kan Bahlam's life likened to those of the deep past. On each panel Kan Bahlam appears in two guises: one his adult self, and the other, as a child; his two selves flank a different central image in each chamber, one the eponymous "cross," in fact, a World Tree.[11] Each shrine is also named as the ritual sweatbath (literally "oven," *pib naah*) where one of Palenque's three patron deities was born. In these texts, Kan Bahlam and his astrologers emphasize a night in 690 when the planets Jupiter, Saturn, and Mars came into close conjunction with the Moon—an event woven into the mythic fabric of the Palenque state. The same date is recorded on a jade pectoral, an item of royal regalia once worn by the king and later cast into the great well or *cenote* of Chichen Itza, far to the north (Plate 118).

In the texts of the Cross Group, Kan Bahlam recapitulated the successes of his decade-old regime. In the Temple of the Sun, he emphasized his military prowess, beginning with his defeat of Palenque's great rival in the mountainous south, Tonina, a subject also addressed on a recently discovered panel from Temple 17. At the Temple of the Cross, Kan Bahlam oversaw the installation of Palenque's one and only carved stela. Given the emphasis on two-dimensional carving at the site, it is something of a shock to see this fully three-dimensional stonework—otherwise unknown at Palenque but highly characteristic of Tonina, from which it may have been sent as a gift, or executed by sculptors from that city in tribute.

During this period of Kan Bahlam's reign ceramic production burgeoned, particularly in the form of terracotta censer stands (Plates 123–126) or censers—usually the elaborately modeled stands for incense burners more rarely made in stone and stucco. Over 100 of these fragile clay sculptures were buried as offerings on the stepped levels of the Cross Group temples, many of which have been carefully re-assembled by archaeologists and conservators (p. 253). Readily available red clay made mass production possible, and artists pursued subtle differences for a standard group of sun deities, particularly the Jaguar God of the Underworld, the solar aspect at night and the god of fire. A few pieces even show the distinctive face of the king himself (Fig. 64). Others portray unknown individuals: the central parting to their hair may indicate that some depict women (Plate 123).[12]

Perhaps distracted by the vast building project at home, Palenque fell prey to military setbacks at the hands of a resurgent Tonina, beginning almost as soon as the Cross Group was completed in 692 (Plates 100, 104).[13] Nonetheless it was only after Kan Bahlam's death in 702 and the succession of his brother K'an Hoy Chitam II, "Precious Tied Peccary" (*k'inich k'an joy chitam*) that Palenque's fortunes took a serious turn for the worse. A truly aged man for his time at 57, K'an Hoy Chitam proved an energetic builder. He expanded the Palace by adding the northern gallery, known today as House AD. This created a grand new public facade, offering vistas onto the vast plain stretching out toward the Gulf of Mexico. At its center was set a huge throne, its back a carved panel of exquisite workmanship now known as the Palace Tablet. Another fine monument, showing K'an Hoy Chitam in the guise of the storm god Chaak and flanked by his parents, demonstrates once again the importance of Pakal to his descendants (p. 244; Fig. 77; Plate 117).

But K'an Hoy Chitam was not to have a peaceful dotage. In a disastrous reversal of fortune, Tonina forces took the old king captive and presumably marched him back to their highland capital

Fig. 68 The Cross Group, Palenque. Each temple shares certain common features: a. A large carved panel on which two images of Kan Bahlam proffer deity effigies or bloodletters to a central image. This example is the tablet from the Temple of the Sun; b. A shrine that houses the panel, itself decorated with panels and sculpted motifs. Illustrated here is the interior of the Temple of the Cross; c. An enclosing sanctuary atop a tiered pyramid platform. The best preserved of these is the Temple of the Sun shown here.

in 711. Although stripped of all but his royal diadem and necklace, he was rendered at Tonina in a sympathetic sculpture and given an unmistakably noble air despite his physical abjection (Plate 101). Characterized by a strong and subtle line, and worked in a two-dimensional format, the stone may have been carved by Palenque artists. Although K'an Hoy Chitam's capture was once thought to be the prelude to his execution or extended imprisonment, today there is good reason to believe that he returned to Palenque to rule once more, with his last mention falling as late as 720.[14] In other cases of this kind the precondition to release was future subservience to the victors, accompanied by regular levies of tribute or perhaps one crippling ransom demand. Long after the king had returned to Palenque, he remained the subject of the Tonina panel, and the work may have been featured in a stairway assemblage.

Recovery and New Heights

K'an Hoy Chitam died within the year and in 721 Ahkal Mo' Nahb III, "Turtle Macaw Sea" (k'inich ahkal mo' nahb) took his place on the Palenque throne. The offspring of Pakal's third, non-ruling son, the new king was a nephew of his two predecessors and thus a grandson of Pakal. Long thought to be a period of little real distinction, Ahkal Mo' Nahb's tenure has been elevated by recent finds to something of a pinnacle for sculptural art at Palenque. Excavations in two of his most important buildings, Temples 19 and 21, have revealed astonishing works in both stone and stucco, opening a whole new vista on Ahkal Mo' Nahb's life and times. Such works betray his primary concerns: the justification of his own position and the delicate balance struck between himself and the local nobility. He was also unusually concerned with establishing the place of his heir, Upakal K'inich, "Shield of the Sun God"—quite possibly his brother, rather than a son—attempting to repeat the fraternal succession of Kan Bahlam and K'an Hoy Chitam. These sets of brothers may have sought to emulate supernatural pairings, like the great Hero Twins and certain Palenque patron gods with fraternal relationships.

Subsidiary lords are portrayed in the earliest of Ahkal Mo' Nahb's works, in scenes whose heightened complexity—with multi-figure compositions in which the king engages with his principal nobles rather than family members—implies new political arrangements. In all likelihood, this regime placed greater reliance on courtiers who needed to be variously rewarded or appeased, as exemplified by the fabulous platform discovered within Temple 19 (Figs. 72, 92, 93). Commissioned in 736, the Temple 19 scene shows Ahkal Mo' Nahb surrounded by his lords, arrayed in orderly rows to his left and right, yet at the same time seemingly ready to crush him from opposing directions. The inscriptions belabor various mythic episodes integral to Palenque's self-perception, as if to enlist supernatural as well as pragmatic political support (pp. 261–264).

A single vertical stone panel, the front facing of a massive pier in Temple 19 may be the most exquisite stone carving known from the ancient New World (Fig. 69). The standing king presses one of his hands into that of a subordinate, while another assistant adjusts the giant supernatural bird mouth—an elaborate costume—within which the king stands. The carving resonates with unresolved erotic tension; eyes do not connect, yet the bodies all press closely together and exchange intimate touches. On the side of the same pier, a flanking polychrome stucco scene gives a side view of the same costume—although this time it is Upakal K'inich who appears in the gaping maw of the supernatural bird (Fig. 70). The scale of this program is very large, evidence that the economic wherewithal for such works was still available to the king and his court.

In a startling discovery in 2002, within Temple 21, archaeologists found a companion platform to the one in Temple 19, carved in the same style and celebrating the same date (Plate 129). This time the center is given over to an unmistakable portrait of Pakal, at this point a long-dead forebear. His

Fig. 69 Detail, panel, Tablet from Temple 19, Palenque. An attendant lord kneels beside his king Ahkal Mo' Nahb. Although badly broken at the time of the building's destruction, this panel displays unsurpassed levels of detail and surface finish.

Fig. 70 Stucco panel, Temple 19, Palenque. Here Upakal K'inich, successor to Ahkal Mo' Nahb, is depicted in a full-color stucco panel. Although the panel was found fallen and smashed into over 3,000 fragments, the patient work of archaeologists and restorers has led to its nearly complete restoration.

caption explains that he is impersonating a legendary king, one who supposedly ruled in a remote 252 BC.[15] Here Ahkal Mo' Nahb both evokes the great patriarch of the city in his quest for legitimization and neatly ties this to Palenque rulers of the ancient past. To the left of the enthroned Pakal, but looking away, as if disengaged, is the portrait of Ahkal Mo' Nahb himself and to the right that of Upakal K'inich. Ahkal Mo' Nahb was only six when Pakal died and we can see this representation as contrived in its depiction of three full-grown adults. At the same time, we see the role that ancestors play in the lives of the living—death had a radically different currency than it does for the modern world. Flanking these lords, in turn, are two pudgy kneeling characters dressed in jaguar suits and holding bouquets of feathers and paper. Despite their bestial appearance, the titles they carry identify them as humans who impersonate supernatural felines.

We lack any date for Ahkal Mo' Nahb's death, though he was duly succeeded by Upakal K'inich (who adopted the name of Pakal on his accession) by at least 742.[16] The new king created at least one carved panel for the Palace, although today it survives only in fragmentary form. There also seems to have been a Kan Bahlam III, to judge from his supervision of a Pomoná king's installation in 751, but no enduring trace at Palenque itself has yet to come to light.[17] A record of a further defeat at the hands of Tonina at about this time may be an important clue to this poorly documented era.

The declining fortunes of Palenque's kings were reflected in the very fabric of the royal court. Unable to commission any major expansion of the Palace, they instead met the rising demand for space by filling the interior courtyards with new buildings, and turning the elegant layout of old into a confused warren. Even the striking and unusual Tower—itself a feat of engineering attesting to the tradition of yore—imposed itself upon the old House E courtyard (Fig. 59). From the Tower's summit, Palenque's elite could look out on the great plain stretching all the way to the Gulf of Mexico. Once the major source of their wealth and power, these northern neighbors would have been viewed much more as the source of potential attack by the mid-8th century.

A brilliant final chapter in Palenque's courtly art was written by a son of Ahkal Mo' Nahb called K'uk' Bahlam II, "Quetzal Jaguar" (*k'inich k'uk' b'ahlam*) (Plate 127). Crowned king in 764, he was still in power two decades later, when he celebrated his *katun* anniversary—the Maya 20-year period—with a magnificent group of artworks. For this occasion, a small atelier of carvers—or perhaps a single master—designed a throne assemblage for the old House E courtyard, built right into the base of the Tower.[18] Although of diminutive scale, the incised workmanship was of exceptional quality, with the carver transferring many of the conventions of brush painting—a carefully weighted, whiplash line—to his stone "page." The Creation Tablet, once the throne back, presents a mythic narrative (Plate 121). Within quatrefoil cartouches—supernatural caves and windows onto another world—we see two deities, one a version of the rain god, Chaak. Each sits on a hieroglyph; the same two glyphs appear as the names of personified stones on the legs that supported the seat (Plates 119, 120). Like Pakal's Oval Palace Tablet, the assemblage developed an internal dialogue, making it animated and self-referential.

Probably once the seat of this throne assemblage, the Tablet of 96 Glyphs has tiny holes drilled through the slab's edges, so that a jaguar pelt cushion could have been tied securely over it. Listing most kings from Pakal onward, the Tablet of 96 Glyphs poised the lord who sat on it as the inheritor of all Palenque (Fig. 71). Even as Palenque lords struggled to retain order, they kept Pakal ever in mind, whether in texts of the time or as they went about their daily lives, where his works, particularly the Temple of Inscriptions, remained at the center of the ceremonial precinct. By consolidating artistic energy into a single, self-contained grouping, the Palenque artist—or perhaps the Palenque king—understood that on a small scale the city's penchant for innovation and imagination could be brilliantly fulfilled even in times of stress.

Fig. 71 Tablet of 96 Glyphs. This finely incised work, commissioned by K'uk' Bahlam c. 784, recalls his ancestry, going back to Pakal. Tiny holes at the edges of the stone indicate that a cushion, perhaps a stuffed jaguar pelt, was tied onto this panel, which probably functioned as the seat of a throne.

These dynamic works, exploring new themes and styles, pointed not to the past but to the future. Yet there was precious little future to be had for this great wave of Maya civilization. Save for a blackware vase incised with the accession date of final, none-too-great Pakal III, in 799, these are the very last creations of Palenque's artisan culture. A rising tide of disintegration—which would see not just Palenque but scores of other cities tipped first into social collapse and then full abandonment—soon extinguished the once vivid flame of Palenque creativity. From the crumbled, tree-choked vestiges of the city, modern researchers seek to retrieve its glorious past, to bring at least some of its one-time magnificence to light, and to color its faded textures with the personalities who brought it into being.

Plate 113
Portrait head of Pakal
Palenque, Mexico
AD 600–900
Stucco
16 7/8 x 6 11/16 in. (43.0 x 17.0 cm)
Museo Nacional de Antropología—INAH, Mexico
10-1285

Palenque sculptors captured the essence of a youthful Pakal the Great in this modeled stucco head, discovered under the sarcophagus in which the king was interred, deep within the Temple of Inscriptions. Broken off at the neck, the head may have been wrenched from a sculpture at the time of the funeral, or it may have been a revered work salvaged from the crippling attack on the city in the mid-7th century.

The small flowers that emerge from the headband may represent the tiny and delicate cacao flowers; his thick turned-forward topknot suggests both maize foliage and the "jester" dangle of *huun*, the Jester God. Pakal's trimmed and stepped bangs reveal the highest of 7th-century hairstyles. Not only did the Maya admire large noses; they may have extended them artificially above the bridge, possibly through a removable cosmetic.

Reference: Ruz 1973

Plate 114

Portrait of an unknown noble

Palenque, Mexico
AD 700–800
Stucco
9 5/8 x 7 7/16 x 4 3/8 in. (24.4 x 18.9 x 11.2 cm)
Museo Nacional de Antropología—INAH, Mexico
10-228046

One of the most affecting and humanistic of personal portraits created by the Maya, this face was once part of an architectural facade, probably set high above the ground. In this context it is likely to depict one of Palenque's rulers. The master stucco artisan has captured a meditative and serene physiognomy that nevertheless suggests intelligence and concentration.

Reference: Schmidt et al. 1998, p. 637

Plate 115

Stucco hieroglyph of a personal title

Palenque, Mexico

c. AD 647 (9.10.14.5.10 3 Ok 3 Pop)

Stucco

6 11/16 x 8 1/2 in. (17.0 x 21.0 x 4.0 cm)

Museo de Sitio de Palenque "Dr. Alberto Ruz L'Huillier"—INAH, Mexico

10-117746

Plate 116

Stucco hieroglyph of the Wind God

Palenque, Mexico

AD 600–800

Stucco

5 1/8 x 5 1/8 in. (13.0 x 13.0 cm)

Museo de Sitio de Palenque "Dr. Alberto Ruz L'Huillier"—INAH, Mexico

10-458704

Experience with the powdered limestone used in both construction and cooking led the Maya to discover the sculptural potential of stucco plaster early in their history. Malleable when freshly mixed but concrete-hard when set, stucco quickly progressed from a simple sealant and mortar on buildings to form decorative programs that enveloped whole facades. By the 7th and 8th centuries these architectural adornments included hieroglyphic texts, of which this is a fine example. It well illustrates the pliant nature of this material, possible only with an advanced understanding of grinding, refining, and mixing processes, as well as

the addition of retardants to slow the drying process and maximize the time for modeling.

This block comes from the Olvidado or "Forgotten" Temple at Palenque—set well to the west of the palace and the main group of ceremonial buildings—where it formed part of a text on an external pier. We have only a partial reading for it, but we do know that it is a personal title establishing the holder's place as "fifth" in some kin-based group: perhaps among a sequence of brothers.

References: Mathews and Robertson 1985; Schmidt et al. 1998, p. 624

This glyphic portrait succeeds in conveying the thin line that can separate Maya art and writing. It depicts the Wind God, the patron of the number three, whose responsibilities partially overlap with the better-known highland Mexican deity Ehecatl. His characteristic features are the plaited headband and flowery medallion he often wears and the T-shaped *ik'* "wind" sign fixed onto his cheek. This hieroglyph once embellished a wall or facade at Palenque, a city with an unusual fascination for this deity and his associated concepts—from the T-shaped windows that appear throughout the royal palace, to the contrived appearances of the day 9 Ik' in mythic texts—a day sacred to the Wind God.

References: Taube 1992, pp. 56–64; Houston and Taube 2000

Plate 117

Carved limestone relief with three figures

(Dumbarton Oaks Panel 2)
Palenque area, Mexico
AD 702–721
Limestone
65 3/4 x 39 3/8 in. (167.0 x 100.0 cm)
Dumbarton Oaks Research Library & Collections,
Washington, D.C.
PC.B.528

Multi-figure scenes were a Palenque specialty, where they were usually mounted on the back walls of temple sanctuaries, or similarly enclosed palace chambers. In this case we see the Palenque king K'an Hoy Chitam dancing in the guise of Chaak, a god of storm and sacrifice—who can be identified by the cross-banded shell diadem worn high in his headdress and his bivalve shell ear ornaments. Here Chaak appears as the maker of storms. In one hand he brandishes a flint axe hafted onto a serpent, a symbol of living lightning with which to strike the earth. In the other he carries an *olla,* a handled water vessel that bears the hieroglyph *ak'ab,* or darkness—to indicate the dark thunderous downpour it contains.

On either side sit K'an Hoy Chitam's parents: to the right the great Pakal and to the left his mother, Lady Tz'akbu Ahaw, both named in captions above their heads. Each holds a small god effigy, respectively the leafy-crowned Jester God, a patron of royal lineage, and the snake-footed K'awiil, a god of lightning.

Originally part of a three-panel composition, only this central section is known. The missing side panels are likely to have been textual, so the inscription as we have it is only an orphaned mid-section. It deals with early events in K'an Hoy Chitam's life, centering on a temple dedication conducted by his father in 657 when the future king was 16 years of age. The temple is called the *waybil,* "sleeping place," of a local storm god called "3-9-Chaak"—mentioned again in a later section—and we might suspect that the impersonation rites performed here are also connected to this deity.

An unusual feature of this monument is its finish: sculptors worked the text and the upper parts of the bodies with finesse, leaving no sign of the chisel and smoothing all edges. By contrast, the feet and lower costume details seem to have been hastily carved and the background left in an unusually rough condition.

References: Coe and Benson 1966, pp. 16–23; Schele and Miller 1986, p. 275; Grube 1992; De la Fuente, this volume, pp. 244–246

Plate 118

Necklace with bar pendant

Chichen Itza, Mexico
c. AD 695
Jade beads (group of 57)
Carved bar pendant
Pendant: 7 5/8 in. (19.4 cm)
Necklace mounted: 16 1/8 x 16 1/8 in. (41.0 x 41.0 cm)
Peabody Museum of Archaeology and Ethnology,
Harvard University
10-56-20/C5969.1(3), 10-70-20/C6048.1, 10-71-20/C5970.1,
10-71-20/C6153.1(3), 10-71-20/C6155, 10-71-20/C6168, 10-
71-20/C6170, 10-71-20/C6200, 10-71-20/C6212, 10-71-
20/C6216, 10-71-20/C6269, 10-71-20/C6275, 10-71-
20/C6318 (pendant), 10-71-20/C6331(31), 10-71-20/C6335.1,
10-71-20/C6342.1(3), 19-37-20/C9257.1 (3), 19-37-
20/C9258.1, 19-37-20/C9263, 17-10-20/C6064)

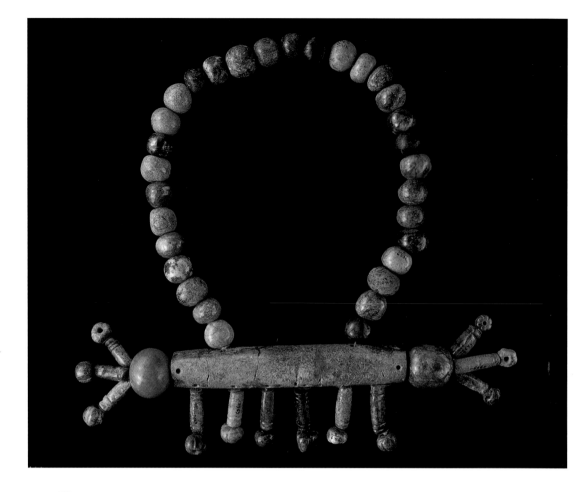

Jade abounds in the rich tombs and caches of
Palenque, whereas other materials valued today—
say, fine ceramic vessels—are nearly absent or of
inferior quality, perhaps revealing that the ancient
Maya had regional, not universal, tastes in luxury.

At the end of the 7th century, the Palenque ruler
Kan Bahlam commissioned this jade pectoral to
celebrate a series of events from his reign, the latest
falling in 695. The text is rudely incised and difficult
to read today, but one of the recorded events was a
rare multi-planetary conjunction of July 690 that
he referred to in several texts, as if he took this
astronomical event to be his personal augury.

The position of the drilled holes on the long
bar determines how the other beads had to be
suspended; the work thus must replicate the sort
of pectoral assemblage depicted on the bar itself.
In other words, this is a self-referential object, in
which the representation and the thing itself engage
in a visual conversation. Additionally, the
suspension holes themselves determine how the
bead is to be worn: Kan Bahlam's portrait must face
up, toward the wearer's chin. In this way the work
is a private one, its most intimate carving visible
only to one viewer.

However, this large jade bead and the 56 other
beads reconstructed here come not from Palenque,
but from the Sacred Cenote at Chichen Itza,
whence they were dredged at the beginning of the
20th century. Whether they were looted from a
Palenque tomb or sent willingly to the "Black
Hole," as the Maya perceived this place of entry
to the Underworld, we will never know.

References: Proskouriakoff 1974; Coggins and Shane
1984, p. 67

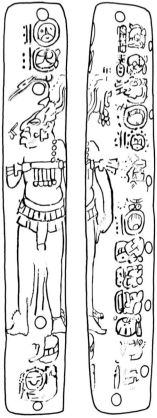

CHRONOLOGY		
9.13.2.13.0	13 Ajaw *18 K'ank'in	(AD 694?)
9.12.18.5.16	*2 Kib 14 Mol	(AD 690)
9.13.2.17.7	9 Manik' 0 Pop	(AD 695)

Plate 119

Throne leg

Palenque, Mexico

c. AD 784

Limestone

10¾ x 7 13/16 x 2¾ in. (27.4 x 19.8 x 7 cm)

Museo Nacional de Arqueología—INAH, Mexico

10-79299

Plate 120

Throne leg

Palenque, Mexico

c. AD 784

Limestone

10⁷/₁₆ x 7 11/16 x 2⅜ in. (26.5 x 19.5 x 6.0 cm)

San Diego Museum of Man, in memory of Jeanne P. Haber

1978–70–1

These small incised panels, now to be found in separate museums, were once the legs of a throne that incorporated two other notable pieces: the Creation Tablet (Plate 121) and the Tablet of 96 Glyphs (Figs. 43, 71). Collectively, they show Palenque's calligraphic style at its most exuberant and unrestrained. They stand witness to the tradition of brush-painting at the city and the appearance of its finest books. Each leg depicts a composite character that blends various identities together in a way much beloved by Maya scribes. They represent mythic locations: with the dominant identity is that of a personified stone, but it also includes features of the storm god Chaak and vegetal motifs that allude to maize.

In their foreheads they carry more explicit glyphic motifs. In the case of the San Diego leg (right) the whole forehead has been turned into a giant eyeball, its shriveled optic nerve shown tapering at left. The cross-hatched pupil is inset with the hieroglyph for *tuun,* "stone." The Mexico City leg (left) has the same word, but differs in incorporating a hieroglyph that depicts the pincers of the infernal centipede, the so-called "jaws of the Underworld." These motifs have direct analogues on the Creation Tablet, where they appear as glyphic thrones for other supernatural characters. Their relative positions to the right and left of that panel would seem to confirm that the two legs beneath originally looked outward, rather than at each other.

References: Robertston 1991; Porter 1994; Houston and Stuart 1996

Plate 121
Creation Tablet
Palenque, Mexico
c. AD 784
Limestone
27½ x 40½ x 2 in. (70.0 x 103.0 x 5.0 cm)
Museo de Sitio de Palenque "Dr. Alberto Ruz L'Huillier"—INAH, Mexico
10–335187

The Creation Tablet is a legacy from Palenque's late florescence of calligraphic carving. Typically, relief carvings seemed to have begun with an artist's sketch or template applied directly to the rock surface. However, to judge from the black painted outlines still to be seen on the sarcophagus of Pakal, these served only as a broad guide for the sculptor, who revised and cut his own forms as the work progressed. In the 8th century the Palenque artists developed a greater interest in the brush style of their best calligraphers—scribes who must have spent most of their careers painting in bark-paper books. In this new technique, the incision faithfully followed the swashes and flourishes produced by the brush, yielding a final effect almost as if an acid ink had etched the work into stone. We can see the style appear first in inscriptions alone, but by the end of the century it had migrated to figural images, such as those seen here.

As James Porter first suggested, the Creation Tablet once formed the back of a throne set at the base of the Palenque Palace's tower. The seat apparently consisted of the Tablet of 96 Glyphs discovered nearby (Fig. 71), while the legs are represented by panels now residing in Mexico City and San Diego (Plates 119, 120). The subject of the tablet, expressed in its two cartouches and their associated texts, is clearly mythological but not well understood. The scalloped cartouches are a very ancient motif that represents a window or portal into a supernatural cave. At right, in a lively but graceful rendering, we see the storm god Chaak—though with some suggestion that this may be a masked impersonator more than a living deity. He sits on hieroglyphs for "eye" and "stone," a supernatural placename also reflected on the leg that once supported this edge of the throne (Plate 120). The upper text talks about the "beheading" of what seems to be a "day fisherman" and a "night fisherman," performed by an important local god— just one of innumerable lost Maya myths.

References: Robertson 1991 (outline painting); Porter 1994

Plate 122

Censer stand with portrait of a noble

Palenque region, Mexico

AD 664

Limestone

16 1/8 x 10 1/4 in. (41.0 x 26.0 cm)

Museo Amparo, Puebla, Mexico

52 22 MA FA 57 PJ 1367

The grandeur of this portrait might lead us to expect that we are in the presence of a K'uhul Ahaw, "holy lord," or king on this censer stand. In fact, this work celebrates a lesser noble of the Ah K'uhuun rank seen at B18, A21, D1, D8, and D22 (Fig. 12c). The 110-block inscription—which runs over the top, sides, and even nestles on the cheeks and in the mouth of the headdress mask—refers to its lordly subject with an undeciphered sign depicting a jawless jaguar, which does at least offer us a suitable nickname (A18, B20, C1, C8, C22). The text begins by describing Jawless Jaguar's death in September AD 647 (A20) and the visiting or re-entry of his tomb in 659. This was an eventful time in the political affairs of Palenque and the neighboring Tabasco region. The tomb ritual takes place just seven days after a famous "arrival" of the Santa Elena king at Palenque and the two events could conceivably be related in some way.

The final section is damaged, but it is likely to name the descendent who commissioned this memorial sculpture in 664. The name of the king to whom Jawless Jaguar was beholden also appears close to the end, but unfortunately it is no longer legible (C25–D25). Although the work is characteristic of Palenque's art, this may celebrate the life of a provincial seat or kingdom under Palenque's control at this time.

This censer stand seems to be made of modeled stucco over a limestone core. This may have been a less expensive way to produce such elaborate works compared with having them carved in stone.

Reference: Easby and Scott 1970, entry 175

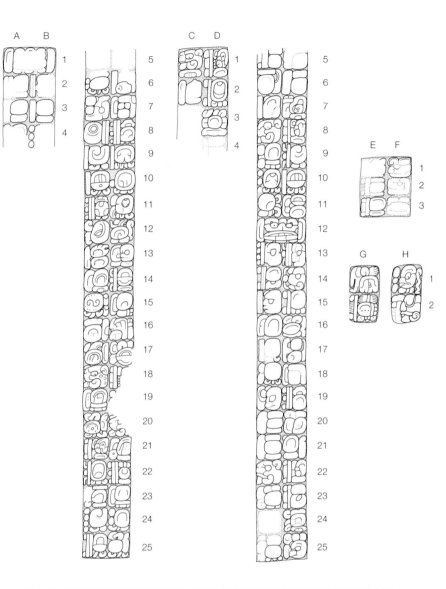

CHRONOLOGY			
9.10.14.15.0	11 Ajaw 13 Yax	(AD 647)	Death of Jawless Jaguar
- 1.5.5			
(9.10.13.9.15)	1 Men 13 Sek	(AD 646)	819-day Count
(9.10.14.15.0	11 Ajaw 13 Yax)	(AD 647)	Death of Jawless Jaguar
+ *3.*0			
(9.10.15.0.0)	6 Ajaw 13 Mak	(AD 647)	15-year Period Ending
(9.10.14.15.0	11 Ajaw 13 Yax)	(AD 647)	Death of Jawless Jaguar
+ 12.2.4			
(9.11.6.17.4)	7 K'an 17 Ch'en	(AD 659)	Tomb ritual
+ 5.2.6			
(9.11.12.1.10)	7 Ok 18 Yax	(AD 664)	Dedication

Plate 123

Censer stand with human face

Palenque, Mexico
AD 700–800
Ceramic
33 1/4 x 11 13/16 x 11 in. (84.5 x 30.0 x 28.0 cm)
Museo de Sitio de Palenque "Dr. Alberto Ruz L'Huillier"—INAH, Mexico
10-479190

The practice of making offerings in elaborate incense burners flourished during Kan Bahlam's reign, and over a hundred have been found to date in the Cross Group. At some point after Kan Bahlam's death, heirs and descendents built Group 15 on the northwestern side, blocking easy access to the complex. At Group 15, the veneration of Kan Bahlam continued. On the temple setbacks some of the most striking of censer stands have been found, including those that include a human face rather than the face of a deity.

As scholars in Mexico have noted, this hairstyle —with its central part and absence of bangs— seems to characterize women at some point in the 8th century. Two particularly beautiful examples of idealized human female faces, in nearly perfect condition, have been reconstructed; other human examples may well represent a posthumous Kan Bahlam, the deified subject of veneration.

Here we see the single most extraordinary censer base known to date. The exquisite human face wears a tiny blue—representative of jade— head as a pendant, atop a stylized vulture head. For a headdress, atop a vertical row of headband beads, the artist has set the large jawless head of a deity, probably the serpent-based K'awiil, which is in turn topped by a small open-mouthed rearing serpent, framed by bird wings. At the very top, just in front of the holder for the actual censer (Plate 126), a handsome noble figure sits on a throne, incense bag in hand. Independent of this assemblage we would recognize him to be an elegant courtly figure; here he is the final icing— even if disconcerting in the leap from larger than life to miniature—on an exceptional work.

Reference: Schmidt et al. 1998, p. 601

Plate 124

Censer stand with sun god
Palenque, Mexico
AD 700–900
Ceramic
43 x 22⅝ x 7½ in. (109.0 x 57.5 x 19.0 cm)
Museo de Sitio de Palenque "Dr. Alberto Ruz L'Huillier"—INAH, Mexico
10–629762

Mesoamerican peoples all prized smoke, in itself both the product of and the evidence for certain kinds of divine manifestations. Although incense burners—usually called braziers or *incensarios*—were made by all Maya, Palenque artists developed the most sophisticated workshops for their manufacture, and they produced them in numbers unknown elsewhere. Teams must have worked together, producing standard individual parts to be assembled as wholes. The human and god faces that dominate the *incensario* received the attention of the most skilled artists.

Maya sun gods come in several aspects, but all are aged faces, like this one, with great oversize —and frequently squinting—eyes. Sun gods usually feature a filed front tooth, often in the shape of the letter T but more rarely a shark tooth, like the tooth of this example.

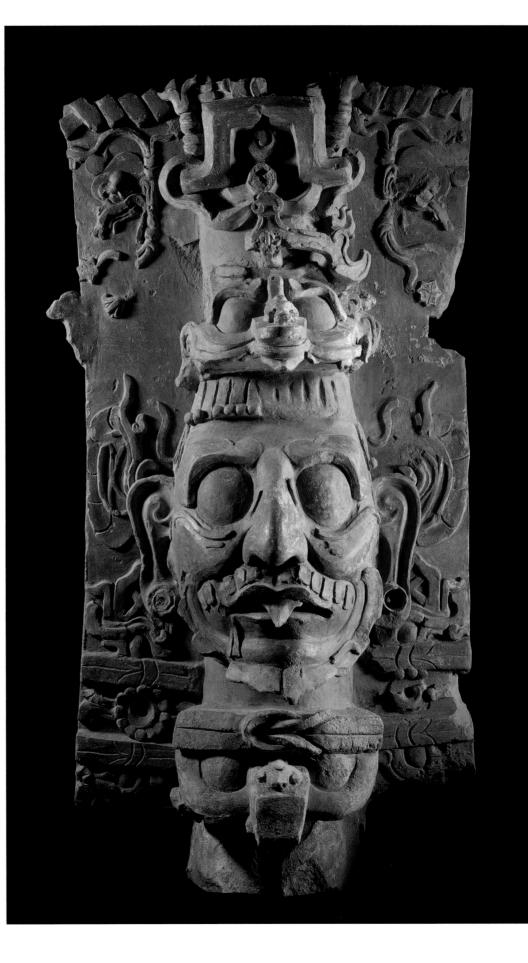

Plate 125
Censer stand
Palenque, Mexico
c. AD 695
Ceramic
39³⁄₈ x 11¹³⁄₁₆ x 11⁷⁄₁₆ in. (100.0 x 30.0 x 29.0 cm)
Museo de Sitio de Palenque "Dr. Alberto Ruz L'Huillier"—INAH,
Mexico
10–629763

This censer stand portrays the sun in the Underworld, making his nightly journey from west to east so that the new day can begin. The Jaguar God of the Underworld, as this solar god is known, features a twisted "cruller," or cord, that runs between and under his eyes; only one of his jaguar ears remains in place. His ragged beard is typical of a solar jaguar who is burned by a young god (Fig. 54), perhaps as an agent of the burning that initiates the growing season.

Here the Jaguar God of the Underworld wears a naturalistic upper snout of a jaguar for his own headdress, who is in turn topped by a serpent-winged bird about to take flight. The open cylinder at top supported the actual incense burner (Plate 126).

Plate 126

Censer pot and lid

Palenque, Mexico
AD 700–900
Ceramic
Pot: 8¹/₄ x 12¹/₈ in. (21.0 x 30.8 cm); lid: 4⁵/₁₆ x 11¹/₄ in.
(11.0 x 28.5 cm)
Museo de Sitio de Palenque "Dr. Alberto Ruz L'Huillier"—INAH,
Mexico
10–479161, 10-479177

The elaborate constructions called "censers" at
Palenque are little more than supports for the actual
holders of incense—plain, simple, lidded vessels like
this one. How such censer stands actually worked is
often no longer in evidence, so archaeologists
welcomed the recent discovery at the Cross Group
of several assemblages with vessels in place to
receive smoking chunks of burning *pom*, as the
Maya call the fragrant crystallized tree sap they
favored as incense.

Plate 127
Censer stand of a king
Palenque, Mexico
c. AD 650–800
Limestone
22 3/8 x 10 9/16 in. (56.7 x 26.8 cm)
Museo de Sitio de Palenque "Dr. Alberto Ruz L'Huillier"—INAH,
Mexico
10–458683

The status and achievements of blood forebears
were important means by which living lords
asserted their own social position and right to
govern. Veneration of these ancestors was an
important feature of Maya life. They believed it
was possible to open conduits to hidden spiritual
realms; through prayer and offerings they brought
the dead into proximity with the living. Offerings
included sacrifices; common "gifts" included blood-
splattered paper and incense. During a century-
long period spanning the 7th and 8th centuries,
sculptors at Palenque began to experiment with
carved stone stands for undecorated incense-
burning pots, modeled in the likeness of historical
forebears.

Excavations by Mexican archaeologists in Group
4, an important secondary court close to the center
of Palenque, produced two sculpted stands in fine
states of preservation (see pp. 256–258); the more
imposing and naturalistic of the pair is represented
here (the other is illustrated as Fig. 89).

This piece carries no hieroglyphic text, but the
headdress combines the image of the quetzal bird
k'uk' with the ears of a jaguar *b'ahlam*. In this way
it spells the royal name K'uk' Bahlam carried by
at least two Palenque kings. Given the role of
this piece in ancestral veneration, it is more likely,
as David Stuart has suggested, that it represents
the "founder" of the human Palenque dynasty,
K'uk' Bahlam I, who ruled the kingdom from
AD 431 to 435.

Plate 128
Standing noble
Palenque, Mexico
AD 700–800
Ceramic
17¾ in. (45 cm)
Museo de Sitio de Palenque "Dr. Alberto Ruz L'Huillier"—INAH, Mexico
10-988898

Mexican archaeologists found this incense burner in Group C during the exploration of this gracious, wealthy palace group a short walk from the ceremonial precinct and adjacent to a crystalline stream. A tiny incense burner about the size of a thimble fits within the cavity of the serpent headdress, making this figure a miniature version of the large Palenque censer stands (Plate 123). As Roberto López Bravo has demonstrated, this figure in turn fit into a yet larger censer stand (pp. 256–258).

With his evocative face, carefully finished ears and mustache, and his intent gaze, this figure portrays a particular lord, probably one of the leaders of the lineage of Complex C. The now-damaged pectoral on his chest depicts a Maya god. An artist added precious Maya blue paint to the figure after firing.

Plate 129

Large carved platform

Palenque, Mexico
AD 736 (9.15.5.0.0 10 Ajaw 8 Ch'en)
Limestone
23⅝ x 89¾ in. (60.0 x 228.0 cm)
Museo de Sitio de Palenque "Dr. Alberto Ruz L'Huillier"—INAH,
Mexico
10–629761

The exquisite execution of this recently discovered panel sets it among the first rank of Palenque reliefs. Buried for over 1,000 years in the rubble of Temple 21, its excavation exposed an almost unblemished surface to the light; traces of original red pigment remain visible (see pp. 264–267). The panel was originally the front face of a low platform, very much like the one found in Temple 19 (see pp. 261–264), and it features five figures with associated captions and longer blocks of hieroglyphic text. In this work, the role of calligraphy, already evident in Palenque's inscriptions, begins to take hold of the figural depiction as well, particularly in rendering of hands and hair.

The work presents a rich interaction between image and text. Analysis by epigrapher Guillermo Bernal Romero makes clear that it was commissioned by Pakal's grandson Ahkal Mo' Nahb III in 736— in celebration of the same Long Count date (9.15.5.0.0) recorded on Temple 19. Though neither relief carries a signature, we can be sure that the same group of sculptors were involved in both— with some elements of glyphic handwriting

suggesting a single hand for the text at least.

At the heart of the scene is not the reigning king himself but the mighty presence of Pakal. His likeness is immediately recognizable, and his hieroglyphic caption confirms his identity. He is dressed in the guise of an ancestral king and holds a stingray spine bloodletter used in personal sacrifice. Also identified by caption are the flanking figures of Ahkal Mo' Nahb and his heir Upakal K'inich. Oddly, both lords look away from Pakal, as if averting their gaze from a painfully luminous presence. They too have portraits we can recognize on other monuments, the reigning king's more refined features contrasting with the stronger profile of the king-to-be. The snarling felines at either side—whose titles name them as masked priests or court functionaries rather than actual beasts—hold complex bouquets of cloth, paper, and leaves.

The date of the ceremony itself is left unstated; but if we are to understand it as a historical event then it must have taken place in the short space of time when both grandfather and grandson were alive, which is to say the years between 678 and 683. Support for this interpretation comes from the

name caption of Ahkal Mo' Nahb where, unusually, he is given his *ch'ok,* "youth," name of Okib. Although shown as the grown men they were in 736, this pair would only have been children at the court of Pakal. If correct, this would serve to place Upakal K'inich in the same generation as Ahkal Mo' Nahb, presumably as his brother. His nomination as heir apparent—and his elevation to king a few years later—would therefore repeat the fraternal succession last seen between Kan Bahlam and K'an Joy Chitam.

For reasons that remain unclear Ahkal Mo' Nahb was much concerned with asserting the rightful inheritance of Upakal K'inich. Their participation in a ritual performed by Pakal served to promote the legitimacy of both lords, whose insecurity seems painfully obvious amid the royal splendor on view. If we consider the monuments of Ahkal Mo' Nahb collectively we see a relentless campaign of legitimization that summons the support of parents, ancestors, nobles, and tutelary gods (see pp. 261–264).

Reference: González Cruz and Bernal Romero 2002

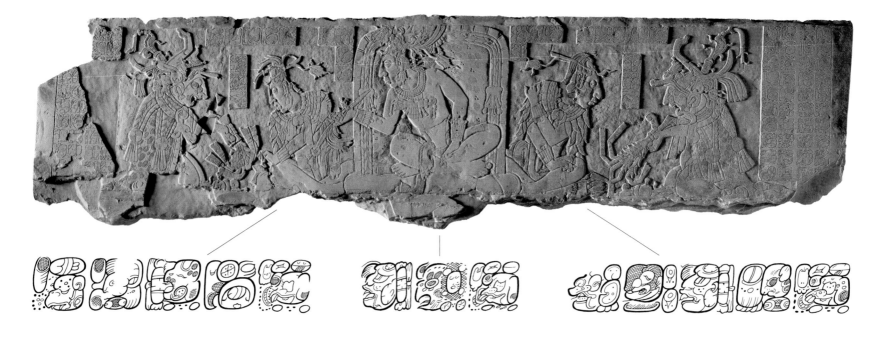

Plate 130

Inscribed jade block

Palenque, Mexico, originally from Pomoná, Tabasco, Mexico

AD 697 (9.13.5.0.0 1 Ajaw 3 Pop)

Jade

3¼ x 1⅞ in. (8.2 x 4.7 cm)

Museo de Sitio de Palenque "Dr. Alberto Ruz L'Huillier"—INAH, Mexico

10-458708

This weighty chunk of greenstone—probably jadeite—was discovered among a sizable offering of jewelry in an empty tomb within Palenque Temple 12. Its front side bears the image of a cross-eyed character, one closely associated with the *axis mundi* or World Tree. The back carries a nine-glyph inscription. This text is self-referential, describing the stone's own dedication on a year-ending in the Maya calendar that fell in AD 697 (9.13.5.0.0 1 Ajaw 3 Pop) (A1–3). After a dedicatory verb (B1) we see the name of the object, consisting of a portrait of our cross-eyed supernatural prefixed by *yax,* "green/beautiful" (B2)—further emphasized by

the following glyph *uk'aba',* "its name" (B3). Our block is then described as *yikatz,* "his burden" (C1); a term which has connotations of gift-giving or tribute payment. The owner of this burden is a king from Pomoná (C3) nicknamed Sunraiser Jaguar (C2). The reference reflects the kind of diplomatic gift-giving that expressed hierarchical relationships between Maya states and probably reflects Palenque's domination of the region at this date. Strangely, inscriptions at Pomoná itself suggest that this king died sometime before this date, so there may be some retrospective quality to the giving of this stone.

Plate 131
Jade necklace
Palenque, Mexico
AD 650–750
Jade
17 5/8 in. (44.7 cm)
Museo de Sitio de Palenque "Dr. Alberto Ruz L'Huillier"—INAH,
Mexico, 10–573801 0/11, 10–573805

Plate 132
Large bead
Palenque, Mexico
AD 650–750
Jade
1 5/8 x 2 3/8 in. (4.1 x 6.0 cm)
Museo de Sitio de Palenque "Dr. Alberto Ruz L'Huillier"—INAH,
Mexico, 10–573806

After Pakal had been interred in the Temple of Inscriptions, other members of the royal family were buried in adjacent buildings. Archaeologists have recently recovered the tomb of a woman of high status from the building immediately adjacent and called her the "Red Queen;" the contents within the next structure to the west, Temple 12, or Temple of the Skull, proved to be more enigmatic.

Deep within the Temple of the Skull lay buried quantities of jade with only fragmentary human remains. The large, heavy beads attest to the wealth accrued by Palenque lords. The single odd bead (Plate 132) may represent a stylized shell.

Plate 133
Belt mask of Pakal
Temple of Inscriptions, Palenque, Mexico
c. AD 650–683
Jade and slate
Mask: 8¾ in. (22.2 cm)
Museo Nacional de Antropología—INAH, Mexico
Mask: 10-001283; celts 10-8699 1/9, 2/9, 3/9

After Pakal had died, his heirs carried his body down the interior stairs of the Temple of Inscriptions and placed it inside the cool, dark sarcophagus, where the body was then dressed for the afterlife. After they had adorned him with jaguar pelt and abundant jade jewelry, a team of assistants slid the sarcophagus lid into place, sealing Pakal in place for over a millennium.

Before leaving the funerary chamber, Pakal's descendents took his royal belt and placed it on the north half of the sarcophagus lid, specifically on the World Tree that grows from Pakal's body. In 1952, more than 1,000 years later, archaeologists recovered dozens of beads and mosaic pieces of what is the finest royal belt ever excavated at a Maya site. Recently, specialists at the Museo Nacional de Antropología have reconstructed the head-and-celt assemblages anew. Although there must have once been three heads, only two are complete. The dangling slate celts would have announced Pakal's movements with bell-like tinkling. For exhibition purposes, a modern replica replaces the now-decayed woven mat from which the celts would have hung.

The Maya valued the youthful representation above all else, but the small mosaic jade heads of Pakal's belt evoke both the wisdom and physical decrepitude of old age, with its attendant tooth loss. A prized possession of Pakal, this head may have represented one of his own ancestors, many of whom are depicted on the carved sides of the sarcophagus.

Reference: Ruz 1973

CHAPTER 7

New Discoveries and Personal Accounts in the Maya West

Fig. 72   Detail, carved platform (west side), Temple 19, Palenque.

GODS OF THE SCRIBES AND ARTISTS
Michael D. Coe

The ancient Maya are unique among world civilizations in that they have endowed their scribes and artists with more supernatural patrons and a richer mythology than any other culture, a tribute to the high status that writing and the arts held in this ancient society. It is true that among the Brahmins of India, Ganesha—the elephant-headed deity—is the lord of writing and learning, and that for the ancient Egyptians, Thoth (in the form of either an ibis or baboon) played the same role. But the scribal pantheon among the Maya is far richer and more abundant.

The identification of specific gods as scribal patrons largely depends upon whether or not they appear to be painting, writing, or carving, and whether they are associated with the tools of these trades. Foremost among the diagnostic objects is the screenfold codex, always depicted in side elevation, usually with the top two pages lifted. Very commonly, the codex has jaguar-skin covers; this may have been the practice in the 7th and 8th centuries, but 16th-century Bishop Diego de Landa describes only boards painted with what sounds like Maya blue pigment. Second in importance is the brush pen, often held in the right hand in the act of writing or painting the codex; but brush pens also appear in the headdresses of deities as well as humans on painted vases. Thirdly, both godly and human scribes very often carry conch-shell paint pots in the left hand.

While the identification of brush pens is generally accepted, less certainly identified are bundles of what seem to be quill pens, worn on the foreheads of many individuals in Maya art, both human and supernatural. From a detailed examination of the Dresden Codex, the most beautiful of the four surviving Maya books, I conclude that only a quill pen could have produced the exceedingly fine lines typical of glyph interiors, and it is almost surely a quill pen that is grasped by the paw of the little Rabbit God scribe on the "Princeton Vase" (Plate 32).

The foregoing paraphernalia was part of the daily toolkit of the Maya artist/scribe. Less obviously taken from "real life" is what Mayanists have called the "computer printout," a strip of what must be bark paper marked with bar-and-dot numbers that emanates from the armpit of scribal deities. However, it may also proceed from the god's mouth, as can be seen with the deity—possibly the rain god Chaak—portrayed on page 73b of the Madrid Codex. On codex-style vases, the "printout" strip ends in fig-shaped leaves, and there is a strong possibility that this strip actually represents the *amate* or strangler-fig tree, from the inner bark of which paper was manufactured.

At the head of this specialized pantheon was Itzamna (*itzamnaaj*), the supreme deity, the aged progenitor of all the gods and of the universe, generally depicted as an old, bearded man seated upon a "sky band" or celestial throne. He wears an elaborate headdress fronted by a flower in which may be imbedded his own nominal glyph. According to our colonial sources, Itzamna was the inventor of writing and books, and the first priest; this intellectual role is confirmed by page eight of the 15th- or 16th-century Madrid Codex, where the god is enthroned on a seat covered with bar-and-dot numbers. His exalted position is indicated on painted Maya vases: where he appears with other scribal gods, they are clearly subordinate to Itzamna.

Lesser divinities were far more involved with scribal and artistic activities than was the probably distant Itzamna. In fact, the first ones to be so identified were the two Monkey Scribes of the Popol Vuh, Huun Bats' and Huun Chuwen (names both standing for the calendar day "One Monkey"). According to the story in this great epic, these were the jealous and boastful half-brothers of the Hero Twins (of whom more below). These latter were hunting birds with blowguns, but their prey became stuck high in a tree. The Twins persuaded their rivals to climb the tree to recover the birds, but once there they were turned into monkeys, and thus figures of fun when they descended to the ground. This humiliation was not the end of their story, for the Popol Vuh goes on to say:

> So they were prayed to by the flautists and singers among the ancient people, and the writers and carvers prayed to them….Even so, they were flautists and singers; they did great things while they lived with their grandmother and mother.[1]

There can be no doubt that the Monkey Scribes were the principal patrons of the arts, including writing, not only among the Maya but elsewhere in Mesoamerica. The high intelligence and dexterity of our primate cousins must have struck the ancient Maya, so it is hardly a surprise that they should have given them a role as the protectors of intellectual activities. The Monkey Scribes are found over and over on painted or carved Maya vases, particularly those in the codex style of the 8th century (Plate 64). They are often shown writing or reading books, or holding brush pen and inkpot. By far the most spectacular representation is the three-dimensional Monkey Scribe sculpture found in the Scribal Palace (Structure 9N-82C), part of the Sepulturas Group at Copan (Plate 63); in this case, the deity has the headdress of Pawahtun (God N), as we shall see, another scribal patron. Another striking Monkey Scribe image, from the 12th or 13th century, is the polychromed effigy *incensario* recently found at Mayapan; as with the Madrid Codex figure, it spews a "computer printout" from its mouth, as well as one from each armpit.[2]

Also high in the scribal pantheon was Pawahtun, a fourfold, sky- and earth-bearing god of the four directions of the world and of the end of the year. Like Itzamna, he is aged and Roman-nosed, but with a headdress resembling a somewhat cylindrical, rolled-up net with crenellated edge. On a remarkable codex-style painted vase, two Pawahtuns act as instructors in a scribal school attended by human novices; one is giving a class in arithmetic, pointing to a codex while reciting bar-and-dot numbers. The other seems to be correcting his young pupil's faulty handwriting.

The episode of the Monkey Scribes appears in an early section of the Popol Vuh that is concerned with events taking place just before the final creation of the universe. In its larger sense, this involves a pair of Hero Twins, Hunahpu and Xbalanque (half-brothers of the Monkey Scribes), whose task it was to rid the world of monsters and to overcome the evil lords of the Xibalba (the Underworld). The Twins' father and uncle—also twins—had been summoned to Xibalba to play a fatal ballgame. In the end, following their trial in various houses of torture, they were sacrificed. Their offspring, the Hero Twins, following their elders' road down to Xibalba, defeated the Underworld lords, and resurrected their father, One Hunahpu.

All three—Hunahpu, Xbalanque, and One Hunahpu—not only are easily recognizable in Maya iconography, but they act as scribal patrons. Hunahpu's body and face are marked by black spots, while pieces of jaguar pelt appear on his twin's face and body. In a tour-de-force of iconographic decipherment, Karl Taube identified One Hunahpu as the Maize God, with the deity's "double-domed," tonsured head taking the form of an ear of maize with its silks. The pious act of paternal resurrection in the Popol Vuh thus replicates the peasant farmer's act of sending the corn kernel into the Underworld, and bringing it out from Xibalba with the coming of the rains. One can see all three of these gods painting codices, particularly on the codex-style painted vessels associated with Nakbe and Calakmul.

Could it be that the association of the Maize God with books stems from the similarity between the preparation of bark paper and the preparation of maize? One step in the conversion of *amate* bark fibers into paper involves boiling them in the very same water that had been used to boil corn kernels before the Maya housewife grinds these into *nixtamal* dough.

These are the principal scribal gods. There are others as well, but they appear in 7th- and 8th-century art with far less frequency. I have already mentioned the now-famous Rabbit God of the "Princeton Vase," but he appears as a scribe only on this lovely object, recording the events taking place in God L's palace. Other such deities occurring sporadically with scribal accoutrements are the Fox God (with Pawahtun headgear) and the Vulture God.

Although these supernaturals must have been largely concerned with writing and the arts, some would probably have had additional functions. For example, one of the Monkey Scribes appears in the Venus pages of the Dresden Codex as the malevolent Morning Star, in the act of hurling a dart at a victim; and among the variants of the *k'in* signs in calendrical records is this self-same deity.

Much of the rich iconography of 7th- and 8th-century Maya art disappears with the great Maya collapse, and many of the Maya scribes may have lost not only their books but also their lives in this huge debacle. But a few of the scribal traditions and beliefs managed to survive into the years before the Spanish Conquest, as testified by the Dresden and Madrid Codices. Nonetheless, the artistic and intellectual glories of Maya palace life were gone forever.

Fig. 73 Codex-style Maya vessel, rollout. Here a scribe who sits in front of a great jaguar-covered throne holds a paint pot and looks at his closed book; his assistant has both brush and paint pot in hand.

DRESSED LORDS AND LADIES

María Teresa Uriarte

At court, lords and ladies donned lavish costumes for ceremonies. There is no better testament to that lost world of wealth and to the variety of Maya finery than the paintings of Bonampak, which make it possible for us to take a closer look at costume. Furthermore, by contemplating these images, we can see some aspects of daily dress for the Maya. We can see how costumes would have been put on the body, and how undergarments were covered by subsequent layers of clothing. The images demonstrate the way in which capes and skirts were secured, as well as unusual features of costume, such as hoods and masks. Unfortunately the paintings of Bonampak have their own limitations, and there are virtually no written records that can provide us with answers to the questions we might pose. Additionally, the humidity and weather throughout most of Mesoamerica have led to the loss of almost all textiles from ancient times.

A few examples from Bonampak offer clues to different techniques employed for the weaving and decoration of garments worn by the elite. The ladies of the court wear costumes fashioned from lightweight, sheer cotton, with designs embroidered in white on white, as can be seen in the royal family grouping sitting on the throne in Room 1 (Fig. 74). Right beside the seated queen stands another woman wearing a yellow *huipil* (a loose, unstitched upper garment worn by women) that shows the image of a serpent as the border of her neckline. Some of these designs were also woven into the cloth, using a technique similar to the brocade that is still used by some modern Maya communities in Guatemala. To the left of the throne, one member of the royal family wears a Tlaloc border on a red *huipil*, edged in green. This same Tlaloc border is also seen on Stela 2, worn by a woman, and by the ruler who dresses on the north wall of Room 1. Time, power, and rain

Fig. 74   Bonampak paintings, Room 1, upper west vault (left). The ruler sits in the center of the throne, with women seated to either side; two others also attend him. Bags of tribute rest beside and in front of the throne.

Fig. 75   Bonampak paintings, Room 1, north wall (above). At right, the principal dancer finishes preparing his attire; a kneeling attendant, below, holds out what may be a mirror for his consultation.

are some of Tlaloc's attributes, introduced from Teotihuacan to the Maya and a symbol of legitimate rulership.

On the north wall of Room 1, we see three dignitaries in the process of dressing (Fig. 75). The scene begins with the moment when they receive magnificent frames of feathers as part of their costume for dance. All three have already put on huge headdresses with an impressive abundance of quetzal feathers in blue-green iridescent tones. Blue-green is the color of the fifth direction, center, indicating the union of celestial, terrestrial, and underworld levels of the cosmos. The ruler stands in the center, completely dressed in his jaguar-skin skirt. He serves the function of mediator, a conduit between sky and earth, between man and deities. Dressed most richly and shown frontally, this royal personage is the most important individual in the scene. Although his eyes, like those of most figures in Room 1, were destroyed in ancient times, I propose that he gazes down, directly into the basket held by a servant on the register below. This servant probably holds out a mirror in the basket, which may have functioned like an oracle.

Mirrors in prehispanic Mexico were used for divination. In many cases, there is archaeological evidence that they were mounted on a base of woven palm or some other perishable material. Although we might first imagine that this is a scene in which the ruler is merely preparing himself in all his finery in front of a mirror, I believe that if we look closely we can see that this mirror is one of the most important features of the entire room. Although it has been suggested that the subject of the room is the presentation of a child,[3] no one turns around to look at the child. In all likelihood, the entire room represents a ritual preceding the sacrifice in Room 2. The seriously damaged scene of a dance can also be connected with the presentation of the mirror, or oracle.

A few other costumes and garments are worth noting. One lord in a white cape wears a skirt of such polychromy that various techniques, among them brocade, embroidery, and even painting, would have been required to produce it (Fig. 76). Additionally, zoologists have provided some insight into the animals that were the sources of feathers, hides, and furs for regal attire. This same lord wears a headdress made of ocellated turkey feathers[4] that provide him with some special distinction. His white cape, like those of others standing near him, is held up by three large brooches. Although they seem to be cut shells, they might also be a particular kind of crab, called *mesh*.[5]

Underneath this finery, Maya men wore undergarments of the sort mentioned in the 16th-century account of Bishop Diego de Landa. Describing one garment, what we would call a loincloth, as consisting of long bands of cloth, he says, "They wound it several times around the waist, so that one end fell in front and one end behind, and these ends the women made with a great deal of care and featherwork."[6]

Some individuals also bear symbols on their skirts or headdresses of different gods. In many cases, elaborate skirts and belts adorn high-status individuals. One man wears a red skirt with a blue serpent; another wears a piece of cloth rolled around his waist like a belt, with symbols alluding to the four corners of the universe, perhaps in association with a year sign. One musician's skirt features what is probably an underworld deity linked to scribes and dance.

Maya fashion was both stylish and functional. In the battle scene in Room 2, warriors wear armor reinforced with layers of cotton or perhaps salt.[7] Others wear jaguar pelt, a costume that the later Aztecs reserved for those who had taken four captives. Some warriors wear skull headdresses that were later called *tzitzimitl* in Central Mexico, an insignia limited to those who had taken two captives.

Clothing at Bonampak not only indicates social rank, as it has throughout human history, but it also reveals ideology and ritual practice. The imagination of the painters at Bonampak can be compared with those of couturiers—the painters who designed, made, and decorated each one of the different outfits of the almost 300 individuals painted on the walls of this exceptional place.

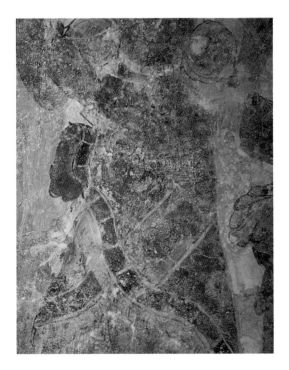

Fig. 76 Bonampak paintings, Room 1, south wall. This fancy and multi-colored overskirt may have been produced using a variety of techniques.

THE MULTIPLE LANGUAGES OF A SINGLE RELIEF
Beatriz de la Fuente

Introduction

Maya relief art of the 7th and 8th centuries is known for varying formal elements that imbue it with a special, unmistakable excellence. Its profound humanistic sentiment, achieved through the portrayal of the human body in innumerable postures and attitudes, is particularly noteworthy. Similarly, the individuality of these works is underpinned by a clearly defined historical awareness.

Palenque is the leading exponent of the Usumacinta style, as demonstrated by the aesthetic ideal embodied in its complex and varied works, whether architectural, pictorial, or sculptural. The artists of Palenque developed a style that stands out from the expressions of other contemporary cities and from those of the region as a whole. The style is characterized by outstanding reliefs such as the Oval Palace Tablet, the sarcophagus lid, the Cross Group tablets, the Palace Tablet, the Scribe and Orator Panels, the Tablet of the Slaves, and the Creation Panel. Within this range of works, what place would Dumbarton Oaks Panel 2 occupy?

The Art of Palenque and Dumbarton Oaks Panel 2

Even though we do not know the exact provenience of Dumbarton Oaks Panel 2, we nevertheless can be sure that it comes from Palenque, based both on its artistic style and three historical figures named in its texts (Fig. 77; Plate 117) . On the left is Lady Tz'akbu Ahaw, and K'an Hoy Chitam and Pakal the Great on the right. This carved panel must once have been set inside a building, like the panels of the Cross Group or Temple 14. The panel is the central one from a three-panel arrangement.[8]

From AD 615 to 790 (ranging from the probable dedication date of the Oval Palace Tablet to the Tablet of 96 Glyphs and Creation Tablet—Plates 119, 120, 121; Fig. 71), a wealth of works of art were created. Because of this, we can see the overarching development of Palenque sculpture, including Dumbarton Oaks Panel 2. Based on stylistic features, the work can be incorporated into the period that some years ago I referred to as the early naturalist-dynamic period (AD 721–751).[9] In creating this category, I took into account the following elements: the axial nature of the composition of three figures; the posture and activity of the three figures; the symbolism of headdresses, offerings, and hand-held objects; and the commemoration of historical events.

At the center of the panel one sees a standing figure, with his head in profile and his body rendered frontally. He lightly lifts his left heel from the ground. He wears the Quadripartite Badge for a headdress; he is ornamented with earspools of spondylus bivalves, jade necklaces and a large pectoral, bracelets, and anklets; a belt over the skirt repeats the pectoral design, also shown in profile. In his right hand, he holds an *ak'bal* bag, while the left, situated above his head, holds an axe fashioned from a serpent's body and incorporating an eccentric flint.

On either side, two seated individuals in profile view one another. They wear headdresses depicting long-nosed gods, together with ear decorations, necklaces, pectorals, bracelets, and sashes representing precious stones. On their laps they hold—as if they were large miniatures—full body images of the god K'awiil and the Jester God (right). Based on their portraits and their glyphs, we know who these characters are: they are the portraits of the same individuals depicted on the Palace Tablet: Lady Tz'akbu Ahaw (left), K'an Hoy Chitam (center), and Pakal the Great.

On Dumbarton Oaks Panel 2, K'an Hoy Chitam dances, as can be inferred from his posture, dress, and adornments. The costume and the posture pertain to a deity known as GI of the Palenque Triad Gods,[10] or Hunal Ye Chaak, who is associated with the aquatic underworld and is one of its foremost inhabitants. In what is a recurring posture in Maya art, K'an Hoy Chitam lifts his heels and engages in a ritual dance. Lords dance at various times—including on entering the Underworld, or Xibalba. The text here makes reference to the entrance to a sacred mountain when K'an Hoy Chitam was a young man, and such an event, too, may have been performed as a dance.

Much of the history of K'an Hoy Chitam's reign remains obscure. He was crowned in AD 702 but was taken prisoner by Baaknal Chaak of Tonina in 711. He may have later returned to Palenque as a very old man, but this remains unclear and hypothetical. What is clear is that, with the

Fig. 77   Dumbarton Oaks Panel 2 (Plate 117), drawing. K'an Hoy Chitam dances at center.

succession to the throne of Ahkal Mo' Nahb III in AD 721 (and with the support of Chak Suts'), renewed impetus was given to artistic expression at Palenque. The new ruler recommended work to extend the Palace, adding House D; he ordered the carving of the panels known today as the "Orator" and "Scribe". At Temple 19, he commissioned two exceptional reliefs for a pillar, and a large carved bench, dedicated in 736. Ahkal Mo' Nahb also ordered the construction of Temples 16 and 17 to commemorate his predecessor, Kan Bahlam II; Temple 18 and its stucco relief to commemorate his parents; as well as Temples 18a and 21. Ahkal Mo' Nahb produced a large number of artistic works to affirm his power and honor his lineage. Dumbarton Oaks Panel 2 was probably produced at the beginning of his reign, perhaps in 722, to commemorate his immediate predecessor.

The Messages of Panel 2

This work underscores the introduction of a new concept of humanity—from the mythical to the historical spheres—through the enrichment of sculptural language. However, in terms of its crafting and formal treatment, Panel 2 differs from other contemporary works, as exemplified by the following factors.

An unusual number of works were created during the reign of Ahkal Mo' Nahb (accession AD 721); after Pakal, Ahkal Mo' Nahb is attributed the greatest number of works so far known (11). In comparison with the existing formal repertory, Panel 2 seems more static than other contemporary reliefs. Relief works of this period are characterized by the presence of new plastic modes, as can be seen on the pillars at House D; the Panels of the Orator and Scribe; the Panel of Temple 21; the stucco relief on the throne and pillar at Temple 19; the "Bundle Panel" at Temple 16; the stucco reliefs at Temples 18 and 18-A, and Panel 2, as discussed here. The considerable number of works created and the short period of time between them (barely 20 years) suggests that Ahkal Mo' Nahb was anxious to finish them. As a result, some works were naturally more refined than others; that is to say, Ahkal Mo' Nahb's artists were hypothetically overburdened. The historical or religious nature of such works may also have had a certain influence on the messages they transmitted.

Through its clear aesthetic expression, Panel 2 of Dumbarton Oaks indicates the movement of Palenque in a new artistic direction. We see the ruler at the height of his power, far beyond the limits of worldly existence, invested with the sumptuous and symbolic garments of a deity. Similarly, reminiscences of the timid emergence of certain features may be discerned in the plastic dynamism in effect at the time. The Panel subsequently stands as one of the pioneering works of a new formal language at Palenque.

Final Considerations

Due to its formal characteristics, Panel 2 is a transitional work situated between two defined moments in the history of Palenque. On the one hand, there are the creations dated between AD 610 and 692, which underline the solid governments of Pakal and Kan Bahlam II, while on the other, there are the efforts of Ahkal Mo' Nahb to enhance his prestige through the bellicose aid of Chak Suts'.

The originality of the relief art at Palenque highlights a solid aesthetic proposal that conjoins an eloquent, clear, precise, and ordered composition with divine and courtly themes. This work unites religious expression with the cult of personality, while also consolidating this paradigmatic city in our historical and artistic consciousness. All of these elements are present in Panel 2 of Dumbarton Oaks, a work that also reflects a history we must strive to discover and comprehend.

THE TECHNIQUES OF THE PALENQUE SCULPTORS
Merle Greene Robertson

Wow. They really did have supervising artist teachers at Palenque. I was working at House A of the Palace and looking at the wrists on the figures of Pier C. One had been broken off, leaving an earlier fully formed wrist underneath ¾ in. (2 cm) of stucco that formed the final wrist. I measured both wrists and found that the sculptor forming the left figure did not go by the instructions for the width of wrists (Fig. 78). The ¾ in. of stucco corrected his error. On another figure, 1⅛ in. (3 cm) of stucco had to be put on top of an already formed hand to make it the correct size. The size of heads also had to conform to the portrait being shaped. Lady Sak K'uk's head on Pier C was ¾ in. (2 cm) longer than the other figures, showing her huge jaw, depicting her probable acromegaly that is even more pronounced in her portrait on the north and south ends of the sarcophagus in the Temple of Inscriptions tomb of her son, Pakal the Great (Fig. 79).

This was now getting exciting. How about the heights of the figures? Simple: they used a template, and then stretched out the central portion of the body and made the torso longer, or reduced it to make it shorter, as I could see looking at the tall figure on Pier D whose clothes were almost completely missing and at the short figure on Pier E. They dressed these figures as though they were real humans, first the underwear, then the jaguar skirts, aprons, loincloths, and last the beads and feathers. However, each piece of clothing was first painted with a thin layer of lime stucco and then the color put on top, even when another garment was to cover the first. Thousands of Munsell color notations of all stucco sculpture at Palenque that I had taken demonstrated that the people there did indeed have an iconographic meaning for color on stucco sculpture. Red stood for the living world, human bodies, and worldly things. Blue represented things divine, such as dwarves, motifs pertaining to rulership like mat symbols, and precious jade beads and feathers. Yellow was the color for the Underworld and included jaguar tails, Underworld plants, and fauna.

Wall-paintings and modified frescos at Palenque do not adhere to the iconographic content of the colors red, blue, and yellow as do the stucco sculptures. On the remains of these wall-paintings and frescos other colors were included in the Palenque palette—purple, orange, green, black, and

Fig. 78   Pier C, House A, Palenque Palace, detail. Maya sculptors made adjustments in stucco.

Fig. 79   Lady Sak K'uk', side of sarcophagus, Temple of Inscriptions, Palenque. Note her oversized jaw.

white, as can be seen on the serpent doorway at the northern end of the west corridor of House E and the east wall of the west corridor of House C.

I often wondered how the sculptors achieved such a smooth surface on their figures. On close scrutiny it suddenly dawned upon me that I was looking at the marks of a smooth tool, probably a flat bone that had been drawn over and over the surface until it almost gleamed. In some places I could detect even the width of the tool and the direction it took. This was really getting exciting now. I could see how the beads were attached. Small holes had been poked into the moist stucco wherever a bead was to be placed, and a very thin coat of red was applied in this hole, then a coat of soft white stucco. Then the stucco bead with a tail-piece at the back was inserted into the hole, thereby making the bead secure. Over and over, everywhere I looked, beads were inserted the same way.

Now knowing how these Maya sculptors completed every garment, even when later covered over, I remarked that there was probably a hidden jaguar mark on one of the skirts under a mirror symbol. There was. One day a tourist removed the mirror symbol, and sure enough, a jaguar spot was underneath where it belonged. I would have much preferred this to be an unproven assumption of mine.

One day I was on scaffolding in the West Court noting the density of the Maya blue on the feather headdresses using the Munsell color designations, when, to my great surprise and delight, I could count the order in which each feather was placed on the headdress (Fig. 80). Where feathers had broken off, I could see that each one had been completely painted before the next feather was laid on top of it. I was so excited that I stayed there on the scaffolding until I could no longer see what I was doing.

These Palenque sculptors were masters at controlling thick masses of fine stucco. On the medallions of House A, a wooden template was used to swing the stucco masses in much the same way as the masters in early New Orleans decorated their Southern mansions with stucco ornamentation by swinging curves with speed and dexterity from one direction to another in even, rhythmic motions. The medallions are all the same size. One day I was projecting slides of them on the screen and came to Medallion 8, and it was different. I thought I had the slide in backwards, but no, when projected upside down, it fit perfectly to the size of all the others. The template was not held steady on Medallion 6, so the cartouche was five degrees off center counterclockwise. Medallion 12 has a slight bulge at the upper right corner, easily accounted for by the pull of the stucco when placing it on the wall. The Maya were humans just like us, who made errors. The figures on the House D piers of the Palace are much more in the round than the flattened figures on the House A piers. The muscular legs are almost in the round, and in some places, held on by only a small mount of stucco at the rear, such as the little flower on Pier D.

We haven't improved on the way earrings are made, as shown on Pier D of House D where the leaf earplug is held on by a tiny cord running through a hole in the ear. Belt buckles were made by these Palencanos 1,300 years ago exactly the same as buckles function today as shown on this same pier, just one of many examples at Palenque.

One day when I was cleaning the green slime off the wall of House B, to my amazement I saw the remains of a stucco mural on the wall. I carefully washed the scum off, revealing a fine incised line outlining the figure that was to be formed in stucco on top of it. All that remained of the figure was one 5⅞-in. (15-cm) piece of a vivid Maya blue feather, and another 4-in. (10-cm) piece of feather farther down, both part of the figure's headdress, but every detail of the face was delicately incised (Fig. 81). At other times the graffiti outlining where stucco sculpture was to go was painted on with a thin brush-stroke of either black or red pigment.

On the Temple of Inscriptions, the stucco is held in place by means of armatures that are placed on top of stucco that adheres to the stone backing of the piers (Fig. 82). Large, flat, smooth stones

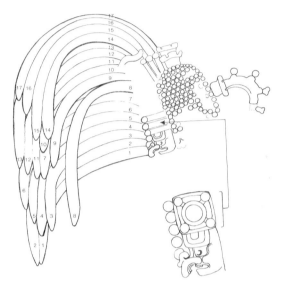

Fig. 80 Headdress, West Court, Palenque Palace, drawing. The Maya artist painted one feather in its entirety before rendering the next.

Fig. 81   Incised figure, House B, Palenque Palace. The artist incised the cartoon before beginning the stucco layers.

Fig. 82   Pier, Temple of Inscriptions, Palenque. Artists built up stucco layers using stone armatures.

form the stomach and chest areas, while large, heavier, long stones form the backing of legs, arms and ribbons. Most of the leg bones are covered with $1\frac{3}{8}$ in. (3.5 cm) of stucco. The child held in the arms of the standing figures is likewise backed with these armatures. The so-called baby seemed much too large for an infant, so I measured dozens of Ch'ol children between the ages of six and seven years and they were the same size as the child on these piers.

The figures on the Inscriptions tomb walls, however, do not have armatures. During the many weeks I was working down in the tomb, I had to be extremely careful not to touch the stucco walls. The stucco of these figures is so fragile it is like seven-minute frosting, a thin crisp coat on the outside and soft stucco behind it. With water seeping in from the exterior, it is a wonder that any of these figures are there today. The coat of lime on them makes it impossible to know in what colors they were once painted. As they are, they have always seemed ethereally beautiful to me, guardians of the sacred king entombed in the sarcophagus.

Who did all of this magnificent stucco work? Was it only men who were the sculptors or were there women sculptors also? I had an answer when working on the west side roof of House B. The stucco lattice work on this roof, to my surprise, is actually woven exactly as weavers go over and under with the warp and weft in making textiles. Now either men knew how to weave or women worked as stucco sculptors also. I like to think it was the latter.

TECHNIQUE, COLOR, AND ART AT BONAMPAK
Diana Magaloni

How did Maya painters manage to create the splendid murals in the city of Bonampak? The answer to this question lies in an interdisciplinary study combining modern scientific techniques to analyze materials, methods of observation and characterization of works used in the discipline of conservation, and the research tools of art history.[11] The results presented in this article form part of a larger research project developed within the framework of the Pre-Hispanic Mexican Mural Painting Project.

Color and Texture, an Inseparable Whole in Bonampak Visual Arts

A detailed observation of the characteristics of the layers of color at Bonampak allows one to appreciate the complexity of the pictorial technique employed there. First, the painters managed to create an enormous variety of colors. Second, they handled transparency and opaqueness of tones with great mastery to create specific expressive effects. Third, they used the agile, calligraphic line of their writing system to draw on color surfaces, defining details, and underscoring material qualities of objects.

Fig. 83 shows a detail of one of the masked figures in Room 1 at Bonampak. It shows that the artist employed a thick, textured application of paint to generate movement, vitality, and a visually attractive contrast between the physicality of the mask and the immateriality of the blue background. In fact, this technique, called impasto, is often used in Western art by great masters of modern painting, such as Vincent van Gogh. At Bonampak, the transparent plane of the blue background is employed in juxtaposition, as shown in the photo. The masks have the texture of earth, while the aqua background has the immateriality of air. The artists contrast opaque pigments and transparent ones to produce two distinct pictorial planes. That is to say, they produce a kind of perspective by accentuating the corporeality of the human figures in the foreground and placing them on an immaterial blue background resembling air.

The identification of pigments made it possible to determine that these layers of textured color were formulated by mixing earthy pigments with paligorskite clay, which made the creation of a dense impasto of color possible. The technique used to create the immaterial appearance of the blue resides in the production of a special tone of the famous pigment known as Maya blue. This pigment was made by dyeing white paligorskite clay with the blue dye of indigo. The Maya achieved more than seven tonalities with this process that range from ultramarine blue to Caribbean sea blue (Fig. 84). Also, as in the case of the blue background at Bonampak, they mixed the Maya blue pigment with other minerals. In optic microscopic photography, we can see Maya blue in combination with azurite, a mineral frequently used in the mural painting of Teotihuacan and that comes from the Central Highlands. The mixture of both pigments results in the translucency of the blue background.

Fig. 85 shows one of the members of the procession in Room 1 at Bonampak. The Maya concern for natural forms led the painters of Bonampak to experiment with color to build up figures with volume. The artist resorted to the use of a dilute layer of red in the cloth tied to the man's waist to produce the effects of the textile in movement and the volume of the human body. The figure's arm was constructed with a white outline, over the brown skin tone; the superimposed layers produce the illusion of volume.

The painters of Bonampak went to great efforts to prepare different suspensions of pigment, allowing them to imitate different qualities of objects. With exquisite detail, the polychrome palette imitates the special transparency of the green tone of jade and the sheerness of cotton, the opaque density of masks and bodies, and the immateriality of the blue of the sky. This visual and material effort, together with specific geographic and environmental conditions that had to be resolved by

Fig. 83 Bonampak paintings, Room 1, north wall. The hoods of two masked figures are painted in thick earthy paint.

Fig. 84 Bonampak paintings, Room 1, west wall. The blue paint of the feathers shifts to green when painted atop the yellow background.

the creators of Bonampak, defines the mural painting technique and places it on a technical and artistic rank of the first order.

Procedures: How Were They Painted?

To understand how the Bonampak murals were painted, it is necessary to examine the relationship that the artists had with an environment unlike and much more complex than the one that we are accustomed to. Therefore, we might imagine that there were "lime specialists" able to distinguish between materials for construction from different materials extracted from the subsoils. One of the most outstanding technical contributions of Maya civilization, and unfortunately one that is rarely spoken of, is the way that their artists and technicians worked lime. Lime plasters were indispensable in the construction of cities in the tropical rainforest.

Laboratory analysis permitted the identification of the wall coating of the Bonampak murals as a cementing mixture made with lime, calcitic sands called *sascab*, and a plant gum that we call *holol*, as an additive. Artists first applied a thick layer with this mixture to make the walls uniform; another thinner layer was applied on top of this to receive the paint. The Maya found that adding *holol* improved the properties of their limestone plaster considerably. By adding gums, they achieved better solubility of calcium oxides, made the lime more plastic, and thus slowed down the hardening process. In this way, Maya technicians resolved the problem of the high temperatures of the environment, so that the lime would be transformed into a good solid, compact and resistant cement.

There also must have been "gum and resin specialists." The Maya obtained adhesives, agglutinants, resins and incense, and the elastic rubber gum for the ballgame from their trees. Sixteenth-century documents and the Maya dictionaries let us know not only that artists used plant gum extracted from *holol* bark, but also that they knew how to classify tree gums based on an interesting taxonomic system:

1 *Holol*, the gum released by the bark when it is submerged in lime water. In pictorial technique, this type of bark gum is used to prepare the lime mixture and to make the plaster coating. These barks with gum are also used to make paper for codices.

Fig. 85 Bonampak paintings, Room 1, west wall. The artist built up layers of color on this figure, including the white outline of his arm.

2 The prefix *its* describes crystalline exudates, for example *its-chakah*, a gum that crystallizes on the *chakah* tree. These gums are what were perhaps used as agglutinants for colors.

3 *Sats* describes substances exuded in the form of whitish tears forming an elastic gum once dry, such as rubber.

4 The particle *kuk* or *kuuk* refers to a sticky, liquid adhesive from the pseudo-bulbs of orchids. In combination with the *its* gums; these substances were probably used for painting.

Therefore, based on laboratory analysis, documentary research, and experimentation, we can propose a reconstruction of the pictorial technique used at Bonampak. The painted surface was made with lime, *sascab* and *holol* gum. This mixture takes a long time to dry because the gums retain considerable moisture. In this way, the painters could execute certain parts of the painting with the wet coat of plaster, such as the background and the base figures, and from there the high resistance of the color layers. However, this does not imply that they worked as if painting a fresco. The pigments were suspended in an agglutinant made of lime water and two types of plant gums. Due to its viscosity, this agglutinant made the different qualities of texture and transparency of the pictorial layer possible. The fine details were applied once the painting and coat of plaster had dried. The quetzal plumes, jade pendants, drawing of textiles, lines defining detail drawn over pictorial surfaces, and hieroglyphic writing were painted directly on an already dried color surface. In reality the Bonampak paintings are not al fresco, but rather are based on the creation of an organic-inorganic agglutinant of lime and plant gums. This is a technical solution that has its origin in Maya alkaline chemistry. Other examples of this are the Maya blue and green pigments that combine an organic tint with a mineral (a clay).

Color

The broad color palette used by the Bonampak painters is truly amazing; the artists produced colors varied in tones, saturation and hues in such a way that their representations took on the magic of the spectrum of visible reality, in addition to colors from the realm of the imagination. We find 28 combinations of minerals that produce distinct colors at Bonampak. This shows that what differentiated mural artists from ceramic vessel painters is their plastic concern with color as a means of expression and that an important artistic value of the paintings resides in the language of color, more than line, contrary to what Tatiana Proskouriakoff had once stated.[12] This fact is even more astonishing if we take into account that Maya culture developed in an environment extremely limited in mineral resources from which to obtain pigments—the Peninsula of Yucatan is geologically composed of a plate of limestone and dolomite rocks.

Maya blue and green pigments represent one of the great technological and artistic advances in Mesoamerica. Their formula differs from those used in traditional European and Asian painting, because it is a stable organic-inorganic complex and not a mineral one. In the Bonampak paintings, we have identified six different tonalities of blue, which indicates that the painters were interested in precisely reproducing each one of the varieties of the "blue" family and used them with precision in each object represented. This observation in itself offers an entirely different conception of the Bonampak murals and the popular "Maya blue" pigment, which has always been considered a single Caribbean sea blue tone. Furthermore, we can see five different tones of green.

The painters at Bonampak used color in narrative form and copied the tones of visible reality. However, the colors have a symbolic and cultural significance that it is important to continue researching.

THE CULT OF PATRON AND ANCESTOR GODS IN CENSERS AT PALENQUE
Martha Cuevas García

Archaeological excavations conducted between 1954 and 1998 at the Temples of the Cross, Foliated Cross, Sun, and Temple 14 and Group 15,[13] uncovered close to 100 composite censers. Their discovery resulted from the exploration of tiered platforms beneath the temples, where most of them had been buried by the ancient inhabitants of Palenque (Figs. 86–88).

The censers were deposited within construction fill composed of rocks and soil. Because these objects were not placed within other receptacles or structures, once they were buried, the impact of the fill broke them into pieces. Different factors led to even more severe deterioration during the time that they remained buried. The high humidity of the environment, and the collapse of the stepped platform structures covering them, as well as the action of plants and animals, all harmed these pieces. These unfavorable conditions made the participation of restorers essential in the process of their study, in order to re-establish the original form of the pieces and keep them in good condition.

Despite the fact that the structures have still not been completely excavated, we have a significant sample of censer deposits, which allows us to see that specific rules determined their placement within structures. The censers tended to be located on the western facades of buildings, where different groups of them were placed in a line inside the platforms. The specimens in each group were normally situated in a vertical position with their faces oriented toward the west or south.

These pieces are known as composite censers because they are composed of two elements: a pedestal base and a brazier-bowl that was placed on top. Plant resin and blood were deposited in the latter to be burned during rituals. The pedestal has a tubular body to which two lateral, rectangular panels were attached. The front side displays a wide variety of iconographic elements, prominent among which are the faces of Palenque Triad Gods (GI, GII, and GIII), mainly those identified as the solar aspects of GI and GIII. Another less numerous group of censers displays human faces modeled in a naturalistic manner, which possibly correspond to the ancestors of the local dynasty.

These objects were of great importance within the ceremonial life of the city. The people of Palenque represented and worshiped divine beings via these censers. They offered their most precious gifts by means of the smoke produced by burning blood together with plant resin. Symbolically the censers formed cosmic trees, elements that made the movement of deities through the cosmos possible during ritual acts. For this reason, the tubular bodies of censers simulate tree trunks, while the Imix monster, marking the union between earthly and underworld levels,[14] is always present in the lowest mask on the censer.

Based on the identification of the beings represented in the central masks and their archaeological context, we can recognize two types of ritual contexts with which these censers are associated. The majority of them, 85 percent, were used to venerate the deities of the Palenque Triad; therefore images alluding to these gods occupy the position of the central masks. These objects come from the Temples of the Cross, Foliated Cross, and Sun, the Cross Group buildings that form the most important ceremonial precinct at Palenque. They were dedicated to the cult of the city's patron gods: the Temple of the Cross was consecrated to GI, that of the Foliated Cross to the god K'awiil (GII, patron of agriculture and the ruling lineage), and that of the Sun, to the god K'inich Ahaw Pakal (GIII), "Sun-faced Shield," the entity that personified the Sun on his journey through the underworld.

The other group of censers come from two structures known as Temple 14 and Group 15, located next to the Temples of the Cross and Sun. The objects display the same morphological and functional characteristics, but they are distinguished by having human faces instead of divine visages. This small assemblage of pieces (nine censers) is associated with the cult of the ancestors, who were venerated by way of these censers. Both the panel from Temple 14, a posthumous, commemorative monument to the ruler Kan Bahlam, and the presence of human burials in the funerary building of Temple 15 and in neighboring structures, suggest this type of ritual activity.

Censers in Rituals of Renewal

After completing the initial excavation seasons, we found it difficult to understand the purpose of burying these objects within buildings. We knew that the appropriate places to conduct veneration ceremonies were within temples or at the facades of these buildings, and not in locations where they were buried within pyramidal platforms. By way of the study of materials, their archaeological contexts, and the analysis of epigraphic texts at Palenque, we have come to understand that the burial of censers in the Temples of the Cross, Foliated Cross, and Sun was the result of a ritual practice of depositing these objects as they were replaced by new specimens.

By means of epigraphic decipherment, we know that censers were referred to in glyphic inscriptions as *ox p'uluut k'uh,* "God-Censers."[15] In addition, the Temple of Inscriptions panels contain clauses in which the participation of these objects is mentioned in *katun*-ending events. In particular, these texts tell us that the god-censers were extinguished when a *katun*-cycle came to an end. In our opinion, these events reflect the custom of the cyclical renewal of these ceremonial implements at the end of *katuns* or other periods.

Based on their beliefs, the Maya of Palenque considered the beginnings of life, death and rebirth, which were exemplified in solar, agricultural, and human life cycles, to be characterized by the god-censers. Therefore, these objects were attributed a life-cycle similar to that of human beings. The censers were consecrated in the sanctuaries of the Temples of the Cross, Foliated Cross, and Sun, with which a group of god-censers were started or "born." On the other hand, objects that had fulfilled their cycle of ritual use during the *katun* that was coming to an end died, and as a consequence, were interred in places destined for their burial.

Figs. 86, 87 Censer bases, as excavated, in the Group of the Cross, Palenque.

Thanks to archaeological remains recovered to date, we have the testimony of rituals of renewal in which these objects were used. The inhabitants of Palenque conducted these activities for more than three centuries (AD 500–800), which explains the enormous quantity of specimens found. It is possible to identify several groups of censers that were deposited simultaneously. The different groups display differences in style, dimensions, and variability of iconographic elements. This indicates to us that, through time, there was stylistic development, greater complexity in iconographic programs, as well as innovations in their techniques of manufacture.

Ethnographic data from the Lacandon Maya provide an important point of reference suggesting to us the possibility that censers would have been buried following a funerary practice similar to that for human beings.[16] The depositing of censers clearly adhered to precise rules. The Maya surely conducted funerary cult rituals prior to burying the objects and, therefore, deposited offerings alongside them. We can infer that during these ceremonies they offered blood and resin that they collected in the censers. At the moment of internment, they deposited the remains of these activities, such as braziers with partially burned resin, obsidian blades, and human toes and fingers, mutilated during auto-sacrifice. The presence of clay receptacles, as well as the bones of animals and seashells, suggests that objects containing food may also have been placed as offerings.

The censers were buried in the sacred space composed of the Temples of the Cross, Foliated Cross, and Sun, because these are locations that symbolized the entrance to the interior of the earth. By depositing them within these sacred mountains, their remains would be safeguarded as seeds, the regenerators of life.

By commemorating the beginning of calendrical cycles, the renewal of life itself was propitiated. From this we can see that the censers were appropriate objects to express the recreation of the cosmos. In the same way that the gods of the Palenque Triad had been born during the creation of the world, as recorded in the mythical texts of the inscriptions from the Temples of the Cross, Foliated Cross, and Sun, so too would the same event to insure the continuity of existence be repeated.

Fig. 88   A magnificent censer stand in the form of the Sun God was found nearly intact alongside the east facade of the Temple of the Sun in 1992.

STATE AND DOMESTIC CULT IN PALENQUE CENSER STANDS
Roberto López Bravo

An analysis of the collection of censer stands from the Cross Group has shown that they were used in temples in the central area for a certain lapse of time, only to be removed from active use and buried in situ. These objects exemplify a state cult at the most important ritual space at Palenque, in which priests and *ajawo'ob*, "lords," communicated with the city's patron deities. By contrast, censer stands excavated in Palenque's elite residential contexts have also made it possible to establish the existence of a domestic cult, in which the heads of families could communicate with venerated ancestors, without the intervention of specialized priests.

Some domestic censer stands display an iconographic array of superimposed masks similar to the censer stands of the Cross Group, but with the central mask replaced by a human face, the portrait of the ancestor commemorated by the object. However, most display formal variability, probably the result of the preferences of each lineage. For example, specimens from Group B show experimentation with a complete effigy attached to a cylinder, while those from Group C display hollow figures representing seated individuals.

Censer stands made of stone deserve special mention. These rare pieces were carved from different qualities of stone. Some were found in temples in the central area, while others bear inscriptions detailing the life of the ancestor represented. We know that they are censer stands because all are designed to hold the burner itself. The fact that they were made of stone suggests a longer duration of use than that of ceramic pieces. Furthermore, the majority were intentionally mutilated, usually on the facial features, particularly the nose.

Fig. 89 Stone censer stand, Building 1, Group 4, Palenque. The noble lord of this stone representation wears a headdress also seen on Plate 104.

Areas of Domestic Ritual Activity at Palenque

Largely constructed during the 8th and 9th centuries, Group B, located to the northeast of the Palace, near the waterfalls of the Otolum, contains the best examples of domestic ritual activity at Palenque known to date, reflecting a common Maya cosmic pattern, in which each one of the cardinal points has a ritual significance. The tombs of the ancestors and the areas of domestic ritual activity are generally associated with buildings flanking the east side of patios and plazas, and facing west. The main patio is framed on the west by Buildings 1, 4, and 5, and on the east by Buildings 2 and 3. The central rooms of the west galleries of the latter buildings had a sanctuary, originally vaulted, similar in plan and construction technique to the sanctuaries of the Temples of the Plaza of the Sun and to the altar of House F in the Palace. Both architectural elements are associated with burials. The sanctuary of Building 2 contained a stone censer stand, in which the human face was completely destroyed. On the other hand, archaeologists recovered two complete censer stands within the sanctuary of Building 3, in addition to ceramic fragments of another along with remains of the sanctuary's decoration. The first censer stand displays a seated human figure—with crossed legs and arms on knees—resting on a throne decorated with Tlaloc motifs. He wears a bird headdress and is framed by two vision serpents. The second censer stand also has a seated, cross-legged individual, who wears a mask and attributes of GIII, such as jaguar claw mittens. The headdress adopts the shape of a helmet decorated with the goggles of Tlaloc.

Group C is located yet farther east, along the Balunte Stream. Here, buildings with different functions surround a large plaza. Most of the structures were built or remodeled during the 8th and 9th centuries, although the initial occupation of the sector dates back to the 1st century AD. Buildings 1 and 3, located on the south and north of the plaza, display galleries subdivided into rooms, some of them with benches. The eastern side of the plaza is closed off by Building 2, composed of

Fig. 90 Group C under excavation.

two small pyramids measuring some 13 ft. (4 m) in height that were later joined by another platform. This structure was the group's area of ritual activity, because the most important burials were found here in addition to several censer stands and their fragments, one of which has been restored (Fig. 91; Plate 128). The censer stands were found behind Building 2, where they had fallen from the upper portion of the same structure.

This piece stands out for the detailed manufacture of the head, elaborated separately and later inserted into the body. Also noteworthy is the unusual treatment of the human figure: the craftsman represented the body in a very simple way, insinuating its existence beneath a cape or mantle, much like the funerary bundles represented in codices from Central Mexico. The figure sits, with legs probably crossed. Originally the arms must have rested on the knees. He wears a conical headdress with a representation of the Mat Bird, while two combs to hold the hair under the headdress may be seen from the back; some of these hair ornaments made of bone have been recovered in some burials, in the exact position indicated by this figure. The face displays traces of blue paint, which once probably covered the entire piece. A pectoral hangs from the neck—also with remains of blue paint—decorated with Tlaloc elements. The body and headdress of the figure are hollow, which makes it possible to insert this piece into a larger censer, of which fragments were found; a miniature censer also fitted into the figure's headdress.

Located to the west of the central zone (and below the modern parking lot), Group 4 was the residence of an important Palenque lineage, based on decipherment of the inscription on the Tablet of the Slaves. Occupied since the 7th century, this elite group underwent architectural modifications and additions through the site's abandonment in the 9th century. Again, the main structures are distributed around a patio, with Buildings 1 and 2 occupying the western position, and Buildings 3 and 4 in the northeastern corner. Buildings 1 and 2 had domestic functions based on archaeological remains, including benches. The excavation of Buildings 3 and 4 showed that both are pyramid platforms with multiple tiers and stairways on the front side, with at least two different construction phases. A number of burials were found in association with these structures, in addition to those excavated in the same area in the 1950s.

Building 1 provided evidence of the veneration of ancestors in the form of two stone censer stands. These sculptures were located on the upper level of the building, facing the patio (toward the east), unlike the pattern identified in Group B, where the sanctuaries of Buildings 2 and 3 face west. The first piece represents an individual with a *yajaw k'ahk'* headdress, identified by the drum shape and associated rings (Fig. 89). Another example of an individual with this type of headdress at Palenque is the figure on the right side of the stone panel of the pilaster from Temple 19 (Fig. 69). A long hieroglyphic inscription covers the front, edges and back portion of the sculpture, with references to at least two individuals, probably ancestors of Chak Suts', a military leader who inhabited the compound during the first half of the 8th century. The second piece (Plate 127) was carved from light greenish stone, probably not of local origins. In this case, the lower mask was eliminated, achieving the effect of a bust in the European sculptural tradition. Mutilated at an undetermined date, the work lacks the lateral flange projections, as well as the upper section of the headdress. The face represented differs from Palenque standards, because the nose is straight, while the eyes seem unfinished. It is framed by a coiffure always used by men, and it bears a quetzal mask—also mutilated—as a headdress. Finally a bar pectoral hangs from the figure's neck. The presence of the bird in the headdress suggests that the name of the individual includes the term *k'uk'*, "quetzal," so the figure may well be K'uk' Bahlam II, *ajaw* of Palenque around the second half of the 8th century. However, because the headdress also includes a *k'in* sign infixed within an ancestor's cartouche, it could instead be a representation of an early ruler of the same name, the founder of the Palenque dynasty.

Final Comments

The excavation of Groups B, C, and 4 has made it possible to establish that the elite lords of Palenque preferred to bury their own ancestors in buildings associated with the east, characteristic of the Maya tradition in this period. However, at Palenque we note two variants of this canon. In the first place, ancestors and their associated ritual were integrated into structures with a specifically funerary and ritual function, such as in the case of the pyramid platforms located on the eastern side of the patios of Groups C and 4. Furthermore, the sanctuaries with burials associated with Group B speak to us of a local variant of the Maya pattern, in which the ancestors and their ritual area were incorporated as a fundamental part of residential buildings.

Fig. 91 Part of censer stand, Building 2, Group C, Palenque. This exquisite, small censer stand had fallen from the top of a structure. A tiny incense-holder fits into the figure's head; the figure itself fitted into a larger censer as well (see Plate 128).

THE DISCOVERIES IN TEMPLE 19, PALENQUE

Alfonso Morales and Julia C. Miller

Temple 19 at Palenque was the source of a series of surprises and exciting discoveries during three excavation seasons. It started quite simply, when in 1998 we wanted to concentrate our project's efforts on a single structure in the area of Palenque known as the Cross Group. Temple 19, the building that we chose, is located at the southern end of that group and faces north toward the famous Temple of the Cross. It was a long mound, covered by forest, in an area of the site that was not visited by tourists very often. Because of its location, we suspected that there was a good chance that we could find a hieroglyphic inscription in Temple 19, which would help to establish this building's relationship to the rest of the structures in the area. However, we didn't expect to find four new inscribed monuments, including a stucco panel, a carved stone panel, a throne with two carved sides, and an inscribed balustrade.

In the first trench started in 1998, in the center of the building, 1.6 ft. (0.5 m) below the surface, the excavators started to uncover pieces of painted and modeled stucco. We called in our restoration team to lift the stucco in the hope that we would find enough pieces to put the panel together again. As the excavations continued to expose the east side of the central pier of the building, we found more stucco fragments and finally, 6.6 ft. (2 m) below the surface, we found a section of the stucco panel that was still complete and in place on the pier. When the excavation reached the floor of the building, we had the lower meter of a modeled and painted stucco panel and more than 3,000 pieces that had fallen from it when the building collapsed. Because the section that was still in place was in danger of falling off the pier, we removed it from the temple and took it to the laboratory to be restored. Nearly a year later, after three restoration specialists and four assistants had labored long hours over it, we ended up with two large sections of the panel. The lower section shows a profile view of Upakal K'inich, one of the last rulers of Palenque, wearing a large bird-head backrack (Fig. 70). The upper section has an inscription with ten hieroglyphs that mention a series of ceremonies that occurred every 900 days. The total height of the stucco panel is 11.5 ft. (3.5 m). The restoration team was never able to join the two sections of the panel, even after adding more pieces found in later excavations, although it was very close.

The second discovery was also made in 1998 when Joshua Balcells, a young archaeology student and Palenque native who had been spending time at the excavations as an apprentice, came to us very excited and tried to explain that there was something behind an unexcavated area close to the

Fig. 92 Carved platform, Temple 19, Palenque. Uncovered in 1998, the Temple 19 reliefs reveal the complexity of Palenque's 8th-century political arrangements.

floor on the north side of the pier with the stucco panel. We asked Christopher Powell to investigate the area that Joshua had noticed. Between of the spaces of the collapsed stones of the building, we could see a finely carved limestone slab attached to the base of the pier. As so often happens in archaeology, this discovery was found at the end of the excavation season. We extended our season for an additional month to excavate the section of the building in front of the pier. The carving was the base of a stone panel with the feet and legs of three people. When the excavation was extended for several square meters in front of the pier, we did not find even a small fragment of the rest of the panel; the floor looked as if it had been swept clean before the collapse of the building. The next year, while investigating the east side of Temple 19, 32.8 ft. (10 m) from the original carving, we found more pieces of the tablet and a year after that, in 2000, we found still more fragments both inside and outside the western end of the building. From the breakage patterns and locations of the pieces, it appears that a group of people, perhaps from Palenque itself, perhaps from another Maya site, came into the building after it had started to collapse and pried the stone panel off the pier. They carried the pieces into different parts of the building and dropped them there, along with parts of an offering that was looted from the throne (see below). Although we only found about two thirds of the panel, after it was restored, we were able to appreciate the scene of Ahkal Mo' Nahb III, an early 8th-century ruler of Palenque, wearing the same bird-head backrack seen on the stucco panel, and supported by two men, one kneeling on either side (Fig. 69). It is fascinating to see two rulers, Ahkal Mo' Nahb on the stone panel shown in frontal view, and Upakal K'inich in profile view on the stucco panel, wearing the same backrack and other costume elements.

The third discovery in Temple 19 discovered itself. The building had been covered by jungle for many centuries and several large trees had grown on top of it. We had decided to stop the excavations before we reached a tree that had grown near the eastern end of the building, to preserve it. One day our foreman, Pedro Cruz, was cleaning the excavation wall in preparation for drawings and photographs when a rock fell out of the wall. In the space left by the rock, Pedro could see hieroglyphs. We were down at the administration building and as we left the office, we got a radio message asking us to come up to the excavations immediately. When we arrived, we found a lot of activity but no one working and we suspected that something important had happened. When we saw the hieroglyphs we knew that it was a major discovery. We extended the excavations the additional 5 in. (15 cm) that was needed to expose the carving and found that it was a limestone panel that formed the western side of a low platform or throne. This panel has four columns of hieroglyphs at each end and three figures with unusual pointed headdresses (Figs. 72, 92). The central figure is holding a bundle of rope and the other figures have a textile band looped around their necks. They carry incense bags, the ends of which connect with the trailing ends of the central rope bundle. After this side was clear, we could see that there was another panel on the south side, and by feeling around the corner, in the spaces between the unexcavated stones, we could tell that there were probably hieroglyphs on that side as well.

The excavation was extended again, but with nearly 8.2 ft. (2.5 m) of building collapse burying the floor in front of the throne, it was slow going. Finally, as we neared the bottom and found the edge of the southern side and confirmed that it was also carved, we ran into a further complication. Resting in a layer of organic material was a large piece of the stone panel. As we expanded the excavation yet again, we discovered that this organic deposit covered an area of 64.6 sq. ft. (6 sq. m) and contained not only several pieces of the stone panel but also a bone earplug, a broken jade bead, small ceramic "luminarios," broken ceramic vessels, turtle shell, bone, obsidian, and other artifacts. As we completed the excavations, we realized that much of this material had originally been part of an offering that had been placed in the center of the throne. It was looted, apparently by the same people who pried the stone panel off the pier. They also took part of the material from this offering and left it in the western end of the building with more of the stone panel.

The south side of the throne also has a central scene flanked by columns of hieroglyphs. On this side, the ruler Ahkal Mo' Nahb is shown receiving a ceremonial headband, surrounded by six supporting lords. The inscriptions describe a ceremony performed by three of the Maya gods, with the earliest mythological date yet found, which Ahkal Mo' Nahb is shown reenacting (Fig. 93).

After the excitement of the west and south sides, everyone was waiting with great anticipation for the excavation of the third side of the throne. We had been sending digital pictures of the hieroglyphs and scenes to David Stuart as they were being uncovered. He would send back the preliminary translation of the inscriptions as fast as he could make them. The history recorded on the south side covered a time period already known from other inscriptions at Palenque so we had great hopes for new material on the east side. But when we uncovered the third panel, it was blank, with a single red line painted partway across its face. The disappointment was momentary, since we already had a wonderful new series of inscriptions on the other two sides.

The excitement and wonder of the discoveries in Temple 19, starting with the stucco panel, growing with the base of the stone panel—and the mystery of the lack of the rest of the panel—and culminating with the throne and the rest of the stone panel, kept the Proyecto Grupo de las Cruces busy for three years. When the inscriptions were read, a new sort of excitement took over, that of learning about two rulers who had been known from the king lists but who had been essentially unknown.

HISTORY, MYTHOLOGY, AND ROYAL LEGITIMIZATION AT PALENQUE'S TEMPLE 19
David Stuart

Before the discovery of the Temple 19 tablets and inscriptions in 1998, little was known of the Palenque king bearing the curious name K'inich Ahkal Mo' Nahb, "The Great Sun Turtle Macaw Sea." Scholars had recognized his existence since first, Heinrich Berlin, and subsequently, Peter Mathews and Linda Schele, established the basic outline of Palenque's 7th- and 8th-century king list.[17] But his name hieroglyphs were long unreadable and the ruler's place in the kingdom's dynastic history was obscure, especially in comparison to his predecessors. The Temple 19 discoveries have changed all of this, and now we can speak of the reign of Ahkal Mo' Nahb as one of the more compelling and complex periods of Palenque history.

Part of the interest in this remarkable king comes from the unusual circumstances surrounding his accession to the throne on 30 December 721 (Julian). Palenque had by this time gone through many ups and downs politically. His immediate predecessor in office was K'an Hoy Chitam, who suffered a military defeat at the hands of the Tonina king, who captured and displayed him in 711. Interestingly, K'an Hoy Chitam continued to rule Palenque after this defeat, probably under Tonina's sway for at least several years. Once this embattled king died sometime shortly before 722, the throne passed to Ahkal Mo' Nahb, who was not the son of the late ruler. Whereas most successions in Maya history went from father to son, the situation was far more complicated in this case. Ahkal Mo' Nahb was instead the son of a nobleman named Tiwohl Chan Mat, who had never occupied the throne.[18] His mother was named Ix Kinuuw Mat, and the parents and the newly installed son are portrayed together on the Tablet of the Slaves, discovered on an outlying residential

Fig. 93 Carved platform, Temple 19, Palenque. Akhal Mo'
Nahb (right) receives a royal Jester God headband from a
liege lord.

compound (Group 4) just west of Palenque's urban center. The king's father was, however, brother
to the deceased K'an Hoy Chitam, and thus a son of Pakal the Great. Two of the older sons of Pakal
ruled Palenque, so we might ask why the third son Tiwohl Chan Mat was left out of the scheme of
succession. The simple answer is that he died during the reign of his elder brother, in AD 680, when
Ahkal Mo' Nahb was only two years of age. As grandson to the heroic Pakal, Ahkal Mo' Nahb certainly could claim a strong royal pedigree, even if the line of succession seems unusually turbulent.

Ahkal Mo' Nahb did much to revive Palenque's fortunes after this unstable period. Reacting
to the poor fortunes of his predecessor and Tonina's dominance in those years, he quickly exerted
Palenque's military force in the years 723–729, when several "axings" (conquests) of neighbors took
place, as recorded on the Tablet of the Slaves. Moreover, within a reign lasting between 15 and 20
years he oversaw an impressive and widespread array of monuments and architectural projects
throughout the ancient city. In addition to the newly excavated Temple 19, the southern sector of the
Cross Group seems to hold several of his buildings, including Temple 18 and possibly Temple 20. We
also find this king's name mentioned on panel fragments from Temple 11, a little-studied but
important pyramid centrally placed in the main plaza, close to the Temple of Inscriptions and the
Palace.

But among all of his artistic accomplishments, little can compare with the small and elegant
sculptures from Temples 19 and 21, two structures dedicated together in AD 734–736 as shrines to the
so-called Palenque Triad, tutelary gods of the dynasty. The decorated platforms from the inner
temple of these structures were clearly conceived by the same team of artisans, and they provide a
large amount of new information about the dynasty of Palenque and particularly its mythological
origins and setting. The function of the 19 and 21 platforms (*yokib'*) is still a mystery, but their carved

faces provide very different historical and ritual narratives about Ahkal Mo' Nahb and his own successor in office, named Upakal K'inich (see González Cruz and Bernal Romero, this volume). The larger 19 platform, which we will focus on here, displays an elaborate scene of seven seated figures on its south side, all named with captions and framed by a lengthy hieroglyphic text (Fig. 93). The format and design of each panel is highly symmetrical, with a central image of a person and flanking portraits and text panels. In many respects this presentation continues the traditional scheme established by earlier Palenque panels, such as the well-known examples of the nearby Cross Group.

The new ruler strikes a pose and gesture that evokes other royal portraits at Palenque, and in this way it can be readily compared to the already familiar Tablet of the Slaves. On the 19 platform a man named Hanahb Ahaw (*janahb' ajaw*) holds before the king a cloth headband, the "crown" of Maya rulership and the essential symbol of the status *ajaw*, "ruler." Hanahb Ahaw was also a grandson of Pakal the Great, and the two men facing one another are thus cousins, if not brothers. The other named attendants seem to be priests and noblemen of the court, some with kin ties to the new king. One who sits directly behind Ahkal Mo' Nahb, next to the large bejeweled headdress, is a priest who seems to have overseen many of the rituals of Temple 19.

The inscription that surrounds the scene establishes the inauguration in its proper mythological setting, and in reading it we encounter one of the most explicit statements of divine kingship among the Maya. The inscription opens with the long count date 12.10.1.13.2, corresponding to a day in 3309, a date far earlier than others known before from Palenque's mythology. The event recorded is "sat in the rulership" and the subject is none other than the god known as GI, a prominent member of the set of three brother gods known as the Palenque Triad, and first identified by Heinrich Berlin.[19] GI is celebrated throughout Palenque's inscriptions, and his birth is mentioned in several texts of the Temple of the Cross. He is in many ways an enigmatic god, without any clear counterpart in the Conquest-period pantheon of Yucatan.

Before the discovery of this text we had no knowledge of GI's accession to office, nor any indication that the god was considered a "ruler" in his own right. As we continue reading this passage, we then find that the accession event was overseen or sanctioned by another god, Itzamna, and that the occasion took place "in the sky." This is an extraordinary statement, for Itzamna is a well-known god who, for most of the 1st millennium, was considered a ruler of the heavens. He is often depicted enthroned atop a sky-band design in portraits on Maya pottery (Plate 61). Evidently, this supernatural monarch established Palenque's GI as a ruler.

After mentioning a mythological sacrifice, the inscription reckons forward some nine centuries to the birth of the Palenque Triad gods, in the proper order GI, GIII and GII. The births of these gods are the major events celebrated in the neighboring Temples of the Cross (GI), Sun (GII), and Foliated Cross (GIII). But how could the deity GI be born some 960 years after his own accession to office? The explanation lies in the fact that the births of the Palenque gods were events of *local* significance; no records of these births are present at other Maya centers, many of which had their own specific sets of patron deities connected to the regional dynasty. GI, however, was celebrated throughout the lowlands in the 1st millennium, and his accession date under the auspices of Itzamna is presented in Temple 19 as a cosmic happening, "in the sky." The birth, or rebirth, of GI was I believe the time at which GI came to be reformulated, along with his two sibling deities, as a Palenque god. Perhaps we should also consider the temporal setting of the births, which came a relatively short time after the turn of Baktun 13, on 13.0.0.0.0 4 Ajaw 8 Kumk'u. This would seem an appropriate time to redesign the relations among the gods, and their own connection to the local Palenque kings.

One of the most important statements in this passage is that the Triad gods were the "creation" (*ch'ab*) of a god or goddess prominently named in other Palenque tablets. This may be an aspect of the Maize God, and according to this and other inscriptions at Palenque, he or she assumed office as a ruler some 35 years after giving birth to the Triad. In the Temple 19 inscription this event is called "the first seating," implying that this creator deity was also a founder of the Palenque political and cosmic order. It is tempting to consider that, as one who had created the Triad gods, this mythical dynast had long ago set the proper relationship or contract between kings and gods. The kings of Palenque, like other Maya lords, had the constant ritual duty of "creating" and sustaining ancestral deities, and the relationship between the parent deity and the Triad seems to have established the pattern.

Temple 19 is not simply a recitation of myth, however. Rather, it strives to link events in the very distant mythological past to dynastic events occurring shortly before the inscription was carved. The design and presentation of the information is extremely careful and deliberate, juxtaposing events and setting them forth as thematically related or even as repetitions of history. For example, most of the key events fell on the day "9 Ik'" (9 Wind), including the three inaugurations (two mythical, one historical). The text opens with GI's accession to office and closes shortly after a record of the king's own inauguration, also on the day "9 Ik'," thus bracketing the narrative contained within.

The stated equivalence between the inaugurations of GI and of the king is made clear in the platform scene as well, where we see Ahkal Mo' Nahb leaning forward to receive the headband emblem of his office from Hanahb Ahaw. In the hieroglyphic captions of these men, we find not only their proper names, but also explicit records that they are "impersonators" of deities. Maya kings and other elite figures apparently often took on ceremonial roles as "embodiments" or active manifestations of certain gods. Here, the ruler is named as the impersonator of none other than GI. The nobleman who faces the king with the headband, named Hanahb Ahaw, is named as the impersonator of Itzamna. The historical accession of Ahkal Mo' Nahb is not simply harkening back to mythical symbolism, but truly becomes a re-creation of that earlier event, where one god installed another in office.

THE THRONE PANEL OF TEMPLE 21 AT PALENQUE
Arnoldo González Cruz and Guillermo Bernal Romero

The Maya city of Palenque has revealed many long-hidden secrets in recent years. Among the most important of these are discoveries that tell the story of the city during the 8th century, particularly during the reign of K'inich Ahkal Mo' Nahb III.

In the fall of 2002, a team of INAH archaeologists, led by Arnoldo Gonzaléz Cruz, in the process of clearing the top of Temple 21, made an important new discovery in the back gallery of the southwest corner of the structure. Here, under about 11.2-ft. (3.4-m) depth of rubble, they uncovered a large carved panel, on which traces of paint still survived (Plate 129). Although archaeologists found no other materials in association with the work, it was clear that the finely carved panel had once served as the base of a beautiful throne. It was perhaps at the abandonment of the site that the panel was ripped from its architectural context, and smashed into 24 large pieces, as well as some smaller ones. At yet a later date the stone vault of the structure collapsed, burying the panel and preserving it until this day.

Fig. 94 Bench relief, Temple 21, Palenque, detail of Plate 129. Ahkal Mo' Nahb turns away from Pakal, at right, who nevertheless extends to him the royal perforator.

The Scene

The central figure of the panel is Pakal the Great, who had died half a century before the carving of this monument. The associated texts indicate that he was the personification of the legendary ruler Ch'away U "K'ix" Kan, whose name is displayed on his diadem. Seated on a throne covered with jaguar pelt, Pakal holds a sharp stingray lancet decorated with the so-called "Perforator God." The head of this entity is tied with three knots to symbolize bloody sacrifice. Pakal offers the sharp tool to Ahkal Mo' Nahb, whose name as a child, according to the text, was Okib (Fig. 94).

In turn, Ahkal Mo' Nahb addresses a supernatural being with a rodent face and feline paws who wears a jaguar pelt cape. This strange character wears a complex headdress, decorated with Jester God medallions, a mirror sign, and maize plant. The associated text identifies this character by the name of *xak'al miht tu-muuy ti-ch'o,* an expression whose significance is unclear. His name is accompanied by a priestly title that David Stuart has pointed out has been erroneously read as *itz'aat,* or "sage," when it probably has the value of *nahb'at,* "anointer," instead. Perhaps this figure represents a priest transfigured in a "nagual," or animal companion spirit.

On the right side is Upakal K'inich, "the young heir to be Sacred Lord of Palenque" (*b'aah ch'ok k'uhul b'aakal ajaw*), probably the first-born son of Ahkal Mo' Nahb, who succeeded his father at some point between AD 736 and 742. He faces a second character named *xak'al miht tu-muuy ti-ch'o,* the mirror image of the rodent-faced figure in jaguar pelt on the other side of the panel.

The Inscription on the Edge of the Top

The texts enclosed in brackets and marked with an asterisk [*] are reconstructions of passages that have been lost. These reconstructions are supported by similar clauses from two monuments from Temple 19: the stucco panel that shows a representation of Upakal K'inich and the stone panel that decorates the western face of the throne or platform.

(ISIG) *b'olon pih oxlajun winik-haab' wuklajuun haab' b'olon winik mih k'in ox ajaw- way u ti' huun sa̱m-iiy hul-iiy* [Glyph 3D*] "Glyph X" *u ch'ok k'aba' winaak lajun ox yaxk'in muut* (?) [*u naah u i'la-el*] ... [*ox ch'ak kab'an*] *mat k'inich k'an* "joy" *chitam k'uhul b'aak ajaw u naah yokob'-il k'ahk' k'uh u suutz icham ajaw wa-waan ta i'ila-el okib' ch'ok u pakal k'inich ch'ok k'uhul b'aak-al ajaw ha'o'b' ki-?-naj ch'am-?-naj ta ch'ab' akab'-il yichnal* "GI" *k'awiil u tz'akaj-_ waklajun waklajuun winik-ij-iiy chan haab'-iiy jun winikhaab'-iiy* [*i-uht b'olon kib way b'olonlajun k'anasiiy* * *och k'ahk' ta' waxak k'inich-lak* (*el?*) *naah ... k'ahk chak p'ul* (?) *naah-il* "GI"*] ...

The Panel Inscription

[*k'inich ahkal mo'nahb' k'uhul b'aak-al ajaw*] *u jun tahn Ix-?- loot nahb' k'uh ix kinuuw mat ix aj ox te' k'uh u yax lo*[*ot*] *sak ik'il jun nahb' naah kan tiwool chan mat ... u tz'ak-aj jun wak winik-ij-iiy cha haab'-iiy i-uht* [*wak kab'an way* "G2" *ti' huun jo' yaxk'in och k'ahk' ox jojol b'aak ... u chak p'ul* (?) *naah-il k'awiil*] *k'inich ... naah* [*u chak p'ul* (?) *naah-il*] *k'inich ajaw pakal, yehtej k'inich ahkal mo'nahb' k'uhul b'aak ajaw yijatej sajal b'olon okib' aj-ich-iiy ox cha winik-ij-iiy lajun ajaw-way naah jo' tuun waxak ik'- sijoom u k'al-aw-Ø tuun k'inich ahkal mo' nahb' k'uhul b'aak-al ajaw yichnal ox p'uluut k'uh* "GI" *k'awiil k'inich ajaw pakal u tz'ak-aj-Ø ox wuk winik-ij-iiy jun haab'-iiy lajun winikhaab'-iiy cha pih-iiy uht-iiy lajun kab'an-way naah ... ? ... ti' huun, jo' muwaan naah otoot-aj- Ø* "GI" *sak b'olon k'awiil u kab'-ij-iiy ch'a-way k'uhul b'aak-al ajaw pih* (?) *ti ich took'* (?) *yax pi* (?) *u naah ... k'an chak* [*p'ul* (?)][*naah-il*]

Translation of the Inscription on the Top

(Initial Series Introductory Glyph) 9 *baktuns,* 13 *katuns,* 17 *tuns,* 19 *winals,* 0 *k'ins* on the day 3 Ajaw, under the regency of the Ninth Lord of the Night, Yik'inal, soon after the arrival of the third lunation, whose name was "X," with a duration of 30 days, on 3 Yaxk'in (June 14, 709), was announced (?) the first *i'la-el* [clear-sightedness?] ... [of Upakal K'inich, under the auspices or in the company of the lord*] Ox Ch'ak Kaban Mat K'inich K'an "Hoy" Chitam, Sacred Lord of Palenque, (on) the first pedestal of the God of Fire, U Suutz' Icham Ahaw. The young Upakal K'inich, the young (heir to be) Sacred Lord of Palenque, is placed as *i'la-el,* (and) they (Upakal K'inich and K'an "Hoy" Chitam II) conjured or invoked in the creation or nocturnal penitence, in the presence of the gods GI and K'awiil. 16 days, 16 *winals,* 4 *tuns* and 1 *katun* passed [and then it was the day (9.15.2.7.16) 9 Kib, 19 K'ayab, January 10, 734 when the fire of the

House of the Eight Braziers, or the Great or Red Incense Burner of the House of god GI enters*]…

Translation of the Panel Inscription

… [for the work (?) of K'inich Ahkal Mo' Nahb, Sacred Lord of Palenque*] the pampered one (the son) of the Lady of the God of the Twin Lakes (?), Lady Kinuuw Mat, lady from Ox te' K'uh, the vital pure breath (the son of the father) First Serpent of the Sole Lake, Tiwool Chan Mat… 1 *k'in*, 8 *winals*, and 2 *tuns* transpired and then it was the day 6 Kab'an, when the Second Lord of the Night ruled, on 5 Yaxk'in (9.15.4.15.17, June 7, 736) [when the fire enters through the three doors … in the Great or Red Incense Burner of the House of the god K'awiil*], and in the House of the Solar Face of the Sky, the Great or Red Incense Burner of the House of the god K'inich Ajaw Pakal, by the work of K'inich Ahkal Mo' Nahb III, Sacred Lord of Palenque, accompanied by Sahal Bolon Okib. From here 3 *kins* and 2 *winals* transpired until the day 10 Ajaw, the first period of five tuns, on 8 Ch'en (9.15.5.0.0, 22 July 736), when the stone of the period is tied (by) Lord Solar Face, Ahkal Mo' Nahb III, Sacred Lord of Palenque, in the presence of the god-censers of the gods GI, K'awiil and K'inich Ajaw Pakal. 3 *kins*, 7 *winals*, 1 *tun*, 10 *katuns* and 2 *baktuns* transpired since it had been the day 10 Kab'an, when G7 governed, the Seventh Lord of the Night [erroneously recorded instead of GI, the First Lord of the Night*] , on 5 Muwan (7.5.3.10.17, July 17, 252 BC), when the gods GI-Sak Bolon and K'awiil were put in a house (a temple), under the auspices or by the will of Ch'away [U "K'ix" Kan*], "He who is Transfigured, Serpent Spine," Sacred Lord of Palenque, (who) wraps the face of flint in the first ceremonial bundle, the First *k'an* offering of the Great or Red Incense Burner (?) of the House (of the god GIII?)."

Summary of Dates:

Initial Series of the top,		9.13.17.9.0,	3 Ajaw, 3 Yaxk'in, June 14, 709 AD
Glyphs 1–16:	+	1.4.16.16	distance number (toward a later date)
Date recorded on the top:		[9.15.2.7.16,	9 Kib, 19 K'ayab, January 10, 734 AD]
	+	2.8.1	distance number (toward a later date)
Panel: C3–D4:		(9.15.4.15.17)	6 Kaban, 5 Yaxk'in, June 9, 736 AD
	+	2.3	distance number (toward a later date)
E4–E5		9.15.5.0.0	10 Ajaw, 8 Ch'en, July 22, 736 AD
	-	2.10.1.7.3	distance number (toward the past)
H3–G5		7.5.3.10.17	10 Kaban, 5 Muwan, July 17, 252 BC

SHIELD JAGUAR AND STRUCTURE 23 AT YAXCHILAN

Roberto García Moll

Beginning in AD 652, or 9.11.0.0.0 in the Maya calendar, Yaxchilan assumed its greatest importance as a regional political entity and urban center, a role that came to an end around AD 810 (9.19.0.0.0). During this period the city exhibited tremendous building activity, as well as a notable increase in the production of sculpture with epigraphic inscriptions. Texts dealing with a wide range of events and exploits in the lives of rulers proliferated, and they also named a larger number of individuals than they had up until this time; furthermore, these texts referred to persons at many more levels of the hierarchy, including particularly powerful women. Externally, Yaxchilan, like its neighbors in this time period, increased its trade contacts: the archaeology reveals a great diversity of non-local products, both from Central Mexico and Central America.

One of the individuals who charted the destiny of Yaxchilan is known to us today as Shield Jaguar. Although we have no record of his birth, we know that he ascended to power in AD 681 (9.12.9.8.1) and that he died in AD 742 (9.15.10.17.14), events that are recorded on several lintels and stelae.[20] A number of military conquests that consolidated and possibly augmented his domain can also be attributed to Shield Jaguar. During his reign, several buildings at the site were erected, including the one that concerns us here, Structure 23, along with a number of important carved monuments.

Structure 23 sits on a raised platform on the southern side of the Great Plaza. Two flights of stairs provide access from the plaza, set against two large setbacks into the natural limestone rise. On the basis of several categories of data, but particularly ceramics (the Yaxkin complex, dating from AD 633 to 732) and architectural style, we have dated Structure 23 to the end of Stage V of the site's urban development—in other words, between AD 672 and 731 (9.12.0.0.0 to 9.15.0.0.0). Structure 23, then, would be coeval with Structures 14, 19, 34, and 44, of which the first two, like 23, are located near what is known today as the Great Plaza. During this period, Shield Jaguar concentrated his major buildings into the west and central portion of the Great Plaza, along with some construction on the southern side of the city, and with important activity in the Lesser Acropolis (first Structure 51, then Structure 44). However, in all likelihood many buildings from this period survive only as substructures to later constructions, particularly those associated with the subsequent ruler, Bird Jaguar IV, whose architectural vision of Yaxchilan is what we see today.

The architectural characteristics common to the end of Stage V include facings that cover both the first and second levels, divided by wide cornices with molding; typically, a large roof comb composed of two vertical openwork sections sits atop the vaults. Abundant modeled stucco decoration, of which little remains today, covered both the horizontal entablature of the second level, as well as the roof comb.

On the northern or main facade, three openings provide access to the interior of the first corridor. Monolithic limestone lintels decorated on both the underside and along the front face, known today as Lintels 24, 25, and 26 (Plates 49–51), spanned each entry. On both the east and west facades, openings provide access to the second corridor, which also has monolithic lintels, but only the lintel on the west facade, Lintel 23, displays additional carved decoration. Both the texts and the figurative representations on the four lintels refer to two important individuals in the life of Yaxchilan: Shield Jaguar and his principal wife, Lady Xok, for whom we know only the date of her death, in AD 749 (9.15.17.15.14).

Structure 23 features two parallel vaults running roughly west to east, along the axis of the building; two internal doorways lead from the first chamber to two smaller rear rooms. Two internal buttresses that support the exterior walls divide the first chamber into three spaces that correspond to the front entrances and Lintels 24, 25, and 26. Of these three small spaces, the two side rooms (Rooms 1 and 3) have benches and niches; they also have niches set into the walls. From the central section (Room 2)—which lacks benches—one gains access to the two rear chambers, each of which is further subdivided by internal buttresses, leaving little interior space (Fig. 95).

Both these small, rear chambers feature a built-in bench. Although information on the final surface layer is fragmentary, the floors, walls, and vaults were completely covered with stucco; decorative stucco elements with evidence of red, blue, and black paint covered the walls of the first vaulted space.

During archaeological exploration of the primary contexts of the first chamber, we recorded two tombs and two deposits. In Room 1 a deposit (known as Element 21) was found on the eastern end of the chamber, under the stucco floor. It consisted of 146 prismatic obsidian blades, each displaying a polished, prepared surface and of lengths ranging from $\frac{3}{8}$ in. to 1 in. (1–2.5 cm). All the blades have two lateral notches on the edges. We have associated this group of obsidian pieces with the Lintel 24 representation of a woman, who performs auto-sacrifice by passing a rope with blades through her tongue. Lintel 24 spans the entry to Room 1.

We found Tomb 3 under Room 2, the central room of the frontal corridor, and the one whose entry is spanned by Lintel 25. The stucco floor covered Element 50, a thick layer of limestone and clay containing a large quantity of obsidian chips, dominated by prismatic blades and totaling 16.5 lb (7.5 kg) on top of an ample stone fill.[21] Smaller amounts of polychrome ceramics and flint chips covered two layers of stone slabs, which in turn covered Tomb 3.

Tomb 3 had a rectangular plan with its major axis running east to west. It was built simply with limestone walls covered with a layer of stucco, on top of which were placed large panels of woven fibers suggesting mats: both impressions and fragments of material survived in the stucco. Five niches at floor level were set into the four walls. Analysis of bones deposited in this tomb revealed that they belonged to an adult woman, of about 40 to 45 years of age.[22] The body was oriented from southeast to northwest, and it must have been wrapped in a shroud, given the anatomical position of the body, extended flat on its back with arms flexed over the thorax.

The associated objects fall into two groups. First, associated directly with the body, within the shroud, were a large perforated mollusk, placed over the face; three cacao beans; 81 bone needles; two bivalves; 431 greenstone beads distributed into four groups; one greenstone disk; 34 obsidian blades; four greenstone earspools; three pearls and one bone awl incised with glyphs. Outside the mortuary bundle we found 27 jaguar claws distributed into six groups and 34 ceramic vessels, one of which depicts an elderly woman. The majority of the vessels are concentrated in the northeastern corner of the tomb.

Under the bench and stucco floor of Room 3, the room that is entered under Lintel 26, at the western end of the frontal corridor, we found Tomb 2. A layer of lime and clay covered two layers of slabs to form the lid of the tomb, with three large ceramic incense burners and a plate on top. The tomb conforms to a rectangular plan with a major east to west axis, with walls built of worked limestone, and with a single niche at the eastern end. Clay covered the walls, and on one section, over the niche, traces of impressions indicated woven mats that had once adorned the walls.

Inside the tomb, the body and offering were deposited on the floor, with the skull at the eastern end and the feet at the west. In the area of the head, there were skull fragments and teeth with incrustations; in the center, remains of the pelvic bone; and to the west, the remains of the subject's left foot, which displayed a severe bone lesion. In order to have survived, the individual must have needed special care for many years. Tomb 2 belonged to an adult male between the ages of 45 and 49, and he was also wrapped in cloth before placement in the tomb.

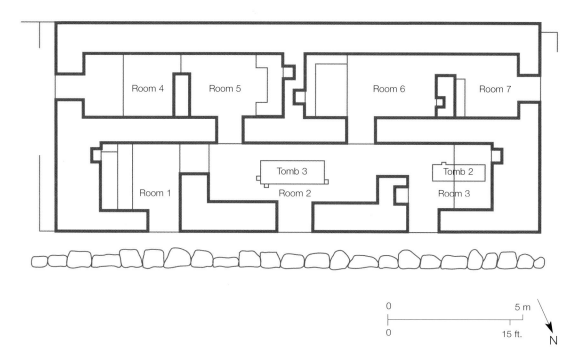

The associated funerary objects may be divided into at least three groups. In the first are pieces directly associated with the body, including a large, perforated mollusk which was found over the face; six rings, five made of greenstone and one of shell; two lip plugs; 469 greenstone beads in 39 groups; two shell beads; four disks, three of greenstone and one of shell; one slate disk with shell, pyrite, and greenstone mosaic; one greenstone earspool; one shell earspool; three pendants, one of shell and two of greenstone, as well as two pearls. At the northwestern end of the tomb, near the individual's feet, there was a large group of objects associated with auto-sacrifice, which must have once been contained in a small bundle. These included two bivalve shells, one ceramic bowl, 78 stingray spines, eight stingray spines carved with glyphs, five flint knives, three prismatic blades, three shell pendants, seven worked bone awls, three deer antler awls carved with glyphs, three worked bones, and five plain awls (Plate 55).

Additionally, outside the mortuary bundle, we found two alabaster vessels (Plate 56), 19 jaguar claws distributed into three groups, one obsidian knife (made from El Chayal obsidian, found in Guatemala), three shells, one obsidian axe (made from Cerro de las Navajas obsidian, in Hidalgo, Mexico, and virtually identical to the one found at San José, Belize[23]), two polishing tools for ceramics, four ceramic vessels, and one incense burner.

The contents of the two tombs in Structure 23 reveal the complexity of a society both in its daily life and rituals. Furthermore, we recognize today the works were created to be a highly refined art. It is important to highlight that all the objects recovered in these tombs, as well as the four other tombs explored at the site, were clearly intended for regular use, given the evidence of normal wear-and-tear.

The context of the two tombs, their associated objects, and the human remains lead us to believe that Tomb 2 belongs to the individual identified in the inscriptions as Shield Jaguar[24] and Tomb 3 to his wife, Lady Xok, who is referred to on some of the awls in Tomb 2. The detailed study of objects and hieroglyphic texts both on the awls as well as on the stingray spines, along with other remains recovered, will lead to a better understanding of Yaxchilan and its key figures.

THE ACROPOLIS OF PIEDRAS NEGRAS: PORTRAIT OF A COURT SYSTEM
Stephen D. Houston

Royal courts of the ancient Maya had two kinds of identities. They were dwellings much like our palaces, opulent homes of kings and courtiers.[25] They were also complex social networks that clustered around an important person, such as a king, noblemen, or priestly figure. The Acropolis at Piedras Negras fit both descriptions (Figs. 96, 97). It was just such a residence, and, along with buildings nearby, it provided an arena for the dense social relations that whirled around the rulers of Piedras Negras *c.* AD 550–800. Recent excavations by Brigham Young University and the Universidad del Valle de Guatemala have shown something of the Acropolis's history and documented how the palace responded to royal needs and whims.[26] But the story ends badly. The vast sprawl of buildings spent its final years in squalor and ruin, with intermittent visits by pilgrims who harbored some memory of its grandeur and sacred status.

In court systems, rulers enjoy a unique position. They are the objects and manipulators of factions but usually stand apart from them, even if slightly. By elevating "favorites," creatures of the king who serve as intimate friends and often begin as playmates from youth, rulers deploy a convenient scapegoat when royal policies go awry. At the same time, in such intimate friendships they find a measure of emotional satisfaction in an atmosphere that otherwise ripples with collective distrust, mutual surveillance, evaluation, and continual brokerage of offices and favors. There is some evidence that Piedras Negras had a favorite of this sort during the reign of the last king, Ruler 7.[27] Many rulers also lavish attention on pets and mentally or physically challenged people, whose affections and motives are less complicated than those of courtiers.[28]

The problem with favorites, and the reason they are often loathed by competitors, is that they tend to control the most important resource at court: access to the ruler. Thus, palaces often reflect, as does the Acropolis at Piedras Negras, minute gradations of open and closed space, leading to ever more restricted locations within the inner precincts of royal life. The Acropolis at Piedras Negras precisely matches such spaces by having areas for the reception of subjects, embassies, tributaries, and prisoners, and more exclusive zones from which members of the court could look out, but few could see in.

Fig. 96 Reconstructed view of Piedras Negras by Tatiana Proskouriakoff. Here the viewer looks across the front of the Acropolis to Structure K-5.

Fig. 97   Reconstructed view of Piedras Negras by Tatiana Proskouriakoff. In this bird's eye view, one sees not only the Acropolis but also the Usumacinta River in the distance.

Most courts, especially Maya ones, remain opaque in the details of their administration. They project the image of smooth organization but almost always involve the opposite—disorder, tension, improvisation, and waste. Another paradox would have troubled the rulers of Piedras Negras greatly: the court housed a unique, nonpareil king but also copied from other courts, which held similar, "unique" rulers. Clearly, courts were affected by the personalities of kings and the particular cultures that enveloped them—in short, they had a history, a cultural setting, and could vary strongly from reign to reign. Some rulers were shy, others egoistic and boastful, a few even insane. Palaces reflect tradition but also the personalities of their occupants.

Against this background we can understand much of the Acropolis at Piedras Negras. It can be dated by two means: by ceramic chronology, which at Piedras Negras is roughly accurate to just under 50 years or so—the productive span of two generations of potters—and by examining the sequence of construction. In no other place at Piedras Negras are the deposits deeper or the building sequence so complicated. These attributes make the Acropolis at once a difficult puzzle and a key opportunity for relating buildings to particular rulers over time.[29] Today, the Acropolis is covered with high trees and lianas in which monkeys cavort and parrots squabble. A few buildings, such as parts of Structures J-9 and J-11—a nomenclature from the 1930s when a team from the University of Pennsylvania excavated there—remain standing in sections, but the slumping of walls and revetments and the destruction of wide wooden lintels make some of the structures difficult to see. Even so, from lowest base, near Structure J-28, to the summit of Structure J-23 the Acropolis stands at least *c.* 262 ft. (80 m) high, at maximum width, *c.* 755 ft. (230 m). Much like other Maya buildings of this size, however, the bulk of the Acropolis consists of a natural hill that has been shaped into terraces, platforms, and patios. When repairs ceased after AD 800, the lateral flow of masonry went unchecked, and buildings such as Structure J-17, a royal sweatbath, began to glide backwards down the sides of the Acropolis.

Visitors to the Acropolis during the period *c.* 300 BC to 175 AD would have seen a virtually untouched hill. The only exception was slight activity below its summit, where a single sherd has been found from this time, wedged into a space hollowed out of bedrock. The Maya often scraped down layers in preparation for others, so it is possible that a small building existed there. During this period most people at Piedras Negras lived in and around the South Group. After a flurry of activity, however, the community went into demographic decline, nearly to the point of depopulation, only to be revived, especially during the phase *c.* AD 350–550. Where these people came from continues to be a matter of debate. To judge from similarities in ceramics, some came from valleys to the south, but many more arrived from the central Peten, Guatemala.[30]

At this juncture the story of the Acropolis begins to involve hazy personages, the early rulers of Piedras Negras. Altar 1, which lies just below Structure J-1 of the Acropolis, on the floor of the West Group Plaza, mentions kings of Piedras Negras at AD 41 and, more plausibly, at AD 297. The references are retrospective, and we can be more certain of the existence of several rulers after about AD 460, all of whom carry the word "Turtle," *ahk*, as part of their name, a pattern that continues through the 8th century. These are the lords who authorized a large series of patios, small temples, and giant revetment walls under the West Group Plaza.[31] However, perhaps between AD 500 and 550 these perishable structures were burned, and the building platforms forcibly leveled, their debris pushed into the patios so as to flatten the West Group Plaza. Our suspicion is that this burning was somehow linked to more general instabilities at the time.

The Acropolis had evidence of similar construction and burning from the period AD 350–550. Parallel buildings, all facing what was to become the West Group Plaza, rose up the Acropolis hill, beginning with Structure J-1-Sub 1, then up a terrace and on to J-11-4th; the summit of the hill, in and around Patio 3, was occupied by small platforms. The struggle against the lateral flow of masonry began with a series of well-built terraces around such platforms. A smear of ceramics from this period has been found just above bedrock in areas without buildings, suggesting that trash was trampled over a stone surface not yet enveloped by mortar and dressed masonry.[32] The overall effect was of openness and of an upward sweep of buildings, each looking over the other, in stepped arrangement, to events occurring in the palaces below. The patios, which became so well-defined in the 7th and 8th centuries, did not yet exist in a clear fashion—the Acropolis was a place for spectators, not, apparently, the central locus of royal events themselves. One episode is registered archaeologically, however: a ceremonial dump in Patio 3 contained crushed jade, fine pottery, and organic materials, along with evidence of burning.[33]

Then the Acropolis changed fundamentally in character, as did the West Group Plaza. This took place at a time just before or partly coincident with the first well-known lord at the site, Ruler 1 or K'inich Yo'nal Ahk. A great deal of burning, evidenced by melted and fused wattle-and-daub (known in Guatemala as *bajareque*), occurs throughout the Acropolis, but especially as part of the destruction of the more open buildings. A second wave of instabilities struck Piedras Negras, probably as a result of hostilities with the neighboring polity of Pomoná, Tabasco.[34] Archaeology does not allow us to tell a more precise story, but it seems likely, given the apparent martial success of Pomoná in this conflict, that Piedras Negras was hit badly. Whether the damage came from external or internal forces is impossible to discern. The ceramics of the city start to incline toward large-scale production of unusual resist polychromes. The dynastic picture suddenly becomes much clearer, too. Scholars can piece together a succession of fathers, sons, and brothers that, on present evidence, would have been undoable earlier. The vestige of the earlier palace was now no more than a memory, perhaps a bad one, to be replaced by an enormous investment of labor during the reign of three kings, Ruler 2, Ruler 3, and Ruler 4. They are the ones who, with architects and builders, engineered a court with increasingly restricted space; from them came a new housing for a court that might have been acutely different from its predecessors in its emphasis on dynastic exclusivity. Ruler 2's role is less clear, but he may have begun the leveling and raising of the West Group Plaza. One wonders if he and his successor were influenced by the creation of palaces at Palenque, with which, ironically, Piedras Negras had poor relations. Such emulation across hostile borders is nothing new in court history. In Ruler 2's time, exceptional calligraphers, working not in paint or ink but clay and stone, were patronized by the court. Embellished with Ruler 2's names and titles, their works appear in pieces of considerable virtuosity found in a deposit within a small residential patio to the west of the West Group Plaza.

Ruler 3 appears to be the great builder of the dynasty, with a fondness for massive bulk and crafted forms that leapt to the sky. He and his builders fashioned a burial pyramid of vast size, Structure J-4, for his father, Ruler 2, thus introducing a mortuary component to the Acropolis and eliminating spaces that had been given over to palace buildings. Traffic up the stairway must have been heavy, for, within a short time, builders enlarged its width twofold, although structural problems may also have contributed to the modification. Panel 15, among the largest of such sculptures discovered in the Maya area, was placed on the upper stairway of Structure J-4 by Ruler 3 to commemorate his father's martial alliances and exploits in war (Fig. 98). Ruler 3's hieroglyphic record appeared in a series of stelae, some with cists (prepared cavities) to house their bases, just in front of his father's mortuary pyramid. During his reign, Ruler 3 drew special attention to a singular date, 9.13.0.0.0 in the Maya long count system, and self-consciously established a connection between that time and the so-called Maya "creation" many thousands of years before, at 13.0.0.0.0; the rulers of Palenque, too, were fascinated by this conjuncture and celebrated it in their Cross Group. A megalithic stairway, involving many times the quantity of stone slabs used in stelae, was invested with a cache of obsidian, eccentric flints, stingray spines, an ear ornament, and bird remains. Elsewhere, such stairways were used for the display of captives and tribute, perhaps evoking the wretches depicted on Panel 15 far above.[35]

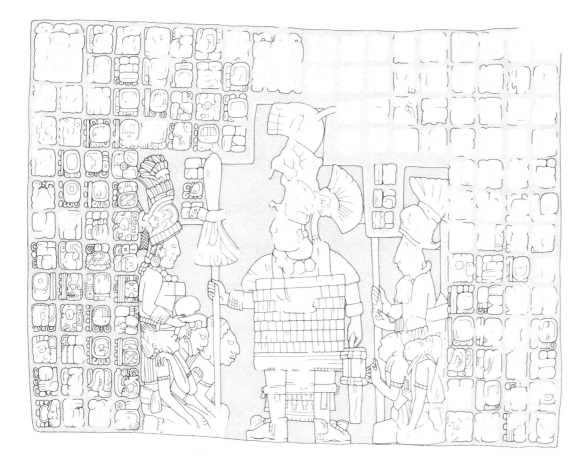

Fig. 98 Panel 15, Piedras Negras, drawing. Found on the upper stairway of J-4, a massive Acropolis funerary monument, Panel 15 depicts Piedras Negras Ruler 2 in his role as military victor, attended by captains and captives.

For the first time, women, including a queen and princess, played a large role in the monuments of Ruler 3, and it may be that this accorded with the harem-like properties of Patios 2 and 3, restricted spaces suggesting a heightened emphasis on a dynastic version of domesticity. Was this the birth of private life among the kings of Piedras Negras? Unfortunately, we have only the footprint of buildings from Ruler 3's time and cannot tabulate the amount of space for his residences. What is certain is that Ruler 3 or Ruler 2 experimented with complicated patios, as under Platform J-7, and then boldly leveled them to create simplified access from one patio to the next. The first throne room may have been built at this time, in Structure J-6. With Structure J-2, Patio 1 was configured as a place for the reception of visitors who had scaled the front of West Group Plaza, passing two guard houses, one containing the tomb of an eternally vigilant prince, sweated across the Plaza, climbed yet another set of stairs, lumbered down into the (at that time) steep Patio 1 entrance, and ended up, much the worse for wear, in front of Structure J-6 and its massive stairway.[36] This was the architecture of impression management, of pauses by visitors entering some new membrane around the court. But it was also the architecture of humiliation. The exhausted effort of visitors would contrast with the stately repose of the ruler in his throne room, surrounded by courtiers.

Oddly, Ruler 3 was then buried, presumably by the enigmatic Ruler 4, in the large but modestly placed Burial 5. The paradox is that this tomb nevertheless contained rich mortuary furniture, including a spondylus-shell vest that he may have inherited from his father. Yet is seems that proprieties were just barely observed. The difference between his father's upward-thrust pyramid and this placement under the shuffling feet of courtiers and royalty ascending the Acropolis could not be more stark. Adding to the mystery is the remains of an unfinished pyramid on the other side of the Acropolis, Structure J-27. The dating of that pyramid may be toward the end of Ruler 3's reign.

Ruler 4, about whom relatively little is known, presided generally over a change in material culture, leading to a new phase (starting *c.* AD 750). It was a ceramic inventory dedicated to enlarged dishes on supports and, presumably, to generous portions for distribution during feasting and other repasts. With Ruler 4, the impression is of someone who breaks with Ruler 3, whose memory is shabbily acknowledged and whose possible pyramid was aborted and, much later, converted into a modest residence attached to Patio 4. Ruler 4's mother is accorded more loving or pious treatment, as evidenced by Stela 40, a rare scene in which Ruler 4 scatters incense into the tomb of this woman, who, to judge from the position of Stela 40, was buried within the J-3 pyramid. With J-4, J-3 framed all frontal entrances to the Acropolis, as though the ruler in between would, when receiving visitors, be flanked by the honored dead. Ruler 4 also shifts focus to his eventual burial place, Structure O-13, perhaps at the cost of his mother's pyramid—that building, too, does not appear to have a finished summit temple. But he must have had a rich court life. Panel 3, among the most intricate of Maya sculptures, shows assembled courtiers, feasting, dancing, in a location that can only have been the Acropolis (Figs. 48, 100).[37]

At this point, the Acropolis had taken its general form, owing largely to the efforts of Ruler 3. The final three kings of Piedras Negras were involved in relatively small-scale ways with the Acropolis. There is circumstantial evidence that the three were brothers, the probable sons, perhaps by different mothers, of Ruler 4. Ruler 5 did not govern long, and his imprint is small on the city. The court is barely detectable. His heir, Ha' K'in Xook, or Ruler 6, is equally obscure, and appeared to have ended his rule with an abdication, an unusual gesture for a sacred lord—was he incompetent? Sickly or unbalanced? To both Rulers 5 and 6 may belong a few of the later masonry buildings in the Acropolis, but of this we cannot be sure.

We are on more secure footing with Ruler 7. Fine masonry buildings were the order of the day. Structures were made of thin slabs of hard limestone, shaped by percussion and laid carefully into walls and vaults, sometimes interspersed with fired clay bricks known as "Granizo Unslipped." These same bricks functioned as armatures for the modeled and painted stucco on building facades in the Acropolis. The architecture of the Acropolis that is visible today comes from Ruler 7 or, just possibly, from his immediate predecessors. An almost frenetic degree of structural modification occurred: relatively narrow buildings were replaced by ones with two corridors and multiple rooms, as in Structure J-11. Later, even finer adjustments were made with further subdivisions of rather poor construction. Evidently, Ruler 7 and his court liked ventilation, something at a premium during the torrential downpours and fungal growth of the rainy season. They accomplished this by ordering buildings with wooden lintels, which, by analogy with Yaxchilan upstream, were most likely carved. These same lintels proved the downfall, literally, of the existing buildings of the Acropolis. Easy to dislodge, burn, and rot, they would, in fall and decay, undermine all standing vaults. Patios 2, 3, and 4 were, for Ruler 7 and his court, restricted spaces that could house only a few non-royal courtiers— Patio 4, at some distance from the finely built structures around Patios 2 and 3, was a possible home for them. It may be for this reason that, on the collapse of the court, Patio 4 continued to thrive with densely placed structures and a profusion of burials.[38] The subdivision of space may hint at a larger court for Ruler 7's reign or at least a need for more varied spaces, including storage chambers and the occasional sleeping bench. These differ from thrones by their solid base, although thrones, too, may be found in more open locations, such as the eastern room of Structure J-11 and the northern, central room of Structure J-18. The preoccupation at Piedras Negras with ritual purification by sweat-bathing was met by the construction of the J-17 bath, among the least accessible at the site.

The glory of the Acropolis during Ruler 7's reign was the Structure J-6 throne, among the most ambitious works attempted by sculptors at Piedras Negras. Ruler 7's favorite, the king of La Mar, makes an appearance on the back of the throne—a literal supporter of the king. (It is possible that the favorite actually commissioned the throne as a gift for his lord.) The text of the throne refers to the night-time abdication of Ruler 6, the carrying of tribute and its placement on a place called the *lam naah*, perhaps a building within the Acropolis, and then, a little over a year later, the arrival of a "celt" or "axe" image, also at *lam naah*, its "first resting" on its journey at the "war place," and then its placement in or around the area of Pyramid O-13, all as a preliminary to his accession.[39] These cryptic events constitute the rationale and justification for his ascent to highest office.

But it was all to end quickly as a result of attacks from Yaxchilan.[40] The throne was shattered in many fragments. The only buildings in continued use were those of Patio 4. Other structures, especially the J-17 sweatbath, by now ruined through lack of terrace maintenance, and Structure J-12 above it, became repositories for great quantities of fetid trash. If this was a court, then it was an extremely dirty one with a striking reduction in quality of life. Patio 4 became densely packed with perishable buildings, whose enduring existence may have resulted from the proximity of water in the Usumacinta below and from anxieties about defense. Later, even these structures fell into disuse, and the "court" of Piedras Negras, such as it was, attempted to create a small throne room in Structure R-8, far to the south. Visible on the surface as a few adobe columns, the room melted away with excavation and seemed not to have any permanent footings. In the Acropolis, a few cremation burials mark the surface of Platform J-7, but they are impossible to date.

In a quiet moment, centuries later, a small group of visitors deposited incense burners in the collapse of Structure J-2, perhaps not daring to venture further into the sacred place. With that small act the Acropolis dies as a Pre-Columbian monument and enters the present age as testimony to the courtly grandeur of the Maya.

TALES FROM THE CRYPT: THE BURIAL PLACE OF RULER 4, PIEDRAS NEGRAS

Héctor L. Escobedo

Introduction

Structure O-13 is the most impressive individual construction in Piedras Negras. It is a five-terraced pyramidal temple elevated *c*. 56 ft. (17 m) above the East Group Plaza. It is a religious building that shares amazing similarities with the Temple of Inscriptions at Palenque, the mortuary pyramid of Pakal the Great. Its superstructure is composed by a large multiple chamber temple with five doorways oriented toward the plaza. Like the Palenque building, the pyramidal superstructure that supports the temple was built in part by taking advantage of a natural hill. This hill was extended and modified with five terraces that integrated the pyramidal base; a monumental stairway led from the plaza to the temple summit. Aside from its impressive size, the importance of O-13 is clearly shown by the presence of ten associated stelae in addition to four panels and one altar. One of those panels, "Panel 2" of Piedras Negras, is included in this volume (Plate 109).

Early Excavations at Structure O-13

Explorations in Structure O-13 were initially directed by J. Alden Mason, director of the University of Pennsylvania Project in 1931 and 1932. Between 1933 and 1936, Frank Cresson and Linton Satterthwaite probed in strategic areas. Tatiana Proskouriakoff created precise plans and profiles while trying to reconstruct the original appearance of the temple. The Penn Project's unpublished data, together with the plans and profiles of the building, demonstrate that the temple had about four construction stages, including a complex series of architectural enlargements, both vertical and horizontal. Penn recovered fragments of the elaborated stucco decoration on the temple excavations, including remains of a possible polychrome mural. The discovery of 56 caches was noteworthy, for these contained hundreds of chert and obsidian eccentrics, often deposited below the floor of the rear chamber of any given building.

Fig. 99 Pyrite disk, Burial 13, Structure O-13, Piedras Negras, drawing. The inscription names this beheaded captive as a lord from the rival kingdom of Hix Witz, "Cat Hill."

Panel 3 and the Burial Place of Ruler 4

One of the strongest motivations in investigating O-13 came from information recorded on Panel 3, a damaged monument found by Mason near the remains of the superstructure's northeast portico (Fig. 48, 100). Although this panel was dedicated to Ruler 7, it actually celebrates Ruler 4's first *katun* anniversary as king on 27 July AD 749 (9.15.18.3.13 5 Ben 16 Ch'en). The sculpture depicts a retrospective courtly scene supervised by Ruler 4, who appears seated on a throne, surrounded by 14 people identified as local nobles and important visitors. Some of the attendants held the Sahal title, a rank employed by important subordinate lords. The most prestigious visitors came from Yaxchilan, including Yopaat Bahlam II, who ruled this site during the ten-year interregnum between Shield Jaguar II and Bird Jaguar IV.

The royal festivities took place two days later on 29 July AD 749 (9.15.18.3.15 7 Men 18 Ch'en), when Ruler 4 did the *ta em mo'*, or "descending macaw" dance, followed by a nocturnal celebration where the celebrants drank cacao. The text goes on to indicate that Ruler 4 died at 56 years of age, on 25 November AD 757 (9.16.6.11.17), to be buried three days later on 28 November AD 757 (9.16.6.12.0 10 Ahaw 3 Pax) in the Ho Hanahb Witz (*ho janahb' witz*) mountain. Although this name normally refers to a mythological place, here it seems to refer to Structure O-13, Ruler 4's ancestral shrine. Even more interesting is the reference to the reentering of the tomb, which took place 24 years later as part of a ritual of purification-by-fire, named as *elnaah umukil*, "house burning at the burial," an event directed by Ruler 7 at the anniversary of the abdication or death of the previous ruler Ha' K'in Xook. It was also just short of the 15-year anniversary of the death and burial of Ruler 4. In reviewing this epigraphic information, we concluded that O-13 represented an ideal opportunity for locating Ruler 4's interment and interweaving historical and archaeological records at Piedras Negras.

New Excavations at Structure O-13

The new excavations in Structure O-13 were directed by the author in 1997 and 1998, with the assistance of Tomás Barrientos and Carlos Alvarado. We started by clearing debris behind the structure and the still-existing chamber on the summit and continued by excavating a pit in front of the center of the temple. After our initial excavations, we tunneled into the base of the pyramid and discovered cache O-13-57, perhaps the largest known cache in the Maya lowlands. This cache was located beneath the monumental stairway, surely marking the axis of the pyramid. O-13-57 contained 129 eccentrics, 57 of chert and 72 of obsidian, placed in groupings of seven or nine equivalent shapes. At the edge of the eccentrics was a small vessel that contained pyrite and jade beads, as well as a large quantity of jade powder, spondylus shells, hematite, pyrite, bird bones, a large bivalve shell, and a marine spiral shell.

Burial 13

The plaza area in front of O-13's main stairway was also explored by Tomás Barrientos, producing a surprising find. In 1997, an initial pit directly in front of O-13's stairway penetrated through a paved floor. The excavation then reached a dense concentration of artifacts and burned human bones that were part of a secondary interment, called Burial 13 by the project (Fig. 101). The excavation of this burial revealed that the stone paving had been placed to cover a pit dug to reenter the tomb in ancient times. The complete deposit was disturbed and intensely burned on that occasion. Many of the bones disappeared and the rest were scattered throughout the tomb and violently compressed by a collapsed vault. The human bones belonged to three individuals, one adult male and two adoles-

Fig. 100 Panel 3, Piedras Negras, detail. Commissioned by Ruler 7 for Structure O-13, the panel features his ancestor, Ruler 4, who sits on the royal throne. The accompanying text describes the re-entry of Ruler 4's tomb, which archaeologists subsequently discovered and called Burial 13.

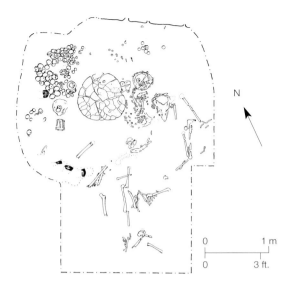

Fig. 101 Burial 13, Structure O-13, Piedras Negras, plan.

cents. The lack of cut marks on the bones suggests that the bodies had decayed prior to being broken and blackened by fire.

The funerary offerings of Burial 13 were very similar to those recovered in Burial 5, the richest tomb discovered by the University of Pennsylvania Project and possible grave of Ruler 3. Among the artifacts found were 128 fragments of a pyrite mosaic, two jade pectorals, one of them representing a crocodile, 50 fragments of spondylus shell that formed a mosaic, four spondylus shells incised with glyphs (one them with an *ik'* "breath, life, wind" symbol carved in its interior, calling forth images of gods and ancestors emerging from shells as at Palenque), various fragments of mother of pearl incised with glyphs, jade earrings, two complete spondylus shells, deer bones and ten broken vessels. Some 211 clay beads, some painted with Maya blue, were found associated with the bones, along with 96 pieces of worked jade fashioned into a necklace. A bag, now disappeared, seemed to have contained a bloodletting "toolkit" with six stingray spines together with two jade and two bone imitations, and a jaguar ulna carved into the head of the rain god Chaak, that probably functioned as a bloodletter handle.

The inscription of one of the shells found in Burial 13 records the date 4 Kib 14 K'ayab, in 747. This corresponds to the reign of Ruler 4, who ruled between AD 729 and 757. Another shell shows the name glyph of Yopaat Balam II of Yaxchilan, who attended the ceremony recorded on Panel 3. A third text on a small pyrite disc displayed the severed head of a captive from Hix Witz, "Cat Hill," a tributary site and sometime enemy of Piedras Negras, located at a short distance from Laguna Perdida (Fig. 99).

Interpretations

Burial 13 and Panel 3 support the identification of this tomb as the crypt of Ruler 4. He was accompanied by two adolescent individuals, following the same pattern as Burial 5, the other identified secure royal tomb found at Piedras Negras. The placement of an impressive number of stelae and caches in Structure O-13 clearly reflects religious fervor, but its deepest motivations may have been political. This very intense ritual focus in a particular temple could be related to the necessity of legitimizing the last rulers of Piedras Negras. As Stephen Houston has pointed out, after Ruler 4's death the succession from father to son shifted to a fraternal one. This transformation of the hereditary system seems to have caused quarrels and problems among the successors of Ruler 4, for they do not mention each other in their monuments. It is probable that Rulers 5, 6, and 7 dedicated monuments in front of the pyramid to emphasize a genealogical bond to Ruler 4. One of them decided to reset Panel 2 at the structure, building a bond to the ancestors named on that work. This connection was, after all, the source of their rights to the throne. Therefore, it is not surprising that Structure O-13 experienced its major transformations during the rulership of Ruler 7, the last known at the site. This king had apparently forced the abdication of Ha' K'in Xook, his brother and predecessor. This would explain why Panel 3 commemorated events in the life of Ruler 4, though it was Ruler 7 who dedicated the monument. Such dynastic conflicts were the prelude to Piedras Negras's defeat by Yaxchilan, an event that accelerated the collapse of what once was the dominant Maya center in the Usumacinta river valley.

Notes

Chapter 1

1 The normal word for "west" in the inscriptions is the Ch'olan *ochk'in,* "sun-enter" (Stuart 1998a, pp. 388–339). However, in the 8th century we begin to see the OCH sign (a hand holding some implement, sometimes with a sun sign *k'in* infixed) partially or wholly replaced with the syllable chi (a hand with touching thumb and forefinger). Some may be phonetic complements, but others appear be independent signs that reflect the Yukatek word for "west," *chik'in.*

2 McAnany 1995.

3 For recent compilations of scholarly work on Maya royal courts see Inomata and Houston 2001–2002; Christie 2003.

4 Stuart 2000, pp. 465–513. The Aztecs, Toltecs, and later Maya all called this sacred place "Tollan," or "place of reeds."

5 Harrison 1970, p. 248.

6 Hohmann and Vogrin 1982, p. 31.

7 Stuart 1998a, pp. 373–425; Martin n.d.

8 Excavated by Alejandro Tovalin and reported on in Schmidt, de la Garza, and Nalda 1998, p. 569.

9 Wurster 2000, pp. 144–149.

10 There is epigraphic evidence that at least some heirs to the thrones of lesser polities lived at the capitals of their political masters. In the known instance, a young lord, probably from La Corona, Guatemala, spent three years at Calakmul (Houston and Stuart 2001, p. 67, Martin 2001a, pp. 182–184; from an observation by Nikolai Grube). Major hegemons such as Tikal and Calakmul may have used de facto hostages such as these as part of their political strategies, and Calakmul in particular is copiously equipped with suitable palace complexes in which to house them (Martin 2001a). In this way, they may have resembled the much later 14th- and 15th-century practice of Mayapan where, the sources tell us, the ruling lineage kept subject lords in long-term residence, supplied by tribute sent from their home towns (Tozzer 1941).

Chapter 2

1 On Mesoamerican gods and the nature of Mesoamerican religion in general, see Coe and Kerr 1998, pp. 101–110; Freidel, Schele, and Parker 1993; Miller and Taube 1993; Townsend 1979, pp. 25–31.

2 The study of Maya religion began with the categorization of Maya gods by alphabetical names at the end of the 19th century by Paul Schellhas (in 1897); the work was translated into English (Schellhas 1904). Karl Taube has been at the forefront of current study (see Taube 1992). For a summary of how terminology has evolved, see Miller and Taube 1993.

3 Tedlock 1996, pp. 145–146.

4 Ibid., p. 91.

5 Ibid., p. 91.

6 Ibid., p. 97.

7 Ibid., p. 99.

8 Ibid., p. 137.

9 See, for example, Izapa Stela 25 (Taube 1992).

10 Taube 1985.

11 Maya writing features two head-forms whose characteristics are frequently blurred and partially overlap. One is female and probably represents the idealized young Moon Goddess. Sometimes identified by a cross-hatched forelock, the head reads both as the female agentive *ix* and as the noun *ixik,* "woman." The other is male and portrays the young Maize God, often distinguished by a jewel worn over the forehead. This seems to read *ixim,* which in modern Maya languages simply means "maize" (David Stuart, personal communication to Simon Martin, 1999).

12 Coe 1989, pp. 161–184.

13 The head of Xbalanque is used in the writing system as the word for "nine," although it also appears as a rare sign for the syllable "ba." Most Mayan languages today use *b'olon* for the number nine, although this syllabic use suggests an internal a-vowel and may therefore favor *b'alun* and its relatives, the word for "nine" in the highland Maya languages of Tzeltal, Tzotzil, Tojolabal, Chuj, Q'anjob'al, Jakaltek, and Motizintlec (see Schele and Freidel 1990, p. 465).

14 A number of tombs at Altar de Sacrificios had a large drilled plate in just this position; other examples are known from Tikal or Uaxactun, although at these sites the practice was less consistent (see Smith 1972, p. 215).

15 "It is black, dark, like a tamal, like mud, appearing like mud. The green maize ear, the ripened maize ear become smutted. Smut forms. It becomes smutted." Sahagún 1963, 11, p. 281.

16 Sahagún 1963, 6, p. 168.

17 One name for God L during the 7th and 8th centuries is spelled 13-? yu-CHAN-na on a ceramic vase (K5359) (Fig.21). The unknown sign resembles the syllable "mu," which would produce a reading of *uxlajuun muy chan.* In a late screenfold book, the Dresden Codex, the name of God L's owl avatar is very similar: *uxlajuun chan kuy,* "Thirteen Sky Owl." Some mystery surrounds God M, a major underworld deity of later times who assumes much of the merchant role previously fulfilled by God L. The name of God M consists of a jaguar deity's eye, the same glyph used as an abbreviated name for the Jaguar God of the Underworld as patron of the month Wo (Thompson 1962, p. 282) and in the lunar series notation of Glyph C in earlier times (also noted by Erik Boot). A direct relationship between these two gods would do much to explain the disappearance of the once important Jaguar God of the Underworld after the 10th century. The pairing of God L and this jaguar-based deity on the Tablet of the Sun at Palenque may therefore be the prototype for the Popol Vuh pairing of One Death and Seven Death (Fig. 68a).

18 See Kerr 1560. http://famsi.famsi.org:9500/dataSpark/maya, or Kerr 1989–2000.

19 See Kerr 5166.

20 Coe and Coe 1996, pp. 98–99.

21 Vargas de la Peña and Castillo Borges 1999 and 2001, pp. 55–56.

22 Gómez-Pompa et al. 1990, pp. 247–257.

23 Sustenance Mountain, the origin mountain of maize, was known as Tonacatepetl (Miller and Taube 1992, p. 120) to Nahua speakers. Among the K'iche Maya, Pan Paxil Pan K'ayala is a sacred mountain near Mexican/Guatemalan border, with cave and spring on slopes, where creator gods acquired maize and water to make the first humans. Teosinte grows in abundance on its slopes (Tedlock 1996, p. 357).

24 Arellano Hernández 2002, pp. 331–357. Arellano has pointed out that several of the capstones specifically identify *kakaw* (351).

25 One vase shows the Maize God in the company of a twin-like partner (see K8540). It may well be the case that some duplicate Maize Gods are actually two distinct but closely related entities, prototypes for the brothers One Hunaphu and Seven Hunaphu in the Popol Vuh (see K6997, 6994). There is no necessary linkage between this second character and cacao, and what relationship we do see may simply be one stage in the various resurrections of the Maize God—as suggested by another painted vessel now in the Popol Vuh Museum, Guatemala City (K5615) (Fig. 28). The female aspects of the Maize God are also to be kept in mind (Bassie-Sweet 1999, pp. 105–125).

Chapter 3

1 See, on Copan: Bell 2002, pp. 89–104; and on Palenque's Red Queen: Tiesler Blos, Cucina, and

Romano Pacheco 2002, pp. 75–78; also:
http://www.mesoweb.com/palenque/features/
red_queen/01.html.

2 Proskouriakoff 1961, pp. 81–99. One might also
note the number of women who entered the field
of Mesoamerican studies, particularly in art history,
after 1960.

3 Hendon 1997, pp. 41–43; McAnany and Plank
2001, pp. 84–129.

4 Houston and Stuart 2001, p. 64.

5 The Mixtec case is useful for comparison:
see Pohl 1994.

6 Murra 1962.

7 Illustrated on p. 7 of Nuttall 1903.

8 The hunter's hat can be seen on many painted
ceramics, and is often worn by Hunahpu, one
of the Hero Twins.

9 Saul and Saul 2002.

10 Reents-Budet 2000, pp. 1022–1037.

11 Taube 1992, pp. 99–101.

12 Siegel 1941, p. 66; Taube, op. cit., p. 68.

13 Rather remarkably this netted skirt forms part
of some Aztec female deities as well (see Matos
Moctezuma and Solís Olguín 2002, Entry 38).

14 Some controversy has focused on Stela H at Copan
and the question of the beaded skirt (see Joyce 2000,
pp. 80–81). Karen Bassie-Sweet has pointed out that
Maize God is reborn from the dead bones of the
Maize Goddess (Bassie-Sweet 2002, pp. 169–190).

15 Schele and Miller 1986, Chapter 4.

16 For the life of Lady Six Sky see Closs 1985,
Martin and Grube 2000, pp. 74–77.

17 The seemingly benign Maize God kicks and
tramples a trio of Underworld Gods on at least
one vessel (K1560) (See Fig. 21).

18 Tate 1992; Schele and Freidel 1990, pp. 262–305.

Chapter 4

1 Tozzer 1941, pp. 27–28. For 16th-century Maya
courts see Restall 2001, pp. 335–390.

2 Stuart 1987, pp. 2–8; see also Stuart 1989,
pp. 149–160;

3 Inomata and Sheets 2000, pp. 5–10.

4 This line was translated by Miguel Leon-Portilla
as "El buen alfarero…enseña al barro a mentir
[the good potter…teaches the clay to lie]" in
Leon-Portilla 1966, p. 267. Charles Dibble and
Arthur O. Anderson translate the same Nahuatl
text more literally as "The good potter is a skilled
man with clay, a judge of clay—thoughtful,
deliberating, a fabricator, a knowing man, an
artist…" (Sahagún 1961, 10, p. 42). Louise Burkhart
points out that no gender is indicated here
(personal communication to Mary Miller, 2003).

5 Coggins 1975, p. 513.

6 Tozzer 1941, p. 169.

7 Tedlock 1996, pp. 23–29.

8 One of very few stone monuments that might
discuss tribute transactions is Naranjo Stela 32
(LeFort and Wald 1995).

9 Coe and Kerr 1998, pp. 148–150.

10 Reents-Budet notes that 137 of 176 ceramic vessels
studied depict the "range" or colonnaded structure
(Reents-Budet 2001, p. 196).

11 Stuart 1999.

12 We use the term "jade" as a non-technical term,
equivalent to chalchiuhuitl among Nahuatl speakers.
It is used commonly to refer to various semi-
precious gemstones, including jadeite and nephrite.
Nephrite (usually found in Asia) is harder than
some steel (Moh's scale, 5.5 to 6.5); jadeite is harder
yet (6.5 to 7). The Maya considered several stones
to be generically "jade," including the principal
material jadeite, but not excluding albite, serpentine,
and diopside. See also Ward 1987, pp. 282–316.
The ancient source of jadeite in Guatemala has
been recently rediscovered (Broad 2002).

13 One large example may be Stela 9 from Calakmul,
the only known slate monument at the site
(Ruppert and Denison 1943, pp. 101–102).
Calakmul was an ally of Caracol, a city close to the
Maya mountains where slate abounds, and this may
be a gift or item of tribute brought from there.

14 Stuart 1990, pp. 9–14; see also Herring 1998,
pp. 102–114.

15 Pasztory 1997, p. 193.

Chapter 5

1 Inomata 1995; Demarest 1993, pp. 95–111; Inomata
et al. 2002, pp. 305–330; Inomata et al. 1998,
pp. 23–39; Inomata 2003, pp. 110–119.

2 "Many yells, horns, and trumpets were heard and
the Indians who showed themselves were armed
with bows and arrows, shields and lances."
Wagner 1942, p. 131.

3 Ibid., p. 147.

4 Stone 1989, pp. 153–172.

5 The historical relationship between the Maya
and Teotihuacan was complex, but receives scant
attention in the inscriptions. Military intervention
may have been of less importance than more subtle
forces, among them intermarriage, religious cults,
and trade agreements, which required other sorts of
contact. Teotihuacan appears to have manipulated
dynastic succession at Tikal in 378—perhaps by
force—and provided some of the impetus or
inspiration for colonizing missions, such as the
one that took a new ruler to Copan in 427 (Martin
and Grube 2000, pp. 29–34, 192–193; Stuart 2000,
pp. 465–513).

6 Stone 1989, pp. 153–172.

7 Stuart 2000.

8 Just 1994; Miller 2000, pp. 177–187; Houston 2001,
pp. 206–219. Juan Yadeun's excavations since the
1980s have brought many of these troubling images
to light.

9 Sixteenth-century sources document the practice of
groveling by touching the earth and then bringing
the hand to the mouth. See Tozzer 1941, pp. 35–36,
n. 175.

10 Baudez and Mathews 1978, pp. 33–34; Benson 1976,
pp. 45–58.

11 Tonina Monument 99 depicts a female captive
with bound arms and cut clothing.

12 Tedlock 2003.

13 Schele 1984, pp. 7–48; Schele and Miller 1986.

14 Baudez and Mathews 1978.

15 The best example would be Yich'aak Bahlam,
"Jaguar Claw," of Seibal, captured by Dos Pilas in
735, yet evidently still ruling his kingdom in 747
(Martin and Grube 2000, pp. 61, 63).

16 Ross Hassig (1992, p. 97) first attempted to assess
the seasonal pattern of Maya warfare "with conquests
largely occurring from December to early June"; see
also Child 1999. Attacks on settlements are reflected
in puluy uch'een, "his town/territory was burned" or
ch'ahkaj uch'een, "his town/territory was chopped".
The former suggests the torching of the highly
combustible pole and palm-thatch houses that made
up the great bulk of Maya cities. Such destruction
would have had a devastating effect on the economy
of the community concerned and take huge efforts
and resources to replace. The latter, to judge from
surviving dictionary entries, seems to be a more
general term for "damage, attack"—at its worst
presumably the sacking of the target city. A more
mysterious expression, och uch'een, seems to combine
a double meaning: a more literal "his town/territory
was entered" with a metaphorical sense of "defeat,
conquest" that seems closely tied to a mythological
episode. The premier field battle, be it conducted
in forest or farmland, was jub'uy, "brought down,"
applied to specific individuals or to their took'
pakal, "flint(s) and shield(s)." The latter was
certainly a war emblem of sorts, but might also
be a prosaic reference to an "army" or "band of
warriors."

17 Buikstra, Price, Wright, and Burton 2003.

18 Landa described the removal of jawbones from
dead opponents. "After the victory they took the
jaws off the dead bodies and with the flesh cleaned
off, they put them on their arms." Tozzer 1941.

19 In his Fifth Letter Cortés wrote, "This town
stands upon a high rock: on one side it is skirted
by a great lake and on the other by a deep stream
which runs into the lake. There is only one
entrance, the whole town being surrounded by a
deep moat behind which is a wooden palisade as
high as a man's breast. Behind this palisade lies a
wall of very heavy boards, some twelve feet tall,
with embrasures through which to shoot their
arrows; the lookout posts rise another eight feet
above the wall, which likewise has large towers
with many stones to hurls down on the
enemy….indeed, it was so well planned with
regard to the manner of weapons they use, they
could not be better defended." (Pagden 2001, 371).
See also Inomata 1997, pp. 337–351, and Webster
1976.

20 Martin and Grube 2000.

Chapter 6

1 According to history inscribed in the 7th century, the dynastic line of Palenque began in 431 with the inauguration of a lord called K'uk' Bahlam, "Quetzal Jaguar." Although none of his records survive, a carved vessel now at Dumbarton Oaks does carry the name of his successor "Casper" (435–487). The turn of the 7th century saw a woman, Ix Yohl Ik'nal, "Lady Heart of the Wind Place" (583–604), on the throne—a 20-year reign notable for the extreme rarity of females using full royal titles and exercising kingly prerogatives. The death of Ix Yohl Ik'nal in 604 led to the accession of an ill-starred king Ah Ne' Yohl Mat, perhaps her son, in 605. He seems to have exerted some political influence over Santa Elena, in Tabasco, but presided over the calamities of 611 and died the following year (Grube in Martin, Zender, & Grube 2002; see also Note 2, below).

2 References to the troubles of this era appear on the East Panel of the Temple of Inscriptions at Palenque. Here we see the expression *ch'ahkaj lakamha'*, "Palenque was axed," an assault or sacking of the city dated to April 611 (Looper and Schele 1991). The protagonist was later identified as Scroll Serpent, king of the "Snake" kingdom, whose capital was Calakmul by *c.* AD 630 (though some uncertainty remains about periods before this, especially given the early references to the same kingdom at the more northerly site of Dzibanche) (Martin 2000, pp. 107–109; Martin and Grube 2000, p. 103). The East Panel goes on to describe the accession of a short-reigning ruler, a namesake of Palenque's founding deity (Schele and Freidel 1990, pp. 226–227). This character remains enigmatic, not least because it is during this period that the normal gifts to the city's patron gods were "not given," their effigies were "not adorned," and lords and ladies were "lost" (Grube 1996, pp. 5–6; Martin and Grube 2000, p. 61).

3 The nature and date of this event have been debated by specialists for a number years. The date was reckoned to be 9.11.1.16.3 6 Ak'bal 1 Yax (AD 654) by Peter Mathews and 9.10.18.8.8 6 Lamat 1 Sip (AD 651) by Floyd Lounsbury (Baudez and Mathews 1978, p. 36; Schele 1994, p. 1). Linda Schele later amended the Lounsbury interpretation by one Calendar Round (52 years) to reach 9.8.5.13.8 6 Lamat 1 Sip (AD 599) (1994, p. 1). This has been the accepted view for some time (e.g. Martin and Grube 2000, p. 159), but at the urging of David Stuart (pers. comm. 2002) a re-appraisal of the casts of this monument in the British Museum was made and the Mathews date confirmed.

Identification of the verb as *ch'ak*, "to chop/damage" (Orejel 1990), revealed the violent nature of the associated event (Schele 1994, p. 2), and subsequently that Palenque itself was the victim (Martin 2000, p. 110–111). The agent of the war is said to come from Calakmul, but is otherwise

unknown. The re-used fragments appear in the North Group of Palenque, built sometime in the 8th century (Robertson 1991, pp. 61–64).

4 A single, tiny, vertical perforation of the wall is interposed between the two more southern doorways, technically giving the building four openings on the west.

5 Stomper 1996.

6 The eastern platform of House C bears the images of six lords captured on a single day in 659. They came from a variety of locations: one from Pomoná, a key kingdom on the Tabascan plain due west of Palenque (Schele 1994, pp. 1–10). The stairway inscription describes these successes, as well as the "arrival" six days later of a certain Nuun Ujol Chaak—not his namesake the king of Tikal, as once thought, but a lord or ruler of a second Tabascan kingdom, Santa Elena (David Stuart, personal communication to Simon Martin, 1999). These events are overtly juxtaposed with the attack Palenque suffered at the hands of Calakmul in 654 (see Note 3). The west side of House C carries the names of five young lords from Santa Elena and a sixth from Pomoná who died in 663. These widely spaced captions were apparently once associated with their own figural sculptures; the spaces for which were later filled in antiquity, but can still be discerned today.

Whatever influence Pakal had gained in Tabasco through these military and diplomatic maneuvers seems to have been short-lived. In 662 a series of closely spaced events began with a joint ceremony between the kings of Piedras Negras and Calakmul in February of that year, signaling some form of collaboration or alliance between them. Six days later Piedras Negras attacked Santa Elena, 24 miles (37.5 km) to its north. In March, Palenque celebrated the taking of two unidentified captives—whose images were incorporated into the gallery of prisoners on the east side of the East Court—which may well be linked to these developments. Just ten days after this the king of Calakmul re-installed the boy-ruler of Moral-Reforma—a third kingdom of the Tabascan plain 21 miles (33.75 km) north of Santa Elena—marking his subordination to this far more powerful ruler. The Moral-Reforma king was to maintain his allegiance to Calakmul for the next three decades (Martin 2003, pp. 44–47).

Although we have only the bare bones of a narrative here, we seem to have a contest for the control of Tabasco between Palenque on the one hand and Calakmul and Piedras Negras on the other. As significant as they may have been, Pakal's successes in Tabasco did not lead to any long-term supervision of the region. Instead, some or all of the region fell under the influence of distant Calakmul, who presumably reaped a material benefit from the rich well-watered soils of this alluvial plain.

7 http://www.famsi.org/reports/ To see the Palenque map, search under Edwin Barnhart, who directed the mapping project.

8 A monumental panel excavated from Structure 16 lists a succession of secondary lords installed by Palenque rulers, stretching from 435 to as late as 768 (Bernal Romero 2002, pp. 401–423). The complex was dedicated either to a particular office or to a lineage that monopolized that office.

9 Alberto Ruz Lhuillier (1906–1979) sometimes called himself Alberto Ruz, or occasionally Alberto Ruz L. He spelled his second surname Lhuillier. Of French origin, this surname is spelled both Lhuillier and L'Huillier in Mexico, France, and the United States. This second spelling of the name is the one used by the site museum at Palenque today. Accordingly, in this text we will use both Lhuillier to refer to the archaeologist and L'Huillier for the museum named in his honor.

10 Kan Bahlam's political prominence is revealed by references to his "overking" status along the Usumacinta River at Anaite and La Mar, and in his reinstallation in 690 of the same Moral-Reforma ruler who had previously been subject to Calakmul (see Note 6). In 692 he suffered defeat at the hands of Baaknal Chaak of Tonina, and several of his vassals were captured at this time or in the years that followed (Martin 2001b; Martin 2003; Martin and Grube 2000, pp. 170, 181–182).

11 The identity of the shorter character pictured on the three tablets of the Cross Group has been debated for many years. Floyd Lounsbury and Moises Morales independently concluded that both figures represented Kan Bahlam—as both an adult and a child—a conclusion also reached by Karen Bassie-Sweet (1991, pp. 202–204, 260). Confirmation of this came with the decipherment of *ub'aah* as "the image of" (Houston and Stuart 1997, pp. 73–101), which in this context clearly ties the smaller figure to the childhood names of Kan Bahlam.

12 One censer stand which also bears a striking resemblence to the young Kan Bahlam now resides in the New Orleans Museum of Art; another was once in the Jay Leff collection. See McDermott 1980, p. 99.

13 In October 692 Kan Bahlam's forces suffered a "star war" defeat at the hands of Baaknal Chaak of Tonina and one of his client lords, K'awiil Mo', was captured. A year later another Kan Bahlam vassal, a lord of La Mar, was also captured, part of a single campaign along in the Usumacinta that included the defeat of Anaite and ultimately seems to have led to Baaknal Chaak's ascendency over Bonampak before 708 (Martin and Grube 2002, pp. 181–184).

14 Tonina Monument 122 ties the capture of K'an Hoy Chitam II to the year 711, although the Palace Tablet suggests his participation in the dedicatory ritual for House AD of the Palenque Palace in 720. Further work on the "K'an Tok" panel (Bernal

Romero 2002) has linked his name there to the year 712 (Peter Mathews, personal communication to Simon Martin, 2000), while David Stuart has since identified a mention of him on Piedras Negras Stela 8 placed to 714 (Stuart, unpublished manuscript at www.mesoweb.com). The most plausible explanation is that K'an Hoy Chitam—like another captive king known from the site of Seibal—survived his ordeal and returned to his throne in some capacity (Martin, Zender, and Grube 2002, p. 39; Stuart, op. cit; Martin and Grube 2000, p. 61, p. 63).

15 The name of this king combines those of the legendary "U-Kix Chan" (986–? BC) and the historical "Casper" (AD 435–487), although he is a separate and previously unknown character from Palenque's legendary past (González Cruz and Bernal Romero 2003, pp. 20–27).

16 Upakal K'inich is named as a full ruler on the "K'an Tok Panel" (Bernal Romero 2002) and as an heir apparent on the stucco pier from Temple 19 (Martin in Morales 1998, p. 3).

17 Porter 1994, pp. 11–18.

18 Martin in Morales 1998, p. 3.

Chapter 7

1 Tedlock 1996, p. 108.

2 Susan Milbrath, personal communication.

3 Miller 1986.

4 Navarijo Ornelas 1999.

5 Gomez Aguirre 1993.

6 Tozzer 1941, p. 36.

7 Tozzer 1941, p. 52.

8 Garcia Moll 1994, p. 23.

9 Fuente 1965.

10 Berlin 1963, pp. 91–99.

11 The CG/SM studies were conducted by Dr. Richard Newman of the Museum of Fine Arts, Boston. DRX studies were carried out by chemical engineer Leticia Baños of the Instituto de Investigaciones en Materiales—UNAM (Institute of Materials Research—National Autonomous University of Mexico). Optic microscopy was carried out by Diana Magaloni thanks to the support of ETS (L'École de Technologie Supérieure) engineer Renato Pancella of the Federal Polytechnic School of Lausanne. Sweeping electronic microscopy and EDS analysis were conducted in collaboration with Dr. Richard Siegel and microscopist Richard Lee of the Argonne National Laboratory.

12 On vase painting, see Reents-Budet 1994; also Proskouriakoff in Ruppert, Thompson, and Proskouriakoff 1955.

13 These excavations were conducted by the following researchers: César Sáenz (1954), Jorge Acosta (1970), Arnoldo González (1991, 1992, and 1993), and Merle Greene Robertson (1997 and 1998).

14 See Cuevas 2000; Cuevas and Bernal 2002b.

15 The epigrapher Guillermo Bernal has made new decipherments in Palenque inscriptions, in which he proposes the reading of glyphs alluding specifically to these objects. See Cuevas and Bernal 2002a.

16 Marie-Odile Marion 1994.

17 Berlin 1968; Mathews and Schele 1974.

18 Ringle 1996.

19 Berlin 1963.

20 Dates and individuals referred to in the Yaxchilan inscriptions are taken from the study by Peter Mathews (1997). The individual that Mathews calls Lady Fist Fish is here called Lady Xok.

21 Brokmann 2000.

22 Internal report submitted by physical anthropologist María Elena Salas Cuesta, who conducted the study of human bones recovered at Yaxchilan between 1973 and 1985.

23 Thompson 1939.

24 The question of the age of the individual in Tomb 2 has arisen, along with the age of the individual buried in the Temple of Inscriptions at Palenque. In both cases epigraphers assign the deceased the age of 80, whereas the bones reveal a different age.

25 "Palaces" are named after Augustus' luxurious residence on the Palatine Hill in Rome, but may also be identified as examples of a *magna domus*, "great dwelling."

26 This project took place because of a permit Héctor Escobedo and I held from the Instituto de Antropología e Historia de Guatemala (IDAEH). Funding came from including Ken Woolley and Spence Kirk, FAMSI (Lewis Ranieri, Chairman, and Sandy Noble, Director), the Ahau Foundation (Dr. Peter Harrison, President), the National Geographic Society, the Ashton Family Foundation, FARMS, the Heinz Foundation, the Peabody Museum of Harvard University, Fulbright-Hays, the National Science Foundation, and Brigham Young University. Four preliminary reports, edited by Escobedo and Houston, have been submitted to IDAEH; final reports will appear as Papers of the New World Archaeological Foundation.

27 Simon Martin and Nikolai Grube describe this figure (2000), p. 153.

28 Katherine MacDonogh (1999, pp. 11–12) provides evidence that pets, human and animal, helped rulers compensate for lives of emotional impoverishment. Reports on dwarves at court include Houston 1992 and V. Miller 1985, p. 28.

29 The ceramics of Piedras Negras are now under study by René Muñoz of the University of Arizona and Mary Jane Acuña and Griselda Pérez of the Universidad de San Carlos de Guatemala. Their work builds on a doctoral thesis by George R. Holley (1983).

30 Early settlements at Piedras Negras are discussed in Houston et al 2003.

31 Houston, Escobedo, Terry, Webster, Veni, and Emery 2002, p. 10.

32 The Early Classic desire to leave such bedrock visible may have been: (1) practical, in that the resources did not yet exist to enclose all natural features; (2) aesthetic, the beauty of masonry contrasting with rough-hewn surfaces; or (3) religious, in that natural stone was thought to be animate. No such scruples hindered Late Classic builders, who favored a thick, artificial "skin" over as much natural rock as possible. Only the hills towering above the northern, eastern, and southern approaches to the city would have remained prominent.

33 Golden 2002.

34 Schele and Grube, unpublished manuscript; Houston, Escobedo, Child, Golden, and Muñoz 2001, pp. 75–77.

35 Houston 2001, pp. 206–219.

36 Fitzsimmons et al, n.d.

37 David Stuart first pointed out these references to speech; some of the references may be to rulers many years before, at *c.* AD 376, a time remarkably close to the burst of settlement at Piedras Negras, Houston and Martin, in preparation.

38 See Golden 2002, pp. 297–305. Golden also notes the unusual concentrations of ceramics and human and animal bone in this zone.

39 Stuart, unpublished manuscript. The event at 9.0.18.16.7, probably a retroactive fiction, corresponds to building activity under Structure 0-13 during the Early Classic period, a feature confirmed by excavations within the pyramid, Escobedo and Alvarado 1998, p. 8.

40 Stuart, 1998, pp. 389–392.

Select Bibliography

Abbreviations
Dumbarton Oaks: Dumbarton Oaks Research Library & Collection
INAH: Instituto Nacional de Antropología e Historia
PARI: Pre-Columbian Art Research Institute (earlier, Pre-Columbian Art Research Center)
The Maya Vase Book: See full listing under Kerr, Justin, ed. 1989–2000 (with Barbara Kerr, ed. 1994–2000)
Royal Courts of the Ancient Maya: See full listing under Inomata, Takeshi, and Stephen D. Houston, eds. 2001
UCLA: University of California, Los Angeles
UNAM: Universidad Autónoma de Mexico

Adams, Richard E. W., and Robert Aldrich. 1980. "A Reevaluation of the Bonampak Murals: A Preliminary Statement on the Paintings and Texts." In *Third Palenque Round Table, 1978.* Pt. 2. Edited by Merle Greene Robertson, pp. 45–59. Austin and London: University of Texas Press.

Álvarez Aguilar, Luis Fernando, María Guadalupe Landa Landa, and José Luis Romero Rivera. 1990. *Los ladrillos de Comalcalco.* Villahermosa: Gobierno del Estado de Tabasco.

Andrews, E., V. Wyllys, and Barbara Fash. 1992. "Continuity and Change in a Royal Maya Residential Complex at Copan." *Ancient Mesoamerica* 3, pp. 63–88.

Ardren, Traci. 1996. "Chocholá Ceramic Style of Northern Yucatan: An Iconographic and Archaeological Study." In *Eighth Palenque Round Table, 1993.* Edited by Martha J. Macri and Jan McHargue, pp. 237–245. San Francisco: PARI, 1996.

——. ed. 2002. *Ancient Maya Women.* Walnut Creek, Ca.: Altamira Press.

Arellano Hernández, Alfonso. 2002. "Textos y contextos: Epigrafía y pintura mural." In *La pintura mural prehispánica en México.* Vol. 2. Series editor, Beatriz de la Fuente, pp. 331–357. Mexico City: Instituto de Investigaciones Estéticas, UNAM.

Arnold, Bruce. 1975. "Attapulgite and Maya Blue: An Ancient Mine Comes to Light." *Archaeology* 28, no. 1, pp. 23–29.

Ashmore, Wendy. 1981. "Some Issues of Method and Theory in Lowland Maya Settlement Patterns." In *Lowland Maya Settlement Patterns.* Edited by Wendy Ashmore, pp. 27–69. Albuquerque: University of New Mexico Press.

——. 1989. "Construction and Cosmology: Politics and Ideology in Lowland Maya Settlement Patterns."

In *Word and Image in Maya Culture: Explorations in Language, Writing, and Representation.* Edited by William Hanks and Don Rice, pp. 272–286. Salt Lake City: University of Utah Press.

——. 1991. "Site Planning Principles and Concepts of Directionality among the Ancient Maya." *Latin American Antiquity* 2, pp. 199–226.

Ayala Falcón, Maricela. 1995. "History of Tonina through Its Inscriptions." Ph.D. dissertation, University of Texas at Austin.

Barnhart, Edwin L. 2001. "The Palenque Mapping Project: Settlement and Urbanism at an Ancient Maya City." Ph.D. dissertation. University of Texas at Austin.

Bassie-Sweet, Karen. 1991. *From the Mouth of the Dark Cave.* Norman: University of Oklahoma Press.

——. 1999. "Corn Deities and the Complementary Male/Female Principle." In *La organización social entre los mayas: Memoria de la Tercera mesa redonda de Palenque,* n.s. Vol. 1. Edited by Vera Tiesler Blos, Rafael Cobos, and Merle Greene Robertson, pp. 105–125. Mexico City and Mérida: INAH and Universidad Autónoma de Yucatán.

——. 2002. "Corn Deities." In *Ancient Maya Gender Identity and Relations.* Edited by Lowell S. Gustafson and Amelia M. Trevelyan, pp. 169–200. Westport, Conn.: Bergin and Garvey.

Baudez, Claude F., and Peter Mathews. 1978. "Capture and Sacrifice at Palenque." In *Tercera mesa redonda de Palenque, Palenque Round Table (3rd session, 1978).* Edited by Merle Greene Robertson and Donnan C. Jeffers, pp. 31–40. Pebble Beach, Ca.: PARI.

Becker, Marshall J. 1991. "Plaza Plans at Tikal, Guatemala, and at other Lowland Maya Sites: Evidence for Patterns of Culture Change." *Cuadernos de arquitectura mesoamericana* 14, pp. 11–26.

Becquelin, Pierre, Claude F. Baudez, and Marie-Charlotte Arnauld. 1982–1984. *Toniná, une cité maya du Chiapas (Mexique). Études mésoaméricaines,* 3 vols. Mexico: Centre d'Études Mexicaines et Centraméricaines.

Bell, Ellen E. 2002. "Engendering a Dynasty: A Royal Woman in the Margarita Tomb, Copán." In *Ancient Maya Women.* Edited by Traci Ardren, pp. 89–104. Walnut Creek, Ca.: Altamira Press.

Benson, Elizabeth P., ed. 1973. *Mesoamerican Writing Systems: A Conference at Dumbarton Oaks, October 30th and 31st, 1971.* Washington, D.C.: Dumbarton Oaks.

——. 1976. "Ritual Cloth and Palenque Kings." *The Art, Iconography and Dynastic History of Palenque.* Pt. 3. In *Proceedings of the Segunda Mesa Redonda de Palenque.* Edited by Merle Greene Robertson, pp. 45–58. Pebble Beach, Ca.: PARI.

Berjonneau, Gérald, and Jean-Louis Sonnery, eds. 1985. *Rediscovered Masterpieces of Mesoamerica: Mexico-Guatemala-Honduras.* Boulogne: Editions Arts.

Berlin, Heinrich. 1963. "The Palenque Triad." *Journal de la Société des américanistes* [n.s.], no. 52, pp. 91–99.

——. 1968. "The Tablet of the 96 Glyphs at Palenque, Chiapas, Mexico." *Archaeological Studies in Middle America.* New Orleans: Middle American Research Institute, Publication 26.

Bernal Romero, Guillermo. 2002. "Análisis epigráfico del Tablero de K'an Tok, Palenque, Chiapas." In *La organización social entre los mayas: Memoria de la Tercera mesa redonda de Palenque.* Vol. 1. Edited by Vera Tiesler Blos, Rafael Cobos and Merle Greene Robertson, pp. 401–423. Mexico City and Mérida: INAH and Universidad Autónoma de Yucatán.

Berrin, Kathleen. 1986. *Feathered Serpents and Flowering Trees: Reconstructing the Murals of Teotihuacan.* The Fine Arts Museums of San Francisco.

——. 1999. "Fine Arts Museums of San Francisco Acquire Maya Stela: Collaboration with Guatemala and Mexico Sets New Standards for Museums." *PARI Newsletter* 28, pp. 6–8, San Francisco.

Boynton, Robert. 1966. *Chemistry and Technology of Lime and Limestone.* New York: John Wiley and Sons.

Broad, William. 2002. "Mother Lode of Jade Comes to Light in Guatemala." *The New York Times,* 23 May 2002.

Brokmann, Carlos. 2000. *Tipología y análisis de la obsidiana de Yaxchilán, Chiapas.* Mexico City: INAH.

Buikstra, Jane E., T. Douglas Price, Lori E. Wright, and James A. Burton. 2003. "Tombs from the Copan Acropolis: A Life-History Approach." In *Understanding Early Classic Copan.* Edited by Ellen E. Bell, Marcello A. Canuto, and Robert J. Sharer, pp. 191–212. Philadelphia: University of Pennsylvania Museum of Archaeology and Anthropology.

Bunzel, Ruth. 1952. *Chichicastenango: A Guatemalan Village.* Publications of the American

Ethnological Society, no. 22. Locust Valley, N.Y.: J.J. Augustin.

Calvin, Inga. 1997. "Where the Wayob Live: A Further Example of Classic Maya Supernaturals." In *The Maya Vase Book*. Vol. 5, pp. 868–883.

Carrasco, David. 1990. *Religions of Mesoamerica*. Religious Traditions of the World, no. 10. New York: Harper & Row.

Carrasco, David, Lindsay Jones, and Scott Sessions, eds. 2000. *Mesoamerica's Classic Heritage: From Teotihuacan to the Aztecs*. Boulder: University of Colorado Press.

Carrasco Vargas, Ramón. 2000. "El cuchcabal de la cabeza de serpiente." *Arqueología mexicana* 7, no. 42, pp. 12–21.

Centro Cultural de la Villa de Madrid. 2002. *El país del quetzal: Guatemala, maya e hispana*. Madrid: Sociedad Estatal para la Acción Cultural Exterior.

Child, Mark. 1999. "Classic Maya Warfare and Its Sociopolitical Implications." Paper presented at the Tercera Mesa Redonda de Palenque, Segunda época, June 1999.

Christenson, Allen J. 2001. *Art and Society in a Highland Maya Community: The Altarpiece of Santiago Atitlán*. Austin: University of Texas Press.

Christie, Jessica Joyce, ed. 2003. *Maya Palaces and Elite Residences: An Interdisciplinary Approach*. Austin: University of Texas Press.

Closs, Michael P. 1985. "The Dynastic History of Naranjo: The Middle Period." In *Fifth Palenque Round Table, 1983*. Vol. 7. Edited by Merle Greene Robertson and Virginia M. Fields, pp. 65–78. San Francisco: PARI.

Coe, Michael D. 1973. *The Maya Scribe and His World*. New York: Grolier Club.

—. 1975. *Maya Vases at Dumbarton Oaks*. Washington, D.C.: Dumbarton Oaks.

—. 1977. "Supernatural Patrons of Maya Scribes and Artists." In *Social Process in Maya Prehistory: Studies in Honor of Sir Eric Thompson*. Edited by Norman Hammond, pp. 327–347. New York: Academic Press.

—. 1978. *Lords of the Underworld: Masterpieces of Classic Maya Ceramics*. Princeton: The Art Museum, Princeton University.

—. 1989. "The Hero Twins: Myth and Image." In *The Maya Vase Book*. Vol. 2, pp. 161–184.

—. 1999a. *Breaking the Maya Code*. Rev. ed. London and New York: Thames & Hudson.

—. 1999b. *The Maya*. 6th ed. London and New York: Thames & Hudson, .

Coe, Michael D., and Elizabeth P. Benson. 1966. *Three Maya Relief Panels at Dumbarton Oaks*. Studies in Pre-Columbian Art and Archaeology, no. 2. Washington, D.C.: Dumbarton Oaks.

Coe, Michael D., and Justin Kerr. 1998. *The Art of the Maya Scribe*. New York: Harry N. Abrams.

Coe, Michael D., and Mark Van Stone. 2001. *Reading the Maya Glyphs*. London and New York: Thames & Hudson.

Coe, Sophie. *America's First Cuisine*. 1994. Austin: University of Texas Press.

Coe, Sophie, and Michael D. Coe. 1996. *The True History of Chocolate*. London and New York: Thames & Hudson.

Coggins, Clemency Chase. 1975. "Painting and Drawing Styles at Tikal: An Historical and Iconographic Reconstruction." Ph.D. dissertation, Harvard University.

Coggins, Clemency Chase, and Orrin Shane. 1984. *Cenote of Sacrifice; Maya Treasures from the Sacred Well at Chichén Itzá*. Austin: University of Texas Press.

Cuevas García, Martha. 2000. "Los incensarios del Grupo de las Cruces, Palenque." *Arqueología mexicana* 45, pp. 54–61.

Cuevas García, Martha, and Guillermo Bernal. 2002a. "*P'uluut K'uh*, 'Dios-Incensario': Aspectos arqueológicos y epigráficos de los incensarios palencanos." In *Memoria de la Tercera mesa redonda de Palenque*, pp. 376–400. Mexico City: INAH.

—. and —. 2002b. "La función ritual de los incensarios compuestos del Grupo de las Cruces de Palenque." *Estudios de cultura maya* 22. Mexico City: Centro de Estudios Mayas, UNAM.

Cuevas García, Martha, and Arnoldo González Cruz. 2001. *Arqueología mexicana*. (Especial) *Los Tesoros de Palenque*.

Demarest, Arthur A. 1993. "The Violent Saga of a Maya Kingdom." *National Geographic Magazine*, February 1993, pp. 95–111.

Diccionario maya Cordemex. 1980. Edited by Alfredo Barrera Vásquez. Mérida, Yucatán: Cordemex.

Diccionario maya-español Calepino de Motul. 1995. Edited by Ramón Arzápalo Marín. Mexico: UNAM.

Diehl, Richard A., and Janet C. Berlo, eds. 1989. *Mesoamerica after the Decline of Teotihuacán, AD 700–900*. Washington D.C.: Dumbarton Oaks.

Easby, Elizabeth Kennedy, and John F. Scott. 1970. *Before Cortés: Sculpture of Middle America: A Centennial Exhibition at the Metropolitan Museum of Art from September 30, 1970 through January 3, 1971*. New York: Metropolitan Museum of Art; distributed by New York Graphic Society.

Escobedo, Héctor, and Carlos Alvarado. 1998. "PN 1: Excavaciones en la estructura O-13." In *Proyecto arqueológico Piedras Negras, informe preliminar no. 2: Segunda temporada, 1998*. Edited by Héctor L. Escobedo and Stephen D. Houston. Guatemala City.

Evans, Susan Toby. 2004. *Ancient Mexico and Central America: Archaeology and Culture History*. London and New York: Thames & Hudson.

Evans, Susan Toby, and Joanne Pillsbury, eds. 2004. *Palaces of the Ancient New World*. Washington, D.C.: Dumbarton Oaks.

Fash, William L. 2001. *Scribes Warriors and Kings: The City of Copán and the Ancient Maya*. Rev. ed. New York and London: Thames & Hudson.

Fields, Virginia M. 1989. "The Origins of Divine Kingship among the Lowland Classic Maya." Ph.D. dissertation, University of Texas at Austin.

—. ed. 1985. *Fifth Palenque Round Table, 1983*. San Francisco: PARI.

Fitzsimmons, James, Andrew Scherer, Stephen D. Houston, and Héctor Escobedo. "Guardian of the Acropolis: The Sacred Space of a Royal Burial at Piedras Negras, Guatemala." Paper under review by *Latin American Antiquity*.

Fragmentos del pasado: Murales prehispánicos. 1998. México: Consejo Nacional para la Cultura y las Artes; Antiguo Colegio de San Ildefonso; Instituto de Investigaciones Estéticas, UNAM.

Freidel, David, Linda Schele, and Joy Parker. 1993. *Maya Cosmos: Three Thousand Years on the Shaman's Path*. New York: William Morrow.

Fuente, Beatriz de la. 1965. *La escultura de Palenque*. Mexico City: UNAM.

—. 1985. *Peldaños en la conciencia: Rostros en la plástica prehispánica*. Mexico City: UNAM (Art collection, 38).

—. series ed. 1996–present. *La pintura mural prehispánica en México*. Mexico: Instituto de Investigaciones Estéticas, UNAM.

Fuente, Beatriz de la, and Alfonso Arellano. 2001. *El hombre maya en la plástica antigua*. Mexico City: UNAM.

Fuerst, Ann H., ed. 1994. *Maya Art Activity Book*. San Diego: San Diego Museum of Man: San Diego Unified School District.

Furst, Peter. n.d. *Art of Ancient America, 1500 BC through 1500 AD: A Guide to the Exhibition*. Santa Fe, N.M.: Museum of New Mexico.

Gallenkamp, Charles, and Regina Elise Johnson, eds. 1985. *Maya: Treasures of an Ancient Civilization*. New York: Harry N. Abrams, in association with the Albuquerque Museum.

García Moll, Roberto. 1994. "Los mayas, arte y memoria." In *México en el mundo de las colecciones de arte*. Vol. 2. Edited by Beatriz de la Fuente, pp. 3–81. Mexico: D.R. Primera.

Golden, Charles W. 2002. "Bridging the Gap between Archaeological and Indigenous Chronologies: An Investigation of the Early Classic/Late Classic Divide at Piedras Negras, Guatemala." Ph.D. dissertation, University of Pennsylvania.

Gómez Aguirre. 1993. "Cacerolita del mar" (*Limulus polyphemus*) en la Península de Yucatán." In *Biodiversidad marina y costera de México*, pp. 650–659. Mexico: Comité Nacional de Biodiversidad y CIQRO.

Gómez-Pompa, Arturo, et al. 1990. "Sacred Cacao Groves of the Maya." *Latin American Antiquity* 1, no. 3, pp. 247–257

González Cruz, Arnoldo, and Guillermo Bernal Romero. 2000. "Grupo XVI de Palenque: Conjuncto arquitectónico de la nobleza provincial." *Arqueología mexicana* 8, no. 45, pp. 20–27.

——. and ——. 2003. *The Throne of Akhal Mo' Nahb' III: A Unique Finding at Palenque, Chiapas.* Mexico City: INAH/Nestlé.

Grube, Nikolai. 1990. "The Primary Standard Sequence on Chocholá Style Ceramics." In *The Maya Vase Book.* Vol. 2, pp. 320–330.

——. 1992. "Classic Maya Dance: Evidence from Hieroglyphs and Iconography." *Ancient Mesoamerica* 3, pp. 201–218.

——. 1996. "Palenque in the Maya World." In *Eighth Palenque Round Table, 1993.* Vol. 10. Edited by Martha Macri and Merle Greene Robertson, pp. 1–13. San Francisco: PARI.

——. ed. 2001. *Maya: Divine Kings of the Rainforest.* Cologne: Könemann Verlagsgesellschaft.

Grube, Nikolai, and Werner Nahm. 1994. "A Census of Xibalba: A Complete Inventory of *way* Characters on Maya Ceramics." In *The Maya Vase Book.* Vol. 4, pp. 686–715.

Gustafson, Lowell S., and Amelia M. Trevelyan. 2002. *Ancient Maya Gender Identity and Relations.* Westport, Conn.: Bergin and Garvey.

Hales, Donald. Unpublished manuscript in possession of the authors.

Hammond, Norman. 1982. *Ancient Maya Civilization.* New Brunswick, N.J.: Rutgers University Press.

Hanau, Kléber, Masschelein-Kleiner, Thissen and Tricot-Marckx. 1966. "Les peintures murales mayas de Bonampak: Analyse des matériaux." *Institute royal de patrimoine artistique, Bulletin* 9, pp. 114–120.

Harrison, Peter d'Arcy. 1970. "The Central Acropolis, Tikal, Guatemala: A Preliminary Study of the Functions of Its Structural Components during the Late Classic Period." Ph.D. dissertation, University of Pennsylvania.

——. 1999. *Lords of Tikal: Rulers of an Ancient Maya City.* London and New York: Thames & Hudson.

Hassig, Ross. 1992. *War and Society in Ancient Mesoamerica.* Berkeley: University of California Press.

Hendon, Julia A. 1997. "Women's Work, Women's Space, and Women's Status among the Classic Period Maya Elite of the Copán Valley, Honduras." In *Women in Prehistory: North America and Mesoamerica.* Edited by Cheryl Claassen and Rosemary A. Joyce, pp. 41–43. Philadelphia: University of Pennsylvania Press.

Herring, Adam. 1998. "Sculptural Representation and Self-reference in a Carved Maya Panel from the Region of Tabasco, Mexico." *Res* 33, pp. 102–114.

Hohmann, Hasso. 1998. *A Maya Palace in Mexico: Structure IV at Becán, Campeche.* Graz: Akademische Druck- u. Verlagsanstalt.

Hohmann, Hasso, and Annegrete Vogrin. 1982. *Die Architektur von Copan (Honduras): Vermessung, Plandarstellung, Untersuchung der baulichen Elemente und des räumlichen Konzepts.* Graz, Austria: Akademische Druck- u. Verlagsanstalt.

Holley, George R. 1983. "Ceramic Change at Piedras Negras, Guatemala." Ph.D. dissertation, University of Southern Illinois.

Houston, Stephen D. 1992. "A Name Glyph for Classic Maya Dwarfs." In *The Maya Vase Book.* Vol. 3, pp. 526–531.

——. 1996 "Symbolic Sweatbaths of the Maya: Architectural Meaning in the Cross Group at Palenque, Mexico." *Latin American Antiquity* 7, no. 2, pp. 132–151.

——. 2001. "Decorous Bodies and Disordered Passions: Representations of Emotion among the Classic Maya." *World Archaeology* 33, no. 2, pp. 206–219.

——. ed. 1998. *Function and Meaning in Classic Maya Architecture: A Symposium at Dumbarton Oaks.* Washington, D.C.: Dumbarton Oaks.

Houston, Stephen D., Héctor Escobedo, Richard Terry, David Webster, George Veni, and Kitty F. Emery. 2002. "Among the River Kings: Archaeological Research at Piedras Negras, Guatemala, 1999." *Mexicon* 22, pp. 97–110.

Houston, Stephen D., Héctor Escobedo, Mark Child, Charles Golden, and René Muñoz. 2001. "Crónica de una muerte anunciada: Los años finales de Piedras Negras." In *Reconstruyendo la ciudad maya: El urbanismo en las sociedades antiguas.* Edited by A. Ciudad Ruiz, Maria J. Iglesias, Ponce de León, and Maria del Carmen Martínez Martínez, pp. 75–77. Madrid: Sociedad Española de Estudios Mayas.

Houston, Stephen D., Héctor Escobedo, Mark Child, Charles Golden, and René Muñoz. 2003. "The Moral Community: Maya Settlement Transformation at Piedras Negras, Guatemala." In *Social Construction of Cities.* Edited by Monica Smith, pp. 212–53. Washington, D.C: Smithsonian Institution Press.

Houston, Stephen D., and Simon Martin. In preparation. "The History of Piedras Negras." In *In the Land of the Turtle Lords: Urban Archaeology at the Classic Maya City of Piedras Negras, Guatemala.* Edited by Stephen D. Houston and Héctor Escobedo.

Houston, Stephen D., and David Stuart. 1989. *The Way Glyph: Evidence for Co-essences among the Classic Maya.* Research Reports on Ancient Maya Writing, no. 30. Washington, D.C.: Center for Maya Research.

——. and ——. 1996. "Of Gods, Glyphs, and Kings: Divinity and Rulership among the Classic Maya." *Antiquity* 70, no. 268, pp. 289–312.

——. and ——. 1997. "The Ancient Maya Self: Personhood and Portraiture in the Classic Period." *Res* 33, pp. 73–101.

——. and ——. 2001. "Peopling the Classic Maya Court." In *Royal Courts of the Ancient Maya.* Vol. 1, pp. 54–83.

Houston, Stephen D., and Karl A. Taube. 2000. "An Archaeology of the Senses: Perception and Cultural Expression in Ancient Mesoamerica." *Cambridge Archaeological Journal* 10, no. 2, pp. 261–294.

Inomata, Takeshi. 1995. "Archaeological Investigations at the Fortified Center of Aguateca, El Peten, Guatemala: Implications for the Study of the Classic Maya Collapse." Ph.D. dissertation, Vanderbilt University.

——. 1997. "Last Day of a Fortified Classic Maya Center: Archaeological Investigations at Aguateca, Guatemala." *Ancient Mesoamerica* 8, no. 2, pp. 337–351.

——. 2003. "Aguateca: New Revelations of the Maya Elite." *National Geographic Magazine,* May 2003, pp. 110–119.

Inomata, Takeshi, et al. 1998. "Residencias de la familia real y de la elite en Aguateca, Guatemala." *Mayab* 11, pp. 23–39.

——. 2002. "Domestic and Political Lives of Classic Maya Elites: The Excavation of Rapidly Abandoned Structures at Aguateca, Guatemala." *Latin American Antiquity* 3, no. 3, pp. 305–330.

Inomata, Takeshi, and Stephen D. Houston, eds. 2001–2002. *Royal Courts of the Ancient Maya.* 2 vols. Boulder: Westview Press.

Inomata, Takeshi, and Payson Sheets. 2000. "Mesoamerican Households Viewed from Rapidly Abandoned Sites: An Introduction." *Mayab* 13, pp. 5–10.

Joyce, Rosemary. 2000. *Gender and Power in Prehispanic Mesoamerica.* Austin: University of Texas Press.

Just, Bryan. 1994. "Captives at Tonina." Manuscript on file, Department of the History of Art, Yale University.

Kerr, Justin, ed. 1989–2000 (with Barbara Kerr, ed. 1994–2000). *Maya Vase Book,* 6 vols. New York: Kerr Associates. Kerr numbers in the text refer to the Maya Vase database, available at http://famsi.famsi.org:9500/dataSpark/maya

Kowalski, Jeff K. 1989. *Mythological Identity of the Figure on the La Esperanza (Chinkultic) Ball Court Marker.* Research Reports on Ancient Maya Writing, no. 27. Washington, D.C.: Center for Maya Research.

Kubler, George, ed. 1986. *Pre-Columbian Art of Mexico and Central America.* New Haven, Conn.: Yale University Art Gallery.

——. 1993. *Art and Architecture of Ancient America: the Mexican, Maya, and Andean peoples.* 3rd ed. New York: Penguin Books.

Laughlin, Robert M., and Carol Karasik, eds. 1988. *People of the Bat: Mayan Tales and Dreams from Zinacantán.* Washington, D.C.: Smithsonian Institution Press.

Leon-Portilla, Miguel. 1966. *Filosofía náhuatl.* Mexico City: UNAM.

Le Fort, Geneviève, and Robert F. Wald. 1995. "Large Numbers on Naranjo Stela 32." *Mexicon* 17, no. 6, pp. 112–114.

Liman, Florence F., and Marshall Durbin. 1975. "Some New Glyphs on an Unusual Maya Stela." *American Antiquity* 40, no. 3, pp. 314–320.

Littmann, Edwin R. 1960. "Ancient Mesoamerican Mortars, Plasters, and Stuccos: The Use of Bark Extracts in Lime Plasters." *American Antiquity* 25, no. 4, pp. 593–596.

Looper, Matthew, and Linda Schele. 1991. Unpublished manuscript. "A War at Palenque during the Reign of Ah-K'an." Texas Notes on Pre-Columbian Art, Writing, and Culture 25. Department of Art, Austin, Texas.

López Bravo, Roberto. Unpublished manuscript. "El Grupo B, Palenque, Chiapas. Una unidad habitacional maya del clásico tardío."

——. "Exploraciones arqueológicos en el Grupo C de Palenque." Cuarto Foro de Arqueología de Chiapas.

——. 2000 "La veneración de los ancestros en Palenque." *Arqueología mexicana* 8, no. 45, pp. 38–43.

McAnany, Patricia A. 1995. *Living with the Ancestors: Kinship and Kingship in Ancient Maya Society.* Austin: University of Texas Press.

McAnany, Patricia A., and Shannon Plank. 2001. "Perspectives on Actors, Gender Roles, and Architecture at Classic Maya Courts and Households." In *Royal Courts of the Ancient Maya.* Vol. 1, pp. 84–129.

McDermott, Betty N., ed. 1980. *Handbook of the Collection.* New Orleans: New Orleans Museum of Art.

MacDonogh, Katherine. 1999. *Reigning Cats and Dogs: A History of Pets at Court since the Renaissance.* London: Fourth Estate.

Magaloni, Diana. 1994. *Metología de análisis de la técnica pictórica mural prehispánica: El Templo Rojo de Cacaxtla.* Mexico: INAH, Colección Científica.

——. 1998. "El arte en el hacer: Técnica pictórica y color en las pinturas murales de Bonampak." In *La pintura mural prehispánica en México: Bonampak.* Series editor, Beatriz de la Fuente, pp. 49–80. Mexico: Instituto de Investigaciones Estéticas, UNAM.

Maldonado C., Rubén, Alexander Voss, and Angel Góngora. 2002. "Kalom Uk'uw, señor de Dzibilchaltun." In *La organización social entre los mayas, Memoria de la tercera mesa redonda de Palenque.* Vol. 1. Edited by Vera Tiesler Blos, Rafael Cobos and Merle Greene Robertson, pp. 79–100. Mexico City and Mérida: INAH and Universidad Autónoma de Yucatán.

Maler, Teobert. 1901–1903. *Researches in the Central Portion of the UsumatsintlaValley: Report of Explorations for the Museum, 1898–1900.* Memoirs of the Peabody Museum of Archaeology and Ethnology, Harvard University, vol. 2. Cambridge, Mass.: Peabody Museum of Archaeology and Ethnology.

Manzanilla, Linda, and Luis Barba. 1990. "Study of Activities in Classic Households: Two Case Studies from Cobá and Teotihuacán." *Ancient Mesoamerica* 1, no. 1, pp. 41–49.

Marion, Marie-Odile. 1994. *Fiestas de los pueblos indígenas. Identidad y ritualidad entre los mayas.* Mexico: Instituto Nacional Indigenista, Secretaría de Desarrollo Social.

Martin, Simon. n.d. "Investigación epigráfica de campo: 1995–1998." In: *Proyecto arqueológico de la biosfera de Calakmul: Temporada 1995–98,* by Ramón Carrasco V. et al., Centro Regional de Yucatán, unpublished report to INAH.

——. 2000. "Nuevos datos epigráficos sobre la guerra maya del clásico." In *La Guerra entre los antiguos mayas: Memorias de la Primera mesa redonda de Palenque.* Edited by Silvia Trejo, pp. 105–124. Mexico City: INAH.

——. 2001a. "Court and Realm: Architectural Signatures in the Classic Maya Southern Lowlands." In *Royal Courts of the Ancient Maya.* Vol. 1, pp. 168–194.

——. 2001b. "The War in the West: New Perspectives on Tonina and Palenque." Paper presented at the Nineteenth Maya Weekend at the University of Pennsylvania Museum of Archaeology and Anthropology: "Four Corners of the Maya World," March 23–25.

——. 2003. "Moral-Reforma y la contienda por el oriente de Tabasco." *Arqueología mexicana* 9, no. 61, pp. 44–47.

Martin, Simon, and Nikolai Grube. 1995. "Maya Superstates." *Archaeology* 48, no. 6, pp. 41–46.

——. and ——. 2000. *Chronicle of the Maya Kings and Queens: Deciphering the Dynasties of the Ancient Maya.* London and New York: Thames & Hudson.

——. and ——. 2002. *Crónica de los reyes y reinas mayas: La primera historia de las dinastías mayas.* Editorial Planeta Mexicana, Mexico City.

Martin, Simon, Mark Zender, and Nikolai Grube. 2002. *Palenque and Its Neighbors: Notebook for the XXVI Maya Hieroglyphic Forum at Texas.* Austin: Maya Workshop Foundation.

Martínez, Maximino. 1987. *Catálogo de nombres vulgares y científicos de plantas mexicanas.* Mexico: Fondo de Cultura Económica.

Mathews, Peter. 1980. "Notes on the Dynastic Sequence of Bonampak, Part I." In *Third Palenque Round Table, 1978.* edited by Merle Greene Robertson, pp. 60–73. Austin: University of Texas Press.

——. 1997. *La escultura de Yaxchilan.* Mexico: INAH Colleccion Cientifica No. 368.

——. 2001. "Dates of Tonina and a Dark Horse in Its History." *PARI Journal* 2, no. 1, p. 16.

Mathews, Peter, and Robertson, Merle G. 1985.

"Notes on the Olvidado, Palenque, Chiapas, Mexico." In *Fifth Palenque Round Table, 1983.* Edited by Virginia M. Fields, pp. 7–17. San Francisco: PARI.

Mathews, Peter, and Linda Schele. 1974. "The Lords of Palenque: The Glyphic Evidence." In *Primera mesa redonda de Palenque.* Pt. 1. Edited by Merle Greene Robertson, pp. 63–76. Pebble Beach, Ca.: Robert Louis Stevenson School.

Matos Moctezuma, Eduardo, and Felipe Solís Olguín. 2002. *Aztecs.* London: Royal Academy of Arts.

Mayer, Karl Herbert. 1980. *Maya Monuments: Sculptures of Unknown Provenance in the United States.* Ramona, Ca.: Acoma.

Mesa redonda de Palenque (Palenque Round Table Series). 1973–present. Various publishers.

Miller, Mary Ellen. 1975. *Jaina Figurines.* Princeton: The Art Museum.

——. 1986. *The Murals of Bonampak.* Princeton: Princeton University Press.

——. 1995. "Maya Masterpiece Revealed at Bonampak." *National Geographic* 187, no. 2, pp. 50–69.

——. 1999. *Maya Art and Architecture.* London and New York: Thames & Hudson.

——. 2000. "Guerra y escultura maya: un argumento en favor del tributo artístico." In *La guerra entre los antiguos mayas: Memoria de la Primera mesa redonda de Palenque.* Edited by Silvia Trejo, pp. 177–187. Mexico: INAH.

——. 2001. *The Art of Mesoamerica,* 3rd edition. London and New York: Thames & Hudson.

Miller, Mary Ellen, and Karl Taube. 1993. *The Gods and Symbols of Ancient Mexico and the Maya: An Illustrated Dictionary.* London and New York: Thames & Hudson.

Miller, Mary Ellen, and Stephen D. Houston. 1987. "The Classic Maya Ballgame and Its Architectural Setting." *Res* 14, pp. 46–65.

Miller, Virginia E. 1985. "The Dwarf Motif in Classic Maya Art." In *Fourth Palenque Round Table, 1980.* Edited by Elizabeth P. Benson, pp. 141–154. San Francisco: PARI.

Montejo, Victor. 1999. *Voices from Exile: Violence and Survival in Modern Maya History.* Norman: University of Oklahoma Press.

Morales, Alfonso. 1998. "INAH-PARI. Group of the Cross Project Season Report." In *PARI Newsletter* 26, pp. 1–3.

Murra, John. 1962. "Cloth and Its Function in the Inca State." *American Anthropologist* 64, no. 4, pp. 710–772.

Navarijo Ornelas, Lourdes. 1999. "Plumas…tocados: Una vieja historia de identidades perdidas." In *La pintura mural prehispánica en Mexico: Area maya, Bonampak,* 11, no. 2, Series editor, Beatriz de la Fuente, pp. 177–191. Mexico City: Instituto de Investigaciones Estéticas, UNAM.

Nuttall, Zelia. 1903. *The Book of the Life of the Ancient Mexicans.* Berkeley: University of California Press.

Orejel, Jorge L. 1990. "The 'Axe-Comb' Glyph (T333) as *ch'ak*." *Research Reports on Ancient Maya Writing* 32. Center for Maya Research, Washington, D.C.

Pagden, Anthony R., trans. and ed. 2001. *Hernán Cortés: Letters from Mexico*. New Haven and London: Yale University Press.

Pasztory, Esther. 1997. *Teotihuacan: An Experiment in Living*. Norman: University of Oklahoma Press.

Piña Chán, Román. 1968. *Jaina, la casa en el agua*. Mexico: INAH.

Pohl, John M.D. 1994. "Weaving and Gift Exchange in the Mixtec Codices." In *Cloth and Curing, Continuity and Exchange in Oaxaca*. Edited by Grace Johnson and Douglas Sharon. San Diego: San Diego Museum of Man. San Diego Museum Papers No. 32.

Porter, James B. 1994. "The Palace Intaglios: A Composite Stairway Throne at Palenque." In *Seventh Palenque Round Table, 1989*. Vol. 9. Edited by Merle Greene Robertson and Virginia M. Fields, pp. 11–18. San Francisco: PARI.

Proskouriakoff, Tatiana. 1950. *A Study of Classic Maya Sculpture*. Washington, D.C.: Carnegie Institution of Washington, Publication no. 593.

——. 1961. "Portraits of Women in Maya Art." In *Essays in Pre-Columbian Art and Archaeology*, pp. 81–90. Cambridge, Mass.: Harvard University Press.

——. 1974. *Jades from the Cenote of Sacrifice, Chichen Itza, Yucatan*. Harvard University: Peabody Museum of Archaeology and Ethnology.

Rands, Robert L. 1987. "Ceramic Patterns and Traditions in the Palenque Area." In *Maya Ceramics: Papers from the 1985 Maya Ceramic Conference*. Edited by Prudence M. Rice and Robert J. Sharer, pp. 203–239. *International Series, 345*. British Archaeological Reports, Oxford, England.

Reents-Budet, Dorie J. 1994. *Painting the Maya Universe: Royal Ceramics of the Classic Period*. Durham, N.C.: Duke University Press.

——. 2000. "Feasting among the Classic Maya: Evidence from the Pictorial Ceramics." In *The Maya Vase Book*. Vol. 6, pp. 1022–1037.

——. 2001. "Classic Maya Concepts of the Royal Court: An Analysis of Renderings on Pictorial Ceramics." In *Royal Courts of the Ancient Maya*. Vol. 1, pp. 168–194.

Restall, Matthew. 2001. "The People of the Patio: Ethnohistorical Evidence of Yucatec Maya Royal Courts." In *Royal Courts of the Ancient Maya*. Vol. 2, pp. 335–390.

Ringle, William M. 1996. "Birds of a Feather: The Fallen Stucco Inscription of Temple XVIII, Palenque, Chiapas." In *Eighth Palenque Round Table, 1993*. Edited by Martha J. Macri and Jan McHargue, pp. 45–61. San Francisco: PARI.

Robertson, Merle Greene. 1983–1991. *The Sculpture of Palenque*, 4 vols. Princeton: Princeton University Press.

——. 1990. "The Celestial God of Number Thirteen." *Triptych*, September/ October, pp. 26–31.

Ruppert, Karl, and John H. Denison, Jr. 1943. *Archaeological Reconnaissance in Campeche, Quintana Roo, and Peten*. Washington, D.C.: Carnegie Institution of Washington.

Ruppert, Karl, J. Eric S. Thompson, and Tatiana Proskouriakoff. 1955. *Bonampak, Chiapas, Mexico*. Washington, D.C.: Carnegie Institution of Washington, Publication no. 505.

Ruz Lhuillier, Alberto. 1952. "Exploraciones en Palenque: 1950." *Anales del Instituto nacional de antropología e historia* 5, pp. 25–45.

——. 1954. "Exploraciones en Palenque: 1952." *Anales del Instituto nacional de antropología e historia* 6, pp. 79–110.

——. 1973. *El templo de las inscripciones, Palenque*. Mexico City: INAH.

Sabloff, Jeremy A., and John S. Henderson, eds. 1993. *Lowland Maya Civilization in the Eighth Century AD: A Symposium at Dumbarton Oaks, 7th and 8th October 1989*. Washington, D.C.: Dumbarton Oaks.

Sahagún, Bernardino de. 1950–1982. *Florentine Codex, General History of the Things of New Spain*. Translated by Charles E. Dibble and Arthur J.O. Anderson. Santa Fe: The School of American Research.

Saul, Julie, and Frank Saul. 2002. "Life and Death: As Recorded in Their Skeletons." Paper read at the Seventh European Maya Conference, London, November.

Scarborough, Vernon L., and David R. Wilcox, eds. 1991. *The Mesoamerican Ballgame*. Tucson: University of Arizona.

Schaffer, Anne-Louise. 1987. "Reassembling a Lost Maya Masterpiece." *Bulletin of the Museum of Fine Arts, Houston* 10, no. 2, pp. 10–13.

Schele, Linda. 1984. "Human Sacrifice among the Classic Maya." In *Ritual Human Sacrifice in Mesoamerica*. Edited by Elizabeth Boone, pp. 7–48. Washington D.C.: Dumbarton Oaks.

——. 1994. "Some Thoughts on the Inscriptions of House C." In *Seventh Palenque Round Table, 1989*, Vol. 9. Edited by Merle G. Robertson and Virginia M. Fields, pp. 1–10. San Francisco: PARI.

——. 1997. *Hidden Faces of the Maya*. Poway, Ca.: Alti Publishing.

Schele, Linda, and David Freidel. 1990. *A Forest of Kings: The Untold Story of the Ancient Maya*. New York: William Morrow.

Schele, Linda, and Nikolai Grube. Unpublished manuscript. "Notes on the Chronology of Piedras Negras Stela 12."

Schele, Linda, Nikolai Grube, and Erik Boot. Unpublished manuscript. "Some Suggestions on the K'atun Prophecies in the Books of Chilam Balam in Light of Classic Period History." Texas Notes on Pre-Columbian Art, Writing, and Culture 72.

Schele, Linda, and Peter Mathews. 1998. *The Code of Kings: The Language of Seven Sacred Maya Temples and Tombs*. New York: Scribner.

Schele, Linda, and Mary Ellen Miller. 1986. *The Blood of Kings: Dynasty and Ritual in Maya Art*. New York: G. Braziller; Fort Worth: Kimbell Art Museum.

Schellhas, Paul. 1904. *Representation of Deities of the Maya Manuscripts*. Papers of the Peabody Museum of Archaeology and Ethnology. Vol. 4, no. 1. Cambridge, Mass.: Peabody Museum of Archaeology and Ethnology.

Schmidt, Peter J., Mercedes de la Garza, and Enrique Nalda, eds. 1998. *Maya*. New York: Rizzoli.

Sharer, Robert J. 1994. *The Ancient Maya*. 5th ed. Stanford: Stanford University Press.

Siegel, Morris. 1941. "Religion in Western Guatemala: A Product of Acculturation." *American Anthropologist* 43, no. 1.

Smith, A. Ledyard. 1972. *Excavations at Altar de Sacrificios: Architecture, Settlement, Burials, and Caches*. Cambridge: The Peabody Museum of Archaeology and Ethnology.

Smith, A. Ledyard, and Alfred V. Kidder. 1951. *Excavations at Nebaj, Guatemala*. Washington, D.C.: Carnegie Institution of Washington, Publication no. 594.

Spinden, Herbert. 1975. *A Study of Maya Art: Its Subject Matter and Historical Development*. 1913. Reprint, New York: Dover Publications.

Stephens, John L. 1841. *Incidents of Travel in Central America, Chiapas, and Yucatan*, 2 vols. New York: Harper & Brothers.

——. 1843. *Incidents of Travel in Yucatan*, 2 vols. New York: Harper & Brothers.

Stomper, Jeffrey. 1996. "Popol Na: A Model for Ancient Maya Community Structure at Copán, Honduras." Ph.D. dissertation, Yale University.

Stone, Andrea J. 1989. "Disconnection, Foreign Insignia and Political Expansion: Teotihuacán and the Warrior Stelae of Piedras Negras." In *Mesoamerica after the Decline of Teotihuacán, AD 700–900*. Edited by Richard A. Diehl and Janet C. Berlo, pp. 153–172. Washington D.C.: Dumbarton Oaks.

Stuart, David. 1987. "Ten Phonetic Syllables." *Research Reports on Ancient Maya Writing* 14.

——. 1988. "The Río Azul Cacao Pot: Epigraphic Observations on the Function of a Maya Ceramic Vessel." *Antiquity* 62, no. 234, pp. 153–157.

——. 1989. "Hieroglyphs on Maya Vessels." In *The Maya Vase Book*. Vol. 1, pp. 149–160.

——. 1990. "A New Carved Panel from the Palenque Area." *Research Reports on Ancient Maya Writing* 32, pp. 9–14.

——. 1992. "Flower Symbolism in Maya Iconography." Paper presented at the VIIIth Symposium on Ancient Maya Writing and Culture, March 1992, *Origins: Creation and Continuity, Mythology and History in Mesoamerica*. University of Texas at Austin.

——. 1998a. "Fire Enters His House: Architecture and Ritual in Classic Maya Texts." In *Function and Meaning in Classic Maya Architecture.* Edited by Stephen D. Houston, pp. 373–425. Washington, D.C.: Dumbarton Oaks.

——. 1998b. "Una guerra entre Yaxchilán y Piedras Negras?" In *Proyecto arqueológico Piedras Negras, informe preliminar no. 2: Segunda temporada, 1998.* Edited by Héctor L. Escobedo and Stephen D. Houston, pp. 389–392. Guatemala City.

——. 1999. "The Meaning of Sacrifice and Bloodletting among the Classic Maya." Paper presented at the Sixth Annual UCLA Maya Weekend, *Communicating with the Gods: Ancient Maya Ritual,* sponsored by UCLA Institute of Archaeology.

——. 2000. "'The Arrival of Strangers': Teotihuacan and Tollan in Classic Maya History." In *Mesoamerica's Classic Heritage: From Teotihuacan to the Aztecs.* Edited by David Carrasco, Lindsay Jones, and Scott Sessions, pp. 465–513. Boulder: University of Colorado Press.

——. 2002. Unpublished manuscript. "Longer Live the King: The Questionable Demise of K'inich K'an Joy Chitam of Palenque." (www.mesoweb.com).

——. Unpublished manuscript. "The Paw Stone: A Toponym and Altar at Piedras Negras, Guatemala."

Tate, Carolyn E. 1985. "Carved Ceramics Called Chochola." In *Fifth Palenque Round Table, 1983.* Edited by Virginia M. Fields, pp. 123–133. San Francisco: PARI.

——. 1992. *Yaxchilan: The Design of a Maya Ceremonial City.* Austin: University of Texas Press.

Taube, Karl A. 1985. "The Classic Maya Maize God: A Reappraisal." In *Fifth Palenque Round Table, 1983.* Edited by Virginia M. Fields, pp. 171–181. San Francisco: PARI.

——. 1992. *The Major Gods of Ancient Yucatan.* Washington, D.C.: Dumbarton Oaks.

——. 1993. *Aztec and Maya Myths.* Austin: University of Texas Press.

——. 1994. "The Birth Vase: Natal Imagery in Ancient Maya Myth and Ritual." *The Maya Vase Book.*

Vol. 4, pp. 652–685.

——. 1999. "Turquoise Hearth: Fire, Self-sacrifice, and the Central Mexican Cult of War." In *Mesoamerica's Classic Heritage: Teotihuacán to the Aztecs.* Edited by Davíd Carrasco, Lindsay Jones, and Scott Sessions, pp. 269–340. Boulder: University Press of Colorado.

Taylor, Dicey. 1992. "Painted Ladies: Costumes for Women on Tepeu Ceramics." In *The Maya Vase Book.* Vol. 3, pp. 513–525.

Tedlock, Dennis, trans. 1996. *Popol Vuh: The Mayan Book of the Dawn of Life.* Rev. ed. New York: Simon & Schuster.

——. trans. 2003. *Rabinal Achi: A Mayan Drama of War and Sacrifice.* Oxford: Oxford University Press.

Thompson, J. Eric S. 1936. "An Eccentric Flint from Quintana Roo, Mexico." *Maya Research* 3, pp. 317–318.

——. 1939. *Excavations at San Jose, British Honduras.* Washington, D.C.: Carnegie Institution of Washington, Publication no. 506.

——. 1962. *A Catalog of Maya Hieroglyphs.* Norman: University of Oklahoma Press.

Tiesler Blos, Vera, Andrea Cucina, and Arturo Romano Pacheco. 2002. "Vida y muerte del personaje hallado en el Templo XIII-Sub, Palenque: 1. Culto funerario y sacrificio humano." *Mexicon* 24, no. 4, pp. 75–78.

Tozzer, Alfred M., trans. 1941. *Landa's relación de las cosas de Yucatan.* Papers of the Peabody Museum, vol. 18. Cambridge, Mass.: Peabody Museum of Archaeology and Ethnology.

Townsend, Richard F. 1979. *State and Cosmos in the Art of Tenochtitlan.* Washington, D.C.: Dumbarton Oaks.

Vargas de la Peña, Leticia, and Victor R. Castillo Borges. 1999. "Ek' Balam: Ciudad que empieza a revelar sus secretos." *Arqueología mexicana* 7, no. 37, pp. 24–31.

——. 2001. "Hallazgos recientes en Ek' Balam." *Méxicon* 23, no. 3, pp. 55–56.

Von Winning, Hasso. 1968. *Pre-Columbian Art of Mexico and Central America.* New York: Harry N. Abrams.

Wagner, Henry Raup, trans. and ed. 1942. *The Discovery of New Spain in 1518 by Juan de Grijalva.* Berkeley: The Cortes Society.

Ward, Fred. 1987. "Jade, Stone of Heaven." *National Geographic Magazine* 172, no. 3 (September 1987), pp. 282–316.

Webster, David. 1976. *Defensive Earthworks at Becan, Campeche, Mexico.* Middle American Research Institute, Publication 41. Tulane University, New Orleans.

——. 2002. *The Fall of the Ancient Maya: Solving the Mystery of the Maya Collapse.* London and New York: Thames & Hudson.

——. ed. 1989. *The House of the Bacabs, Copan, Honduras.* Studies in Pre-Columbian Art and Archaeology, no 29. Washington, D.C.: Dumbarton Oaks.

Webster, David, AnnCorinne Freter, and Nancy Gonlin. 2000. *Copan: the Rise and Fall of an Ancient Maya Kingdom.* Fort Worth: Harcourt College Publishers.

Whittington, E. Michael, ed. 2001. *The Sport of Life and Death: The Mesoamerican Ballgame.* London and New York: Thames & Hudson.

Whittington, Stephen L., and David M. Reed. 1997. *Bones of the Maya: Studies of Ancient Skeletons.* Washington, D.C.: Smithsonian Institution Press.

Willey, Gordon R., and Jeremy A. Sabloff. 1980. *A History of American Archaeology.* 3rd ed. New York: W.H. Freeman.

Wurster, Wolfgang W. ed. 2000. *El sitio Maya de Topoxté: Investigaciones en una isla del Lago Yaxhá, Petén, Guatemala.* Mainz am Rhein: P. von Zabern: KAVA.

Yadeun Angulo, Juan. 1992. *Toniná.* Mexico City: Citibank.

——. 1993. *Toniná: El laberinto del inframundo.* Tuxtla Gutiérrez: Gobierno del Estado de Chiapas.

Glossary

by Mary Miller, Dina Solomon, and Simon Martin

GLOSSARY OF HISTORICAL FIGURES

Palenque

Pakal (*k'inich janahb' pakal*)—Ruler of Palenque from 615 to 683; the most famous of all Maya kings and known for his remarkable burial within the Temple of Inscriptions at the age of 80. Father of two successive kings and revered by his lineage. Child of Lady Sak K'uk' and K'an Mo' Hix, who did not rule; Lady Tz'akb'u Ajaw was his wife.

Kan Bahlam II (*k'inich kan b'ahlam*)—Ruler of Palenque from 684 to 702; son of Pakal; constructed the Group of the Cross; his portraits are among the most distinctive of any Maya king with his imperious nose and full lower lip. No known offspring or spouse.

K'an Hoy Chitam II (*k'inich k'an joy chitam*)—Second son of Pakal, ruler of Palenque from 702–c. 721. Although captured by Tonina king in 711, he seems to have returned to Palenque by the following year.

Ahkal Mo' Nahb III (*k'inich ahkal mo' nahb'*)—Ruler of Palenque, he came to power in 721 and revitalized the kingdom after a demoralizing series of defeats. Little known until recent excavations, he now emerges as a major commissioner of monuments and buildings.

Upakal K'inich—The *baah ch'ok* or "head youth" or "heir" *c.* 736 and perhaps brother to Ahkal Mo' Nahb. Upakal K'inich later ruled as Pakal II *(upakal k'inich janahb' pakal),* installed by at least 742.

K'uk' Bahlam II (*k'inich k'uk' b'ahlam*)—Acceded in 764; ruled for at least 20 years. The last Palenque king to make substantial additions to the Palace.

Yaxchilan

Shield Jaguar II (*itzamnaaj b'ahlam*)—Ruler of Yaxchilan from 681 to 742. Wives included Lady Xok and Lady Ik' Skull of Calakmul. Son of Bird Jaguar III and father of Bird Jaguar IV.

Lady Xok (*ix k'ab'al xook*)—The principal wife of Shield Jaguar II of Yaxchilan. Temple 23 was dedicated to her and probably held both her tomb and that of her husband.

Bird Jaguar IV ("the Great")—Son of Shield Jaguar II and Lady Ik' Skull of Calakmul (b. 709). Acceded to office in 752, following ten-year interregnum; ruled until 768 and completed unprecedented building programs at the site.

GLOSSARY OF TERMS

Ah K'uhuun (*aj k'uhuun*)—A noble title carried by both men and women. It does not yet have a secure translation, so the functions it referred to remain unclear.

Ahaw (*ajaw*)—Literally "lord, ruler," this title was carried by the upper stratum of royal figures in Maya society, including women. In the form of an **Emblem Glyph**, the Ahaw was elaborated and used to refer to the "holy lord" or *k'uhul ajaw,* the supreme ruler of the kingdom.

Atlatl—A dart-thrower, the most effective long-range weapon in ancient Mesoamerica. Used in Central Mexico from about AD 100 onwards, the *atlatl* was sometimes adopted by the Maya, who persisted in representing it as a foreign weapon.

Aztecs—This term came into widespread use in the 19th century to refer to the Nahuatl-speaking peoples of Central Mexico in the early 16th century. Centered at their capital of Tenochtitlan, modern-day Mexico City, the Aztecs dominated much of Mesoamerica through trade, tribute, and warfare.

Balche'—A fermented honey drink, similar to a mead, consumed by the Maya.

Ballgame—A ritualized game played throughout Mesoamerica in which teams of two players or more competed to control the ball without using their hands and to make contact with stone markers or rings. The game was played with a heavy rubber ball, requiring the players to wear protective garments. Ball courts consist of two parallel structures with either straight or sloping sides and are found at the center of many Maya cities.

Bloodletting—A practice conducted throughout Mesoamerica for ritual purposes, in which men and women lacerated certain body parts with **stingray spines** or pieces of obsidian to produce the blood necessary to appease the gods and conjure visions. Blood was the most important offering that could be made to the gods; the shedding of human blood was the supreme sacrifice.

Cacao (*kakaw*)—The cocoa plant whose seed was used for money or used to make a frothy, liquid chocolate drink beloved by the Maya elite. Dried cacao was

ground with chili, honey, water, and occasionally flowers and then poured from one vessel to another to yield a desirable frothy foam.

Caiman—Spanish term for alligator; the particular species known among the Maya is *Caiman crocodilus.* This carnivorous amphibian was often identified with the surface of the earth; the Maya also identified an aspect of **Itzamna** with this creature.

Calendar—A means of reckoning days, years, and longer periods of time. The Maya kept track of days by both a 260-day divinatory calendar and a 365-day solar calendar, among others; they also charted a continuous count of days in the **Long Count**.

Calendar Round—A 52-year period of time that elapses in order for the 260-day calendar and 365-day calendar to return to their starting points.

Capstone—The flat stone that caps a **corbel vault**. Some Maya examples, particularly in Yucatan, were painted with images and glyphic texts.

Cenote—A sinkhole found in karst limestone landscapes. Cenotes served both as a source of fresh water and as a place of ritual deposit. They are especially common in Yucatan where they form a partial ring that mirrors the buried crater of a meteorite that struck the earth during the Cretaceous period.

Celt and Belt Assemblage—An ornament worn at the waist and typically composed of three thin celts (symbolic stone axe heads) dangling from a large head or mask. Jade celts of this sort yield a loud bell-like sound. They are often depicted in Maya painting and sculpture. A belt with three heads and their attendant celts was found atop Pakal's sarcophagus (see Plate 133).

Censer—A vessel in which incense, usually the Maya resin *pom*, could be burned (see Plate 126). Maya censers (*incensarios* in Spanish) were supported by elaborate stands. Most of the censers in this exhibition would have supported plain vessels.

Chaak—The Maya god of rain and storms. He is often depicted as a fisherman and is a patron of agriculture because he presides over water; he can be recognized by catfish-like whiskers, blunt reptilian snout, body scales, or a **spondylus** shell earpiece. Chaak also presides over sacrifice, and is rarely depicted without an axe in hand.

Chak Chel—An old goddess considered to be a woman warrior, midwife, diviner, and the patron of weavers; she both delivered infants and brought on destructive floods at the end of the world. Chak Chel is Goddess O of the Schellhas system.

Cinnabar—The red mineral also known as vermilion; it occurs naturally in any volcanic environment. The Maya used it as a pigment, rubbed into ritual objects, and covered their dead with it. When heated, cinnabar yields mercuric oxide, from which mercury is rendered.

Codex—A folding-screen book made from either strips of pounded bark paper or deer hide painted on both sides with a fine coating of white lime gesso. They were painted with intricate scenes, outlined with black and filled with color; the codices contain information about all aspects of Mesoamerican life, including gods and rituals, religion, history, flora, fauna, and trade and tribute. Only a handful of Maya books survive today.

Codex-style—A painting style used for ceramic vessels in the Calakmul and Nakbe regions, defined by a fine black line on creamy backgrounds, often rimmed by red paint. The name comes from what is assumed to be the similar appearance to Maya screenfold books, or codices.

Copal—The most common native incense of Mesoamerica; made from the resin from trees of the *Bursera* genus; often burned with rubber, blood, and other offerings for the gods. The Maya call it *pom* today.

Corbel Vault—A characteristic of Maya architecture in which courses of stone approach each other until they can be spanned by a single **capstone**.

Directions—north, east, south, west, and center; each also associated with a color and a particular bird. The red is always east, but other colors are not consistent.

Dwarf—often portrayed with the **Maize God** on painted vases from the Naranjo-Holmul region, perhaps an allusion to the smaller second ear of maize frequently issued by the **maize** plant. Dwarves and hunchbacks often served as counselors to the highest ranking lords.

Earflare or Earspool—An ear decoration, often round (hence "spool") threaded through ear and balanced by counterweights. Both men and women wear them; the finest examples are made of jade or other hard stones.

Ebet—"Messenger." This title usually appears in the texts in possessed form: *yebet,* or "his messenger."

Eccentric Flint—Blades of flint knapped and flaked into multifaceted symbols of sacred power. Usually made into abstract shapes, some depict multiple human and god profiles. The most common of these deities was the lightning god **K'awiil**, whose essence was believed to create flint when lightning strikes the earth.

Emblem Glyphs—Hieroglyphs that share a common structure but with individual toponyms or place-names embedded, so that versions are unique to individual Maya sites. Each represents a personal title as, for example, *k'uhul b'aakal ajaw,* "Holy Lord of Palenque."

Glyph—The basic component of Maya writing. Some glyphs (or "hieroglyphs") are logographs, that is, signs that represent whole words (for example, the head of a **quetzal** bird that reads *k'uk',* "quetzal"); or syllables that spell words phonetically (for example, the duplicated signs k'u-k'u combining to read *k'uk*).

God K—*see* K'awiil.

God L—A principal god of the Underworld. God L may represent one of the two death gods who appear in the Popol Vuh, and he may have partnered with the **Jaguar God of the Underworld** in such a role. He usually sits on a throne, wears an **owl** headdress and fancy woven cape; he has jaguar aspects, and can have either a human or a square eye. He is also the principal merchant god and patron of tobacco.

God N—A god who often is portrayed emerging from or wearing a conch or turtle shell; he seems to have had the responsibility of supporting the sky and frequently appears on throne legs.

Graffiti—among the Maya, graffiti refer to informal sketches, notations, and incisions, often found scratched into the stucco-surfaced walls of palace chambers.

Hacha—Spanish word for "axe"; usually refers in Mesoamerican ritual to a piece of **ballgame** equipment fixed to a wide belt or yoke rather than a true axe. They often take the form of a human, animal, or god head.

Hero Twins—The twins Hunahpu and Xbalanque who defeat the gods of the Underworld in the K'iche Maya creation story, the **Popol Vuh**; they hunt with blowguns and play the **ballgame**. The Hero Twins are sons of the **Maize God** and half-brothers to the **Monkey Scribes**.

Huipil—A blouse-length or full-length garment usually made of cotton and worn by Maya women. Maya noble women wore long, extravagant versions, particularly as depicted on Yaxchilan lintels.

Incensario—Spanish for "censer." The term *incensario* usually refers not to the burner itself but the heavy clay or stone stand that supported an undecorated flared vessel for burning incense such as copal. Other Maya censers feature spikes that would stay cool even with burning contents.

Itzamna (*itzamnaaj*)—The paramount sky god of the Maya, often depicted as an enthroned ruler together with the **Moon Goddess** and presiding over lesser gods. Otherwise he appears in his avian aspect, a great supernatural bird. Itzamna is closely associated with the scribal arts and art-making.

Ixchel—principal Maya goddess at the time of the Spanish invasion, particularly revered for her powers over the female dominion—childbirth, weaving, etc. Evidently the same as the earlier **Chak Chel**.

Jade—A term referring to two types of rock, jadeite and nephrite. Jadeite occurs in Mesoamerica as rocks and boulders; its sources in Guatemala have recently been rediscovered. Jade was the most precious material in Mesoamerica, exceeding gold's value at the time of the Spanish invasion. Its green color was identified with maize and water. Jade, the hardest material in Mesoamerica, was worked with string saws, tubular drills, jade powder, and jade tools.

Jaguar—Lords identified themselves with the big cat, who like them occupied the top of the food chain. They used its pelt for royal clothing and for the covers of cushions and books. Many Underworld gods have jaguar aspects; cats were seen as nocturnal spirits who ruled the night.

Jaguar God of the Underworld—One of several Maya deities with jaguar associations; this god is identified by his feline ears and claws and by the "cruller," a twisted rope that circles the eyes and nose. The Jaguar God of the Underworld represents the sun at night, during its Underworld journey from dusk to dawn.

Jaina Island—An island off the coast of Campeche, where most of the ceramic Maya figurines have been found. The Maya may have journeyed from other regions to make burials there.

Jester God—A god who takes his name from the tri-pointed crest that dangles over his forehead like that of a medieval court jester. When tied onto a cloth or paper headscarf—collectively known as *huun*—he becomes a key element of lordly insignia.

Kakaw—*see* Cacao.

Kaloomte'—A lordly epithet of very high status, it was originally ascribed only to the most powerful and prestigious of kings. Though not fully deciphered, has versions associated with each of the cardinal directions and could be linked with supernatural *te'* "trees" at the corners of the world.

K'awiil—Formerly known as God K and the Manikin Scepter, K'awiil is a complex and incompletely understood character in Maya religion. His forehead features a **mirror** punctured by a stone celt or some flaming device: either a cigar or torch. His body often displays scales and one leg and foot are usually depicted as a writhing snake. This serpent appears to be an embodied bolt of lightning, pointing to his close association with storms. But K'awiil is also associated with **maize** and other foodstuffs, perhaps because lightning is associated with freeing these items from a sacred mountain. K'awiil was particularly important to elite lineages and rulers and his portrait formed the scepter used in royal accession ceremonies.

Kill Hole—A drilled or smashed hole in previously fired pottery that ostensibly released the power that the object had accumulated through use. In Maya tombs plates were sometimes laid over the faces of the deceased and drilled in this way. In this case they were probably designed to allow the departure of the soul or other vital essences rather than "killing" the vessel itself.

K'inich Ahaw—The Maya Sun God, identified by the four-petaled *k'in* (sun) sign placed upon his head or body. Generally aged, he is cross-eyed and has his upper incisors filed into the form of the T-shaped wind sign *ik'*.

Limestone—A porous rock formed from compressed layers of calcareous sea deposits, mostly consisting of calcium carbonate. Limestone forms the bedrock of the entire Maya lowlands. It was cut into blocks by the Maya to make sculpture and architecture and burned to make lime, an important element used for Maya food preparation as well as for building mortar and stucco.

Lintel—A slab of stone or series of thick wooden planks spanning a doorway. At Yaxchilan stone lintels were commonly carved.

Long Count—A Maya system of dating and counting that records the total number of days elapsed since a mythological starting point; this date fell in 3114 BC. Like all Maya numbers, this dating system was vigesimal, that is, based on the number 20. Time was reckoned by days, periods of 20 days, years (of 360 days), 20-year periods, and 400-year periods.

Mesoamerica—a cultural area that encompassed most of modern-day Mexico and north-western Central America.

Maize—Commonly, corn, or what is often called "field corn," to distinguish it from "sweet corn." Maize was the most important food crop of Mesoamerica. The Maya depicted maize ears as human heads, as if corn was a sentient being.

Maize God—A youthful male god with stylized **maize** attributes. One of the most important Maya deities, the Maize God was Hun Hunahpu of the **Popol Vuh** epic, the father of the **Hero Twins** who was sacrificed in the Underworld but ultimately reborn, replicating the life cycle of the plant.

Metate and *mano*—Stone tools used to grind maize; the *metate* is the large stone on which the lime-soaked grain is placed. The *mano* is a smaller stone tool (or rock), often shaped like a small rolling pin, used to grind corn or other grains.

Mirror—made of polished hematite or pyrite pieces fitted together in a mosaic, Maya mirrors were used at court for divination, particularly for a ruling lord, who consulted them and even allowed mirrors to "speak" during official audiences.

Monkey Scribes—Older half-brothers to the **Hero Twins**, the Monkey Scribes inherit their artistic gifts from their father, the **Maize God**, Hun Hunahpu. They may be human or simian in their aspect.

Moon Goddess—represented as young and beautiful by the Maya, often sitting in the crescent of the Maya glyph for moon. She sometimes holds the **rabbit** Mesoamericans see in the moon's disk and she may be regarded as its mother.

Olmec—the oldest civilization in Mesoamerica, a precursor and important influence on the Maya as well as cultural developments in other parts of the region. The Olmecs thrived along the Gulf of Mexico, and in Central Mexico from about 1400–400 BC.

Owl—owls in general, but particularly a small screech owl with a penetrating and chilling nighttime call, played a role in Maya religious belief. Companion of **God L** (the bird sits atop his hat), the owl appears as a messenger from **Xibalba**.

Palenque Triad—Heinrich Berlin identified three god names used in sequence at Palenque and named them GI, GII, and GIII. Although each may be related to or an aspect of a more common Maya deity (**Chaak**, **K'awiil**, and a fusion of **K'inich Ahaw** and the **Jaguar God of the Underworld**), each is also specific to Palenque.

Pectoral—An ornament or decoration worn on the chest; the Maya often created such key important items of regalia out of **jade**.

Peten—In Mayan, *peten* means "island" but also refers to broader ideas of "territory." Today, it is the name of the northernmost province of Guatemala, but also used as a more general designation for the heart of the Maya region which also encompasses the southern portion of the Mexican states of Campeche and Quintana Roo.

Popol Naah—literally "Mat House," but in effect the "council house," where nobles met.

Popol Vuh—The sacred book of the K'iche Maya of highland Guatemala. Transcribed into alphabetic writing in the 16th century, the Popol Vuh preserves important mythic narratives from ancient times. It contains three parts: the creation of the earth and its first inhabitants, the story of the **Hero Twins** and their forebears, and the legendary history of the founding of the K'iche dynasties.

Pseudo-glyphs—a common feature of painted ceramics, these glyphs mimic the appearance of real writing but have no actual meaning. They seem to have been created by illiterate artists who wanted to give their works higher prestige.

Puh—Literally, rushes or reeds. The Maya may have thought of distant **Teotihuacan** as a "Place of rushes." The word **Tollan** refers to the same concept in Central Mexico, where it served as the name of any of a number of revered cities.

Pyrite—Fool's gold. An iron sulfide, pyrite was prized by the Maya for the bright, reflective surface it acquired when polished. Small pieces were skillfully assembled to form mosaic mirrors.

Quetzal—*k'uk'* in Mayan, the resplendent trogon, *Pharomachrus mocinno*, lives in the restricted ecological niche of the tropical cloud forest, at 3000–4000 ft. (915–1220 m). The blue-green iridescent tailfeathers of the male run 3 ft. (0.9 m) in length and were the prized elements of any ruler's headdress.

Rabbit—*t'ul* in Mayan, the rabbit had an important place in Maya belief. Mesoamericans saw its image on the face of the full moon and believed it to be the companion or child of the **Moon Goddess**. The Maya considered the rabbit a trickster; he played key roles in both the **Popol Vuh** and in more ancient painted stories, where he contributed to the downfall and humiliation of **God L**.

Sahal (*sajal*)—A high title borne by lords, and not a few ladies, who served in the courts of ruling kings or governed provincial centers on their behalf.

Scepter—An object held in the hand of a ruler as a symbol of rulership itself; Maya rulers are often portrayed holding one.

Serpent—*chan* or *kan* in most Mayan languages, snakes have varied roles in Mesoamerican religion and religious symbolism. They are known as vehicles of rebirth and transformation because of their ability to swallow prey whole and to shed their skins. Among the most important snakes in the region are the boa constrictor, the fer-de-lance (a ferocious pit viper), and the rattlesnake.

Shaman—A religious specialist who becomes the actual vehicle for the supernatural through ecstatic trance and spirit-possession.

Shells—The Maya valued seashells from Atlantic, Pacific, and Caribbean waters, particularly species of conch, from which they made trumpets, and spondylus, or spiny oyster, the probable source of pearls found occasionally in Maya tombs. Halves of spondylus (valves) are defining features of the **Maize God**'s costume, along with copious **jade** adornments.

Spondylus—*see* shell.

Stela (pl. stelae)—A prismatic stone slab, erected on significant dates and carved with hieroglyphs and portraits to celebrate the reigns and ritual passages of Maya rulers. Stelae were usually made from limestone, but local stones—particularly sandstone and volcanic tuff—are also used where available.

Stingray spine—The sharp, barbed tail spine of the stingray that was used to puncture the skin for ritual **bloodletting**; often found in burials of male nobility.

Stucco—A cement that covers many Maya buildings, plazas, and roads. Stucco is made of water and lime (CaO; yielded by complete combustion of limestone), sometimes with sand added, and hardens to a stone-like surface.

Sun God—*see* K'inich Ahaw.

Sweatbath—Chamber for ritual cleansing; stones heated in firebox release clouds of steam. A feature of some elite Maya residential quarters.

Tamale—**Maize** dough made from ground lime-soaked kernels and then steamed inside cornhusks. This is the principal foodstuff depicted in courtly scenes, sprinkled with sauces and often containing meats, such as turkey, deer, or iguana.

Teotihuacan—Located just northeast of modern Mexico City, Teotihuacan was the largest city of the 1st millennium AD in Mesoamerica and capital to a long-lived and influential civilization.

Tlaloc—a Central Mexican god of rain, storms, war, and sacrifice; the Maya adopted him principally as a war god.

Tollan—"Place of *tules*," or "rushes." A number of Mesoamerican cities may have been known as a *tollan*, or sacred city, though the best known are **Teotihuacan**, Tula, and Cholula.

Tribute—Goods or services of skilled individuals that were given to a major site from a subsidiary one; a Sajal or Ah K'uhuun would oversee the delivery of tribute.

Tripod Vessel—A type of Maya pottery vessel with three legs, a shape introduced to the Maya from **Teotihuacan** in the 4th century.

Tumpline—a burden strap that runs across the forehead to carry on the back, thus distributing weight of load across the upper half of the body. Ancient Mesoamerica had no beasts of burden, so the transport of goods over land required teams of bearers.

Turtle—*Ahk* to the Maya and present in the sky as the three bright stars read by the Greeks as Orion's belt. The turtle's rounded and segmented carapace was understood to symbolize the surface of the earth.

Usumacinta River—The river that today forms the border between the state of Chiapas, Mexico, and Guatemala.

Venus—A planet of largely baleful and inauspicious augury; the Maya recognized both Morning Star and Evening Star aspects and charted its 584-day period.

Vigesimal—A counting system based on 20, rather than our own decimal (base 10), and the standard across Mesoamerica.

Vision Serpent—Maya nobles used **bloodletting** and hallucinogens to conjure up images of rearing serpents whose mouths belch gods and ancestors; these Vision Serpents probably functioned as visual metaphors for birth and rebirth, whether of divinities or humans.

War Serpent—Usually donned by warriors in scenes of war or sacrifice, the War Serpent's body is formed by mosaic segments or plates. As a miniature, it is also held in the hand as a weapon or scepter. It seems to be of Central Mexican origin and known to the Maya as *waxaklajuun ub'aah kan*, "18 [are the] images of the snake."

Way—A soul-like spirit companion or *nahual*, which often takes animal form, and may belong to a human or a god. Some seem to characterize particular Maya sites or kingdoms. Many are menacing and dangerous and could well be associated with particular diseases and misfortunes.

Xibalba—The K'iche Maya word for the Underworld, literally "place of fright." Xibalba was entered through a cave. Neither burning nor freezing, this parallel universe was ruled by the gods One Death and Seven Death in the **Popul Vuh**.

Yoke—Wide, padded deflectors worn as a mid-body belt during the **ballgame** to protect vital organs and control the ball. Maya yokes were made of perishable materials, although elsewhere in Mesoamerica ceremonial pieces were rendered in stone.

Guide to Spelling and Transliteration

The spelling and pronunciation of Mayan words in this volume require a few brief comments. First of all, most scholars use the word "Mayan" exclusively when referring to language, as opposed to "Maya," which is applied to the culture, people, or things. In ancient times two Mayan language groups predominated in the region, the Yukatekan and Ch'olan, although it is clear that the hieroglyphic script developed among the latter and reflects Ch'olan grammar and word construction. Nonetheless the boundary between these groups was permeable and the script was adapted to include Yukatek characteristics in its northern homelands. Today, some 28 different Mayan languages are spoken across the region. Some thrive—Kekchi, Yukatek, K'iche, Ch'ol, among them—while others, Itza, for example, struggle and may be on the verge of extinction.

The decipherment of Mayan script is still incomplete and many questions remain about its phonology and morphology, not to mention the basic readings of many less common signs. In some cases readings are tentative or entirely unknown, and here long-standing nicknames or glosses are often employed in their place. Linguists and epigraphers have developed common rules for the transliteration of Mayan words and we hold to these conventions wherever possible. No system of representation is flawless, however: there are always conflicts and compromises in translating one system into another.

We want to be sure that names mentioned in the text can be sounded out by English-speaking readers. Vowels should be pronounced as they would be in Spanish: A as in Los Angeles, E as in El Paso, I as in Domingo, O as in Los, and u as in Tula. Since the script makes distinctions between short and long vowels we indicate these where necessary. Long vowels are represented by doubled letters, as in Hawaii. One of the most common examples in this book is the god name K'awiil.

Regarding consonants: the letter "x" in Mayan words has the value it had in 16th-century Mexico; that is, the sound "sh"—as in Yaxchilan, which is pronounced "Yashchilan." More difficult to grasp are the sounds of glottalized consonants, indicated by apostrophes, such as the one in K'awiil. These sounds involve a constriction of the glottis in order to create an accompanying "click." They are vital constituents of Mayan languages; the absence or presence of "glottal stops" distinguishes, for example, *chak,* "red/great," from *ch'ak,* "to chop/damage." In the standard Mayan orthography all b-sounds carry an apostrophe. But since this does not reflect a true glottal distinction we have included them only in the more accurate transliterations given in italics within parentheses, e.g. Baah (*b'aah*).

Another problem arises where the script distinguishes between hard and soft h-sounds—just as Spanish orthography does today. Here, in the Spanish fashion, the hard h-sound (as in Bach) is represented by a "j." The soft version (as in house) is conveyed by the normal "h." Since the letter "j" distracts English readers, it is another feature restricted to the fuller spellings in parentheses, e.g. Ahaw (*ajaw*).

All place-names are given standard Spanish spellings, but those based on Mayan words have not been Hispanicized: Tonina rather than Toniná.

List of Lenders

American Museum of Natural History
New York, New York

The Art Institute of Chicago
Chicago, Illinois

John G. Bourne Foundation
Santa Fe, New Mexico

The British Museum
London, United Kingdom

The Cleveland Museum of Art
Cleveland, Ohio

Dallas Museum of Art
Dallas, Texas

The Denver Art Museum
Denver, Colorado

Dirección de Estudios Arqueológicos—INAH
Mexico City, Mexico

Duke University Museum of Art
Durham, North Carolina

Dumbarton Oaks Research Library & Collections
Washington, D.C.

Fine Arts Museums of San Francisco
San Francisco, California

Instituto Hondureño de Antropología e Historia
Copán, Honduras

Kimbell Art Museum
Fort Worth, Texas

Los Angeles County Museum of Art
Los Angeles, California

The Metropolitan Museum of Art
New York, New York

Museo Amparo
Puebla, Mexico

Museo Arqueológico de Campeche "Fuerte de San Miguel"—INAH
Campeche, Mexico

Museo de Sitio de Comalcalco—INAH
Comalcalco, Chiapas, Mexico

Museo de Sitio de Palenque "Dr. Alberto Ruz L'Huillier"—INAH
Palenque, Chiapas, Mexico

Museo de Sitio de Toniná, Chiapas—INAH
Toniná, Chiapas. Mexico

Museo Nacional de Antropología—INAH
Mexico City, Mexico

Museo Nacional de Arqueología y Etnología de Guatemala
Guatemala City, Guatemala

Museo Regional de Chiapas
Tuxtla Gutiérrez, Chiapas, Mexico

Museo Regional de Yucatán "Palacio Canton"—INAH
Merida, Yucatán, Mexico

The Museum of Fine Arts, Houston
Houston, Texas

National Gallery of Australia
Canberra, Australia

National Gallery of Victoria
Melbourne, Australia

National Museum of the American Indian, Smithsonian Institution
Washington, D.C.

New Orleans Museum of Art
New Orleans, Louisiana

Peabody Museum of Archaeology and Ethnology
Cambridge, Massachusetts

Princeton University Art Museum
Princeton, New Jersey

Private Collection
San Francisco, California

Private Collection
Switzerland

Sainsbury Centre for Visual Arts
Robert and Lisa Sainsbury Collection
Norwich, United Kingdom

The Saint Louis Art Museum
Saint Louis, Missouri

San Diego Museum of Man
San Diego, California

Seattle Art Museum
Seattle, Washington

The Utah Museum of Fine Arts
Salt Lake City, Utah

Virginia Museum of Fine Arts
Richmond, Virginia

Yale University Art Gallery
New Haven, Connecticut

Zona Arqueológica de Palenque—INAH
(Proyecto Arqueológico Palenque)
Mexico

Anonymous lenders

Authors and Contributors

Authors

Mary Miller is Vincent Scully Professor of the History of Art and Master of Saybrook College, Yale University. She is the author of *The Art of Mesoamerica, Maya Art and Architecture*, and the co-author of *The Blood of Kings* (with Linda Schele) and *Gods and Symbols of Ancient Mexico and the Maya* (with Karl Taube).

Simon Martin is a Research Specialist at the University of Pennsylvania Museum of Archaeology and Anthropology. He is the co-author of *Chronicle of the Maya Kings and Queens: Deciphering the Dynasties of the Ancient Maya* (with Nikolai Grube).

Contributors

Guillermo Bernal Romero is the Epigraphic Investigator for the Instituto Nacional de Antropología e Historia archaeological project at Palenque, Mexico.

Kathleen Berrin is Curator-in-Charge of the Arts of Africa, Oceania, and the Americas at the Fine Arts Museums of San Francisco.

Michael D. Coe is McCurdy Professor of Anthropology Emeritus and former Curator of the Peabody Museum of Natural History at Yale University.

Martha Cuevas García is Director of the Instituto Nacional de Antropología e Historia archaeological project "Los Incensarios del Grupo de las Cruces" at Palenque, Mexico.

Héctor L. Escobedo is Professor of Archaeology at the Universidad del Valle de Guatemala.

Beatriz de la Fuente is Professor Emeritus at the Instituto de Investigaciones Estéticas at the Universidad Nacional Autónoma de México.

Roberto García Moll is an archaeologist and researcher at the Dirección de Estudios Arqueológicos, Instituto Nacional de Antropología e Historia.

Arnoldo González Cruz is Director of the Instituto Nacional de Antropología e Historia archaeological project at Palenque, Mexico.

Stephen D. Houston is the Jesse Knight University Professor at Brigham Young University.

Roberto López Bravo is Director of the Museo de Sitio "Dr. Alberto Ruz L'Huillier" in Palenque, Mexico.

Diana Magaloni is an art historian at the Instituto de Investigaciones Estéticas at the Universidad Nacional Autónoma de México.

Julia C. Miller is Co-Director of the Instituto Nacional de Antropología e Historia archaeological project "Grupo de las Cruces" at Palenque, Mexico.

Alfonso Morales is the Principal Investigator for the Instituto Nacional de Antropología e Historia archaeological project "Grupo de las Cruces" at Palenque, Mexico.

Merle Greene Robertson is Chairman of the Board of the Pre-Columbian Art Research Institute.

David Stuart is Senior Lecturer in Anthropology at Harvard University.

María Teresa Uriarte is Director of the Instituto de Investigaciones Estéticas at the Universidad Nacional Autónoma de México.

Acknowledgments

Courtly Art of the Ancient Maya could not have been realized without the support and generous help of many. Kathleen Berrin and Mary Miller—co-curators of the project from its inception in San Francisco in 1998 until its initial presentation in Washington, D.C., in the spring of 2004—formed the perfect team to realize the project's creative possibilities and address its ever-changing parameters. British epigrapher Simon Martin served admirably as primary scholarly consultant. Throughout the years of the exhibition's development, San Francisco's Director of Museums, Harry S. Parker III, provided the overriding enthusiasm and vision for the project that helped make it a reality.

From Mexico, support from the Consejo Nacional para la Cultura y las Artes and the Instituto Nacional de Antropología e Historia was indispensable at the highest levels. We would like to extend special appreciation to the very distinguished Sari Bermúdez and to Jaime Nualart, as well as to Sergio Raúl Arroyo, Moisés Rosas Silva, Felipe Solís Olguín, José Enrique Ortiz Lanz, Fernando Arechavala, Ricardo Armijo, Rosana Calderón, Ernesto de Jesús Vargas Rodríguez, and Agenor Torres García. For assistance during the initial years of development on the project, special thanks also go to María Teresa Franco and Mercedes de la Garza. Elvira Báez García and Ivonne Morales in Mexico City were highly effective in their abilities to direct and coordinate a myriad of loan details. Both museums are grateful to the government and people of Chiapas for lending treasures celebrating the ancient heritage of the Maya; particular gratitude goes to Bianca Margarita González Rodríguez, Laura Pescador, and Roberto Ramos Maza.

The U.S. Embassy in Mexico City, Ambassador Antonio O. Garza Jr. with the support of Jeffrey Brown, Marjorie Coffin, Bertha Cea Echenique, and Martha Chávez, proved essential to our project. Scholars and museum personnel in Mexico gave the project great distinction. Deserving special recognition are the efforts of Beatriz de la Fuente, as well as Martha Cuevas García, Roberto García Moll, Arnoldo González Cruz and Guillermo Bernal Romero, Diana Magaloni, Alfonso Morales and Julia C. Miller, María Teresa Uriarte, and Juan Yadeun. We are also grateful to Marco Antonio Carvajal Correa and Carlos Vidal in Campeche, Juan Antonio Ferrer and Roberto López Bravo in Palenque, Angeles Espinosa and the staff of the Amparo Museum in Puebla, Miriam Judith Gallegos Gomora and Ricardo Armijon Torres in Tabasco, and Omar Alor Jacobo in Tonina.

Loans from other parts of Latin America were important to our project. In Guatemala we wish to thank Héctor Escobedo, Fernando Moscoso, Mónica Pérez, and Federico Fahsen. At the U.S. Embassy in Guatemala City, we are grateful for the support of Mary Thompson-Jones, Ida Eve Heckenbach, Carmen M. de Foncea, and, during earlier phases of the project, Peter Samson. We are indebted to Margarita Durán de Galvez, Ricardo Agurcia, and, formerly, Olga Joya in the government of Honduras. The U.S. Embassy in Tegucigalpa facilitated communications through the efforts of Melissa Cooper and Carmen L. Urcuyo.

This project and Maya studies in general owe special thanks to the following for their insights, passion, and inspiration: Michael D. Coe, Stephen D. Houston, Merle Greene Robertson, and David Stuart. For select areas of technical expertise we are grateful to our friends Ron Dammann, Prajna Desai, Bill Fash, Gillett Griffin, Heather Hurst, David Joralemon, Edward Merrin, Debra Nagao, Jay Oles, Megan O'Neil, Matthew Robb, Joel Skidmore, Dina Solomon, James Terry, Mónica del Villar, and Mark Zender.

Courtly Art of the Ancient Maya underwent several creative reconfigurations that required institutional forbearance and patience. The cooperation and assistance of the directors and staff of many lending institutions in the United States are gratefully acknowledged: Charles Spencer and Kristin Mable at the American Museum of Natural History in New York; James Wood, Richard Townsend, and Barbara Battaglia at the Art Institute of Chicago; Katharine Lee Reid and Susan Bergh at the Cleveland Museum of Art; Charles Venable and Carolyn Robbins at the Dallas Museum of Art; Timothy Standring, Margaret Young-Sanchez, and Carole Lee at the Denver Art Museum; Michael Mezzatesta at the Duke University Museum of Art; Jeffrey Quilter, Loa Traxler, and Jennifer Younger at Dumbarton Oaks Research Libraries & Collections; Timothy Potts, Patty Decoster, and Michelle Bennett at the Kimbell Art Museum; Virginia Fields at Los Angeles County Museum of Art; Julie Jones at the Metropolitan Museum of Art; Peter Marzio, Frances Marzio, and Erika Franek at the Museum of Fine Arts, Houston; Erik Satrum of the National Museum of the American Indian, Smithsonian Institution; John Bullard and Paul Tarver of the New Orleans Museum of Art; William Fash, Steven LeBlanc, Viva Fisher, and Victoria Cranner at the Peabody Museum of Archaeology and Ethnology; Susan Taylor, Rebecca Sender, and, formerly, Gillett Griffin at the Princeton University Art Museum; John Nunley, Patricia Woods, and Angie Carter at the Saint Louis Museum of Art; Grace Johnson at the San Diego Museum of Man; Barbara Brotherton at the Seattle Art Museum; E.F. Sanguinetti of the Utah Museum of Fine Arts; Michael Brand, Kathy Morris, and Mary Sullivan at the Virginia Museum of Fine Arts; and Jock Reynolds and Susan Matheson at the Yale University Art Gallery.

Loans from England and Australia were of tremendous importance. Works from the British Museum were especially essential to our story and we would like to thank Neil MacGregor, John Mack, Colin McEwan, and Alison Deeprose for their collective support. A loan from the Sainsbury Centre for Visual Arts was made possible through the efforts of Nichola Johnson and Emma Hazell. At the National Gallery of Australia in Canberra, we would like to thank Ron Ramsey, Leanne Handreck, and, formerly, Andrew Fyfe; and at the National Gallery of Victoria in Melbourne, we gratefully acknowledge Gerald Vaughan and Judith Ryan.

Most of the work for this exhibition was the responsibility of two museums. At the National Gallery of Art grateful appreciation goes to the director, Earl A. Powell III, and to D. Dodge Thompson, Mark Leithauser, and Susan Arensberg for their collective energy, enthusiasm and discernment in developing special exhibitions; they were solidly supported in their efforts by Ann Robertson, Wendy Battaglino, Mervin Richard, and Michelle Fondas. Carroll Moore, Lynn Matheny, and Elizabeth Laitman Hughes were responsible for the exhibition film.

The Fine Arts Museums of San Francisco, as the organizing institution, relied on the unsparing efforts of the entire staff, with special thanks to the following individuals: Jennifer Williams Moore and Suzy Peterson could not have been more exacting or dedicated to clarifying the most essential curatorial details. Other staff members who gave valuable support were Lesley Bone, Anne-Marie Bonfilio, Barbara Boucke, Therese Chen, Gerry Chow, Krista Davis, Brian Marston, Joseph McDonald, Ron Rick, William White, and, formerly but importantly, Kathe Hodgson.

The coordination skills and innate good sense of Ann Heath Karlstrom at the Fine Arts Museums guided this publication to its fruition. The entire staff of Thames & Hudson was a pleasure to work with, and special thanks go to Jamie Camplin, Susan Dwyer, Susan Crouch, Sheila McKenzie, Mark Lane, Jill Barrett, Neil Palfreyman, and Colin Ridler, and to the designer, Maggi Smith. Mary Miller's exhaustive and exacting editorial efforts that went far above and beyond the call of duty are very deeply appreciated. Simon Martin's many insights into academic accuracy and complex detail proved important and enlightening. Many scholars have generously shared their drawings: Ian Graham, David Stuart, Stephen Houston, Stefanie Teufel, Merle Greene Robertson. Among the many photographers who supplied the beautiful images that appear on these pages, several must be mentioned specially for providing numerous images quickly and generously in response to urgent requests: Justin Kerr, assisted by Barbara Kerr, and Javier Hinojosa, Jorge Pérez de Lara, and Michel Zabé.

Illustration Credits

Figures

1: © Michel Zabé; 2: Simon Martin; 3: ML Design; 4: Stephen Houston; 5: © Justin Kerr (K6135); 6: Hasso Hohmann; 7: Mary Miller; 8: © Merle Greene Robertson 1986; 9: Jorge Pérez de Lara; 10: Simon Martin; 11: Drawing David Stuart and Stephen Houston; reproduced courtesy Arthur Demarest; 12: Simon Martin; 13: © Justin Kerr; 14: Simon Martin; 15: © Justin Kerr (K6979); 16: © Justin Kerr (K1892); 17: Simon Martin (after Barbara Fash); 18: Simon Martin; 19: Simon Martin; 20: Linda Schele; 21: Simon Martin (K5359); 22: Simon Martin (K1560); 23: © Justin Kerr (K1398); 24: © Enrico Ferorelli; 25: Maricel Presilla; 26: Simon Martin (K631); 27: Simon Martin; 28: Simon Martin (K5615); 29: Jorge Pérez de Lara; 30: Ian Graham; 31: Joseph McDonald; 32: Simon Martin; 33: Simon Martin (K501 & K2733); 34: © Justin Kerr (K559); 35: Mark Van Stone; 36: Matthew H. Robb, reconstruction based on drawings by Ian Graham; 37: Ian Graham; 38: Ian Graham; 39: Jorge Pérez de Lara; 40: Simon Martin (K1523); 41: © Justin Kerr; 42: Simon Martin; 43: Simon Martin; 44: Simon Martin; 45: Helen Trik; 46: David Stuart; 47: Simon Martin (after John Montgomery); 48: © Justin Kerr; 50: © Bonampak Documentation Project, Heather Hurst with Leonard Ashby; 51: Simon Martin; 52: © Michel Zabé; 53: Simon Martin; 54: Simon Martin 54b (K1299); 55: © Photo Javier Hinojosa; 56: © Michael Calderwood/Arqueología Mexicana/Raíces/INAH, 2003; 57: Bibliothèque Nationale de France, Paris; 58: Simon Martin; 59: Tracy Wellman; 60: © Merle Greene Robertson 1986; 61: David Drew (a), Simon Martin (b); 62: Mary Miller; 63: © Michel Zabé; 64: Javier Hinojosa; 65: Mary Miller (left), Philip Winton (right); 66: Yale Visual Resources; 67: © Merle Greene Robertson 1967; 68: Linda Schele (a), Tatiana Proskouriakoff (b), Jorge Pérez de Lara (c); 69: Mary Miller; 70: © Michel Zabé; 71: © Michel Zabé; 72: Jorge Pérez de Lara; 73: © Justin Kerr; 74: Bonampak Documentation Project; 75: Bonampak Documentation Project; 76: Bonampak Documentation Project; 77: Linda Schele; 78: © Merle Greene Robertson; 79: © Merle Greene Robertson; 80: © Merle Greene Robertson; 81: © Merle Greene Robertson; 82: © Merle Greene Robertson; 83: Bonampak Documentation Project; 84: Bonampak Documentation Project; 85: Bonampak Documentation Project; 86: Martha Cuevas García; 87: Martha Cuevas García; 88: Martha Cuevas García; 89: © Michel Zabé; 90: Roberto López Bravo; 91: Roberto López Bravo; 92: Jorge Pérez de Lara; 93: Jorge Pérez de Lara; 94: © Michel Zabé; 95: Roberto García Moll; 96: Tatiana Proskouriakoff; 97: Tatiana Proskouriakoff; 98: Stephen Houston; 99: Stephen Houston; 100: Mary Miller; 101: Alfredo Roman and Tomás Barrientos.

Plates

1: © Michel Zabé; drawing Simon Martin; 2: © Justin Kerr; 3: Bruce M. White; 4: Dumbarton Oaks Research Library & Collections (still); © Justin Kerr (K4338) (rollout); 5: Dumbarton Oaks Research Library & Collections; 6: © Justin Kerr (still); The British Museum (rollout); 7: National Gallery of Victoria; 8: Bruce M. White; 9: Photograph © 1981 The Metropolitan Museum of Art; 10: © Michel Zabé; 11: © Museum of New Mexico 2002, Photography by Blair Clark; 12: Photograph © 2004 Museum Associates/LACMA; 13: Bruce M. White; 14: © Justin Kerr; 15: © Michel Zabé; 16: Bruce M. White; drawing Stefanie Teufel; 17: Joseph McDonald (still); © Justin Kerr (rollout); 18: Joseph McDonald; 19: James Austin; 20: © Michel Zabé; drawing Simon Martin; 21: © Justin Kerr; 22: Photograph by Robert Hashimoto, reproduction, © The Art Institute of Chicago; drawing Ian Graham; 23: © Justin Kerr; drawing Simon Martin; 24: © Michel Zabé; 25: © Michel Zabé; 26: © Photo: Javier Hinojosa; 27: © Photo: Javier Hinojosa; 28: National Gallery of Australia; drawing Simon Martin; 29: New Orleans Museum of Art; 30: © Michael D. Coe; 31: Amparo Museum; 32: © Justin Kerr (K511) (rollout); Bruce M. White (still); 33: Dumbarton Oaks Research Library & Collections; drawings Simon Martin; 34: Dumbarton Oaks Research Library & Collections; 35: © Justin Kerr (K2796); 36: © The Museum of Fine Arts, Houston; drawing courtesy of Donald Hales, Hermosa Beach, California (© all rights reserved, 1986); 37: © Photo: Javier Hinojosa; 38: Joseph McDonald; 39: Joseph McDonald; 40: © Photo: Javier Hinojosa; 41: © Michel Zabé; 42: © Michel Zabé; 43: Jorge Pérez de Lara; 44: © Justin Kerr; 45: © Justin Kerr (K2803); 46: Joseph McDonald; drawing Simon Martin; 47: © Michel Zabé; 48: Joseph McDonald; 49: © Justin Kerr; 50: © Justin Kerr; 51: © Michel Zabé; 52: © Justin Kerr (K5345); 53: © Michel Zabé; 54: © Justin Kerr (K4022); drawing Simon Martin; 55: Jorge Pérez de Lara; 56: © Photo: Javier Hinojosa; 57: Jorge Pérez de Lara; 58: Jorge Pérez de Lara; 59: Dumbarton Oaks Research Library & Collections; 60: Jorge Pérez de Lara; 61: Katherine Wetzel © Virginia Museum of Fine Arts (still); Justin Kerr (K504) (rollout); 62: © Photo: Javier Hinojosa; 63: © Justin Kerr; 64: © Justin Kerr; 65: © The Cleveland Museum of Art, 2003, John L. Severance Fund. 1994.12.1; 66: © The Cleveland Museum of Art, 2003, John L. Severance Fund. 1994.12.2; 67: © Justin Kerr; 68: Bruce M. White; 69: © Justin Kerr; 70: Jorge Pérez de Lara; drawing Ian Graham; 71: Jorge Pérez de Lara; 72: Saint Louis Art Museum; drawing Simon Martin; 73: © Photo: Javier Hinojosa; 74: © Michel Zabé; drawing Simon Martin (after David Stuart); 75: © Photo Javier Hinojosa; drawing Simon Martin (K7727); 76: © Justin Kerr; drawing Simon Martin; 77: © Justin Kerr; 78: Jorge Pérez de Lara; 79: NGM 1989/10 492 Kenneth Garrett; 80: Dumbarton Oaks Research Library & Collections; 81: Dumbarton Oaks Research Library & Collections; 82: Dumbarton Oaks Research Library & Collections; 83: Museo Nacional de Arqueología y Etnología de Guatemala; 84: Museo Nacional de Arqueología y Etnología de Guatemala; 85: © Justin Kerr (K635); 86: © Photo Javier Hinojosa; 87: © Photo Javier Hinojosa; 88: Bruce M. White (still); © Justin Kerr (K791) (rollout); 89: © Photo Javier Hinojosa; drawing Simon Martin; 90: © Photo Javier Hinojosa; drawing Simon Martin; 91: © Photo Javier Hinojosa; 92: © Photo Javier Hinojosa; 93: © Bonampak Documentation Project, Heather Hurst with Leonard Ashby; 94: National Museum of the American Indian, Smithsonian Institution; 95: © Justin Kerr; 96: Yale University Art Gallery; 97: Yale University Art Gallery; 98: © Photo Javier Hinojosa; 99: Ignacio Guevara; 100: © Photo Javier Hinojosa; 101: © Photo Javier Hinojosa; 102: © Photo Javier Hinojosa; 103: J. Beckett; 104: Jorge Pérez de Lara; drawings Simon Martin; 105: © Justin Kerr (K767 and K3412); 106: © Photo Javier Hinojosa; 108: Photographer: Michael Bodycomb 2001. © 2003 by Kimbell Art Museum (still); © Justin Kerr (K638) (rollout); 109: Peabody Museum, Harvard University Photo T229 © President and Fellows of Harvard College, 2003; 110: © Susan Dirk; 111: © Justin Kerr; 112: © Photo by the Denver Art Museum 2003; 113: Michel Zabé; 114: Jorge Pérez de Lara; 115: © Photo Javier Hinojosa; 116: © Photo Javier Hinojosa; 117: Dumbarton Oaks Research Library & Collections; 118: Peabody Museum, Harvard University Photo T219 © President and Fellows of Harvard College, 2003; drawing Simon Martin; 119: Jorge Pérez de Lara; 120: Dan Kramer; 121: © Photo Javier Hinojosa; 122: Amparo Museum; drawing Simon Martin; 123: © Photo Javier Hinojosa; 124: © Photo Javier Hinojosa; 125: © Photo Javier Hinojosa; 126: © Photo Javier Hinojosa; 127: © Photo Javier Hinojosa; 128: © Photo Javier Hinojosa; 129: © Michel Zabé; drawing Simon Martin; 130: © Photo Javier Hinojosa; drawing by Simon Martin; 131: © Photo Javier Hinojosa; 132: © Photo Javier Hinojosa; 133: Jorge Pérez de Lara.

Index

Page numbers in *italics* refer to illustrations